OXFORD MONOGRAPHS IN INTERNATIONAL LAW

General Editors

PROFESSOR VAUGHAN LOWE QC

Chichele Professor of Public International Law in the University of Oxford and Fellow of All Souls College, Oxford

PROFESSOR DAN SAROOSHI

Professor of Public International Law in the University of Oxford and Fellow of The Queen's College, Oxford

PROFESSOR STEFAN TALMON

Professor of Public International Law in the University of Oxford and Fellow of St. Anne's College, Oxford

State Responsibility for International Terrorism

OXFORD MONOGRAPHS IN INTERNATIONAL LAW

The aim of this series is to publish important and original pieces of research on all aspects of international law. Topics that are given particular prominence are those which, while of interest to the academic lawyer, also have important bearing on issues which touch the actual conduct of international relations. Nonetheless, the series is wide in scope and includes monographs on the history and philosophical foundations of international law.

State Responsibility for International Terrorism

Problems and Prospects

KIMBERLEY N. TRAPP

OXFORD

UNIVERSITY PRESS

Great Clarendon Street, Oxford OX2 6DP

Oxford University Press is a department of the University of Oxford.
It furthers the University's objective of excellence in research, scholarship,
and education by publishing worldwide in

Oxford New York

Auckland Cape Town Dar es Salaam Hong Kong Karachi
Kuala Lumpur Madrid Melbourne Mexico City Nairobi
New Delhi Shanghai Taipei Toronto

With offices in

Argentina Austria Brazil Chile Czech Republic France Greece
Guatemala Hungary Italy Japan Poland Portugal Singapore
South Korea Switzerland Thailand Turkey Ukraine Vietnam

Oxford is a registered trade mark of Oxford University Press
in the UK and in certain other countries

Published in the United States
by Oxford University Press Inc., New York

British Library Cataloguing in Publication Data
Data available

Library of Congress Control Number:
2011924624

Typeset by SPI Publisher Services, Pondicherry, India
Printed in Great Britain
on acid-free paper by
CPI Group (UK) Ltd, Croydon, CR0 4YY

ISBN 978–0–19–959299–9

3 5 7 9 10 8 6 4 2

Acknowledgments

This book is based on my doctoral research at the University of Cambridge. The road to completing a PhD-cum-book is long and there are invariably many people whose support, assistance, or indeed forbearance make the journey easier. My own journey started and ended with the unwavering support of my parents, twin sister, and younger twin brothers, and my debt to them is incalculable. Alex, my partner in life throughout this book project, also smoothed the road considerably. His unfailing love (and excellent espressos) made sitting down to even the likes of footnotes and copy-editing a pleasure.

Throughout my PhD, Girton College proved a warm and inspiring academic environment, and provided generous financial support for my research. This research was also funded by the Canadian Council on International Law, the International Security Research Programme of the Canadian Department of Foreign Affairs and the Faculty of Law, Cambridge. Newnham College has been my home throughout the book project, and I am greatly indebted to the College for its generous research funding, and in particular to Dr Catherine Seville, who is a more kind and supportive colleague than anyone could hope for. I would also like to thank Merel Alstein and Ela Kotkowska at Oxford University Press for their support and guidance.

I am very grateful to Dr Guglielmo Verdirame, whose supervision of my PhD was open, thoughtful, and always challenging. Throughout this project, I had occasion to discuss my research with a number of scholars, and I am indebted to them for helping catalyse my thinking. In particular, discussions with Professor James Crawford assisted me in my early conceptualization of this project, and an insightful examination of the PhD by Judge Christopher Greenwood and Professor Stefan Talmon helped shape its development into a book. My research also benefited from the time I spent at Columbia Law School as a visiting scholar, and I am grateful to Professor José Alvarez for his helpful comments on an early draft of Chapter 4. The year I spent at the International Court of Justice, between the 2nd and 3rd years of the PhD, was one of the most intellectually engaging of my life. I am deeply indebted to Vice-President Al-Khasawneh and Judge Simma for their insights and encouragement, and the example they set of academic excellence. This research also profited immeasurably from discussions with Dr Chris Tooley, Dr Isabelle Van Damme, Dr Douglas Guilfoyle, Dr Daniel Joyce, Dr Marko Milanovic, and Professor Geert De Baere. I am fortunate not only to have found in them colleagues who contributed greatly to the stimulating academic environment of the University of Cambridge and the Faculty of Law, but to count these scholars as my dear friends. The importance of their support and friendship throughout the writing process cannot be overstated.

Kimberley N. Trapp

March 2011

General Editors' Preface

The international legal regime governing the relationship between acts of terrorism and States is both complicated and, in almost every case, concerned with covert activity, so that its exact nature and content is very difficult to establish in any given case. While it is rare for States openly to engage in acts of terrorism this does not mean that they should not be held responsible for terrorist acts. Most analyses focus on the question of the attributability of terrorist acts to States, and on the implications thereof for the legality of uses of force in self-defence against States harbouring terrorists. Dr Trapp, in a refreshing approach, takes the question futher. Her study focuses on the substantive obligations to prevent and punish acts of international terrorism and the implementation of State responsibility, both judicially and otherwise, in response to the breach of those obligations. It is an important and timely contribution to a debate that brings together two topics which are the subject of intense contemporary academic and public interest—terrorism and State responsibility.

AVL, DS, ST

Oxford, April 2011

Table of Contents

Table of Cases

PERMANENT COURT OF INTERNATIONAL JUSTICE / INTERNATIONAL COURT OF JUSTICE

NUREMBERG / INTERNATIONAL TRIBUNAL FOR THE FORMER YUGOSLAVIA / INTERNATIONAL CRIMINAL TRIBUNAL FOR RWANDA

ARBITRAL AWARDS

HUMAN RIGHTS JUDGMENTS, DECISIONS AND OPINIONS

GATT AND WTO REPORTS

DOMESTIC JURISPRUDENCE

Table of Treaties

List of Abbreviations

AB	Appellate Body (WTO)
CAT	Committee against Torture
CTC	Counter-Terrorism Committee
CTITF	Counter-Terrorism Implementation Task Force
DSB	Dispute Settlement Body (WTO)
EC	European Community
ECOSOC	United Nations Economic and Social Council
ECtHR	European Court of Human Rights
EU	European Union
ICAO	International Civil Aviation Organization
ICC	International Criminal Court
ICJ	International Court of Justice
ICRC	International Committee of the Red Cross
ICTR	International Criminal Tribunal for Rwanda
ICTY	International Criminal Tribunal for the Former Yugoslavia
IHL	International Humanitarian Law
ILC	International Law Commission
IMO	International Maritime Organization
INTERPOL	International Criminal Police Organization
NAM	Non-Aligned Movement
OAS	Organization of American States
OAU	Organization of African Unity
OIC	Organization of the Islamic Conference
SWGCA	Special Working Group on the Crime of Aggression (ICC)
TSC	Terrorism Suppression Convention
UN	United Nations
UNCLOS	United Nations Convention on the Law of the Sea
UNGA	United Nations General Assembly
UNHCR	United Nations High Commissioner for Refugees
UNIIIC	United Nations International Independent Investigation Commission
UNSC	United Nations Security Council
UNSG	Union Nations Secretary-General
WTO	World Trade Organization

1

Introduction

The concept of 'terrorism' has long been a subject of legal and political discourse and a site of contestation for the international community. During the de-colonization process, 'terrorism' was the label used by developing states to characterize the means used by imperial powers to repress colonial populations,[1] and by the Western world to describe a tool of proxy war employed by weaker states in opposing them.[2] At least since the 1930s, attention has been focused on the use of non-state terrorist actors[3] as an instrument of foreign policy.[4] Today, the 'war on terror' is focused on transnational non-state groups who act frequently with the support or acquiescence of states.[5] Throughout, terrorism has been treated as a phenomenon that straddles the legal regimes of criminal law enforcement, international peace and security, and State responsibility.

The mechanisms available for holding individual terrorist actors criminally responsible for their crimes have been the subject of much study.[6] Equally, the Security Council's response to international terrorism under Chapter VII of the UN Charter, and the applicability of Article 51 of the UN Charter to defensive uses of force in response to terrorist attacks, have attracted much academic comment.[7]

---

[1] See UNGA Resolution 3034 (1972).

[2] See the negotiation of the UN Definition of Aggression, UNGA Resolution 3314 (1974), Annex, discussed in Section 2.1.1.

[3] For the purposes of this book, 'non-state terrorist actors' or 'non-state actors' is the term used in reference to individuals who are not formally state organs or part of a state's apparatus, although their conduct may be attributable to the state on the basis of the control exercised by that state.

[4] King Alexander of Yugoslavia was assassinated in Marseilles on 9 October 1934 by Yugoslav *émigrés* operating from Hungary. Yugoslavia brought the incident to the attention of the Council of the League of Nations, and accused Hungary of complicity in the terrorist activities of the Yugoslav *émigrés*. See League of Nations, Official Journal 1934 (July–December) 1712–14; Liais (1935). See further Sections 3.2 and 6.4.1 for a discussion of the terrorism suppression convention drafted by the League of Nations in response to the assassination.

[5] The 21st century regime of Security Council Chapter VII resolutions addressing terrorism was adopted initially in response to the terrorist attacks of 11 September 2001 ('9/11') carried out by Al Qaeda with at least the acquiescence of the *de facto* Afghan government.

[6] See generally Gross (1973); Bassiouni (1978); A.E. Evans (1978); Murphy (1985); Wise (1987); Kellman (2001); Joyner (2003); Pellet (2003); Schabas and Clémentine (2003); Cassese (2004); Kolb (2004); Proulx (2004); Schabas (2004); Stephens (2004); Arnold (2006); Saul (2006). See further Section 6.4.

[7] See generally Schachter (1989); Lobel (1999); Rostow (2002); Szasz (2002); Alvarez (2003); Happold (2003); Rosand (2003); Ward (2003); Fassbender (2004); Gehr (2004); Rosand (2004); Sur (2004); Donnelly (2005); Happold (2005); Rosand (2005); Saul (2005); Talmon (2005); Bianchi (2006); Bianchi (2006a); Nesi (2006); Santori (2006); Klein (2007); Boulden (2008). See further Section 2.2.3.

Ensuring that individual actors are held criminally responsible for their terrorist offences and responding to terrorism through a security paradigm, however, does not fully address the systemic consequences of un-remedied breaches of international law. States are under a primary obligation to refrain from engaging in and to prevent acts of international terrorism, and to extradite or submit terrorist actors for prosecution. Holding states responsible for breaches of these obligations can play an important role in maintaining respect for international law,[8] 'confirm the validity of fundamental international norms'[9] relating to terrorism, and can prevent the escalation of threats to international security by promoting the reconciliation of the relevant states and restoring 'confidence in a continuing relationship'.[10] Indeed, the possibility of state responsibility has been described as a pre-requisite for the existence of international law itself: 'if one attempts [. . .] to deny the idea of State responsibility because it allegedly conflicts with the idea of sovereignty, one is forced to deny the existence of an international legal order'.[11] The General Assembly took note of the Articles on State Responsibility adopted on second reading by the International Law Commission ('ILC') in December 2001,[12] only two months after the 9/11 terrorist attacks. While studies on particular aspects of state responsibility for international terrorism have been undertaken following the adoption of the ILC Articles on State Responsibility,[13] there has yet to be a comprehensive assessment of the way in which state responsibility for international terrorism is or might be implemented.

The aim of this book is to explore the primary and secondary rules of state responsibility, with a view to identifying both the problems and prospects for effectively holding states responsible for internationally wrongful acts related to terrorism.[14] In seeking to identify problems and prospects, this book focuses principally on aspects of state responsibility that are contested in the terrorism context. This book also engages critically with arguments that the rules on state responsibility are inadequate to meet the threat of terrorism. Sweeping changes have been suggested to the secondary rules of state responsibility as they apply to terrorism (in particular as regards the rules of attribution) and the aim of this book,

---

[8] See Commentary to Part Two, Chapter I, Draft Articles on Responsibility of States for Internationally Wrongful Acts, with Commentaries, in Report of the International Law Commission on the work of its fifty-third session, UN Doc. A/56/10 (2001), 31 [hereinafter 'ILC Articles on State Responsibility'], para 1.

[9] Scobbie (2009), 283.

[10] See Crawford (2000), para 57, discussing the secondary obligations of cessation and assurances of non-repetition.

[11] Ago (1971), 205, para 31. See further Pellet (2010), 4.

[12] See UNGA Resolution 56/83 (2001).

[13] See e.g. Malzahn (2002); Brown (2003); Travalio and Altenburg (2003); Chase (2004); Dupuy (2004); Guillaume (2004); Barnidge (2005); Duffy (2005); Proulx (2005); Becker (2006). In French, see Martin (2006). See also, prior to 9/11, Lillich and Paxman (1977); Condorelli (1989); Franck and Niedermeyer (1989); Sucharitkul (1989); Schreiber (1998).

[14] This book explores state responsibility for acts of terrorism, including sponsorship and support of terrorism and counter-terrorism failures. This book does not address the important question of state responsibility for *excessive* counter-terrorism measures (for instance torture, abductions, extrajudicial killings, or unfair trials).

in part, is to evaluate whether such changes are necessary. In particular, this book considers the extent to which identified problems with the implementation of state responsibility for international terrorism are the result of difficulties inherent in the primary or secondary rules themselves; difficulties resulting from a misunderstanding or misapplication of those rules; or indeed whether such problems are the implication of the particular nature of terrorism or the general consequence of a consensual system of international law based on sovereign equality.

This chapter sets out the legal context within which state responsibility for international terrorism will be examined. Section 1.1 sets out the basic framework of state responsibility, both as contemplated in the ILC Articles on State Responsibility and as a matter of state practice, and outlines the structure of the analysis in this book. Section 1.2 then considers the international legal framework applicable to terrorism, focusing on the overlapping regimes of international law that address and respond to the threat of international terrorism. Finally, Section 1.3 defines international terrorism for the purposes of the book, drawing on elements of the international legal framework applicable to terrorism.

1.1 The framework of state responsibility

The initial project of codifying the law of state responsibility, as conceived by ILC Special Rapporteur Garcia-Amador, was in the form of a code of substantive rules bearing on responsibility for injuries to aliens and their property.[15] Very little progress was made on the project until Special Rapporteur Ago took the helm, and began work based on his proposal that the codification project 'give priority to the definition of the general rules governing the international responsibility of the State'.[16] In this proposal was born the distinction between the primary rules of international law, consisting of the substantive international obligations of states under customary and treaty law,[17] and the secondary rules of state responsibility, of general application, bearing on the identification of a breach of the primary rules and the consequences of any such breach.[18] The ILC Articles on State Responsibility, as adopted on second reading, maintained the distinction between primary and secondary rules,[19] and this book adopts the framework of analysis suggested

---

[15] See e.g. Garcia-Amador (1957); Garcia-Amador (1958); Garcia-Amador (1961).

[16] Ago (1963), 228, para 5.

[17] See Crawford (2002), 16.

[18] *Ibid.* Special Rapporteur on State Responsibility James Crawford queried whether the intellectual origin of the distinction between the primary and secondary rules of state responsibility lies in H.L.A. Hart's *Concept of Law*. See Crawford (2002), 14. See further Mills (2009), 19, 100–1, arguing that H.L.A. Hart's distinction is not reflected in the law of state responsibility, but underlies developments in international constitutional law.

[19] There is some question in the literature as to whether all of the articles in the ILC Articles on State Responsibility are in fact secondary rules, or whether some are primary or even tertiary rules. The question is posed in particular in reference to circumstances precluding wrongfulness (Part One, Chapter V, ILC Articles on State Responsibility) and aid or assistance in the commission of an internationally wrongful act (Art. 16, ILC Articles on State Responsibility). This theoretical question is not one examined in this book, most particularly because the ICJ has treated

thereby. Chapters 2 and 3 examine the substantive obligations bearing on states in relation to international terrorism ('international terrorism obligations') and explore the application of the rules of attribution which determine the primary rule that is engaged by a state's terrorist activities. Chapters 4, 5 and 6 then examine the mechanisms available to give effect to a state's responsibility for international terrorism.

Conduct that is in breach of a primary obligation of international law gives rise to the wrongdoing state's responsibility for the internationally wrongful act by operation of the law.[20] A wrongdoing state is under a secondary obligation, which arises in virtue of its international responsibility, to cease the internationally wrongful act (if it is continuing),[21] and to make full reparation for the injury (whether material or moral) caused by the internationally wrongful act.[22] A further secondary obligation that might arise in virtue of a state's international responsibility is to 'offer appropriate assurances and guarantees of non-repetition, *if circumstances so require*'.[23]

In cases of terrorism carried out by or on behalf of a state, the breach of the primary obligation (examined in Chapter 2) is unlikely to be continuing, given that the breach will terminate on completion of the act of terrorism. As such, cessation will not always be a relevant secondary obligation. In cases, however, where a state supports terrorist activities, or fails to prevent terrorism or to extradite or submit terrorist actors to prosecution, breach of the primary terrorism obligation will certainly be continuing, and the secondary obligation to cease the internationally wrongful conduct will therefore be engaged. There is some debate about whether the obligation of cessation is genuinely a secondary obligation or whether it is merely incidental to the obligation to respect the primary obligation.[24] As injured states tend to address cessation as part of their invocation of responsibility, cessation will be treated in this book as one of the secondary obligations that arise for the wrongdoing state by virtue of its international responsibility.

---

circumstances precluding wrongfulness (in particular, necessity and countermeasures, which are examined in Chapter 5) and the rule prohibiting aid or assistance (examined in Chapter 4) as rules of customary international law. See *Gabčíkovo–Nagymaros Project (Hungary v. Slovakia)*, Judgment, paras 51 and 82–7; *Bosnia Genocide Case*, Judgment, para 420. As a result, whether these rules can strictly be qualified as secondary or not, they are accepted elements of the international legal framework bearing on state responsibility and will be treated as such in this book.

[20] Commentary to Art. 43, ILC Articles on State Responsibility, para 2; Crawford (2010), 23.

[21] Art. 30(a), ILC Articles on State Responsibility. See further Corten (2010), discussing the obligation of cessation as one which gives effect to the general principle of respect for the rule of law.

[22] Art. 31, ILC Articles on State Responsibility.

[23] Emphasis added. Art. 30(b), ILC Articles on State Responsibility. As the obligation to offer appropriate assurances and guarantees of non-repetition is an obligation bearing on future conduct, rather than one which attends to past conduct (as does the obligation to make reparation), the ILC considered that it was best addressed with the obligation of cessation (also concerned with future conduct). See Crawford (2000), para 57; Crawford (2002), 32. This classification of the obligation to offer assurances has yet to be confirmed by the International Court of Justice. See *LaGrand (Germany v. US)*, Judgment, paras 124–5, in which the Court held that the US had met German demands for a general assurance of non-repetition, but did not discuss the legal basis of any such obligation, including whether it was an aspect of cessation or reparation.

[24] See Corten (2010), 546, on the debate.

While the ILC considered that assurances and guarantees of non-repetition would not always be appropriate, and are indeed of a 'rather exceptional character',[25] injured states often request them in regard to the breach of international terrorism obligations (as examined in Section 5.1.4). The Commentary to Article 30(b) of the ILC Articles on State Responsibility acknowledges that the appropriateness of assurances and guarantees will depend on the nature of the obligation breached and the seriousness of the breach[26]—the implication being that the more fundamental the primary rule breached, and the more serious the breach, the more appropriate (and less exceptional) assurances and guarantees of non-repetition might be. As will be examined in Chapter 2, a state's direct participation in an act of terrorism can amount to an act of aggression, and a state's military support for an act of terrorism can amount to a prohibited use of force. State involvement in terrorism therefore breaches primary obligations that lie at the very foundations of the contemporary international legal order, which means that assurances and guarantees of non-repetition will often be appropriate. Finally, the secondary obligation to make reparation can take a number of forms, including restitution (which will often be materially impossible in the terrorism context), compensation (the principal mode of reparation in the terrorism context, as shown by the examination of state practice in Section 6.2), and satisfaction (examined in Section 6.3).[27]

The existence and nature of the secondary obligations set forth above have long been accepted as the consequence of state responsibility,[28] even if calculating compensation or determining appropriate satisfaction is sometimes complicated in the circumstances. As a result, this book focuses on the mechanisms available under international law for giving effect to a state's responsibility. The precise content and application of the secondary obligations is explored incidentally—through an exploration of the mechanisms available under international law for securing a wrongdoing state's compliance with its obligations of cessation and reparation.

Following initial protests by an injured state, wrongdoing states generally refuse to acknowledge responsibility for international terrorism, as evidenced in important cases like the Rainbow Warrior incident[29] and the *Lockerbie Case*.[30] To the extent that a wrongdoing state does not acknowledge its responsibility for an internationally wrongful act related to terrorism and fails to comply with the secondary obligations resulting from its responsibility, the injured state is entitled to take action to secure the wrongdoing state's compliance with its obligations of cessation and reparation. Special Rapporteur Arangio-Ruiz referred to the mechanisms available for implementing state responsibility as the '*facultés* relating to the ways and means—the instrumentalities—by which an injured State may seek to obtain

---

[25] Commentary to Art. 30, ILC Articles on State Responsibility, para 13.
[26] *Ibid.* See further Barbier (2010).
[27] Art. 34, ILC Articles on State Responsibility.
[28] See Crawford (2002), 28.
[29] See Section 2.2.1.
[30] See Sections 4.3 and 6.2.1.

cessation and reparation'.[31] Special Rapporteur Riphagen referred to this implementation as the '*mise en oeuvre*' of state responsibility.[32] Chapters 4, 5 and 6
examine the *facultés* or mechanisms available to states under international law to
effect the *mise en oeuvre* of a wrongdoing state's responsibility for international
terrorism.

The two methods of implementing state responsibility contemplated in the ILC
Articles are (i) the invocation of responsibility and (ii) the adoption of countermeasures.[33] A formal invocation of state responsibility[34] includes (but is not
limited to) filing an application before a competent international tribunal.[35] In
order that the institution of proceedings amount to an effective invocation of
responsibility for breach of the series of international terrorism suppression conventions (discussed in Section 4.4 below), however, it must be preceded by efforts
to negotiate a settlement and to arbitrate. This is because the ICJ's jurisdiction is
subject to these conditions of seisin.[36] Were the institution of proceedings the first
protest of responsibility by the injured state, the conditions of seisin in the
terrorism suppression conventions would not be met, and the Court would lack
jurisdiction—resulting in the ineffectiveness of judicial settlement as a mechanism
for implementing state responsibility.

Dispute settlement was also explored by the ILC as a general obligation in
reference to any dispute regarding 'the interpretation or application of the
present articles [on state responsibility]'[37] and as a possible condition for the
adoption of countermeasures.[38] As the scope of the obligation to settle disputes

---

[31] Arangio-Ruiz (1994a), 21. See also Vereshchetin (1994), 55, arguing that countermeasures
belong not to the substantive, but to the procedural consequences of state responsibility as a means
of law enforcement and implementation of the substantive (and secondary) rules of state responsibility.

[32] Riphagen (1983), 8, para 33.

[33] See Part Three, ILC Articles on State Responsibility.

[34] The invocation of responsibility does not result merely from criticism of a wrongdoing state's
conduct. It requires further action, for instance a demand for reparation, or a request to negotiate the
terms of responsibility (see Commentary to Art. 42, ILC Articles on State Responsibility, para 2).
States have long made public statements criticizing other states for their policies (or lack thereof) in
regard to international terrorism. For instance the UK Prime Minister, while on a visit to India in
July 2010, commented that: '[W]e cannot tolerate in any sense the idea that [Pakistan] is allowed to
look both ways and is able, in any way, to promote the export of terror'. <http://www.bbc.co.uk/
news/uk-10831580>. Similarly, in his statement to the General Assembly in September 2010, the
Indian Minister of Foreign Affairs claimed that '[i]f [. . .] Pakistan were to live up to its commitment not to allow use of its soil by terrorists acting against India, this would significantly help
reduce the trust deficit that impedes the development of better bilateral relations between our two
countries'. See UN News Centre, 'Pakistan must rein in terrorism, top Indian official tells UN',
29 September 2010, <http://www.un.org/apps/news/>. Such critiques do not amount to the
invocation of state responsibility.

[35] See Commentary to Art. 42, ILC Articles on State Responsibility, para 2.

[36] Each of the terrorism suppression conventions contains a compromissory clause which requires
disputing states to negotiate, failing which, to seek arbitration, failing which, the clause confers
jurisdiction on the ICJ.

[37] See Arts. 54 and 56, ILC draft Articles on State Responsibility adopted on first reading, in Report
of the International Law Commission on the work of its forty-eighth session, UN Doc. A/51/10 and
Corr. l, 125 (1996) [hereinafter '1996 ILC draft Articles on State Responsibility'].

[38] Article 48(2) of the 1996 ILC draft Articles on State Responsibility required compulsory third
party dispute settlement (in the form of arbitration). See further Art. 5, Institut de droit international

(framed in terms of negotiation and compulsory conciliation) in the draft articles adopted on first reading in 1996 was overbroad,[39] and states were not prepared to accept compulsory settlement for all disputes relating to state responsibility,[40] this feature was not included in the final draft articles adopted by the ILC on second reading. Furthermore, proposals regarding dispute settlement as a condition for the adoption of countermeasures put the machinery of dispute settlement at the disposal of the targeted state, i.e. the *wrongdoing* state.[41] States were certainly not prepared to accept that they might be forced into dispute settlement, to which they had not given prior consent, by the wrongdoing state. As a result, use of mechanisms of dispute settlement is treated in the ILC Articles as a means of invoking a wrongdoing state's responsibility (which is itself a means for implementing state responsibility), rather than as a means for implementing state responsibility in its own right.

For present purposes, both the institution of proceedings before a competent international tribunal and the adoption of countermeasures are treated as mechanisms for implementing state responsibility. The goal of both mechanisms is to give effect to the obligations of cessation and reparation which arise for a wrongdoing state. Former Special Rapporteur Crawford described countermeasures as 'measures of later (if not final) resort aimed at securing compliance', which were appropriately addressed in the ILC Articles chapter on the implementation of state responsibility.[42] The judicial settlement of disputes is equally a tool used by injured states to 'secure compliance' with the secondary obligations of wrongdoing states, although need not be (and if available, should not be) a 'later (if not final) resort'.[43] Both the judicial settlement of disputes and the adoption of countermeasures pressure wrongdoing states, albeit in different ways, to comply with their secondary obligations. The judicial settlement of a dispute regarding international terrorism does not, by itself, enforce compliance with the secondary obligations resulting from a wrongdoing state's responsibility. But neither does the adoption of countermeasures. This is in the nature of an international legal community based on the sovereign equality of its constituent members. In both cases, the wrongdoing state may be impervious to the pressures of international opinion or the disadvantages resulting from the countermeasures adopted against it, and these mechanisms for implementing state responsibility may ultimately be ineffective. They are

---

(1934); Riphagen (1983), 19; Riphagen (1985), 11–12; Arangio-Ruiz (1991), 20; Arangio-Ruiz (1992), 19–22.

[39] Given that disputes regarding state responsibility cannot be resolved without first resolving any dispute as to the source/breach of the relevant primary rule, the articles in the 1996 draft conceivably required negotiation and compulsory conciliation for 'every dispute as to the existence of an internationally wrongful act of a State or its consequences within the field of responsibility'. Crawford (2002), 10. See also Crawford (2001), para 14.

[40] See Crawford (2002), 58. See further Simma (1988), 307–9; Simma (1994), 103.

[41] Art. 48, 1996 ILC draft Articles on State Responsibility. See further Crawford (1999a), paras 384–7.

[42] See Crawford (2010b), 932.

[43] While the judicial settlement of a dispute does not, in itself, result in the adoption of measures against a wrongdoing state, a decision by the ICJ is a platform from which the adoption of such measures can be contemplated (as explored in Chapters 4 and 5), and decisions of domestic courts and tribunals can catalyze invocations of responsibility (as explored in Chapter 6).

nevertheless the tools available under international law on which injured states rely to re-equilibrate their legal relationships with wrongdoing states.[44] The real difference between the judicial settlement of disputes and the adoption of countermeasures as mechanisms for implementing state responsibility is that the former is contingent on the consent of both the injured and wrongdoing states (however expressed) while the latter is unilateral, adopted at the discretion of the injured state. This difference informs the analysis of the problems and prospects of these two mechanisms for implementing state responsibility for international terrorism in Chapters 4 and 5.

The principal objective of this book is to explore the implementation of state responsibility for an internationally wrongful act related to terrorism by injured states, as defined in Article 42 of the ILC Articles on State Responsibility.[45] In the terrorism context, injured states will generally be states in whose territory, against whose nationals, or against whose interests terrorist attacks have been committed. The reason for the focus on injured states is that the benefit of the full range of secondary obligations resulting from a wrongdoing state's responsibility is only available to the injured state as defined in Article 42 of the ILC Articles on State Responsibility,[46] and the injured state is the only state with a recognized right to adopt the full range of measures aimed at securing the wrongdoing state's compliance with its secondary obligations, including the adoption of countermeasures.[47]

1.2 The international legal regimes applicable to terrorism

International terrorism is subject to several different regimes in international law— understood both in terms of accountability and substantive law. This section introduces the different regimes of law that are potentially applicable to international terrorism and the regime interaction issues which will be explored in this book.

1.2.1 Regimes of accountability applicable to international terrorism

The international community has consistently addressed terrorism as a criminal phenomenon through the adoption of treaties that aim to secure the individual

---

[44] In the collection of essays entitled *The Law of International Responsibility* edited by (among others) former Special Rapporteur Crawford, the judicial settlement of disputes in matters of state responsibility is considered in Part V of the collection, entitled 'The Implementation of International Responsibility'. See Crawford, Pellet, et al. eds, *The Law of International Responsibility* (Oxford: Oxford University Press, 2010). In that edited collection, see Cottereau (2010), 1115, referring to the pacific settlement of disputes as a means of implementing international responsibility.

[45] A state is an 'injured state' under Article 42 of the ILC Articles on State Responsibility if the obligation breached is owed to it individually, or specially affects that state. Injured states are to be distinguished from 'interested states', which can also invoke a wrongdoing state's responsibility if the obligation breached is 'owed to the international community as a whole', but does not specially affect the interests of that state. Art. 48(1), ILC Articles on State Responsibility.

[46] Interested states can only claim cessation, assurances and guarantees of non-repetition, and the 'performance of the obligation of reparation [...] *in the interests of the injured state* or the beneficiaries of the obligation breached'. Emphasis added. Art. 48(2), ILC Articles on State Responsibility.

[47] See Section 5.1.2.

responsibility of terrorist actors.[48] To date, there are thirteen international conventions and protocols that require state parties to (i) criminalize a particular manifestation of international terrorism under domestic law; (ii) co-operate in the prevention of that terrorist act, and (iii) take action to ensure that alleged offenders are held responsible for their crime (through the imposition of an obligation to extradite or submit the alleged offender to prosecution).[49] Collectively, these conventions are referred to in this book as the 'Terrorism Suppression Conventions' or the 'TSCs'.[50] Terrorism, however, is not merely a tool of the dispossessed. It is equally a tool used by states to achieve, in a deniable fashion, their foreign policy objectives. As a result, international law addresses the state as a potential terrorist actor, and states are subject to an obligation to refrain from participating in, supporting, or acquiescing in acts of international terrorism.

Acts of terrorism carried out with the active participation, support, or acquiescence of states, such as the attack on the 'Rainbow Warrior' in New Zealand and the terrorist attacks against the Vienna and Rome international airports in 1985, the

---

[48] The first international effort to address terrorism as a criminal phenomenon followed the assassination of King Alexander of Yugoslavia in 1934. See Sections 3.2 and 6.4.1 for a discussion of the terrorism suppression convention drafted by the League of Nations in response to the assassination.

[49] Convention for the Suppression of Unlawful Seizure of Aircraft, signed at the Hague on 16 December 1970, 860 UNTS 105 [hereinafter 'Hague Convention']; Protocol Supplementary to the Convention for the Suppression of Unlawful Seizure of Aircraft, done at Beijing on 10 September 2010 [hereinafter '2010 Protocol to the Hague Convention' (not yet in force)]; Convention for the Suppression of Unlawful Acts against the Safety of Civil Aviation, signed at Montreal on 23 September 1971, 974 UNTS 177 [hereinafter 'Montreal Convention']; Protocol for the Suppression of Unlawful Acts of Violence at Airports Serving International Civil Aviation, signed at Montreal on 24 February 1988, ICAO Doc. 9518 [hereinafter '1988 Protocol to the Montreal Convention']; Convention on the Suppression of Unlawful Acts Relating to International Civil Aviation, done at Beijing on 10 September 2010 [hereinafter 'Beijing Convention' (not yet in force)]; Convention on the Prevention and Punishment of Crimes against Internationally Protected Persons, including Diplomatic Agents, adopted by the General Assembly of the United Nations on 14 December 1973, 1035 UNTS 167 [hereinafter 'Internationally Protected Persons Convention']; International Convention against the Taking of Hostages, adopted by the General Assembly of the United Nations on 17 December 1979, 1316 UNTS 205 [hereinafter 'Hostages Convention']; Convention for the Suppression of Unlawful Acts against the Safety of Maritime Navigation, done at Rome on 10 March 1988, IMO Doc. SUA/CONF/15/Rev.1 [hereinafter 'SUA Convention']; Protocol for the Suppression of Unlawful Acts against the Safety of Fixed Platforms Located in the Continental Shelf, done at Rome on 10 March 1988, IMO Doc. SUA/CONF/16/Rev.2 [hereinafter '1988 Protocol to the SUA Convention']; Protocol of 2005 to the Convention for the Suppression of Unlawful Acts against the safety of Maritime Navigation, done at Rome on 14 October 2005, IMO. Doc. LEG/CONF.15/21 (2005) [hereinafter '2005 Protocol to the SUA Convention']; International Convention on the Suppression of Terrorist Bombings, adopted by the General Assembly of the United Nations on 15 December 1997, UN Doc. A/RES/52/164 (1997) [hereinafter 'Terrorist Bombing Convention']; International Convention for the Suppression of the Financing of Terrorism, adopted by the General Assembly of the United Nations on 9 December 1999, UN Doc. A/RES/54/109 (1997) [hereinafter 'Terrorism Financing Convention']; International Convention for the Suppression of Acts of Nuclear Terrorism, adopted by the General Assembly of the United Nations on 13 April 2005, UN Doc. A/59/766 (2005) [hereinafter 'Nuclear Terrorism Convention'].

[50] The TSCs negotiated under the auspices of the International Civil Aviation Organization ('ICAO') in force at the time of writing, in particular the Hague Convention, Montreal Convention and 1988 Protocol to the Montreal Convention, are referred to in this book as the 'ICAO TSCs'. The TSCs negotiated under the auspices of the International Maritime Organization ('IMO'), such as the SUA Convention, 1988 Protocol to the SUA Convention and 2005 Protocol to the SUA Convention, are referred to as the 'IMO TSCs'.

Lockerbie bombing in 1988, and the 9/11 terrorist attacks against the World Trade Center and the Pentagon, bring into sharp relief the interaction between the different regimes of accountability applicable to acts of terrorism under international law. For instance, when a state actively participates in an act of terrorism, fails to prevent a terrorist offence, or fails to extradite or submit a terrorist actor to prosecution, the one act of terrorism may give rise to both individual criminal and state responsibility.[51] Concurrent responsibility may arise in a strict sense when conduct results in both individual criminal and state responsibility for breach of the same norm, as was alleged in the *Bosnia Genocide Case*,[52] or where the same act gives rise to individual criminal and state responsibility, but the primary rule breached (or the source of the primary rule breached) is in fact different, as in the Rainbow Warrior case.[53] In both cases, the state is held 'directly' responsible for the relevant terrorist act through the mechanism of attribution.[54] Concurrent responsibility may also arise in a looser sense when the individual actor is held criminally responsible for terrorist conduct, but the state is held responsible for its failure to act appropriately in relation to such conduct, by failing to prevent, or to extradite or submit to prosecution. In such a case, state responsibility is 'indirect' in that the state is not held responsible for the terrorist act itself, but for its own failure to act in regards to the terrorist act. The terrorist conduct acts as a catalyst[55] for the state's responsibility.

While both individual and state responsibility are intended to hold a wrongdoer to account, their objectives are very different. Criminal responsibility is punitive in nature. State responsibility is not punitive, nor is it civil in character.[56] State

---

[51] This book refers to the overlap of individual criminal and state responsibility as 'concurrent responsibility'. On the relationship between individual criminal and State responsibility, see generally Nollkaemper (2003); Degan (2002); Dupuy (2002). See further Chapter 6, discussing the relationship in the terrorism context.

[52] Individual Bosnian Serbs have been charged with the crime of genocide before the International Criminal Tribunal for the Former Yugoslavia (see e.g. *Popović et al.* (ICTY-05-88), Indictment), on the basis of the Tribunal's Statute which incorporates the prohibitions set forth in the Convention on the Prevention and Punishment of the Crime of Genocide, 9 December 1948, 78 UNTS 277 [hereinafter 'Genocide Convention']. Bosnia also alleged that Serbia was directly responsible for genocide on the basis of the attributability of the genocide committed by Bosnian Serbs. See *Bosnia Genocide Case*, Judgment. Concurrent responsibility in the sense of the *Bosnia Genocide Case* would be possible in the terrorism context if an individual were held criminally responsible for a terrorist crime, and the state were held responsible for the terrorist crime on the basis of its attributability, both pursuant to a Terrorism Suppression Convention. See *supra* note 49 for a list of the Terrorism Suppression Conventions, and Section 4.2 for a discussion of the TSCs as a basis of direct state responsibility for acts of terrorism.

[53] The French secret service agents prosecuted for the Rainbow Warrior attack were found guilty of manslaughter and wilful damage to a ship by means of an explosive (see Section 6.2.4), but France's conduct amounted to an unlawful use of force (see Section 2.1.2).

[54] See Section 2.2 on the rules of attribution as they apply in the terrorism context. On whether a state's acceptance of its direct responsibility for an act of international terrorism bars prosecution of the individual state official who carried out the act on the basis of immunity *ratione materiae*, see Section 3.2.2 below.

[55] Special Rapporteur Ago first introduced the notion of private conduct as a catalyst for state responsibility in his Fourth Report on State Responsibility. See Ago (1972), 71, para 65. The work on state responsibility by Condorelli also adopts the term 'catalyst'. See Condorelli (1984), 100; Condorelli (1989), 240.

[56] See Kelsen (1953), 87.

responsibility is 'purely and simply international',[57] and its purpose is restorative. The process of invocation of responsibility by the injured state and compliance with the secondary obligations of cessation and reparation by the wrongdoing state restores the equilibrium between sovereign states. Nevertheless, the possibility of state criminal responsibility for the perpetration of international crimes was long contemplated by the ILC in its codification project on state responsibility.[58] The ensuing debate over a regime of criminal responsibility for states (both in the extensive literature on the subject[59] and in state comments on the codification project) covered a broad range of issues, including the absence of an appropriate institutional infrastructure to implement the criminal responsibility of states,[60] the impact of such responsibility on the still developing regime of individual criminal responsibility under international law,[61] and the form sanctions might take in the event of such responsibility.[62] While none of these issues raise insoluble conceptual difficulties,[63] highlighting instead the difficulties involved in giving effect to a regime of criminal responsibility between sovereign and equal states, they were sufficiently divisive to result in the 'depenalisation of state responsibility' within the framework of the ILC Articles on State Responsibility.[64] This book takes *pour acquis* the non-punitive nature of state responsibility as it now exists in the ILC Articles on State Responsibility, which is instead conceptualized as a vehicle for restoring the primary legal relationship between the wrongdoing and injured states, including through full reparation for any injury caused by the internationally wrongful act.[65]

State responsibility for internationally wrongful acts related to terrorism, in addition to overlapping with individual criminal responsibility, may equally give rise to a threat to international peace and security to which the Security Council could respond under Chapter VII of the UN Charter. That said,

---

[57] Crawford (1998), 9, para 60. See also *Bosnia Genocide Case*, Judgment, paras 65–6; Crawford (2010), 22.

[58] State criminality was first raised by Special Rapporteur Garcia-Amador (see Garcia-Amador (1956), 239–45), and was formalized in what became the famous 'Article 19' by Special Rapporteur Ago (see Ago (1976), 3). In support of the creation of a regime of criminal responsibility for states, see generally Jørgenson (2000).

[59] See e.g. Mohr (1987); Dominicé (1989); Dupuy (1989); Elias (1989); Graefrath (1989); Jiménez de Aréchaga (1989); Simma (1994a), 301–21; Bowett (1998); Pellet (1997); Pellet (1999); Jorgensen (2000).

[60] See e.g. ILC, Comments and Observations received from Governments on State Responsibility, UN Doc. A/CN.4/488 (1998), 51 (Austria), 54 (France).

[61] *Ibid*, 51 (Austria), 135 (Germany).

[62] See Crawford (1998), 3, para 51.

[63] See Crawford (2002), 19.

[64] See Crawford (2002), 36. The concern that certain breaches of international law are more serious than others, which was initially framed in terms of state crimes, was addressed through provisions in the ILC Articles on State Responsibility relating to serious breaches of peremptory norms and breaches of international obligations owed to the international community as a whole. See Arts. 40, 41 and 48, ILC Articles on State Responsibility. See generally Crawford (2010a). On the abandonment of the vocabulary of criminal law in reference to serious breaches of obligations 'essential for the protection of fundamental interests of the international community', see Pellet (1999); Pellet (2010).

[65] See generally Crawford (2002), Introduction; Commentary to Art. 31, ILC Articles on State Responsibility.

the purpose and limits of Chapter VII measures are driven by a security paradigm, rather than one concerned with questions of legal responsibility. The Security Council Chapter VII framework is legally and conceptually different from that of state responsibility, both in the purpose of its interventions (which is 'to maintain or restore international peace and security',[66] to be distinguished from that of state responsibility, which is to re-establish the primary *legal* relationship between the wrongdoing and injured states) and the scope of conduct to which it can respond (which is not limited, as is state responsibility, to the breach of international obligations). As a result, the ILC Articles on State Responsibility are 'without prejudice to the Charter of the United Nations',[67] reflecting the hierarchical position of the UN Charter.[68]

But neither the UN Charter nor the ILC Articles on State Responsibility suggest that state conduct that is in breach of an international obligation and also falls within the Security Council's Chapter VII competence is, by virtue of the latter, exempted from the regime of state responsibility. The Commentary to Article 40 of the ILC Articles on State Responsibility (in regard to serious breaches of *jus cogens* obligations) notes that '[i]n the case of aggression, the Security Council is given a specific role by the Charter',[69] but does not suggest that the Security Council's role is exclusive. Indeed, given the list of *jus cogens* obligations listed in the ILC Commentary to Article 40 (including the prohibition of genocide and apartheid), which fall within the scope of the Security Council's Chapter VII competence, the very existence of a supplementary regime of state responsibility to address the breach of those obligations suggests that the Security Council's role in respect thereof was not considered exclusive. There is the additional question, however, of whether the Security Council, in addressing conduct that amounts to a threat to international peace and security *and* a breach of an international obligation, could displace or suspend the regime of state responsibility in respect of the breach (including an injured state's right to demand cessation and assurances of non-repetition, or to adopt countermeasures to induce the wrongdoing state to comply with its secondary obligations of cessation and reparation). The question remains an open one,[70] but there is no Security Council practice that has suspended the regime of state responsibility as it applies to the breach of an international obligation. This book therefore examines the regime of state responsibility as it applies to breaches of international terrorism obligations, even though the breach of those obligations is also likely to fall within the scope of the Security Council's Chapter VII competence.

---

[66] Art. 39, Charter of the United Nations, 26 June 1945, 1 UNTS XVI [hereinafter 'UN Charter'].

[67] Art. 59, ILC Articles on State Responsibility.

[68] On the different approaches taken to the interaction between the law of state responsibility and the UN Charter throughout the drafting history of Article 59, see Gowlland-Debbas (2010).

[69] Commentary to Art. 40, ILC Articles on State Responsibility, para 9. On terrorism as an act of aggression, see Section 2.1.1.

[70] See generally Gowlland-Debbas (2010). But see Sicilianos (2010), 1141–2, arguing that the Security Council sanctions regime under Chapter VII is exclusive, and once the Security Council has adopted sanctions, non-injured states (i.e. those acting in the collective interest) must suspend any countermeasures they adopted in response to the internationally wrongful act.

Prior to the 9/11 terrorist attacks, the Security Council treated the possibility of impunity for terrorist offences as a threat to international peace and security, and put its Chapter VII 'muscle' behind requests for the extradition or surrender of accused individuals made by injured states.[71] As such, there was a great deal of interaction between the criminal law enforcement regime applicable to acts of international terrorism and the UN Charter framework for the maintenance of international peace and security. Following 9/11, the Security Council's approach to international terrorism shifted. The Council defined the phenomenon of international terrorism as a threat to international peace and security and began 'legislating',[72] adopting Chapter VII resolutions that impose substantive obligations on states to refrain from engaging in, and to suppress, international terrorism.[73] For the most part, the Chapter VII obligations duplicate those that exist under customary international law and the TSCs (although the Security Council did effectively impose such obligations on states irrespective of whether they were party to relevant Terrorism Suppression Conventions). This book examines the Security Council's response to international terrorism in so far as it has had an impact on or relates to the application of the general law of state responsibility in the terrorism context.

Finally, terrorist attacks that are launched from a foreign state's territory might give rise to both the territorial state's responsibility for supporting terrorism or failing to diligently prevent harm emanating from its territory and the victim state's right to use force in self-defence in that foreign state's territory (against the terrorist attackers). Defensive force is not used in foreign territory for the purposes of holding the participating or acquiescing state (or individual terrorist actors) to account for their wrongdoing. Instead, it serves to protect the security interests of the injured (and victim) state. This book explores the right to use force in self-defence against terrorist attacks only in so far as developments with respect thereto affect (or have been argued to affect) the law of state responsibility, in particular the secondary rules of attribution.[74]

---

[71] See Section 4.3 discussing the *Lockerbie Case* and Section 6.2.5 discussing the attempted assassination of President Mubarak. See also the preambles of the Terrorism Financing Convention and the draft comprehensive terrorism suppression convention (discussed below, *infra* notes 80–2 and accompanying text), which highlight the overlap between regimes of criminal responsibility and threats to friendly relations amongst states and international peace and security.

[72] The legitimacy of the Security Council's assuming the role of international legislature has been debated in the academic literature (see e.g. Szasz (2002); Happold (2003); Rosand (2005); Talmon (2005)), but in practice, states have complied with at least the reporting obligations imposed on them pursuant to relevant Security Council Chapter VII resolutions.

[73] See e.g. UNSC Resolution 1373 (2001), imposing obligations on states to prevent and criminalize acts of terrorism and the financing of terrorism, and to refrain from actively or passively supporting persons or entities involved in terrorist acts; UNSC Resolution 1540 (2004), imposing obligations on states to prevent the proliferation of weapons of mass destruction ('WMDs') to non-state actors, criminalize the development or acquisition of such weapons by non-state actors, and to refrain from supporting non-state actors in their efforts to acquire WMDs.

[74] See Section 2.2.

1.2.2 Regimes of substantive law applicable to international terrorism

There are two separate regime interaction issues in relation to the substantive law applicable to international terrorism. The first, in reference to acts of terrorism carried out by or on behalf of a state or with the support of a state, concerns the relationship between rules prohibiting states from engaging in terrorism and the broader corpus of international law regulating the activities of states in their international relations. This book argues (in Chapter 2) that the terrorism-specific prohibition is merely an instantiation of rules under general international law that regulate the use of force. International terrorism engaged in by states, against other states, is but a particular form of using force in international relations, and the use of force in international relations is amply regulated by the UN Charter and customary international law. This book therefore accepts and advocates the continued relevance and appropriateness of the *jus ad bellum* in a post-9/11 world.

The second potential area for interaction in regard to applicable substantive law in the terrorism context regards conduct during an armed conflict. While it is clear that international humanitarian law ('IHL') prohibits acts of terrorism, the issue considered in this book is the extent to which the Terrorism Suppression Conventions also apply to acts committed during the course of an armed conflict that meet the elements of offences defined in the Conventions. The question, examined in Sections 3.3 (in reference to armed conflicts in which a people are fighting in exercise of their right of self-determination) and 4.2.2 (in reference to the military activities of states), is effectively one of treaty interpretation, as a number of the TSCs contain clauses that may exclude (to a greater or lesser extent) such conduct from their scope. The analysis in Chapters 3 and 4 suggests that the TSCs which address this question of regime interaction generally supplement, but do not supplant, IHL as the body of law applicable to armed conflicts.

1.3 Defining international terrorism

This book defines terrorism as states have done, through the Terrorism Suppression Conventions, and relevant General Assembly and Security Council resolutions, and examines the regime of state responsibility as it applies to violence that states have singled out as particularly in need of regulation. These instruments evidence a general agreement that terrorism should be prohibited and punished, and general agreement on what 'terrorism' looks like in its *actus reus* and *mens rea* elements (as discussed further below), but there is continuing disagreement about who a 'terrorist' might be. The manifestation of this disagreement is the seemingly interminable debate on whether a distinction should be drawn between acts of terrorism and acts of violence committed in furtherance of a struggle for self-determination.

1.3.1 The self-determination debate as a question of regime interaction

Some members of the international community (in particular members of the Non-Aligned Movement ('NAM')),[75] have long insisted that the definition of international terrorism is not only about the elements of terrorist offences, but is equally about who is entitled to use violence,[76] and for what purposes.[77] It is this potential element of the definition of terrorism that the international community has struggled with since the Secretary-General first placed international terrorism on the General Assembly's agenda in 1972.[78] The early position of NAM members in this debate was to emphasize the legitimacy of struggles for self-determination and to argue that those waging such struggles are entitled to use any means at their disposal.[79] While this position has slowly been qualified, in favour of one that accepts limitations on means and methods of warfare in exercising the right of self-determination (as discussed further in Section 3.3), some states continue to insist that the issue goes to the very definition of 'terrorism'. The latest United Nations initiative to define terrorism generally as an offence (rather than in reference to particular acts of terrorism under the TSCs) has been through the elaboration of a comprehensive terrorism suppression convention.[80] Work on the draft comprehensive terrorism suppression convention has been ongoing for over ten years.[81] To date, there has been no consensus on whether acts committed in furtherance of a people's right of self-

---

[75] See <http://www.nam.gov.za/> for a list of members.

[76] See Saul (2006), 4.

[77] See e.g. summary record of the 5th meeting of the *Ad Hoc* Committee on International Terrorism, UN Doc. A/AC.160/SR.5 (1977), para 10 (Algeria); summary record of the 8th meeting of the *Ad Hoc* Committee on International Terrorism, UN Doc. A/AC.160/SR.8 (1977), para 35 (Tanzania). See further Section 3.3.

[78] The Secretary General attempted to de-politicize the issue of international terrorism by claiming that he had the general issue, and no specific incident, in mind (see 'Questions related to international terrorism', 26 Yearbook of the United Nations (1972) 639, 640), but it is widely believed that the impetus for the Secretary General's request was (i) the murder of eleven Israeli athletes participating in the Olympic Games at Munich by the Black September Organization on 5 September 1972 and (ii) the attack on civilian passengers at Lod Airport in Israel by Japanese terrorists (working with the PLO) on 30 May 1972, killing twenty-eight and wounding seventy-eight. See Sofaer (1986), 903; Lambert (1990), 32; Romanov (1990), 295.

[79] This position was consistently articulated during the negotiation of the Hostages Convention. Members of NAM emphasized that the UN had condemned practices of apartheid and could not tie the hands of the victims of those practices in their attempts to recover their freedom. See e.g. summary record of the 8th meeting of the *Ad Hoc* Committee on the drafting of an International Convention against the Taking of Hostages, UN Doc. A/AC.188/SR.8 (1978), paras 1–6 (Algeria); para 24 (Lesotho); para 28 (Tanzania). This position continues to be adopted by some members of NAM during negotiation of the draft comprehensive terrorism suppression convention. *Infra* note 82 and accompanying text.

[80] India first proposed a draft comprehensive terrorism suppression convention in 1996. See Letter dated 1 November 1996 from the Permanent Representative of India to the United Nations addressed to the Secretary-General, UN Doc. A/C.6/51/6 (1996).

[81] Pursuant to UNGA Resolution 53/109 (1998), the General Assembly charged the 51/210 *Ad Hoc* Committee with consideration of a comprehensive terrorism suppression convention.

determination should be excluded from the definition of terrorist acts in the convention.[82]

Opponents of distinguishing between acts of terrorism and acts committed in furtherance of a people's right of self-determination (principally Western states) generally highlight that the legitimacy of a cause does not itself legitimize the use of certain forms of violence, especially against the innocent.[83] These opponents consider that the proposed distinction conflates limiting a people's right to self-determination (which is impermissible) with limiting means and methods of exercising that right (which is both permissible and necessary). In the same way that the right of states to defend themselves is not undermined or affected by the limitations on methods and means of warfare imposed by the laws of war, the right of self-determination is not undermined or affected by limitations imposed on the methods and means of exercising that right. The position taken by Western states, which distinguishes between a right and methods and means of exercising that right, appears to the present author to be the more principled position. The difficulty with the position taken by Western states is that they then tend to conflate imposing limitations on the methods and means of fighting in exercise of the right of self-determination with the prohibition of terrorism, when such limitations should be a question for humanitarian law.

Conflicts in which a people are fighting in exercise of their right of self-determination have long been recognized as armed conflicts to which humanitarian law applies (although whether such conflicts should be legally characterized as international armed conflicts has proven more controversial). As discussed in Chapter 3, Article 1(4) of Additional Protocol I to the Geneva Conventions of 12 August 1949 incorporates factually non-international armed conflicts in which a people is fighting in exercise of their right of self-determination into the legal definition of international armed conflict.[84] Given that the international community has recognized that the right of self-determination is something worth fighting for,

---

[82] UNGA, 56th Session, 12th meeting, UN Doc. A/56/PV.12 (2001), 3; Report of the *Ad Hoc* Committee established by General Assembly Resolution 51/210 of 17 December 1996, UN Doc. A/59/37 (2004), Annex I, paras 15–17. See in particular, proposals that self-determination be excluded from the definition of terrorism, UNGA, Sixth Committee, UN Doc. A/C.6/55/SR.27 (2000), paras 41–5 (Qatar and Egypt); UNGA, Sixth Committee, UN Doc. A/C.6/55/L.2 (2000), Annex III, para 30 (Malaysia). See also UNGA, Sixth Committee, UN Doc. A/C.6/60/L.6 (2005), Annex, paras 2–17. No progress has been made on this issue. See Reports of the *Ad Hoc* Committee established by General Assembly Resolution 51/210 of 17 December 1996, UN Doc. A/61/37 (2006), Annex I, para 2; UN Doc. A/62/37 (2007), Annex, paras 5 and 11–21; UN Doc. A/63/37 (2008), Annex I, paras 5–6; UN Doc. A/64/37 (2009), para 6; UN Doc. A/65/37 (2010), paras 3 and 11.

[83] See Report of the *Ad Hoc* Committee on International Terrorism, UN Doc. A/9028 (1973), paras 22–3; summary record of the 6th meeting of the *Ad Hoc* Committee on International Terrorism, UN Doc. A/AC.160/SR.6 (1977), para 3 (Austria); summary record of the 4th meeting of the *Ad Hoc* Committee on International Terrorism, UN Doc. A/AC.160/SR.4 (1979), para 31 (US).

[84] The circumstances under which a non-international armed conflict will amount to an international armed conflict because a people is fighting in exercise of a right of self-determination, as envisioned in Article 1(4) of the Protocol Additional to the Geneva Conventions of 12 August 1949, and Relating to the Protection of Victims of International Armed Conflicts, 8 June 1977, 1125 UNTS 3 [hereinafter 'API'], is not defined clearly in the Additional Protocol. The Commentary to API suggests optimistically that it is a question of 'common sense'. See ICRC (1987), 56.

acts of war carried out by a people in furtherance of that right should be evaluated on the basis of their compliance with humanitarian law. Indeed, given that the NAM was the principal architect of Article 1(4) API, which situated struggles for self-determination within the context of armed conflicts (and thereby accepted that persons fighting in exercise of the right of self-determination are subject to restrictions on means and methods of warfare imposed by humanitarian law), it makes little sense to approach the terrorism/self-determination debate as one bearing on the definition of terrorism. Instead, the debate is really about regime interaction—in particular whether acts of violence committed in furtherance of a struggle for self-determination should be evaluated on the basis of the terrorism suppression regime or humanitarian law—and will be treated as such in this book. While a regime interaction approach to the distinction (if any) between terrorism and self-determination is increasingly the approach taken by NAM delegates in negotiating the draft comprehensive terrorism suppression convention,[85] and is indeed the approach taken in the existing TSCs (given that self-determination has not been not addressed as a matter of definition, but purely as a matter of exclusion from the scope of the TSCs),[86] there are still some states that insist on characterizing the matter as a question of definition.[87]

Even as a question of regime interaction, however, negotiations have not always managed to leave acts of war committed in furtherance of a struggle for self-determination to be evaluated on the basis of humanitarian law. Uneven ratification of API, and the absence of an international criminal law enforcement framework in the context of humanitarian law treaties applicable to non-international armed conflicts, has meant that certain acts of war committed in furtherance of a right of self-determination that should be evaluated on the basis of humanitarian law also fall to be evaluated pursuant to the Terrorism Suppression Conventions.[88] To the extent that such acts of violence are genuinely carried out in the context of an armed conflict (even if one that is legally characterized as non-international), this is perhaps a regrettable result. But that result is a matter for the negotiated principles of regime interaction and the particularities of humanitarian law as applied in the context of non-international armed conflicts, rather than a question of the definition of terrorism. The issue of self-determination is therefore explored in this book in reference to the scope of application of the Terrorism Suppression Conven-

---

[85] In an oral report to the working group on measures to eliminate international terrorism, the Coordinator of the 51/210 *Ad Hoc* Committee described the approach taken to negotiations on the draft comprehensive terrorism suppression convention as follows: 'the approach taken [...] sought to (a) proscribe, as comprehensively as possible, through inclusionary clauses, the particular conduct; and then (b) provide particular exclusionary "safeguards" in respect of certain activities. [...] [T]he approach in the current negotiations was that such exclusions formed the essence of "applicable or choice of law" and "without prejudice" clauses, [and had] been agreed upon following intense debates and delicate negotiations. [...] [T]here had been at least some common ground in that the activities which were to be excluded were the subject of regulation by other legal regimes, including the law under the Charter of the United Nations, international humanitarian law, and aspects of international and national "security law"'. UNGA, Sixth Committee, UN Doc. A/C.6/64/SR.14 (2009), para 16.

[86] See further Section 3.3.

[87] *Supra* note 82.

[88] See Section 3.3.

tions—whether limited through exclusion clauses or through the adoption of reservations on ratification—and their interaction with humanitarian law.

1.3.2 An emerging definition of 'international terrorism'?

Through the series of Terrorism Suppression Conventions, states have co-operated to suppress the kind of violent conduct that is criminalized in most domestic jurisdictions, coupled with an added element of (i) prohibited means or method (bombing,[89] hostage taking,[90] hijacking,[91] shipjacking,[92] or use or transport of biological, chemical or nuclear weapons)[93]; (ii) prohibited target (internationally protected persons,[94] civil aircraft,[95] international airports,[96] maritime navigation,[97]

---

[89] The offences defined in Article 2 of the Terrorist Bombing Convention include delivering, placing, discharging or detonating explosives in a place of public use, a state or governmental facility, a public transportation system or an infrastructure facility, with the intent of causing death, serious bodily injury or major economic loss.

[90] The offences defined in Article 1 of the Hostages Convention include detaining and threatening to kill, injure or continue to detain a person in order to compel a third party, namely a state, an international governmental organization, a natural or juridical person, or a group of persons, to do or abstain from doing any act as an explicit or implicit condition of the release of that person.

[91] Article 1 of the Hague Convention defines unlawfully seizing or threatening to seize control of an aircraft as an offence.

[92] Article 3 of the SUA Convention adopts the framework of the Hague Convention and Montreal Convention in defining offences in reference to maritime navigation. In particular, unlawfully seizing or threatening to seize control of a ship and acts likely to endanger the safety of the ship or its safe navigation are offences under the SUA Convention.

[93] Possession of a nuclear weapon (with intent to cause death or serious bodily injury or substantial damage to property or the environment) and the use of a nuclear weapon or causing damage to a nuclear facility in a manner which releases or risks the release of radioactive material (both with intent to cause death or serious bodily injury, substantial damage to property or the environment, or with the intent to compel a natural or legal person, an international organization or a state to do or refrain from doing an act) are the offences defined under Article 2 of the Nuclear Terrorism Convention. Article 4(5) of the 2005 Protocol to the SUA Convention and Article 1 of the Beijing Convention (not yet in force) require states to criminalize the transport by ship or civil aircraft (respectively) of explosive or radioactive material (with knowledge that it is intended to be used to cause death, serious bodily injury or damage, for terrorist purposes (as defined below)), and the use on, against or from a ship or civil aircraft (respectively) of explosives or biological, chemical or nuclear weapons ('BCN weapons').

[94] Article 2 of the Internationally Protected Persons Convention requires state parties to criminalize attacks (murder and kidnapping included) against the person or liberty of internationally protected persons, or violent attacks upon their official premises, private accommodation or means of transport where such attack is likely to endanger the internationally protected person.

[95] See the Hague Convention and 2010 Protocol to the Hague Convention (not yet in force, which does not define any new primary offences, but adds accessory offences to those listed in the Hague Convention, including organizing or directing others to commit an offence under the Hague Convention, and assisting a person who has committed such an offence to evade justice); the Montreal Convention (which requires states to criminalize acts likely to destroy an aircraft in service, or render it incapable of flight or endanger its safety in flight); and the Beijing Convention (not yet in force, which requires states to criminalize the use of an aircraft to cause death or bodily injury – as was the case in the 9/11 terrorist attacks).

[96] Article II of the 1988 Protocol to the Montreal Convention requires states to criminalize unlawfully and intentionally using any device, substance or weapon to perform an act of violence against a person at an international airport which is likely to cause death or serious bodily injury, or destroy or seriously damage the facilities of an international airport or aircraft not in service located at an international airport, if such act endangers safety at the airport.

[97] See the SUA Convention and 2005 Protocol to the SUA Convention.

fixed platforms on the continental shelf,[98] or civilians)[99]; or some combination thereof. The earlier Conventions, in particular the Hague Convention, Montreal Convention, 1988 Protocol to the Montreal Convention, and the Internationally Protected Persons Convention, all require states to criminalize conduct without qualifying the relevant conduct as 'terrorist' and without defining the relevant offences in reference to what might be characterized as a terrorist purpose (in particular the purpose of intimidating a population, or compelling a government or an international organization to do or to abstain from doing any act). These Conventions have nevertheless long been considered part of the terrorism suppression regime.[100]

In other cases, a prohibited method or target must be coupled with a terrorist purpose to amount to an offence under the relevant TSC. For instance, hostage taking is defined partly in reference to a terrorist purpose.[101] States have also defined the ancillary offence of threatening to carry out a particular offence in reference to the terrorist purpose of the threat, even when the definition of the principal offence contains no element of terrorist purpose—as is the case under the SUA Convention (regarding unlawful acts against the safety of maritime navigation) and the 1988 Protocol to the SUA Convention (regarding unlawful acts against the safety of fixed platforms). Finally, some offences, like nuclear terrorism, require either a general intent to cause bodily injury or death, or a terrorist purpose.[102] Under the Nuclear Terrorism Convention, terrorist purpose, coupled with the *actus reus* elements of an act of nuclear terrorism, is therefore a sufficient but not a necessary element of the defined offence.

---

[98] See the 1988 Protocol to the SUA Convention.

[99] Terrorism is increasingly being defined as to encompass a prohibition on violence against non-combatants or civilians, when such violence is committed for a terrorist purposes. See Art. 2(1)(b), Terrorism Financing Convention; Slaughter and Burke-White (2002).

[100] See *International Instruments related to the Prevention and Suppression of International Terrorism* (New York: United Nations, 2004). See further Art. 2(1)(a) of the Terrorism Financing Convention, which prohibits the financing of terrorism and defines acts of terrorism in reliance on the TSCs in force at the time the Terrorism Financing Convention was adopted (including the Hague Convention, Montreal Convention, Internationally Protected Persons Convention, and 1988 Protocol to the Montreal Convention).

[101] Article 1 of the Hostages Convention reads: 'Any person who seizes or detains and threatens to kill, to injure or to continue to detain another person (hereinafter referred to as the "hostage") *in order to compel a third party, namely, a state, an international intergovernmental organization, a natural or juridical person, or a group of persons, to do or abstain from doing any act as an explicit or implicit condition for the release of the hostage* commits the offence of taking of hostages [...] within the meaning of this Convention'. Emphasis added. By including natural or juridical persons in the list of persons who might be the subject of compulsion, the Hostages Convention also requires states to criminalize hostage takings committed for purely private purposes—in addition to those committed for terrorist (and public) purposes.

[102] Article 2(1)(b) of the Nuclear Terrorism Convention reads as follows: 'Any person commits an offence within the meaning of this Convention if that person unlawfully and intentionally: (b) uses in any way radioactive material or a device, or uses or damages a nuclear facility in a manner which releases or risks the release of radioactive material: (i) with the intent to cause death or serious bodily injury; or (ii) with the intent to cause substantial damage to property or to the environment; or (iii) with the intent to compel a natural or legal person, an international organization or a State to do or refrain from doing an act'.

Some offences in the more recent TSCs are defined without reference to any terrorist purpose, suggesting that the prohibited method or target is sufficient to qualify the act as terrorism. For instance, the Terrorist Bombing Convention, both in its title and preamble, characterizes the subject matter of the Convention as terrorism. But the Terrorist Bombing Convention requires states to criminalize any bombing against a place of public use, a state or government facility, a public transportation system or an infrastructure system (committed with the intent to cause death, serious bodily injury or extensive damage resulting or likely to result in major economic loss), whether committed for political purposes or for purely private purposes.[103] While some commentators have argued that a political or terrorist purpose is an essential feature of any definition of 'terrorism' as a crime,[104] and that TSCs which apply to acts committed for purely private motives are 'overbroad',[105] states appear to consider that terrorism can be both a question of purpose and a question of consequence, although not necessarily with any consistency or grand design (as discussed below). It is certainly true, however, that detonating an explosive (whether nuclear or not) with the intention of causing serious bodily injury, death or extensive damage causes terror among the general population, whatever the perpetrator's motive.

Finally, the TSCs adopted under the auspices of the IMO in 2005 and ICAO in 2010 respond to concerns raised by the 9/11 terrorist attacks and require states to criminalize the use of maritime shipping or civil aircraft to cause death or bodily injury.[106] They also respond to the some of the concerns addressed in Security Council Resolutions 1456 (2003) and 1540 (2004) regarding access to and use of BCN weapons by non-state terrorist actors. The 2005 Protocol to the SUA Convention and the Beijing Convention (adopted by the ICAO on 10 September 2010 and not yet in force) require states to criminalize (respectively) the use of maritime shipping or civil aircraft from which to discharge explosives or BCN weapons in a manner that causes or is likely to cause death, serious injury or damage. Only the offence of using explosives or BCN weapons against or from maritime shipping is defined in reference to a terrorist purpose. The offence of using such weapons against or from civil aircraft contains no element of terrorist purpose.[107] It may well be that the terrorist element is

---

[103] Article 5 of the Terrorist Bombing Convention does require state parties to adopt 'such measures as may be necessary, including, where appropriate, domestic legislation, to ensure that criminal acts within the scope of this Convention, *in particular where they are intended or calculated to provoke a state of terror in the general public or in a group of persons or particular persons*, are under no circumstances justifiable by considerations of a political, philosophical, ideological, racial, ethnic, religious or other similar nature and are punished by penalties consistent with their grave nature'. Emphasis added. Terrorist purpose is not required as an element of the offence, but the Convention expressly stipulates that defences (most relevantly in regard to political offences) must not be made available for bombings as defined under the Convention, *particularly* where committed for a terrorist purpose.

[104] See e.g. Saul (2006), 39.
[105] Levitt (1986), 115; Saul (2006), 10.
[106] See Art. 4(5), 2005 Protocol to the SUA Convention; Art. 1(f) Beijing Convention.
[107] See Art. 4(5), 2005 Protocol to the SUA Convention; Arts. 1(g) and 1(h), Beijing Convention. States are also required to criminalize the transport of explosives or BCN weapons on maritime

implicit in some offences, for instance using explosives or BCN weapons against civil aircraft undoubtedly causes a state of terror among the general population, even if committed for purely private purposes. It is hard to see, however, why the same should not be true in reference to the use of explosives or BCN weapons from or against maritime shipping. These inconsistencies in approach reflect the difficulties in identifying the core and essential elements of an act of terrorism. What can be said is that the process of defining acts of terrorism is an ongoing one. The series of Terrorism Suppression Conventions, each adopted in response to particular terrorist attacks, reflect lessons learned from both the use of violence and previous efforts to suppress that violence through the adoption of international conventions. The fact that a terrorist purpose is not necessary in reference to all offences defined in the TSCs suggests prohibited methods and targets, in certain circumstances, more than account for the need to co-operate internationally in their suppression. Whether prohibited methods and targets ought to be sufficient to properly characterize these offences as 'terrorism' is an entirely different question, and for present purposes, largely irrelevant. This book examines state responsibility for acts of international terrorism as in fact defined by states.

To amount to an act of terrorism under the TSCs, the act of violence must also have a transnational component. For instance, the Hague Convention, 2010 Protocol to the Hague Convention, and the Montreal and Beijing Conventions require that the aircraft on board which or from which the offence is committed take-off or land in a state other than the state of registration.[108] Article 1 of the Internationally Protected Persons Convention limits the scope of the Convention to offences committed against internationally protected persons when they are in a foreign state. The Hostages Convention, Terrorist Bombing Convention, Terrorism Financing Convention, and Nuclear Terrorism Convention do not apply to offences which are committed within a single state, of which the alleged offender and victim(s) are nationals, when the alleged offender is found in the territory of that State.[109] Finally, the SUA Convention and its Protocols do not apply unless the ship is navigating or is scheduled to navigate into, through or from waters beyond the outer limit of the territorial sea of a single state.[110]

Together, the TSCs define the core of activities that states consider terrorist for the purposes of international law. Broader definitions adopted in General Assembly and Security Council Resolutions, and in the draft comprehensive terrorism suppression convention, include the offences defined in the TSCs, in addition to acts of violence that do not use any of the prohibited methods against prohibited targets as yet singled out by states, but which nevertheless have a terrorist purpose.

---

shipping or civil aircraft if it is known that such weapons are intended to be used to cause death, serious injury or damage for the purpose of intimidating a population, or compelling a government or an international organization to do or to abstain from doing any act. Art. 4(5), 2005 Protocol to the SUA Convention; Art. 1(1)(i), Beijing Convention.

[108] Art. 3, Hague Convention; Art. 4(2), Montreal Convention.

[109] Art. 13, Hostages Convention; Art. 3, Terrorist Bombing Convention. Arts. 3 and 7(2), Terrorism Financing Convention; Arts. 3 and 9(2), Nuclear Terrorism Convention.

[110] Art. 4(1), SUA Convention.

For instance, the UN General Assembly has defined terrorism generally as '[c]riminal acts intended or calculated to provoke a state of terror in the general public, a group of persons or particular persons for political purposes'.[111] The draft comprehensive terrorism suppression convention is more specific in its reference to the *actus reus* element of terrorist offences (i.e. an act which intentionally causes, by any means, serious injury, death or serious damage to public or private property), but equally relies on terrorist purpose to limit the scope of the definition. As a result, the draft convention requires that conduct be criminalized 'when the purpose of the conduct, by its nature or context, is to intimidate a population, or to compel a Government or an international organization to do or to abstain from doing any act'.[112]

Finally, the Security Council has adopted a general definition of terrorism that mirrors the terms of the definition in the draft comprehensive terrorism suppression convention,[113] but that restricts the generality of that definition by limiting its scope of application to offences that are already defined as terrorist offences in the series of TSCs. The Security Council definition of an act of terrorism is therefore narrower than the cumulative definition of such acts set forth in the TSCs because Security Council Resolution 1566 introduces an element of terrorist purpose into all such offences, even though (as discussed above) a number of the TSCs do not include terrorist purpose as an element of the offence. As a result, the conduct defined as terrorist by the Security Council is narrower than, but included in, the series of definitions set out in the TSCs. Part of the reason for this qualification is undoubtedly that the Security Council was attempting to restrict its novel use of legislative power to obligations that already existed under international law. As states (party to the TSCs) are already under an obligation to prevent and punish offences defined in the TSCs, calling on states to fulfil such obligations in the context of a Chapter VII Resolution does not expand the scope of obligations, although does impose them on states not yet party to the TSCs.

The draft comprehensive terrorism suppression convention, on the other hand, is intended to supplement the sectoral approach to defining terrorism.[114] Its very purpose is to be broader than the TSCs and to cover acts that would not otherwise be subject to international cooperation under the present terrorism suppression regime, while leaving conduct falling within the scope of the TSCs to the regulation of the existing Conventions. For instance, causing the pollution, fouling or poisoning of drinking water or food or wilfully destroying railways or damaging power installations belonging to public services without the use of explosives[115] (provided committed with a terrorist purpose) would meet the

---

[111] UN Declaration on International Terrorism, UNGA Resolution 49/60 (1994), Annex, para 3.

[112] See Art. 2, Draft comprehensive convention against international terrorism: Consolidated text prepared by the coordinator for discussion, UN Doc. A/59/284 (2005), Appendix II.

[113] UNSC Resolution 1566 (2005) adds the following prohibited terrorist purpose to those set forth in the draft comprehensive terrorism suppression convention: 'to provoke a state of terror in the general public or in a group of persons or particular persons'.

[114] See Art. 3, Draft comprehensive convention against international terrorism: Consolidated text prepared by the coordinator for discussion, UN Doc. A/59/284 (2005), Appendix II.

[115] Contemplating such possible acts of terrorism, see Fourth International Conference for the Unification of Penal Law, Brussels, 26–30 June 1930, Actes de Conférence (Brussels: Office de

general definition of terrorism under the draft convention, but states are not required to criminalize such conduct under the existing TSCs.

For the purposes of this book, the term 'terrorism' is understood as reflecting the emerging international consensus (reflected in the instruments discussed above) on the relevant elements of a terrorist offence. An act of terrorism is therefore defined as any act falling within the scope of a Terrorism Suppression Convention, in addition to:

> any act intended to cause death or serious bodily injury, or extensive damage to property, when the purpose of such act, by its nature or context, is to intimidate a population, to provoke a state of terror in the general public, a group of persons or particular persons for political purposes, or to compel a government or an international organisation to do or abstain from doing any act.[116]

In keeping with the approach of the Terrorism Suppression Conventions, the terms 'act of terrorism' or 'terrorist offence' are only used in this book to denote conduct meeting the definition set out above which has a transnational component, in that the alleged offender or victims are not nationals of the state within which the offence was committed.

---

publicité, 1931); Sixth International Conference for the Unification of Penal Law, Copenhagen, 31 August – 2 September 1935, Actes de Conférence (Paris: Éditions A. Pédone, 1938); Scharf (2001), 393.

[116] This definition is slightly broader than that proposed by the Report of the High Level Panel on Threats, Challenges and Change, A more secure world: our shared responsibility, UN Doc. A/59/565 (2004), para 164, which does not address property damage. As many of the TSCs do so, the definition proposed above merely recognizes that extensive property damage caused by violent conduct is a concern to states, and that the regime of TSCs does not necessarily cover all ways in which such damage might be caused.

2

The prohibition of state terrorism
and questions of attribution

Former UN Secretary-General Kofi Annan has argued that '[i]t is time to set aside debates on so-called "State terrorism". The use of force by States is already thoroughly regulated under international law'.[1] This statement of principle, denying the existence of a *lex specialis* prohibiting acts of terrorism carried out by states, is one that is confirmed by the examination of general international law set out below. Nevertheless, the term 'state terrorism' is a useful one—principally because the term 'terrorism' describes a sphere of violent conduct that states have singled out as requiring particular regulation through the regime of TSCs and relevant General Assembly and Security Council resolutions,[2] and the term 'state terrorism' merely highlights the possibility of state sponsorship and support for acts that fall within that regime.

State sponsorship of terrorism is the term used in this book to denote terrorist conduct that is carried out by or on behalf of a state,[3] i.e. terrorist conduct which is attributable to the state. State support for terrorism refers to a state's assistance in the commission of terrorist acts in cases where the act is not attributable to the state. State support can take many forms, including training, financial support, provision of arms and/or technology, assistance with diplomatic assets (provision of passports and other forms of cover), provision of transportation or intelligence and permitting use of territory as a base of operations.[4] The distinction between state sponsorship and state support for terrorism (examined in Section 2.1 below) plays a role in determining which primary rule is engaged by a state's involvement in terrorism, in particular whether the state can be held responsible for an act of aggression, a prohibited use of force, or an intervention in the domestic affairs of a foreign state. The rules of attribution as they apply in the terrorism context are examined in Section 2.2.

---

[1] UNSG Report, In larger freedom: towards development, security and human rights for all, UN Doc. A/59/2005 (2005), para 91. See also Report of the High Level Panel on Threats, Challenges and Change, A more secure world: our shared responsibility, UN Doc. A/59/565 (2004), para 160; Saul (2006), 195.

[2] See Section 1.3.

[3] Murphy (1989), 33–4; Murphy et al. (1991), 19.

[4] *Ibid.*

2.1 The prohibition of state terrorism

The prohibition of state sponsorship of and support for acts of terrorism was the subject of much debate during consultations on the UN Definition of Aggression and the UN Declaration on Friendly Relations.[5] The UN Declaration on Friendly Relations in particular considers state terrorism through the prism of the UN Charter,[6] and thereby confirms the argument that terrorism, particularly with state involvement, 'is not a discrete topic of international law with its own substantive legal norms', but a contemporary phenomenon to which existing international law applies.[7] The precise scope of states' obligations to refrain from engaging in or supporting acts of international terrorism is therefore best examined through its Charter-related development as regards the prohibition of aggression, the prohibition of the use of force, and the principle of non-intervention (considered in turn below). While the prohibition of state terrorism features expressly in the UN Declaration on Friendly Relations, both in reference to prohibited uses of force and impermissible interventions, it was not ultimately included in the UN Definition of Aggression. Nevertheless, state sponsorship of an act of terrorism will, in certain circumstances, amount to a prohibited act of aggression as defined in the UN Definition of Aggression.

It bears noting that the UN instruments discussed below do not define terrorism, although they do treat terrorism as a type of state violence meriting particular attention. States have, however, defined terrorism in other contexts, particularly through the negotiation of the TSCs and more recently in General Assembly and Security Council resolutions.[8] Even though these instruments are aimed principally at acts of terrorism carried out by individuals, they are indicative of the type of violence that states consider to be 'terrorist'—and therefore fall within the prohibition of state terrorism as an instantiation of general prohibitions on state violence under international law.

2.1.1 The prohibition of aggression

The Special Committee on the Question of Defining Aggression spent a great deal of time debating whether the definition of aggression should include 'indirect armed aggression', in particular, acts of state-sponsored or supported terrorism.[9]

---

[5] What amounts to an act of terrorism was not discussed during the negotiations of either the UN Definition of Aggression, UNGA Resolution 3314 (1974), Annex, or the UN Declaration on Friendly Relations, UNGA Resolution 2625 (1970). Instead, terrorism was generally used as a term referencing indirect uses of force by states. *Infra* notes 9 and 32 and accompanying text.

[6] See also the GA Resolution on the Inadmissibility of State Terrorism, UNGA Resolution 39/159 (1984), which characterizes state terrorism as a violation of Article 2(4) of the UN Charter and the principle of non-intervention.

[7] Higgins (1997), 13–14. See also Murphy et al. (1991), 29; Beres (1995), 239; Saul (2006), 195.

[8] See Section 1.3.

[9] See Report of the Special Committee on the Question of Defining Aggression, UN Doc. A/8019 (1970), paras 26–30.

It was generally agreed that state terrorism would amount to a breach of the peace or an illegal intervention in the domestic affairs of another state.[10] Western states, however, insisted that the 'organization, instigation of, assistance or participation in terrorist acts in other states' should figure in the definition of aggression.[11] The Soviet Union preferred to distinguish between aggression and indirect aggression,[12] while the Non-Aligned Movement raised objections to the concept of indirect aggression altogether. The NAM was pre-occupied with the relationship between the definition of aggression and the definition of an armed attack under Article 51 of the UN Charter.[13] They were particularly concerned that a failure to limit the definition of aggression to direct (attributable) state action raised the possibility of powerful states disingenuously accusing weaker states of acquiescing in armed bands operating from their territory to justify an aggressive use of force (under the guise of self-defence) against that weaker state.[14] On the other hand, Western states supporting the inclusion of indirect aggression in the definition argued that failing to do so would threaten international peace as it would encourage states to engage in wars by proxy emboldened by the belief that they could not be charged with aggression.[15] As a result of the impasse, the UN Definition of Aggression does not address terrorism as such. Several delegates expressed discontent with the final text because it omitted acts that they thought should have been covered.[16]

The definition of aggression finally adopted by the General Assembly is clearly limited to acts carried out by a state. Article 1 of the UN Definition of Aggression defines aggression as 'the use of armed force *by a State* against the sovereignty, territorial integrity or political independence of another State [. . .]'.[17] The use of armed force, however, need not be carried out by a state's military forces: 'sending by or on behalf of a State of armed bands, groups, irregulars or mercenaries, which

---

[10] *Ibid*, para 127.
[11] See Report of the Special Committee on the Question of Defining Aggression, UN Doc. A/8719 (1972), Appendix B, Section A.
[12] See Report of the Special Committee on the Question of Defining Aggression, UN Doc. A/8019 (1970), para IV.B (7).
[13] See Reports of the Special Committee on the Question of Defining Aggression, UN Doc. A/7620 (1969), paras 26–9, 62, and 69–72; UN Doc. A/8019 (1970), Annex I, para 7; UN Doc. A/8419 (1971), paras 27–8; UN Doc. A/8719 (1972), Section C. But see Bowett (1958), 256–60, correctly arguing that the identification of the concepts of aggression and armed attack should be rejected, because aggression is defined for the purposes of triggering the United Nations' collective security apparatus, whereas an armed attack triggers a state's right to use force in self-defence unilaterally.
[14] See Report of the Special Committee on the Question of Defining Aggression, UN Doc. A/7620 (1969), para 127.
[15] *Ibid*, para 128. See also Ferencz (1973), 419–21, for a summary of the debate. Note that at the time of negotiation, 'armed attack' under Article 51 of the UN Charter was generally understood to be restricted to armed attacks that are attributable to states. The concern of Western states might have been alleviated had 'armed attack' equally been understood as an attack by non-state actors giving rise to a right to use force in self-defence in cases where the territorial state could not be relied on to prevent its territory from being used as a base of terrorist operations, as argued in Section 2.2.3.
[16] See Report of the Special Committee on the Question of Defining Aggression, UN Doc. A/9019 (1973), Appendix A.
[17] Emphasis added. Art. 1, UN Definition of Aggression, UNGA Resolution 3314 (1974), Annex. See also Stone (1977), 232.

carry out acts [amounting to aggression], or its substantial involvement therein' also amounts to aggression.[18] Article 3 of the UN Definition of Aggression is intended to provide a non-exhaustive list of acts that amount to aggression within the meaning of Article 1. As such, the 'sending by or on behalf of a State of armed bands [...], or [...] substantial involvement therein' must be interpreted as a *lex specialis* threshold for attributing the aggression carried out by the armed bands to the state sending them,[19] thereby maintaining the Article 1 requirement that an act of aggression be a 'use of armed force *by a State*'.[20] Some commentators argue that 'sending' does not invoke a standard of attribution, and question whether it might include permitting or tolerating the activities of armed bands.[21] Such an argument, however, is inconsistent with the terms of Article 1 of the UN Definition of Aggression. Indeed, proposals to minimize the level of state involvement required for an act of aggression, including 'assistance to', 'knowing acquiescence in', or 'collaboration in'[22] (all of which would amount to active or passive support for, rather than sponsorship of, armed bands) were rejected in favour of the 'sending by or on behalf of' standard. As such, no form of indirect aggression made its way into the UN Definition of Aggression, which applies only to state sponsorship of terrorism, and not to state support for terrorism involving some lesser form of assistance to non-state terrorist actors.[23]

---

[18] Art. 3(g), UN Definition of Aggression, UNGA Resolution 3314 (1974), Annex.

[19] 'Sending by or on behalf of a State' is not a basis of attribution specifically set forth in the ILC Articles on State Responsibility, and therefore can be regarded as a *lex specialis* basis of attribution, although it closely tracks the attribution threshold set forth in Article 8 of the ILC Articles. *Infra* note 21.

[20] Emphasis added. Art. 1, UN Definition of Aggression, UNGA Resolution 3314 (1974), Annex. See the ICJ's treatment of Article 3(g) in its *Nicaragua (Nicaragua v. US)* and *Armed Activities on the Territory of the Congo (DRC v. Uganda)* decisions, *infra* notes 142 and 148 and accompanying text. But see Becker (2006), 179–80, arguing that the 'sending by or on behalf of a State of armed bands' threshold in Article 3(g) is not a standard for attributing the conduct of those armed bands to the state, but is rather the act of aggression itself. This argument ignores the fact that Article 1 of the Definition of Aggression defines aggression as a use of armed force by a state. 'Sending armed bands' is not in itself a use of armed force, and it must therefore be that the use of armed force by the armed bands, attributable to the state on the basis of the act of sending, is what satisfies the elements of Article 1 coupled with Article 3(g) of the Definition of Aggression.

[21] See e.g. Franck (2002), 65. But see Zanardi (1986), 112, arguing that 'sending' implies that the armed bands act as *de facto* organs of the sending state. Zanardi's view on Article 3(g) as a standard of attribution is consistent with the *travaux préparatoires* for the UN Definition of Aggression (see Report of the Special Committee on the Question of Defining Aggression, UN Doc. A/9019 (1973)), but these do not necessarily support attribution on the basis of the *de facto* organ status of the armed bands, which standard of attribution requires a high level of dependence on the state sending them. See *infra* note 90 and accompanying text. Article 3(g) as a standard of attribution accords more closely with the 'acting on instructions of [the state]' standard set forth in Article 8 of the ILC Articles on State Responsibility, as discussed in Section 2.2.2.

[22] See Report of the Special Committee on the Question of Defining Aggression, UN Doc. A/9019 (1973).

[23] See Lillich and Paxman (1977), 273; Daudet (1997), 203–4. But see the dissenting opinions in *Nicaragua*, which considered a state's substantial involvement in the sending of armed bands to amount to an act of aggression by that state. *Nicaragua (Nicaragua v. US)*, Merits, Dissenting Opinion of Judge Schwebel, paras 162–71; *Nicaragua (Nicaragua v. US)*, Merits, Dissenting Opinion of Judge Jennings, 543.

An act of terrorism amounting to aggression carried out by non-state actors that is attributable to a state (in virtue of that state having *sent* the armed bands) will constitute aggression. As a result, Article 3(g) of the UN Definition of Aggression elaborates part of the customary international law content of the obligation to refrain from engaging in acts of terrorism.[24] The circumstances under which a state's sponsorship of terrorism will amount to an act of aggression as defined in the UN Definition of Aggression are rare, but not entirely unlikely. For instance, consider the nineteen men who hijacked American Airlines ('AA') Flight 11, United Airlines ('UA') Flight 175, AA Flight 77, and UA Flight 93 on 11 September 2001 and flew the aircraft into the World Trade Center north and south towers, the Pentagon and an empty field in Pennsylvania respectively.[25] That the 9/11 attacks amounted to acts of terrorism as defined in Chapter 1 is indisputable: they were acts intended to cause death or serious bodily injury to civilians, and their purpose was certainly to provoke a state of terror and to compel a government to do or abstain from doing any act.[26] It is equally clear that the use of force by the hijackers (using commercial aircraft as targeted missiles against civilian and military targets) was of such gravity that it would have amounted to an act of aggression had it been carried out by a state's military.[27] Had a state sent the suicide hijackers, the 9/11 terrorist attacks would therefore have met the definition of aggression, in that the 'sending by or on behalf of a State' test for aggression would be met.[28]

2.1.2 The prohibition of the use of force

The UN Declaration on Friendly Relations codified and progressively developed[29] the prohibition of the use of force set out in Article 2(4) of the UN Charter,[30] but has since been held to reflect customary international law.[31] It characterizes the prohibition of state terrorism as an instantiation of the general prohibition of the use of force, and affirms that it is the duty of every state to 'refrain from organizing,

---

[24] The prohibition of sending armed bands to carry out acts of armed force amounting to aggression has been determined to reflect customary international law. *Nicaragua (Nicaragua v. US)*, Merits, para 195.

[25] National Commission on Terrorist Attacks Upon the United States, 1–14.

[26] In claiming responsibility for the 9/11 terrorist attacks, Bin Laden reportedly threatened new attacks if the policies of the US Government did not change. CBC, 'Bin Laden claims responsibility for 9/11', 29 October 2004, <http://www.cbc.ca/world/story/2004/10/29/binladen_message041029.html>.

[27] For instance the attacks could be likened to bombardment by the armed forces of a state against the territory of another state, defined as an act of aggression in Article 3(b), UN Definition of Aggression.

[28] Art. 3(g), UN Definition of Aggression, UNGA Resolution 3314 (1974), Annex. But see Gaeta (2007), 637.

[29] Preamble, UN Declaration on Friendly Relations, UNGA Resolution 2625 (1970).

[30] Article 2(4) of the UN Charter reads that states 'shall refrain in their international relations from the threat or use of force against the territorial integrity or political independence of any state, or in any other manner inconsistent with the purposes of the United Nations'.

[31] *Nicaragua (Nicaragua v. US)*, Merits, para 191. See also *Armed Activities on the Territory of the Congo (DRC v. Uganda)*, Judgment, para 162, in which the ICJ holds that the prohibition of state terrorism set forth in the UN Declaration on Friendly Relations, UNGA Resolution 2625 (1970), is also customary international law.

instigating, assisting or participating in acts of civil strife or terrorist acts in another State or acquiescing in organized activities within its territory directed toward the commission of such acts, when the acts referred to in the present paragraph involve a threat or use of force'.[32]

State sponsorship of terrorism amounts to an illegal use of force pursuant to the UN Declaration on Friendly Relations in that states are prohibited from *participating* in terrorist acts in another state. The direct participation of state organs in a terrorist attack would result in that attack being attributable to the state. France's use of a state organ (secret service agents) to destroy the 'Rainbow Warrior' Greenpeace ship in Auckland Harbour[33] amounted to state sponsorship of terrorism, and therefore a prohibited use of force pursuant to the UN Declaration on Friendly Relations. Furthermore, organizing terrorist acts is related to the concept of direction or control in Article 8 of the ILC Articles on State Responsibility. To the extent that a state's organizational role amounted to either instructions to act or met the threshold level of control under Article 8 of the ILC Articles on State Responsibility, terrorist acts organized by a state would be attributable thereto on that basis and would amount to a prohibited use of force.[34]

A curious feature of the UN Declaration on Friendly Relations, as interpreted by the International Court of Justice ('ICJ'), is that state support (assistance) for terrorism will only amount to a prohibited use of force if the modalities of assistance themselves amount to a threat or use of force. For instance, the ICJ held that the arming and training of the *contras* amounted to a breach of the prohibition of the threat or use of force, while financing the *contras* did not.[35] The distinction must lie in the nature of the support, because the use of force by the non-state actors being supported remains the same, whatever form of support the state provides. The ICJ's decision implies that support which is necessarily ancillary to a use of force and military in nature will amount to a threat or use of force, while financing (which is perhaps neutral as to the threat or use of force) will not. The difficulty with the ICJ's distinction is that it misinterprets the UN Declaration on Friendly Relations. '[O]rganizing, instigating, assisting or participating in acts of civil strife or terrorist acts in another State or acquiescing in organized activities within its territory directed toward the commission of such acts, when the acts referred to in the present paragraph involve a threat or use of force' amounts to a prohibited use of force.[36] The phrase 'when the acts referred to in the present paragraph involve a threat or use of force' qualifies 'the acts of civil strife or terrorist

---

[32] 1st Principle, UN Declaration on Friendly Relations, UNGA Resolution 2625 (1970). See further UN Declaration on International Terrorism, UNGA Resolution 49/60 (1994), para 4; Supplement to the UN Declaration on International Terrorism, UNGA Resolution 51/210 (1996), Annex, para 5; World Summit Outcome Document, UN Doc. UNGA Resolution 60/1 (2005), para 86, all reiterating the prohibition on state terrorism (without defining terrorism) through the prism of the UN Charter and the prohibition on the use of force.
[33] See Sections 2.2.1 and 6.2.4 for full details of the Rainbow Warrior incident.
[34] See Section 2.2.2.
[35] *Nicaragua (Nicaragua v. US)*, Merits, para 228.
[36] 1st Principle, UN Declaration on Friendly Relations, UNGA Resolution 2625 (1970).

acts in another State', and not 'organizing, instigating, assisting or participating'. In the case of terrorism, support (whether military or financial) should therefore amount to a prohibited threat or use of force when the terrorist act itself amounts to such a use of force.[37] As the ICJ's reasoning on this point has not been reconsidered in later judgments,[38] it remains the Court's position that training in military combat tactics and the provision of weapons, weapons systems, or ammunition to non-state actors for the purposes of assisting in the commission of terrorist acts will amount to a prohibited use of force, while financing terrorist acts (or perhaps providing diplomatic or intelligence support) will not.

Finally, the UN Declaration on Friendly Relations requires a state to refrain from passively supporting international terrorism in that states are under a duty to refrain from acquiescing in the commission of terrorist acts in another state.[39] While the obligation itself is not framed as a positive duty to act, it will only be complied with through positive action, given that it could be breached through omission or inaction on the part of the state. A state that does nothing in the face of known activities within its territory directed toward the commission of terrorist acts in another state is acquiescing in such activities. A state that takes positive measures to counter such activities is refraining from acquiescing. Given that compliance with the obligation to refrain from acquiescing in terrorist activities requires positive action, it mirrors to a large extent the obligation to prevent terrorism examined in Chapter 3. Indeed, developments in international law following the 9/11 terrorist attacks have led to a *rapprochement* between the obligation to refrain from acquiescing in terrorism and the obligation to prevent terrorism, as discussed in Section 3.1.3 below.

2.1.3 Non-intervention in the domestic affairs of another state

The UN Declaration on Friendly Relations also considers state terrorism to be a violation of the principle of non-intervention.[40] Unlike negotiation of the UN Definition of Aggression, there was virtually no disagreement in the Special Committee on Friendly Relations regarding whether the principle of non-intervention incorporated a prohibition of state terrorism.[41] The principle of non-intervention, considered a principle of customary international law by the ICJ,[42] stipulates 'the duty not to intervene in matters within the domestic jurisdiction of any State,

---

[37] See further *infra* note 49 and accompanying text.

[38] See *Armed Activities on the Territory of the Congo (DRC v. Uganda)*, Judgment, paras 161–5.

[39] *Supra* note 32 and accompanying text. That acquiescence amounts to a prohibited use of force pursuant to the UN Declaration on Friendly Relations, UNGA Resolution 2625 (1970) further calls into question the distinction the ICJ draws between military and financial support in its *Nicaragua* decision. If passive support for terrorist conduct amounts to a prohibited use of force, active support for such conduct, whether financial or military in nature, should equally amount to a prohibited use of force.

[40] 3rd Principle, UN Declaration on Friendly Relations, UNGA Resolution 2625 (1970).

[41] See generally Report of the 1966 Special Committee on Principles of International Law Concerning Friendly Relations and Co-operation among States, UN Doc. A/6230 (1966).

[42] *Nicaragua (Nicaragua v. US)*, Merits, para 202.

in accordance with the Charter'.[43] The terrorism-specific instantiation of the principle of non-intervention prohibits organizing, assisting, fomenting, financing, inciting or tolerating 'subversive, terrorist or armed activities directed toward the violent overthrow of the regime of another State, or interfer[ing] in civil strife in another State'.[44] While the prohibited purposes of terrorist activities (and a state's organization, assistance or tolerance thereof) are more circumscribed than those set out in the general formulation of the principle of non-intervention, the prohibition of state terrorism should be interpreted within the broader context of that principle as equally prohibiting state sponsorship or support of terrorist activities with general interventionist aims.

In part, the principle of non-intervention gives rise to the same prohibitions in regard to state sponsorship of or support for terrorism as does the prohibition of the use of force. The distinction lies in the purpose or objective of the terrorist activities being sponsored or supported. Where that purpose or objective is interference with 'matters in which each State is permitted, by the principle of State sovereignty, to decide freely',[45] then the prohibition on sponsorship of or support for such activities falls within the scope of the principle of non-intervention.[46] The requirement of an interventionist purpose, however, does not really serve to restrict the type of terrorist conduct that might fall within the scope of the principle of non-intervention. The prohibited purposes are so broad that the principle of non-intervention has been described as one that can subsume the whole of international law.[47]

To the extent that a state is sponsoring or *militarily* supporting terrorist activities (thereby breaching the prohibition of the use of force as understood by the ICJ) and the terrorist activities have as their objective interference in the domestic affairs of another state, the state's conduct will breach both the prohibition of the use of force and the principle of non-intervention.[48] In order to fall within the principle of non-intervention as articulated in the UN Declaration on Friendly Relations, however, a state's support for terrorism need not itself amount to a threat or use of force. For instance, the ICJ held that US financing of the *contras* did not amount to a breach of the prohibition of the use of force, although it was an illegal intervention in the

---

[43] 3rd Principle, UN Declaration on Friendly Relations, UNGA Resolution 2625 (1970).

[44] *Ibid.*

[45] *Nicaragua (Nicaragua v. US)*, Merits, para 205.

[46] *Ibid.* The ICJ considered that, when one state, with a view to the coercion of another state, supports and assists armed bands whose purpose is to overthrow that other state's government, it is illegally intervening in the internal affairs of the other, whether or not the political objective of the state giving such support is as far reaching as that of the armed band. *Nicaragua (Nicaragua v. US)*, Merits, para 241.

[47] Conforti (1991), 467. Consider also the UN Declaration on the Inadmissibility of Intervention in the Domestic Affairs of States, UNGA Resolution 2131 (1965), para 1: 'No State has the right to intervene, directly or indirectly, for any reason whatever, in the internal or external affairs of any other State. Consequently, armed intervention and *all other forms of interference* or attempted threats against the personality of the State or against its political, economic and cultural elements, are condemned'. Emphasis added. In *Nicaragua (Nicaragua v. US)*, Merits, para 202, the ICJ considered the principle of non-intervention to be a corollary of the principle of sovereign equality of states, and equated the principle to that requiring respect for territorial sovereignty and political integrity.

[48] *Nicaragua (Nicaragua v. US)*, Merits, para 205.

domestic affairs of Nicaragua.[49] By analogy, assistance with diplomatic assets or providing transportation or intelligence, none of which, by themselves, imply a use of force, could amount to a breach of the principle of non-intervention, but not the prohibition of the use of force.

The prohibition of state support for terrorism, as set out in both the prohibition of the use of force and the principle of non-intervention in the UN Declaration on Friendly Relations, is directed at support for the *terrorist act*, not the terrorist actor.[50] This will sometimes be a distinction without a difference, but may involve complicated questions of fact. For instance, providing funds to a particular person or group of persons would not amount to financing terrorist acts unless the financier intended to finance terrorist activities,[51] or at least had reasonable notice that such funds were to be used for terrorist purposes.[52] Such notice will likely be inferred in many circumstances, for example where it is notorious that the person or group of persons use collected funds to finance terrorist attacks.[53] Assume, for example, that a state is providing financial support to Al Qaeda. Al Qaeda is not only known for its terrorist activities, but the subject of sanctions under UN Security Council Resolution 1390 (2002). It could therefore be inferred that the state was providing funds to finance terrorism (and not, for example, to finance medical care or education for Al Qaeda operatives),[54] and such conduct could amount to a breach of the customary international law principle of non-intervention. On the basis of the distinction between military and other forms of support set out in the ICJ's *Nicaragua* decision, such financing would not, however, amount to a prohibited use of force.[55] Likewise, training a group of non-state actors in intelligence gathering, surveillance, use of sophisticated communications

---

[49] *Ibid*, para 228. It might be argued that the distinction drawn by the ICJ between military and other types of support is based in part on the fact that financing terrorist activities is prohibited as an instantiation of the principle of non-intervention, but is not listed as prohibited conduct *vis à vis* terrorist activities under the prohibition of the use of force. 1st Principle and 3rd Principle, UN Declaration on Friendly Relations, UNGA Resolution 2625 (1970). There is no evidence in the *travaux préparatoires*, however, to suggest that a deliberate distinction was being drawn.

[50] *Supra* notes 32 and 43.

[51] Murphy et al. (1991), 18. In its *Nicaragua* decision, the ICJ required a measure of intentionality on the part of the supporting state in order that support for non-state actors amount to intervention. The ICJ attributed the interventionist aims of the *contras* to the US on the basis of US awareness of those aims. *Nicaragua (Nicaragua v. US)*, Merits, para 205.

[52] The requirement of reasonable notice can be inferred generally from principles of due diligence discussed in Section 3.1.1, and from the Terrorism Financing Convention (in so far as it may be deemed to apply directly to state financing of terrorism, on which see Section 4.2), which only holds a person criminally responsible for financing terrorism if he or she intended that the funds be used, or acted in the knowledge that they were to be used, to finance terrorist acts. Art. 2(1), Terrorism Financing Convention.

[53] Knowledge need not always be proven directly, but in some contexts can be inferred from the circumstances. See for instance the ICJ's analysis of Serbian knowledge of the serious risk of genocide being perpetrated in Srebrenica. *Bosnia Genocide Case*, Judgment, paras 436–7.

[54] See *Nicaragua (Nicaragua v. US)*, Merits, paras 242–3, holding that humanitarian assistance to armed groups cannot be regarded as unlawful intervention or in any other way contrary to international law, subject to the proviso that such assistance is strictly for the purposes of alleviating human suffering and to protect life and health, and is given without discrimination.

[55] *Supra* notes 35–6 and accompanying text.

equipment, explosives etc., does not, in itself, amount to a breach of the obligation to refrain from supporting acts of terrorism (as an instantiation of the
general prohibition of the use of force, or, depending on the purpose of the
terrorist acts, the prohibition of intervention). Only if the assistance is provided
for the purpose of assisting in the commission of terrorist acts is the prohibition
of state terrorism engaged. The determination of a state's purpose in providing assistance will be a question of fact but will generally be inferable from
a state's notice of the non-state actors' own purposes in seeking or accepting
the assistance.[56]

2.1.4 Conclusion

The prohibition of state sponsorship or support for acts of international terrorism is
an instantiation of rules under general international law, in particular the prohibition of aggression, the prohibition of the use of force, and the principle of non-
intervention. The analysis above identifies four factors that are relevant to determining which primary rule is breached by a state's involvement in terrorism. The
first factor is the extent to which the terrorist conduct is attributable to the state.
The distinction between state sponsorship of and state support for terrorism turns
on the application of the secondary rules of state responsibility (examined in
Section 2.2 below)—and affects the primary rule that can be engaged by the state's
conduct. The second factor bears on the intensity or gravity of the use of terrorist
force (from minor attacks to a use of terrorist force equivalent to an act of
aggression). Together, these two criteria determine whether a state's involvement
in a terrorist attack amounts to an act of aggression (as defined in the UN
Definition of Aggression) or a prohibited use of force (as set out in Article 2(4)
of the UN Charter and the UN Declaration on Friendly Relations). In order that a
state's involvement in terrorism amount to an act of aggression, the terrorist attack
must be attributable to the state and be of such gravity as to amount to an act of
aggression had it been carried out by the state's military forces. If the terrorist attack
is not grave enough to be characterized as an act of aggression, but is nevertheless
attributable to the state, the state's conduct amounts to a prohibited use of force.
The third factor that determines which primary rule is engaged by a state's
sponsorship or support of terrorism bears on the purpose or aim of the terrorist
use of force. To the extent that the purpose of terrorist force is an intervention in
the domestic affairs of another state, state sponsorship of terrorism (in addition to
being an act of aggression or a prohibited use of force) will amount to a prohibited
intervention. Where conduct is not attributable to a state, and the state is only
supporting (rather than sponsoring) international terrorism, the fourth factor that
determines which primary rule is engaged by the state conduct is the form of
support. Support that itself amounts to a use of force breaches the prohibition

---

[56] See *Nicaragua (Nicaragua v. US)*, Merits, para 241. See also *Bosnia Genocide Case*, Judgment,
para 421.

of the use of force,[57] while other forms of support, to the extent that the aim of the terrorist force is interventionist (very broadly defined), breach the principle of non-intervention.

2.2 Attribution

In order for a state to be held 'directly' responsible for the commission of a terrorist act, such act must both be attributable to the state and amount to the breach of an international obligation.[58] Section 2.1 above explored the international obligations that might be engaged by a state's sponsorship of an act of terrorism. A state, however, only acts through natural persons.[59] The rules of attribution in Part One, Chapter II, of the ILC Articles on State Responsibility define the circumstances in which the acts of natural persons (whether acting individually or as part of a group or entity) will be considered acts of the state for the purposes of that state's responsibility.[60] The following sections examine the application of the different rules of attribution in the terrorism context, and consider the extent to which these rules are adequate to respond to the threat posed by state participation in acts of international terrorism.

2.2.1 Organs of the state

Under Article 4 of the ILC's Articles, 'the conduct of any State organ shall be considered an act of that State under international law'.[61] This rule of attribution provides the clearest legal standard for attributing conduct to a state, but its successful application in the terrorism context is complicated by difficulties in situating terrorism within a sphere of legitimate state activity.

It has long been accepted that a state is responsible for the conduct of its organs even if they have exceeded their competence under municipal law or disobeyed instructions (*ultra vires* conduct), as long as the organ acted in an official capacity.[62]

---

[57] But see Condorelli (1989), 245, arguing that, where the terrorist act is not attributable to the state, support therefor does not amount to an act of direct or indirect aggression, or to a violation of the prohibition on the use of force, but can only amount to a grave intervention in the internal affairs of another state.

[58] In the absence of attributability, state support for a terrorist act still amounts to a breach of that state's international obligations, but the state is not 'directly' responsible for the terrorist conduct. See Fox (2002), arguing that 'direct' and 'indirect' responsibility serve to indicate the degree of participation of a state in the wrongful act.

[59] See *German Settlers Advisory Opinion*, 22.

[60] Commentary to Part One, Chapter II, ILC Articles on State Responsibility, para 1.

[61] Art. 4(1), ILC Articles on State Responsibility.

[62] See e.g. League of Nations, Conference for the Codification of International Law, Bases of Discussion for the Conference Drawn up by the Preparatory Committee, Vol. III (Responsibility of States for Damage Caused in their Territory to the Person or Property of Foreigners), LN Doc. C.75. M.69.1929.V, 75; League of Nations, Acts of the Conference for the Codification of International Law Held at The Hague from 13 March to 12 April 1930, Vol. IV (Minutes of the Third Committee), LN Doc. C.351(c) M.145(c).1930.V, 237; Ago (1972), 75–92, paras 11–52; Report of the International

This rule is articulated in Article 7 of the ILC Articles on State Responsibility. Because *ultra vires* conduct, by definition, will not be in the *actual* official capacity of the state organ (but beyond it, while connected to it), official capacity is determined both in reference to the real and apparent authority of a state organ.[63] Apparent authority exists when the state organ acts under 'cover of [its] official character'[64] or while 'cloaked with governmental authority'.[65] Effectively, the state is responsible for conduct actually within the official capacity of a particular state organ, and conduct that appears to be within its official capacity to third parties (usually the victims of the relevant conduct) given that the state organ is acting under colour of its official capacity and using tools placed at its disposal by virtue of that capacity. *À contrario*, the state is not responsible for the conduct of a state organ when that organ acts in a purely private capacity. While the commentaries to the ILC Articles on State Responsibility warn against confusing *ultra vires* conduct with purely private conduct,[66] Special Rapporteurs on State Responsibility have acknowledged that it may be difficult in practice to distinguish conduct exceeding or contravening instructions from conduct that is so far removed from the sphere of the state organ's official functions that it amounts to private conduct.[67] Jurisprudence that addresses the distinction in the context of crimes committed by state organs relies on the cover of official status under which the relevant persons acted: based on the fact that a state organ appeared to be acting within its official capacity, and used the tools at its disposal by virtue of that capacity, the conduct is characterized as official (even if *ultra vires*) instead of purely private.[68]

The distinction between *ultra vires* and purely private conduct is particularly problematic to apply in the terrorism context given that acts of terrorism carried out by state organs will virtually always be in the form of covert operations, carried out by secret service agents who do not display any outward manifestation of the authority under which they act. The state organs will appear to be private citizens, engaging in private conduct. As a result, such acts of terrorism could not be said to have been carried out under colour of authority. A finding of attributability will therefore require holding that, in carrying out acts of terrorism, the state organ was acting in its *actual* (rather than *apparent*) official capacity. But such a determination will invariably involve policy judgments as to the proper sphere of state activity. If a court was not

---

Law Commission on the work of its twenty-fifth session, UN Doc. A/9010/Rev.1 (1973), 191–3; Brownlie (1983), 145.

[63] Commentary to Art. 7, ILC Articles on State Responsibility, para 3.
[64] League of Nations, Acts of the Conference for the Codification of International Law Held at The Hague from 13 March to 12 April 1930, Vol. IV (Minutes of the Third Committee), LN Doc. C.351 (c) M.145(c).1930.V, 237.
[65] *Petrolane v. Iran* (Iran–US Claims Tribunal, 1991), 92.
[66] Commentary to Art. 4, ILC Articles on State Responsibility, para 13; Commentary to Art. 7, ILC Articles on State Responsibility, para 7.
[67] Ago (1972), 93, para 56; Crawford (1998a), 29–31, paras 238–43.
[68] See e.g. *Youmans Case* (US–Mexico General Claims Commission, 1926), 115–16; *Caire Case* (France–Mexico Mixed Claims Commission, 1929), 531; *Velásquez-Rodríguez Case* (Inter-American Court of Human Rights, 1988), para 170.

willing to hold that a terrorist offence fell within the actual official capacity of a state organ, it would have to hold that the conduct was carried out in the private capacity of the state organ, thereby making it unattributable.

The practical difficulties of distinguishing between conduct carried out in an official capacity (but *ultra vires*) and conduct carried out in a private capacity are illustrated by the Rainbow Warrior case. The 'Rainbow Warrior' was a Greenpeace ship, moored in Auckland Harbour, preparing to protest against French nuclear testing in the South Pacific. Shortly before midnight on 10 July 1985, explosive devices attached to the hull of the 'Rainbow Warrior' were detonated, blowing an eight-foot wide hole into the ship below the waterline. The ship sank within minutes of the explosion, killing a photographer on board. Two days after the explosion, two French secret service agents were interviewed regarding their role in the destruction of the Greenpeace ship. Alain Mafart and Dominique Prieur were arrested following their interviews.[69] France initially denied any official link between the French citizens in New Zealand's custody and the French government, and offered France's full co-operation in New Zealand's investigations into the 'criminal outrage committed on [New Zealand] territory'.[70] France subsequently admitted that Mafart and Prieur were Direction Générale de la Sécurité Extérieure ('DGSE') agents, and acknowledged that DGSE agents had been sent to New Zealand to gather intelligence on Greenpeace, but continued to deny responsibility for the explosions aboard the 'Rainbow Warrior' on the basis that neither the French government nor the DGSE had ordered the attack.[71]

To acknowledge that Mafart and Prieur were organs of the state, yet deny responsibility for their conduct, the French government's argument could only have been that the DGSE agents were acting in their private capacity when they participated in the bombing of the 'Rainbow Warrior'. Had the question of France's responsibility been put to an international court, it could not have found that the agents, carrying Swiss passports and posing as tourists,[72] were acting under colour of authority. The only basis of attributability would be the organ status of the DGSE agents and a finding that acts of terrorism fell within the sphere of official functions entrusted by the French State to the DGSE. The fact of organ status would certainly have created a presumption of attributability, and it would have been for France to argue that acts of terrorism are not official acts within the meaning of Article 7 of the ILC Articles on State Responsibility. That said, qualifying criminal conduct as falling within the official functions of an organ of the French State would have been a sensitive determination for an international court to make. Under mounting media pressure, however, the French Government acknowledged that the DGSE agents were acting in their actual official capacity.

---

[69] See Communiqué from the French Prime Minister dated 22 September 1985, 74 International Law Reports 261; *UNSG Rainbow Warrior Ruling* (1986); *R. v. Mafart and Prieur*, New Zealand (High Court, 22 November 1985), 74 International Law Reports 243, 250.

[70] See Letter from the President of France to the Prime Minister of New Zealand, 8 August 1985, 74 International Law Reports 262.

[71] See <http://www.greenpeace.org/international/rainbow-warrior-bombing/spy-story>.

[72] *Ibid.*

Prime Minister Laurent Fabius admitted that the French secret service had ordered the attack on the 'Rainbow Warrior' and accepted international responsibility for the attack.[73] France and New Zealand could not agree on the amount of compensation to be paid by France, or on the fate of the two secret service agents (who had been convicted of manslaughter in the interim). Both issues were put to the UN Secretary-General for a binding ruling.[74]

2.2.2 Instructions, direction or control

Notwithstanding the Rainbow Warrior case examined above, acts of international terrorism are rarely carried out by organs of a state. States are more likely to conduct terrorist activities through private persons or groups who act on their behalf while remaining outside the formal structure of the state.[75] The applicable standard of attributability is therefore set out in Article 8 of the ILC Articles on State Responsibility, which reads:

The conduct of a person or group of persons shall be considered an act of a State under international law if the person or group of persons is in fact acting on the instructions of, or under the direction or control of, the State in carrying out the conduct.[76]

Acting on the instructions of a state was first codified as a basis for attributing the conduct of non-state actors to a state in the draft ILC Articles on State Responsibility adopted on first reading,[77] and subsequently confirmed by the ICJ in its *Tehran Hostages* decision.[78] The Commentaries to the ILC Articles on State Responsibility highlight that the 'acting on the instructions of' standard applies even if the persons involved are private individuals and are not exercising 'governmental authority'.[79] As a result, the practical difficulties involved in distinguishing between official and private conduct under Article 4, particularly in situating

---

[73] See Communiqué from the French Prime Minister dated 22 September 1985, 74 International Law Reports 261.

[74] See *UNSG Rainbow Warrior Ruling* (1986); Apollis (1987). See also Section 3.2.2 below for a discussion of the Ruling in reference to issues of immunity *ratione materiae* from domestic criminal proceedings.

[75] See Byman (2005), Chapter 2; Hoffman (2006), 27.

[76] Art. 8, ILC Articles on State Responsibility.

[77] Art. 8(a) and Commentary, Report of the International Law Commission on the work of its twenty-sixth session, UN Doc. A/9610/Rev.1 (1974), 283, para 1 and 285, para 8. There is, however, some ambiguity in the Commentaries as to whether acting in concert with or at the instigation of a state might also form the basis for attributing non-state conduct to a state (both of which seem lower standards than acting on instructions of). *Ibid*, 284, para 5. See also Crawford (1998a), para 200; Kress (2001), 102.

[78] The ICJ held that the conduct of the revolutionaries 'might be considered as itself directly imputable to the Iranian State *only if it were established that*, in fact, on the occasion in question the militants acted on behalf on the State, having been charged by some competent organ of the Iranian State to carry out a specific operation'. Emphasis added. *Tehran Hostages (US v. Iran)*, Judgment, para 58. Having concluded that the revolutionaries were not acting on the instructions of the Iranian State, the ICJ then considered a state's *post facto* adoption of private conduct as a basis for attributing that conduct to the adopting state. *Tehran Hostages (US v. Iran)*, Judgment, para 74.

[79] Commentary to Art. 8, ILC Articles on State Responsibility, para 2.

terrorism within a sphere of legitimate state activity (discussed in Section 2.2.1 above), do not complicate the application of Article 8 in the terrorism context. The Commentaries to the ILC Articles on State Responsibility further describe the application of the 'acting on instructions' standard of attribution as applying where:

> State organs supplement their own action by recruiting or instigating private persons or groups who act as 'auxiliaries' while remaining outside the official structure of the State [. . . including persons] sent as 'volunteers' to neighbouring countries, *or* who are instructed to carry out particular missions abroad.[80]

The clear implication of the Commentary is that sending volunteers (mirroring the language of Article 3(g) of the UN Definition of Aggression), *or* instructing volunteers on a particular mission, will fulfil the standard of attribution set out in Article 8 of the ILC Articles on State Responsibility. According to the Commentary, particular instructions on a mission are *not* required in regard to the sending of volunteers. The ICJ, however, has not interpreted Article 8 in this way. In its *Bosnia Genocide Case* decision, the Court held that it must be shown that 'the State's instructions were given in respect of each operation in which the alleged violations occurred, not generally in respect of the overall actions taken by the persons or groups of persons having committed the violations'.[81]

Given the improbability of an applicant state being able to prove that terrorist conduct was undertaken on the specific instructions of the respondent state,[82] this section focuses instead on state *control* over non-state actors as a basis for attribution in the terrorism context. It examines the *Nicaragua* decision, the partial codification of that decision by the ILC, reformulation of the *Nicaragua* control standard for attribution by the International Criminal Tribunal for the Former Yugoslavia ('ICTY') in its *Tadić* decision, and the ICJ's reaction to that reformulation in its *Bosnia Genocide Case* decision.

(i) International jurisprudence and the ILC's codification of the rules on attribution

In *Nicaragua*, the ICJ considered the conditions under which the conduct of non-state actors, in particular that of the *contras*, would be attributable to the US. Nicaragua alleged that the US was responsible for breaching the prohibition of the use of force, the principle of non-intervention, and the duty not to kill, wound or kidnap citizens of Nicaragua, through its active participation in and support for military and paramilitary activities in and around Nicaragua. Before setting forth

---

[80] Emphasis added. *Ibid.*

[81] *Bosnia Genocide Case*, Judgment, para 400. The ICJ's decision was in application of Article 8 of the ILC Articles on State Responsibility, and therefore did not say anything about the *lex specialis* rule of attribution under Article 3(g) of the UN Definition of Aggression, UNGA Resolution 3314 (1974), Annex.

[82] See Commentary to Art. 7, ILC Articles on State Responsibility, para 3, citing the Italian position that there is 'no practical way of proving that [an] agent had or had not acted on orders received' in support of the rule that the state should be responsible for all conduct of its organs, even if *ultra vires*.

the legal standard for attribution, the ICJ made a number of factual determinations regarding the relationship between the US and the *contras*. Importantly, the Court determined that the US did not create the armed opposition *contra* forces, although the size of the *contras* increased dramatically with its military and financial assistance.[83] The Court considered it to have been established that the US financed the *contras*,[84] provided significant logistical support in the form of uniforms (including boots), ammunition, and communications and military equipment,[85] supplied the *contras* with intelligence on the movement of Nicaraguan troops,[86] and trained the *contras*.[87] The Court also found that a number of the *contras'* paramilitary operations were decided and planned in close collaboration with US advisers,[88] and that the US selected targets for the *contras'* armed activities.[89]

There are three levels of potentially attributable conduct raised in *Nicaragua*: the *contras'* paramilitary campaign in general; specific paramilitary operations; and humanitarian law violations committed during the course of specific paramilitary operations. The ICJ considered the attributability of the *contras'* paramilitary campaign *en bloc* to turn on the *de facto* organ status of the *contras*. Had the *contras* amounted to a *de facto* organ of the US, the US would have been directly responsible for all their activities, including humanitarian law violations committed by the *contras* in the course of some of their paramilitary operations. But the ICJ concluded that the level of US involvement in the *contras'* activities did not signify that 'the relationship of the *contra* to the United States Government was so much one of dependence on the one side and control on the other that it would be right to equate the *contras*, for legal purposes, with an organ of the United States Government, or as acting on behalf of that Government'.[90] As a result, the ICJ did not consider the *contras'* paramilitary campaign as a whole to be attributable to the US.

The second level of potentially attributable conduct the ICJ might have considered relates to specific and identifiable paramilitary operations, for instance the targeting of a particular military installation. Nicaragua's pleadings addressed the *contras'* use of force on an operation by operation basis,[91] but did not break

---

[83] *Nicaragua (Nicaragua v. US)*, Merits, paras 94 and 108. One commentator has argued that the ICJ's decision on attribution may well have been different if the US had created the *contras*. See de Hoogh (2001), 269.

[84] *Nicaragua (Nicaragua v. US)*, Merits, paras 100 and 108.

[85] *Ibid*, para 100.

[86] *Ibid*, para 106.

[87] *Ibid*, paras 101–2.

[88] *Ibid*, para 106. The ICJ did not consider it to have been established that 'all the operations launched by the *contra* force, at every stage of the conflict, reflect strategy and tactics wholly devised by the United States'. *Ibid*.

[89] *Ibid*, paras 112 and 115.

[90] *Nicaragua (Nicaragua v. US)*, Merits, para 109. In its *Bosnia Genocide Case* decision, the ICJ characterized this test as determinative of *de facto* organ status, and conduct carried out by *de facto* organs would be attributable to a state on the basis of Article 4 of the ILC Articles on State Responsibility. *Bosnia Genocide Case*, Judgment, paras 390–1 and 397. But see Griebel and Plücken (2008), 612–13, arguing that the dependence test set forth in the *Nicaragua* decision should not be characterized as a *de facto* organ test. For a vigorous critique of Griebel and Plücken's argument, see Milanovic (2009).

[91] *Nicaragua (Nicaragua v. US)*, Merits, Memorial of Nicaragua, paras 37–59.

down US support for the operations in the same manner. Instead, the pleadings addressed US support for the *contras'* activities in a general manner, without tying such support to specific paramilitary operations.[92] The ICJ did not formulate a standard for attribution in relation to specific paramilitary operations, and regarded the US to have violated the prohibition of the use of force based on its own conduct *vis à vis* the *contras* (i.e. training and arming the *contras*),[93] rather than on the basis of the attributability of specific paramilitary operations.[94]

The third level of potentially attributable conduct in *Nicaragua* is in relation to the humanitarian law violations committed during the course of particular paramilitary operations. The ICJ elaborated an 'effective control' standard as the relevant basis for attribution, and held that general control over paramilitary forces and operations, such as that exercised by the US over the *contras*, was not sufficient for the purposes of attributing the humanitarian law violations.[95] While the ICJ acknowledged that the US selected military and paramilitary targets for the *contras* and planned its operations, it held that these elements did not necessarily imply that the US 'directed and enforced the perpetration of the acts contrary to human rights and humanitarian law' committed by the *contras* during the course of those operations.[96] The ICJ held that:

such acts could well be committed by members of the *contras* without the control of the United States [and that for] such acts to give rise to the legal responsibility of the United States, it would in principle have to be proved that the State had *effective control* of the military and paramilitary operations *in the course of which the alleged violations were committed.*[97]

The ICJ's decision in *Nicaragua* was considered by both the Trial Chamber and Appeals Chamber of the ICTY in their *Tadić* decisions.[98] In determining which body of humanitarian law applied to the case, the Trial Chamber relied on the rules of state responsibility, in particular the rules of attribution, to decide whether the conflict in Bosnia was of an international or non-international character. The Trial Chamber adopted the 'effective control' test set out in the ICJ's *Nicaragua* decision, and held that the Former Republic of Yugoslavia ('FRY') did not exercise effective control over the Bosnian Serb forces ('VRS'). As a result, the Trial Chamber held that the VRS military campaign in Bosnia could not be attributed to the FRY and that the FRY could not be considered a party to the conflict on that basis—thereby

---

[92] *Ibid*, paras 255–62.
[93] *Nicaragua (Nicaragua v. US)*, Merits, para 228. But see *Tadić* (ICTY-94-1-A), Separate Opinion of Judge Shahabuddeen, paras 8–12.
[94] The ICJ did address specific military operations (i.e. an attack on Sandino International Airport on 8 September 1983 and an attack on oil storage facilities at Benjamin Zeledon on 2 October 1983) when considering the attributability of certain non-state conduct (carried out by the so-called Unilaterally Controlled Latino Assets) because the specifics of US involvement in those operations was addressed in the pleadings. See *Nicaragua (Nicaragua v. US)*, Merits, para 81.
[95] *Ibid*, para 115.
[96] *Ibid*.
[97] Emphasis added. *Ibid*.
[98] *Tadić* (ICTY-94-1-T); *Tadić* (ICTY-94-1-A).

rendering the conflict non-international for the purposes of applicable humanitari-an law.[99] The Prosecutor appealed the decision, and argued that '[i]t would lead to absurd results to apply the rules relating to state responsibility to assist in determin-ing' which body of humanitarian law applied to the conflict.[100] The Appeals Chamber, however, upheld the Trial Chamber's approach to the issue, and held that:

[i]nternational humanitarian law does not contain any criteria unique to this body of law for establishing when a group of individuals may be regarded as being under the control of a State, that is, as acting as *de facto* State officials. Consequently, it is necessary to examine the notion of control by a State over individuals, laid down in general international law, for the purpose of establishing whether those individuals may be regarded as acting as *de facto* State officials.[101]

Having determined that the general law of state responsibility was applicable in the circumstances, the ICTY Appeals Chamber rejected the *Nicaragua* 'effective control' test as the only control-based test for attributing non-state military operations to a state. The Appeals Chamber drew a distinction between the level of control to be exercised over private individuals or unorganized groups of individuals and that to be exercised over militarily organized groups. In regard to the latter, the Appeals Chamber held that it is by no means necessary that the controlling state should plan all the operations of the military units dependant on it, choose their targets or give specific instructions on military operations (amounting to effective control over those operations) in order that those operations be attributable to the state. Instead, the Chamber held that 'overall control', which exists where the state has a role in organizing, coordinating or planning the military operations of a group, in addition to financing, training, equipping or providing operational support for such military operations, is sufficient for the purposes of attribution.[102] Whether or not the ICTY correctly relied on the rules of state responsibility to determine the applicable humani-tarian law,[103] its decision is of interest in that it addresses the relevant standard of attribution for particular military operations, without regard for whether humanitarian law violations were committed in the course thereof.

Following the decision in *Nicaragua*, Special Rapporteur Crawford revised Article 8 of the ILC Articles on State Responsibility, incorporating a control standard, but without specifying the threshold of control that it required.[104] The Commentaries to Article 8 note that the ICJ addressed the relevant degree of

---

[99] *Tadić* (ICTY-94-1-T), paras 592–604.
[100] *Tadić* (ICTY-94-1-A), Prosecution Brief, paras 2.21–2.23.
[101] *Tadić* (ICTY-94-1-A), para 98.
[102] *Tadić* (ICTY-94-1-A), para 137. The Appeals Chamber subsequently reaffirmed its *Tadić* 'overall control' test, holding that '[t]he "overall control" test could thus be fulfilled even if the armed forces acting on behalf of the "controlling State" had autonomous choices of means and tactics although participating in a common strategy along with the "controlling State"'. *Delalić et al.* (ICTY-96-21-A), para 47.
[103] See Commentary to Art. 8, ILC Articles on State Responsibility, para 5; *Bosnia Genocide Case*, Judgment, para 404.
[104] Crawford (1998a), 4; Art. 8, ILC Articles on State Responsibility.

control in *Nicaragua* and highlight the 'effective control' standard elaborated in that decision.[105] The Commentaries do not, however, limit the standard of control in Article 8 to the *Nicaragua* effective control test. Although critical of the ICTY Appeals Chamber's foray into the law of state responsibility, the Commentaries to Article 8 do not reject the 'overall control' test set out in *Tadić*, acknowledging that '[i]n any event it is a matter for appreciation in each case whether particular conduct was or was not carried out under the control of a State, to such an extent that the conduct controlled should be attributed to it'.[106]

The ICJ, however, has not adopted such a flexible approach to the standard of control articulated in Article 8 of the ILC Articles on State Responsibility. In its *Bosnia Genocide Case* decision, the ICJ reprimanded the ICTY Appeals Chamber for its incursion into the law of state responsibility[107] and rejected the 'overall control' test for attribution set out in the *Tadić* Appeals Chamber decision as 'stretch[ing] too far, almost to breaking point, the connection which must exist between the conduct of a State's organs and its international responsibility'[108] (albeit without explaining why this should be so). The Court instead reaffirmed the 'effective control' standard first set out in *Nicaragua*. Indeed, the Court held that Article 8 of the ILC Articles on State Responsibility must be 'understood in the light of the Court's jurisprudence on the subject, particularly [its decision in *Nicaragua*]',[109] rendering 'effective control' the exclusive standard of control under Article 8.[110] Whether that is appropriate, particularly in the context of state responsibility for terrorism, remains to be considered below.

(ii) Article 8 of the ILC Articles on State Responsibility in the terrorism context

Commentators who regard the 'effective control' test as too strict for the purposes of addressing state terrorism have broadly supported a reading of Article 8 of the ILC Articles on State Responsibility that leaves room for a flexible adaptation of the standard of control.[111] Some states have also read Article 8 in a way that leaves room for such flexible adaptation. For instance, the Netherlands has suggested that the words 'direction or control' in Article 8 of the ILC Articles on State Responsibility allow for the application of both a strict standard of 'effective control', as used by the ICJ in *Nicaragua*, and a more flexible standard as applied by the Appeals

---

[105] Commentary to Art. 8, ILC Articles on State Responsibility, para 4.

[106] *Ibid*, para 5.

[107] *Bosnia Genocide Case*, Judgment, paras 403–4.

[108] *Ibid*, para 406. But see *Bosnia Genocide Case*, Judgment, Dissenting Opinion of Vice-President Al-Khasawneh, para 39.

[109] *Bosnia Genocide Case*, Judgment, para 399.

[110] *Ibid*, para 400.

[111] See e.g. Condorelli (1989); Reisman (1999), 39; Dinstein (2005), 182–3; Slaughter and Burke-White (2002), 20; Chase (2004), Becker (2006). For general remarks on whether 'effective control' remains the only standard of control, see Kress (2001); Griebel and Plücken (2008), 618–20. See also Brownlie (2008), 419, suggesting that attribution may take different forms, depending upon the primary rule applied.

Chamber of the ICTY in its *Tadić* decision. In its view, this inbuilt ambiguity is a positive element and offers scope for progressive development of the legal rules on state responsibility.[112] In addition, members of the ILC, when endorsing Special Rapporteur Crawford's formulation of Article 8, suggested that varying degrees of sufficient control were required in different legal contexts.[113] Such flexible approaches to 'control' under Article 8 of the ILC Articles on State Responsibility have in fact been adopted in other judicial dispute settlement contexts.[114]

The difficulty with 'effective control' as the only applicable control threshold is that the standard, as adopted by the ICJ in *Nicaragua*, was driven by the particular facts of the case. In *Nicaragua*, the ICJ was dealing with two separate levels of activity: the first was the paramilitary operations of the *contras* (which the Court did not consider separately for the purposes of attribution); the second level of activity involved violations of humanitarian law perpetrated in the course of those paramilitary operations. The humanitarian law violations, however, were a non-inherent feature of the military operations of the *contras*, and the ICJ's 'effective control' test is formulated to ensure that responsibility for such violations only arises where a state's control extends to those non-inherent features of a military campaign. In the terrorism context, however, there is no second level of activity—the breach of international law is inherent in terrorist operations. Contrary to the case in *Nicaragua*, it is difficult to argue that material military support (including logistical, munitions, and military training) for terrorist activities does not necessarily imply support for the offences committed by the terrorists in the course of their use of force.[115] There is therefore no need for the added layer of effective control, in addition to a more general level of control over the group's operations (through its support thereof), to ensure that a state is only held responsible for that over which it exercised sufficient control.

Special Rapporteur Crawford recognized that the decision in *Nicaragua* related specifically to the extent of the obligation of the state to control irregular forces or

---

[112] ILC, Comments and Observations received from Governments on State Responsibility, UN Doc. A/CN.4/515 (2001), 23. See also *Blaškić* (ICTY-95-14-T), Declaration of Judge Shahabuddeen, arguing that any control over non-state actors, for the purposes of attribution, needs to be effective—and what threshold of control amounts to effective control will depend on the circumstances.

[113] Report of the International Law Commission on the work of its fiftieth session, UN Doc. A/53/10 and Corr.1 (1998), para 395. See also Dupuy (2004), 10, arguing that the ambiguity in Article 8 was likely deliberate, in order to leave some flexibility for different possible interpretations. But see *Bosnia Genocide Case*, Judgment, para 401: '[t]he rules for attributing alleged internationally wrongful conduct to a State do not vary with the nature of the wrongful act in question in the absence of a clearly expressed *lex specialis*'.

[114] See *Bayindir v. Pakistan* (ICSID, 2009), para 130: 'Finally, the Tribunal is aware that the levels of control required for a finding of attribution under Article 8 in other factual contexts, such as foreign armed intervention or international criminal responsibility, may be different. It believes, however, that the approach developed in such areas of international law is not always adapted to the realities of international economic law and that they should not prevent a finding of attribution if the specific facts of an investment dispute so warrant'.

[115] Non-military support raises more complicated issues because several organizations designated by the West as 'terrorist' equally carry out governance functions in the regions within which they operate, for instance Hamas in Gaza and Hezbollah in Lebanon. As a result, financial and other forms of non-military assistance may well be intended for the purposes of assisting the organization in carrying out its governance-related responsibilities.

auxiliaries acting under its auspices and that it might present a *lex specialis* in the context of the rules of attribution. He concluded, however, that it is not clear why conduct of auxiliary armed forces in operations under specific direction or control should be attributable to the state, but not analogous conduct under state direction and control in other spheres.[116] The question Special Rapporteur Crawford might have asked is whether there are any circumstances in which a lower threshold for attribution might be appropriate, particularly given that the added measure of control injected into the attribution test for the purposes of the ICJ's decision in *Nicaragua* seems unnecessary in the terrorism context, or indeed in any other context where the operation is itself an offence defined under international law.[117]

However unsuitable the 'effective control' standard might be to the terrorism context, the *Bosnia Genocide Case* decision does suggest that the ICJ will neverthe-less apply it when considering the attributability of non-state conduct to a state. That said, the facts of the *Bosnia Genocide Case* are not dissimilar from those in *Nicaragua*. The VRS were fighting a civil war—and genocide is a non-inherent feature of civil wars. As a result, the Court reaffirmed the applicability of the standard of control it first established in *Nicaragua*, in reference to the attribut-ability of non-inherent features of military campaigns. Were the Court confronted with a state's overall control of a terrorist campaign, it might well realize that a different threshold of control is sufficient for the purposes of attributing inherent features of a use of force. This would be particularly important because state support for terrorism, no matter how substantial, will not generally satisfy the 'effective control' test. In his study of state terrorism, Byman concludes that the most common forms of support for non-state terrorist actors are training (in explosives particularly), the provision of intelligence, the supply of arms, financing, the provision of logistical assistance (for example issuing passports and helping terrorist actors obtain visas through state-fronted companies or non-governmental organizations), ideological direction and sanctuary.[118] While states often support terrorist activities by offering several or indeed all these forms of support,[119] together they do not amount to effective control over particular terrorist operations, even if the state chooses the target of the terrorist operation. But states do not necessarily exercise operational control over terrorist attacks that are committed on their behalf, which is what the 'effective control' standard of attribution would require. It would be more accurate to consider state sponsorship of terrorism as based on a general control over terrorist operations (including the selection of targets). Such control would satisfy the 'overall control' test articulated in the ICTY Appeals Chamber's decision in *Tadić*. Were the flexible approach to Article 8 advocated by states and ILC members adopted, it could incorporate the 'overall control' standard as a basis of attribution, and thereby respond to the particularities

---

[116] Crawford (1998a), 23, para 216.
[117] Regarding the unsuitability of the 'effective control' test for the attribution of genocide, see *Bosnia Genocide Case*, Judgment, Dissenting Opinion of Vice-President Al-Khasawneh, para 39.
[118] Byman (2005), 54–66.
[119] Byman (2005), 54.

of the terrorism context in a way that rigid adherence to the *Nicaragua* standard does not.

2.2.3 Complicity revisited

The sections above examine the broadly accepted bases of attribution reflected in the ILC Articles on State Responsibility, as they apply in the terrorism context. The sufficiency of those grounds of attribution has recently been challenged in academic commentary on the basis of state practice in the *jus ad bellum* context. This section examines the extent to which this challenge is justified and the implications, if any, of proposed changes to the rules of attribution applicable in the terrorism context. The contested territory on the rules of attribution centre on concepts of complicity or acquiescence—which occupy the boundary between 'direct' and 'indirect' responsibility.

If conduct is not attributable to a state on the basis of the rules of attribution set out in the ILC Articles on State Responsibility (including on the basis of organ status, or instructions, direction or control, as examined in Sections 2.2.1 and 2.2.2 above), the state can only be held responsible for its own wrongdoing in relation to that private conduct.[120] This lends itself to a clear distinction between a state's 'direct' responsibility for a terrorist attack (in virtue of that attack being attributable to the state) and a state's 'indirect' responsibility for breach of its obligations in relation to a terrorist attack—including obligations to refrain from supporting terrorism, to act in prevention of acts of terrorism, and to extradite or submit terrorist actors to prosecution—without the state being responsible for the terrorist attack itself. In the latter case, particularly as regards the obligations to prevent terrorism and to extradite or submit terrorist actors to prosecution,[121] the private terrorist conduct is not the basis of responsibility in the sense implied by attribution. Rather, the private terrorist conduct is the catalyst for the state's responsibility,[122] in that it triggers the state's obligation to act, failure of which constitutes the internationally wrongful act.

The distinction between 'direct' responsibility for attributable conduct, and 'indirect' responsibility for failures to act in anticipation of or in response to conduct not attributable to a state, was not always clear. In the late nineteenth and early twentieth centuries, states were held 'directly' responsible for private conduct (in the sense implied by attribution) based on their complicity or acquiescence therein—put in evidence through a failure to prevent or punish the private conduct.[123] This artificial way of linking private conduct to the state, rather than focusing on whether the state had an independent obligation to prevent or punish the conduct,[124] was gradually abandoned in the inter-war

---

[120] See Commentary to Part One, Chapter II, ILC Articles on State Responsibility, para 9.
[121] See Chapter 3 on the obligations to prevent and extradite or submit to prosecution.
[122] See Ago (1972), 71, para 65.
[123] See e.g. *Cotesworth and Powell Case (Great Britain/Colombia)*, 2082; *Poglioli Case (Italy/Venezuela)*, 689; Eagleton (1928), 77; Starke (1938), 367–9. See also de Frouville (2010), tracing the movement away from complicity as a basis of attribution from Grotius to the present day ILC Articles on State Responsibility.
[124] For a critique of the artificiality of the link, see Christenson (1983), 322.

period.[125] The ILC and international jurisprudence have since firmly rejected complicity or acquiescence in private conduct as a basis of attribution.[126] Nevertheless, complicity-based theories of attribution are not dead: recent state practice, coupled with a reading of the ICJ's jurisprudence that suggests a strict attribution-based definition of 'armed attack' under Article 51 of the UN Charter, have breathed new life into them.

The state practice on complicity or acquiescence as a basis for attribution in the terrorism context that is treated as relevant in the literature derives generally from states' recent exercise of their right to use force in self-defence against non-state terrorist actors. The scope of the right to use force in self-defence is set out in Article 51 of the UN Charter, which reads in relevant part that '[n]othing in the present Charter shall impair the inherent right of individual or collective self-defence if an armed attack occurs against a Member of the United Nations'.[127] A use of force in self-defence is therefore only legitimate under the Charter to the extent that it is in response to an armed attack.[128] The ICJ's jurisprudence has been interpreted as limiting 'armed attacks' to uses of force by or attributable to a state.[129] On the basis of such a definition, defensive force in response to a terrorist attack emanating from foreign territory would only be legitimate under Article 51 of the UN Charter if the

---

[125] The US–Mexico Claims Commission's decision in the *Janes Case* (1926), paras 114–15, was the first clear rejection of complicity as a basis of direct state responsibility for underlying criminal conduct, at least in relation to a failure to punish. See also *British Property in Spanish Zone of Morocco Case (UK/Spain)*, 641–2. Even though codification efforts did not unambiguously distinguish between state responsibility based on the negligent failure to prevent private conduct where there was an international obligation to do so and responsibility based on the attributability of the unprevented private conduct (see e.g. Institute of International Law (1927), 229; American Institute of International Law (1929), 232; Harvard Law School (1929), 187–9; League of Nations, Conference for the Codification of International Law, Bases of Discussion for the Conference drawn up by the Preparatory Committee, Vol. III (Responsibility of States for Damage caused in their Territory to the Person or Property of Foreigners), LN Doc. C.75.M.69.1929.V, 515–18, 534), scholarly opinion was more in line with the *Janes Case* distinction between direct and indirect responsibility. See Borchard (1915), 217; Brierly (1928); Rice (1934), 249.

[126] See Ago (1972), 119–20, para 135. See also *Bosnia Genocide Case*, Judgment, para 420, in which the ICJ considered state responsibility for complicity in genocide, an ancillary offence under the Genocide Convention, and clearly distinguished it from a standard of attribution. But see Sohn and Baxter (1974), 235. See *infra* Chapter 4, notes 67–72 and accompanying text for a discussion of state responsibility for accessory crimes (like accomplice liability) defined in the TSCs.

[127] Art. 51, UN Charter.

[128] See Brownlie (1963). But see Bowett (1958) and Schwebel (1972), arguing that the 'inherent' nature of the right of self-defence recognized in the Charter preserves earlier customary law, including anticipatory self-defence. On the debate, see Gray (2008), 117–19.

[129] See e.g. Cassese (1989), 596–7 (requiring attributability under the law of state responsibility, but, in line with the dissents in *Nicaragua (Nicaragua v. US)*, Merits, describing state support and acquiescence in terrorism as a 'grey' area in the law that might form the basis of attribution); Zanardi (1986); Condorelli (2001), 838; Corten (2002), 55. But see *Palestinian Wall Advisory Opinion*, Separate Opinion of Judge Higgins, para 33 (questioning the ICJ's conclusion in *Nicaragua*, given that there is nothing in the language of the Charter itself that restricts 'armed attacks' to uses of force by a state); *Palestinian Wall Advisory Opinion*, Separate Opinion of Judge Kooijmans, para 35; *Armed Activities on the Territory of the Congo (DRC Uganda)*, Judgment, Separate Opinion of Judge Kooijmans, para 28; Wedgwood (1999), 564; Franck (2000), 840; Murphy (2002), 50; Paust (2002), 534; Greenwood (2003), 419–21; Stahn (2003), 42.

attack[130] were carried out by the territorial state's organs or if it were otherwise attributable to the state from whose territory it emanated (and in whose territory defensive force was used).

The difficulty with a strict attribution-based definition of 'armed attack' is that it fails to account for recent uses of defensive force in response to terrorist attacks carried out by non-state actors (that were not attributable to the state on the basis of the ILC Articles on State Responsibility or Article 3(g) of the UN Definition of Aggression) that were widely accepted as legitimate by the international community, most particularly the US-led coalition military campaign in Afghanistan in 2001 ('Operation Enduring Freedom'). In order to square the legitimacy of Operation Enduring Freedom against a strict attribution-based reading of 'armed attack', scholars have been forced into the uncomfortable position of having to resuscitate old bases for attributing non-state conduct to the state in whose territory force was used defensively, including complicity in terrorist activities or harbouring terrorists,[131] or to deny the legality of the defensive force based on the non-attributability of the relevant terrorist attacks to Afghanistan (and its *de facto* Taliban government), despite the overwhelming international support it received.[132] Neither of these solutions is satisfactory. The first one reinvigorates a standard of attribution that has long been rejected as too tenuous a basis for direct responsibility. The second ignores the facts to maintain legal coherence.[133]

Implicit in the view that complicity is a basis of attribution is the argument that any change to the rules of attribution that are necessary to respond to the security context will be carried through to the law of state responsibility.[134] But there is no good reason why the rules of attribution, as they may or may not need to develop for the purposes of defining the limits of the right to use force in self-defence, would also need to develop for the purposes of holding a state delictually responsible. Indeed, any changes to the rules of attribution that may be necessary to address state practice under Article 51 of the UN Charter would best be characterized as *lex specialis*.

Even if, however, changes in the rules of attribution in the *jus ad bellum* context were generalized for the purposes of state responsibility, the view that complicity has re-emerged as a basis of attribution (on the grounds of post-9/11 *jus ad bellum* practice) is rooted in a misinterpretation of the ICJ's jurisprudence and the relevant state practice. This section examines both, and argues that a careful reading of the ICJ's jurisprudence, coupled with the increasing recognition of a right to use force

---

[130] The terrorist attack committed by the non-state actors must also be of sufficient gravity to amount to an armed attack within the meaning of Article 51 of the UN Charter. See *Nicaragua (Nicaragua v. US)*, Merits, para 195; *Oil Platforms (Iran v. US)*, Judgment, para 51.

[131] See Randelzohfer (2002), 801; Jinks (2003); Jinks (2003a); Brunnée and Toope (2004), 795; Janse (2006), 168–9; Tams (2009), 385. But see Trapp (2009).

[132] See Sassòli (2001), 223; Paust (2002), 540–3; Guillaume (2004), 545–7.

[133] See Simpson (2004), 335.

[134] See Becker (2006), suggesting that the attribution-based approach to state responsibility (which he refers to as the 'agency paradigm') needs to be reconceptualized in order to respond properly to (among other things) the realities of state practice under Article 51 of the UN Charter. See Trapp (2006) for a critique of this argument. See also discussion in Tams (2009); Trapp (2009); and Tams (2009a).

in self-defence against non-state terrorist actors in foreign territory, alleviates the need to play 'fast and loose' with the rules of attribution or to ignore the acknowledged legitimacy of certain recent defensive operations.

(i) Rejection of an attribution-based definition of 'armed attack'

Uses of force in self-defence against non-state terrorist actors can take two separate forms. The first involves a use of force that only targets the non-state actors and their bases of operation in foreign territory. The second is where the use of force equally, or perhaps only, targets the state from whose territory the non-state actors operate. A majority of the ICJ has consistently held that a use of defensive force in response to an attack by non-state actors is a legitimate exercise of rights under Article 51 of the UN Charter if (and only if) the armed attack is attributable to the state in whose territory defensive force is used. The ICJ's insistence on the attributability of an armed attack, however, can be explained by the distinction set out above. In both the contentious cases addressing the right to use force in self-defence against non-state actors, the use of force was not directed solely at the non-state actors alleged to have launched armed attacks—it was equally (if not exclusively) directed at the state from whose territory the non-state actors operated. The fact that the ICJ required armed attacks launched by non-state actors to be attributable to the state in whose territory defensive force was used may thus be understood as a direct consequence of the fact that the territorial state was itself the target of defensive force. The ICJ's refusal to address the circumstances under which a state has a right to use force in self-defence against (and only against) non-state actors, however much lamented in the separate opinions,[135] is therefore justified on the facts of each case and should not be read as precluding such uses of defensive force.

In *Nicaragua*, the ICJ considered whether US assistance to the Nicaraguan *contra* forces[136] amounted to a legitimate exercise of the right of collective self-defence. The US claimed to be acting (primarily) in defence of El Salvador, which was the victim of armed attacks by rebel groups allegedly supplied with arms through Nicaragua with the active support, or at the very least complicity, of the Nicaraguan Government.[137] The *contras*' main targets were Sandinista troops, although there were numerous reports of attacks on non-combatants[138] and Nicaragua alleged a US-devised strategy for the *contras* to attack 'economic targets like electrical plants and storage facilities' in Nicaragua.[139] The ICJ noted that, to defend El Salvador

---

[135] See e.g. *Armed Activities on the Territory of the Congo (DRC v. Uganda)*, Judgment, Separate Opinion of Judge Simma, para 8; Separate Opinion of Judge Kooijmans, para 25.

[136] The ICJ held that the US was responsible for financing, training, and providing logistical support to the *contras* (including the supply of intelligence as to Nicaraguan troop movements). *Supra* notes 83–9 and accompanying text.

[137] The ICJ held that Nicaragua was not in fact responsible for the arms traffic, to the extent such arms traffic existed. *Nicaragua (Nicaragua v. US)*, Merits, paras 154–5.

[138] *Nicaragua (Nicaragua v. US)*, Merits, para 113. See Section 2.2.2 for a discussion of the ICJ's decision on the attributability of humanitarian law violations committed by the *contras* during the course of their paramilitary operations to the US.

[139] *Nicaragua (Nicaragua v. US)*, Merits, para 105.

against rebel attacks, the US might have arranged for a strong patrol force in El Salvador along its frontiers with Nicaragua, and that 'it is difficult to accept that [the US] should have continued to carry out military and paramilitary activities against Nicaragua if their only purpose was, as alleged, to serve as a riposte in the exercise of the right of self-defence'.[140] Given that the US-supported *contras* were directly targeting the Nicaraguan Government and military, the circumstances under which a state could legitimately use force against non-state actors (and only against non-state actors) in foreign territory was not in issue. Furthermore, the conditions under which a state could use force *against* another state in response to armed attacks by non-state actors were not met. The ICJ held that the legitimate exercise of the right of self-defence required that an armed attack by rebel groups be attributable to the state *against which* defensive force was used.[141] But Nicaragua's alleged assistance to rebel groups (in the form of provision of weapons and logistical support) did not meet the threshold for attributing the conduct of those groups to Nicaragua,[142] and such support did not itself amount to an armed attack.

In its *Palestinian Wall Advisory Opinion*, the ICJ gave brief consideration to whether Israel's construction of a security wall within the Occupied Palestinian Territories might be justified as a measure of self-defence. The ICJ considered Israel's justification for the construction of the wall to be one based on the right of states to defend themselves against terrorist attacks under Article 51 of the UN Charter, as recognized in Security Council Resolutions 1368 (2001) and 1373 (2001). But the Court held that:

Article 51 of the Charter [. . .] recognizes the existence of an inherent right of self-defence in the case of armed attack by one State against another State. However Israel does not claim that the attacks against it are imputable to a foreign State.[143]

While the Court might be understood as reaffirming the position it took in *Nicaragua* that armed attacks giving rise to the right of self-defence must be attributable to a foreign state, it might also be understood as merely articulating the conditions for the applicability of Article 51 of the UN Charter. In particular, Article 51 serves to justify a use of force that would *otherwise* be inconsistent with Article 2(4). As the Court considered the West Bank to be occupied territory, Israel's use of force in the West Bank (ignoring for the moment that building a wall does not in fact amount to a use of force) could not engage the Article 2(4)

---

[140] *Ibid*, para 156. The ICJ's argument is effectively a commentary on the necessity of the US operation. See Sohn (1989), 874.

[141] Scholars writing at the time of the decision were divided on the attribution-based definition of 'armed attack' advanced by the Court. Arguing that an 'armed attack' is limited to uses of force by one state against another, see e.g. Brownlie (1963), 278–9; Zanardi (1986). But see Dinstein (1987), 144–6; Combacau (1986), 26.

[142] *Nicaragua (Nicaragua v. US)*, Merits, para 195. The ICJ applied Article 3(g) of the UN Definition of Aggression, UNGA Resolution 3314 (1974), Annex, as a standard of attribution. See further the Court's treatment of Article 3(g) as a standard of attribution for the purpose of defining an 'armed attack' in its *Armed Activities on the Territory of the Congo (DRC v. Uganda)* decision, *infra* note 148 and accompanying text.

[143] *Palestinian Wall Advisory Opinion*, para 139.

prohibition which only applies as between sovereign states, thereby rendering Article 51 inapplicable. The ICJ also took a narrow approach to the applicability of Security Council Resolutions 1368 (2001) and 1373 (2001), and held that the territories from which terrorist attacks were launched were under Israeli control and could therefore not be considered in the context of resolutions that addressed the 9/11 terrorist attacks, where attacks were directed from abroad.[144] The Court's refusal to genuinely engage the justification of self-defence has subjected it to severe criticism,[145] but is arguably defensible based on the occupied status of Palestinian Territories and the availability of an alternative legal framework within which to assess Israeli conduct. In addition, the legal difficulty regarding a state's right to use defensive force directly against non-state actors in foreign territory results from the apparent irreconcilability of a state's right to defend itself and the inviolability of the territorial state's sovereignty. In the Israeli/Palestinian context, given the occupied status of the territory from which terrorist attacks are launched, the ICJ could not have shed any light on this issue in its decision.

In *DRC v. Uganda*, the ICJ held that the attacks carried out by rebel groups operating from the DRC's territory against Uganda were 'non-attributable to the DRC',[146] and because the legal and factual circumstances giving rise to a right to use force in self-defence were not satisfied, 'there [was] no need to respond to the contentions of the Parties whether and under what conditions contemporary international law provides for a right of self-defence against large-scale attacks by irregular forces'.[147] The ICJ reaffirmed its position, taken in *Nicaragua*, that a state's sending armed bands into another state, within the meaning of Article 3(g) of the UN Definition of Aggression, amounts to an armed attack giving rise to the right of self-defence against the sending state.[148] The Court did not elaborate on the standard of 'sending of armed bands' as a basis for attribution because it did not consider there to be 'satisfactory proof of the involvement in [the attacks by anti-Ugandan rebel forces against Uganda], direct or indirect, of the Government of the DRC'.[149] The ICJ's insistence that armed attacks be attributable to a state before they can give rise to a right to use force in self-defence, however, has to be

---

[144] *Palestinian Wall Advisory Opinion*, para 139. But see *Palestinian Wall Advisory Opinion*, Separate Opinion of Judge Higgins, para 34; Declaration of Judge Buergenthal, para 6.

[145] See Tams (2005); Murphy (2005). But note that the ICJ's opinion has been interpreted as at least implicitly recognizing a right to use force in self-defence against non-state terrorist actors in foreign territory, even though refusing to accept such a right as applicable in the circumstances based on the occupied status of the territory from which the terrorist attacks emanated. See Canor (2006), 132.

[146] *Armed Activities on the Territory of the Congo (DRC v. Uganda)*, Judgment, para 146.

[147] *Ibid*, para 147.

[148] *Armed Activities on the Territory of the Congo (DRC v. Uganda)*, Judgment, para 146. Interestingly, both the DRC and Uganda, in their pleadings, accepted a lesser degree of state involvement than that set out in *Nicaragua* as a basis for attributing the activities of armed bands to the host state for the purposes of self-defence. In particular, the DRC considered that a state's support for rebel groups, *including by deliberately allowing them access to its territory*, could be characterized as an 'armed attack' within the meaning of Article 51 of the UN Charter, justifying a unilateral response. *Armed Activities on the Territory of the Congo (DRC v. Uganda)*, Judgment, CR 2005/03 (translation), 12 April 2005, para 21.

[149] *Armed Activities on the Territory of the Congo (DRC v. Uganda)*, Judgment, para 146.

understood in the context of its findings of fact. The ICJ emphasized that Uganda's defensive measures were carried out *against* the DRC,[150] particularly noting the fact that Ugandan military action was directed largely against towns and villages far removed from the territory from which anti-Ugandan rebels operated.[151] One should therefore read the ICJ's decision as reflecting the distinction set out above between force used in self-defence *against* the territorial state (which would require that the armed attacks being responded to are attributable to that state), and force used in self-defence directed against non-state actors *within the* territorial state, while expressly refusing to address the conditions under which the latter use of force would be permissible. The ICJ's opinion should not be read as ruling out uses of defensive force in foreign territory that exclusively target non-state actors.

(ii) State practice

Broad support for the Operation Enduring Freedom military campaign in 2001 and subsequent state practice suggests that, if it ever was established, a strict attribution-based definition of 'armed attack' no longer is.[152] In particular, post-9/11 practice confirms that a use of force directly targeting non-state terrorist actors who have launched an armed attack is a legitimate exercise of the right of self-defence. Operation Enduring Freedom, however, targeted both non-state terrorist actors and the Taliban regime (in their capacity as *de facto* Government of Afghanistan). As such, in addition to using defensive force directly against non-state terrorist actors (consistently with an increasingly recognized right to do so, and not inconsistently with the reading of the ICJ's jurisprudence suggested above), the 2001 military campaign in Afghanistan was a broadly supported use of force directed against a state, in response to an armed attack by non-state actors whose conduct is not attributable to that state on the basis of the ILC-sanctioned rules of attribution. The widely accepted legitimacy of the operation therefore raises the question whether, post-9/11, complicity is re-emerging as a basis on which to attribute non-state terrorist conduct to a state. This section examines the state practice as a means of evaluating the possibility that 9/11 was a turning point in international law on the use of force and the rules of attribution as applied in the *jus ad bellum* context.

In response to the 1998 terrorist attacks on its embassies in Tanzania and Kenya, the US attacked terrorist training camps in Afghanistan and a pharmaceutical plant in Sudan. In a letter dated 20 August 1998 to the Security Council, the US claimed to have been exercising its right of self-defence. The US noted that its use of force was only directed against installations and training camps used by the Bin Laden organization and was 'carried out only after repeated efforts to convince the Government of the Sudan and the Taliban regime in Afghanistan to shut

---

[150] *Ibid*, paras 118 and 147.
[151] *Ibid*, paras 81–6.
[152] Commentators are also increasingly arguing in support of a right to use force in self-defence in response to armed attacks by non-state actors. See e.g. Franck (2000), 840; Murphy (2002), 50; Paust (2002), 534; Greenwood (2003), 522; Dinstein (2005), 204–7; Lubell (2010), 35; Moir (2010), 54.

these terrorist activities down and to cease their cooperation with the Bin Laden organization'.[153] The US charged the Taliban and Sudan with acquiescing in Bin Laden's terrorist activities, and based its right to specifically target non-state actors in foreign territory on an inability to rely on the host states' counter-terrorism efforts. The international community widely condemned the attacks in Sudan— primarily based on an absence of evidence that the pharmaceutical plant was used for anything other than civilian purposes.[154] There was no similar condemnation of the use of force in Afghanistan, which was directed solely against Al Qaeda facilities, and not against the Taliban.[155] The failure to condemn should not necessarily be viewed as indicating broad support for the US military operation.[156] But given past practice of complaining to the Security Council, the absence of condemnation is significant and signals the beginning of the emerging consensus that uses of force specifically targeting non-state terrorist actors, in response to armed attacks they launch from foreign territory, is a legitimate exercise of the right of self-defence.

Operation Enduring Freedom, launched in response to the 9/11 terrorist attacks, targeted Al Qaeda (non-state terrorist actors) operating from Afghan territory. The US and coalition military operations equally targeted the Taliban (Afghanistan's *de facto* Government). The US, in its letter to the Security Council dated 7 October 2001, informed the Council that it had:

initiated actions in the exercise of its inherent right of individual and collective self-defence following the armed attacks that were carried out against the United States on 11 September 2001[. . .]. The attacks on 11 September 2001 and the ongoing threat to the United States and its nationals posed by the Al-Qaeda organization have been made possible by the decision of the Taliban regime to allow the parts of Afghanistan that it controls to be used by this organization as a base of operation [. . .]. In response to these attacks, and in accordance with the inherent right of individual and collective self-defence, United States armed forces have initiated actions designed to prevent and deter further attacks on the United States. These actions include measures against Al-Qaeda terrorist training camps and military installations of the Taliban regime in Afghanistan.[157]

---

[153] Letter dated 20 August 1998 from the Permanent Representative of the United States of America to the United Nations addressed to the President of the Security Council, UN Doc. S/1998/780.

[154] The Sudan, in a letter to the Security Council, denied that the pharmaceutical plant in Khartoum was used for terrorist purposes. Letter dated 21 August 1998 from the Permanent Representative of The Sudan to the United Nations addressed to the President of the Security Council, UN Doc. S/1998/786. The League of Arab States and Non-Aligned Movement condemned the US for its attack on the Sudan. Letter dated 21 August 1998 from the Chargé D'Affaires a.i. of the Permanent Mission of Kuwait to the United Nations addressed to the President of the Security Council, UN Doc. S/1998/789; Letter dated 24 August 1998 from the Chargé D'Affaires a.i. of the Permanent Mission of Kuwait to the United Nations addressed to the President of the Security Council, UN Doc. S/1998/800; Letter dated 21 September 1998 from the Permanent Representative of the Sudan to the United Nations Addressed to the President of the Security Council, UN Doc. S/1998/879.

[155] The US position at the time was that Al Qaeda operated on its own, without having to depend on a state sponsor for support (although depending on state acquiescence). See Murphy (2000), 367.

[156] But see Franck, effectively arguing that a failure to condemn reflects international acceptance of a particular operation. Franck (2002), 65–6.

[157] Letter dated 7 October 2001 from the Permanent Representative of the United States of America to the United Nations addressed to the President of the Security Council, UN Doc. S/2001/946. While accusing the Taliban of acquiescence, the letter stopped short of alleging that the Taliban was directly responsible for the 9/11 terrorist attacks.

The Security Council is widely considered to have endorsed and even invited the US position that the 9/11 terrorist attacks gave rise to the right to use force in self-defence.[158] In particular, Security Council Resolution 1368 condemned the 9/11 terrorist attacks and '*[r]ecogniz[ed]* the inherent right of individual or collective self-defence in accordance with the Charter'.[159] Both NATO and the Organization of American States, which at their inception required armed attacks to be attributable to a state before force in self-defence would be justified,[160] invoked their collective security arrangements in response to the 9/11 terrorist attacks.[161] States informing the Security Council of measures taken in Afghanistan in exercise of the collective right of self-defence emphasized that uses of force were directed against *both* Al Qaeda bases and the Taliban which supported and harboured Al Qaeda (but not against the Afghan people or Islam).[162] Unlike the military campaign in 1998, states invoking the right of self-defence viewed both Al Qaeda and the Taliban as legitimate targets of defensive force.[163] If we accept the interpretation of the ICJ's decisions in *Nicaragua* and *DRC v. Uganda* suggested above—namely that they do not preclude uses of defensive force targeted exclusively at non-state terrorist actors, but that attributability will be required if the territorial state is *itself* the target of defensive force—then the targeting decisions in the 2001 US-led campaign appear to support the argument that a state's acquiescence in (or harbouring of) terrorist actors operating from its territory was accepted as a basis for attributing the 9/11 terrorist attacks to Afghanistan.[164] Some authors have argued that support for targeting the Taliban in 2001 is indeed based on the attributability of the 9/11 terrorist attacks, but reject acquiescence as the basis of attribution. Rather, they argue that the close relationship between Al Qaeda and the Taliban, and the Taliban's support for Al Qaeda, forms the basis for attribution.[165] These arguments, while correctly refusing to stretch the grounds on which conduct will be attributable to a state, do not

---

[158] See Gray (2008), 199; Greenwood (2003), 421. But see Cassese (2001), 996.

[159] UNSC Resolution 1368 (2001). The Council again reaffirmed the right to individual and collective self-defence in UNSC Resolution 1373 (2001).

[160] See US Senate, Report of the Committee on Foreign Relations on the North Atlantic Treaty, Executive Report No. 8, 13; Art. 3, Inter-American Treaty of Reciprocal Assistance, 2 September 1947, 21 UNTS 77.

[161] See NATO update, 2 October 2001, <http://www.nato.int/docu/update/2001/1001/e1002a. htm>; Inter-American Treaty of Reciprocal Assistance, 24th Ministers Meeting, 19 September 2001, <http://www.oas.org>.

[162] See Letter dated 9 October 2001 from the Permanent Representative of Belgium to the United Nations addressed to the Secretary-General, UN Doc. S/2001/967; Letter dated 24 October 2001 from the Chargé D'Affaires a.i. of the Permanent Mission of Canada to the United Nations addressed to the President of the Security Council, UN Doc. S/2001/1005; Letter dated 29 November 2001 from the Permanent Representative of Germany to the United Nations addressed to The President of the Security Council, UN Doc. S/2001/1127; Letter dated 17 December 2001 from the Permanent Representative of New Zealand to the United Nations addressed to the Secretary-General, UN Doc. S/2001/1193.

[163] But see Paust (2002), 540–3, arguing that Al Qaeda was a legitimate target of defensive force, but that the Taliban, to which the 9/11 terrorist attacks could not be attributed (because acquiescence is not a basis for attribution), was not a legitimate target.

[164] For an argument to this effect, see Jinks (2003); Jinks (2003a); Janse (2006), 168–9.

[165] See Murphy (2002); Ratner (2002), 913; M.E. O'Connell (2002), 32; Byers (2002); Stahn (2003), 42–9.

account for the fact that states invoking the right of collective self-defence emphasized the Taliban's acquiescence in (not support for) Al Qaeda's terrorist activities.[166] It is also unlikely that the Taliban's refusal to accede to US and Security Council demands to surrender Bin Laden[167] amounts to a *post facto* adoption of Al Qaeda's conduct for the purposes of attribution. The Taliban made it clear that the refusal to surrender Bin Laden was based on Muslim customs, and did not imply acknowledgment or adoption for the purposes of perpetuating terrorist conduct, as would be required under Article 11 of the ILC Articles on State Responsibility.[168]

In the post-9/11 world, Operation Enduring Freedom remains the only case in which the international community accepted a state's right to use force in self-defence against both non-state terrorist actors *and* the state from whose territory such terrorist actors operated, when the terrorist attack being responded to was not attributable to the territorial state. Subsequent invocations of the right to use defensive force in response to terrorist attacks have been limited to the use of force exclusively targeting non-state terrorist actors.

For instance, following a terrorist attack on a café in Haifa in 2003, Israel launched a guided missile attack in Syrian territory, targeting what it claimed to be a terrorist base used by a Syrian and Iranian sponsored terrorist group (Islamic Jihad) responsible for terrorist attacks against Israel (including the Haifa café attack).[169] Following the example of the 1998 and 2001 US military campaigns in Afghanistan, Israel accused Syria of complicity in terrorist attacks by Islamic Jihad, but was very careful to emphasize that its military operation was directed specifically at the Ein Saheb terrorist base.[170] The Security Council considered the matter following letters of complaint by Syria[171] and Lebanon.[172] Despite Islamic Jihad being recognized as a terrorist organization by the EU,[173] EU member states condemned Israel's military response to the Haifa bombing,[174] as did most other states appearing before the Security Council.[175] The Secretary-General condemned both the Israeli attack in Syria and the preceding terrorist attack in Haifa.[176] While the expressions of condemnation before the Security Council have been interpreted

---

[166] *Supra* notes 157 and 162. See also 9/11 Commission Report, which called into doubt the degree of control the Taliban exercised over Al Qaeda, instead finding that senior officials in the Taliban regime were opposed to the 9/11 terrorist attacks.

[167] UNSC Resolution 1267 (1999); UNSC Resolution 1333 (2000).

[168] See Commentary to Art. 11, ILC Articles on State Responsibility; *Tehran Hostages (US v. Iran)*, Judgment, para 74. See further Rowe (2002), 308; Stahn (2002), 220–1; Moir (2010), 66–8.

[169] SC 4836th meeting (2003), 5.

[170] *Ibid.*

[171] Letter dated 5 October 2003 from the Permanent Representative of the Syrian Arab Republic to the United Nations addressed to the President of the Security Council, UN Doc. S/2003/939.

[172] Letter dated 5 October 2003 from the Permanent Representative of Lebanon to the United Nations addressed to the President of the Security Council, UN Doc. S/2003/943.

[173] Council Common Position 2005/847/CFSP of 29 November 2005, 2005 Official Journal of the European Union (L 314/41).

[174] SC 4836th meeting (2003), 9 (Spain, UK), 10 (Germany), 11 (France).

[175] See SC 4836th meeting (2003). Only the US, which also characterizes Islamic Jihad as a terrorist organization, did not condemn the Israeli attack, and instead admonished Syria for 'harbouring and supporting the groups that perpetrate terrorist acts'. *Ibid.*

[176] UN Doc. SG/SM/8918 (2003).

as an absence of general support for a wide right to use force against terrorist training camps in foreign territory,[177] this is not necessarily the lesson to be drawn from the condemnations. Most states firmly situated their comments on the terrorist attack in Haifa and the Israeli response thereto within the broader framework of the Middle East peace process. Their expressions of condemnation were based on the effect both attacks would have on the implementation of the Road Map devised by the Quartet, which was released in between the attack in Haifa and Israel's military campaign in Syria.[178] None of the delegations making presentations before the Security Council addressed the legality of defensive force specifically targeting terrorist bases in foreign territory given an inability to rely on that state to prevent terrorist operations planned or launched from its territory.

In July 2006, Hezbollah abducted two Israeli soldiers and launched a number of rockets from southern Lebanon into northern Israeli towns. In response, Israel launched a large-scale military campaign against Hezbollah in Lebanese territory. As has been Israel's consistent practice, it claimed not to be acting against the territorial host state, but primarily against non-state terrorists.[179] The scale of Israel's use of force in Lebanese territory, particularly as regards the destruction of all three runways at Beirut International Airport[180] and the significant number of civilian deaths,[181] militated against broader acceptance of Israel's characterization of its defensive measures.[182] Nevertheless, Israel consistently maintained that it was targeting Hezbollah strongholds or weapons delivery routes, and that any civilian casualties were the result of Hezbollah's practice of using civilians as human shields.[183] A majority of Security Council members recognized Israel's right to defend itself.[184] Given the non-attributability of Hezbollah's conduct to Lebanon, such recognition amounts to acceptance of a right to use force in self-defence against non-state actors. These states also underlined the need for Lebanon to extend its exclusive control over all of its territory and to act in prevention of

---

[177] See Gray (2008), 237.

[178] Released 30 April 2003. See <http://www.un.org/News/dh/mideast/roadmap122002.pdf>.

[179] Israel claimed that it 'has repeatedly been compelled to act not against Lebanon, but against the forces and the monstrosity which Lebanon has allowed itself to be taken hostage by'. SC 5503rd meeting (2006), 4. Israel also suggested that Lebanon, Iran and Syria were responsible for Hezbollah's activities, but did not appear to be suggesting attributability for the purposes of a defensive use of force. See SC 5489th meeting (2006), 6.

[180] See BBC, 'Israel Imposes Lebanon Blockade', 13 July 2006, <http://news.bbc.co.uk/2/hi/middle_east/5175160.stm>.

[181] See BBC, 'Q&A: Mid-East War Crimes', 21 July 2006, <http://news.bbc.co.uk/2/hi/middle_east/5198342.stm>; Human Rights Watch, 'Israeli Indiscriminate Attacks Killed Most Civilians', <http://www.hrw.org/en/news/2007/09/05/israellebanon-israeli-indiscriminate-attacks-killed-most-civilians>; Amnesty International, 'Deliberate destruction or "collateral damage"? Israeli attacks on civilian infrastructure', <http://web.amnesty.org/library/print/ENGMDE180072006>.

[182] See SC 5489th meeting (2006), 9; SC 5492nd meeting (2006), 3; SC 5493rd meeting (2006), 14; SC 5498th meeting (2006), 6.

[183] See SC 5508th meeting (2006), 5.

[184] SC 5489th meeting (2006), 9–17; SC 5493rd meeting (2006), 17. The Secretary General also acknowledged Israel's right to defend itself against Hezbollah attacks under Article 51 of the UN Charter. SC 5492nd meeting (2006), 3; SC 5498th meeting (2006), 3.

Hezbollah's attacks against Israel.[185] Taken together, these positions accept that defensive force in foreign territory against non-state actors is sometimes necessary given the host state's failure (rather than its unwillingness)[186] to prevent its territory from being used as a base for terrorist operations.[187] All but one of the states recognizing Israel's right to act in self-defence also characterized Israel's use of force in July 2006 as disproportionate or excessive,[188] referencing Israel's use of force beyond its immediate border region with Lebanon (from which Hezbollah operated).

Turkey has long claimed a right to resort to measures that are imperative to its own security, including uses of force directed against Kurdistan Workers Party ('PKK') non-State actors operating from Iraqi territory. Turkey based its right to use force in foreign territory on its inability to rely on Iraq to control its northern border and prevent cross-border terrorist attacks.[189] Turkey undertook military operations against PKK training bases in Iraq in January 1994,[190] March 1995,[191] and again in May and September of 1997.[192] Consistent with earlier approaches to an attribution-based definition of 'armed attack', Turkey's right to respond to PKK attacks (which were not attributable to Iraq) with force in Iraqi territory was not broadly supported.[193] More recently, however, the international community has

---

[185] SC 5489th meeting (2006), 9–17. See also the statement of the Secretary General to the Security Council, SC 5492nd meeting (2006), 4 and UNSC Resolution 1559 (2004), paras 1–3; UNSC Resolution 1583 (2005), paras 3–4; UNSC Resolution 1655 (2006), paras 3, 6 and 8; UNSC Resolution 1680 (2006), preamble; UNSC Resolution 1701 (2006), para 3.

[186] Lebanon expressly acknowledged that it needed to extend its authority throughout its territory. SC 5493rd meeting (2006), 13.

[187] See Section 3.1.2 regarding incapacity to prevent international terrorism as a limitation on state responsibility for such failure. On the use of defensive force against non-state actors in the territory of a state that is incapable of fulfilling its duty of diligent terrorism prevention, see Dinstein (1987), 146. See also *Armed Activities on the Territory of the Congo (DRC v. Uganda)*, Judgment, Separate Opinion of Judge Kooijmans, paras 27–31.

[188] SC 5489th meeting (2006), 9 (Argentina), 12 (Japan), 12 (UK), 13–14 (Tanzania considered Israel's use of force as disproportionate without having expressly recognized Israel's right to use force in self-defence), 14 (Peru), 15 (Denmark), 16 (Slovakia), 16 (Greece), 17 (France). The US is the only state to have explicitly recognized Israel's right to defend itself without characterizing Israel's defensive measures as disproportionate or excessive. The Secretary General also condemned Israel's excessive use of force. SC 5492nd meeting (2006), 3; SC 5498th meeting (2006), 3. See further Kirgis (2006).

[189] See e.g. Letter dated 24 July 1995 from the Chargé D'Affaires a.i. of the Permanent Mission of Turkey to the United Nations addressed to the President of the Security Council, UN Doc. S/1995/605; Identical letters dated 27 June 1996 from the Chargé D'Affaires a.i. of the Permanent Mission of Turkey to the United Nations addressed to the Secretary-General and to the President of the Security Council, UN Doc. S/1996/479; Identical letters dated 16 July 1997 from the Chargé D'Affaires a.i. of the Permanent Mission of Turkey to the United Nations addressed to the Secretary-General and to the President of the Security Council, UN Doc. S/1997/552. Turkey notably failed to invoke Article 51 of the UN Charter in its communications with the Security Council, or to clearly characterize its targeted use of force against the PKK as in exercise of the right of self-defence.

[190] Keesing's, Vol. 40, January 1994, 39834.

[191] Keesing's, Vol. 41, March 1995, 40473.

[192] Keesing's, Vol. 43, May 1997, 41651; Keesing's, Vol. 43, October 1997, 41877.

[193] Identical letters dated 14 June 1997 from the Permanent Representative of Iraq to the United Nations addressed to the Secretary-General and to the President of the Security Council, UN Doc. S/1997/461; Keesing's, Vol. 41, March 1995, 40474; Keesing's, Vol. 41, April 1995, 40522. See also Ruys (2005), 295–6. According to Libya, the US did however support Turkish uses of force against the PKK as a legitimate exercise of the right of self-defence. See Letter dated 12 July 1995

softened to the Turkish position. Between the summer and fall of 2007, high level discussions were held between Turkish, Iraqi and US delegates, in which the latter two promised to significantly step up efforts to prevent PKK cross-border attacks.[194] Turkey rejected the proposals as inadequate,[195] and in response to an escalation in PKK violence across the Iraqi–Turkish border[196] began its largest military campaign to date, targeting PKK bases in December 2007.[197] Turkey maintained throughout that it was exclusively targeting the PKK and other terrorist targets,[198] and avoided claiming a broader right to use force against Iraq's autonomous Kurdish region or Iraq itself. The international response to the campaign has not been entirely supportive, largely based on the impact thereof on the precarious peace and security situation in the region.[199] Iraq initially characterized the use of force as a violation of its sovereignty,[200] but subsequent statements by its foreign minister suggest that, to the extent that Turkey asserts a right to defend itself against PKK attacks, the right must be limited to PKK targets—and that civilians and civilian infrastructure should be left untouched.[201] Similarly, the US acknowledged that it was warned of the December 2007 Turkish military operation, and claimed to have urged Turkey to limit its action to precise targeting of PKK targets.[202] The attitudes of Iraqi and US authorities implicitly acknowledge a right to use force in foreign territory against non-state terrorist actors, while rejecting uses of force against the territorial state in cases of non-attribution. In June 2010, Turkey again attacked PKK insurgents (and only PKK insurgents) in Iraqi territory in response to their attacks on its border forces, without any official reaction from the Iraqis or US.[203]

On 1 March 2008, Colombia launched a targeted military operation against a Colombian Revolutionary Armed Forces ('FARC') training camp in Ecuador, two miles from the Colombian border.[204] The raid, while limited to FARC targets, was immediately condemned by Ecuador, followed by Venezuela, each of which broke

---

from the Chargé D'Affaires a.i. of the Permanent Mission of the Libyan Arab Jamahiriya to the United Nations addressed to the President of the Security Council, UN Doc. S/1995/566.

[194] See Keesing's, Vol. 52, July 2006, 47377–8; Keesing's, Vol. 52, July 2006, 47377–8; Keesing's, Vol. 53, October 2007, 48219.

[195] Keesing's, Vol. 53, October 2007, 48219.

[196] Keesing's, Vol. 52, July 2006, 47377–8.

[197] Keesing's, Vol. 53, December 2007, 48316. Turkish forces had carried out a number of more limited military operations against PKK fighters in the fall of 2007. See Al Jazeera, 'Turkey "hits PKK targets in Iraq"', 24 October 2007, <http://english.aljazeera.net/NR/exeres/14FA7823-911C-4456-B8DB-6CD27C4DE07F.htm>.

[198] BBC, 'US denies backing Turkey PKK raid', 17 December 2007, <http://news.bbc.co.uk/2/hi/europe/7147375.stm>.

[199] See e.g. Keesing's, Vol. 53, June 2007, 48009.

[200] Al Jazeera, 'Toll rises in Turkey-PKK conflict', 25 February 2008, <http://english.aljazeera.net/NR/exeres/3E14DD15-F2D1-4C65-8148-5200DFB3E975.htm>.

[201] See BBC, 'Iraq warns Turkey over incursion', 23 February 2008, <http://news.bbc.co.uk/2/hi/europe/7260478.stm>.

[202] *Ibid.*

[203] BBC, 'Turkish troops "pursue Kurdish rebels into Iraq"', 16 June 2010, <http://www.bbc.co.uk/news/10334276>.

[204] Keesing's, Vol. 54, March 2008, 48456.

off diplomatic ties with Colombia.[205] Colombia claimed to be acting in self-defence, and partly invoked Ecuadorian (and Venezuelan) support for FARC as justification for its violation of Ecuadorian sovereignty.[206] The matter was put to an emergency ministerial level meeting at the Organization of American States, which adopted a resolution recognizing every state's right to defend itself, but positioning the right in the context of the principles of sovereignty and non-intervention. The resolution considered that Colombia's incursion constituted 'a violation of the sovereignty and territorial integrity of Ecuador and of principles of international law',[207] for which Colombia issued an apology.[208] The swift South American condemnations and Colombian apology, both of which took place in the broader context of the inter-American system, highlight the lack of a broad acceptance, on the facts, that Ecuador is supporting FARC. Nevertheless, Colombia's assertion of its right of self-defence against non-state terrorist actors in foreign territory is consistent with other assertions of the right, and had some support in the international community.[209]

(iii) Complicity in terrorism

All invocations of the right to use force in self-defence against terrorist attacks since the 2001 US-led campaign in Afghanistan purport to be based on a right to use defensive force against non-state terrorist actors.[210] In each case, the victim state has accused the territorial state of acquiescence or complicity in, or active support for, the terrorist attacks emanating from its territory, but has not claimed a right to also use force directly against the territorial state (as distinguished from *in* the territorial state's territory, but against non-state actors). While the 2003 Israeli campaign was criticized, largely in the context of its negative impact on the Middle East peace process, the right to use force in foreign territory in a targeted and proportionate

---

[205] Keesing's, Vol. 54, March 2008, 48456.
[206] *Ibid.*
[207] OAS, Convocation of the Meeting of Consultation of Ministers of Foreign Affairs and Appointment of a Commission, 5 March 2008, CP/RES. 930 (1632/08).
[208] Speech of Colombian Ambassador to OAS, 4 March 2008, <http://www.oas.org/speeches/speech.asp?sCodigo=08-0021>.
[209] See BBC, 'Ecuador seeks to censure Colombia', 5 March 2008, <http://news.bbc.co.uk/2/hi/americas/7278484.stm>.
[210] See also claims by the Russian Federation that, despite Georgian assurances that it was restoring order along its border with Russia, Georgia was in fact unwilling to take measures to halt terrorist attacks against Russian territory from its border region. On the basis of Georgia's failure to address terrorism emanating from its territory, Russia asserted a right to use force directly against non-state actors in Georgian territory. Letter dated 31 July 2002 from the Chargé D'Affaires a.i. of the Permanent Mission of the Russian Federation to the United Nations addressed to the Secretary-General, UN Doc. S/2002/854; Letter dated 11 September 2002 from the Permanent Representative of the Russian Federation to the United Nations addressed to the Secretary-General, UN Doc. S/2002/1012. Georgia claimed that Russia's characterization of the facts was inaccurate. Letter dated 13 September 2002 from the Permanent Representative of Georgia to the United Nations addressed to the Secretary-General, UN Doc. S/2002/1035; Identical letters dated 15 September 2002 from the Permanent Representative of Georgia to the United Nations addressed to the Secretary-General and the President of the Security Council, UN Doc. A/57/408–S/2002/1033 (2002).

manner against non-state actors was recognized in Israel's 2006 campaign. Equally, Turkey's right to use force directly against PKK terrorist actors in Iraqi territory was implicitly recognized by Iraq and the US, the most immediately interested states. This state practice strongly supports the argument that, despite the ICJ's failure to engage the issue, there is a right under international law to use force directly against non-state terrorist actors operating from foreign territory. An attribution-based reading of 'armed attack' under Article 51 of the UN Charter should therefore be laid to rest.

The only role a state's complicity with, or acquiescence in, international terrorism plays in evaluating whether there is a right to use force in self-defence against non-state actors in foreign territory is that it responds to the requirement that the use of force be necessary, given an inability to rely on the host state to prevent its territory from being used as a base for terrorist operations.[211] In cases where a state is acting diligently to prevent the terrorist activities of non-state actors operating from its territory, in compliance with its obligation to prevent international terrorism examined in Section 3.1 below, a victim state's use of force against non-state actors in that state's territory (amounting to a violation of that state's territorial integrity) is an unnecessary use of force, particularly given that necessity is generally evaluated in terms of whether force is a 'last resort'.[212] Such uses of force amount to the substitution (and imposition) of the victim state's views on how to respond to terrorist threats emanating from the host state's territory for those of the host state. To the extent that the victim state believes that further action should be taken by the host state to respond to the terrorist threat, the issue should be dealt with through co-operative arrangements with the host state.[213] This does not suggest that victim states must consult with unfriendly states that they know will not (or cannot) act to counter terrorist attacks launched from their territory before they react in self-defence. But states that have proven themselves co-operative in counter-terrorism should not be subject to violations of their territorial integrity.

Where, however, a host state is unwilling (or, in some cases, unable)[214] to prevent its territory from being used as a base of terrorist operations, the victim state is left with little choice. Either it respects the host state's territorial integrity at great risk to its own security, or it violates that state's territorial integrity in a limited and targeted fashion, using force against (and only against) the very source of the

---

[211] See Cassese (2001), 997; Beard (2002), 580–2.

[212] See Green (2009), 79, evaluating the state practice and concluding that 'the interpretation of the necessity criterion as requiring that forcible action in self-defence may be taken only as a "last resort" is correct'. See also Ago (1980), para 120; Gardam (2004), 152–3. But see Schachter (1991), 152.

[213] For instance, US raids against militants in Pakistan have been condemned by Pakistan as an intrusion on its sovereignty. Pakistan further contends that such raids threaten to hurt progress being made against the militants by Pakistani forces, and that any US military operations need to be decided in cooperation with the Pakistani authorities. See Reuters, 'U.S. raids hurt terrorism fight: Pakistan minister', 2 October 2008, <http://www.reuters.com/article/topNews/idUSTRE4910AA20081002>. To the extent true, doubts regarding Pakistan's commitment to the 'war on terror' might justify US uses of force in Pakistani territory (targeting and only targeting non-state terrorist actors) as necessary given an inability to rely on the host state to prevent its territory from being used as a base of terrorist operations.

[214] See Section 3.1.3 for a discussion of the *rapprochement* between the obligation to refrain from acquiescing in, and the obligation to prevent, terrorism.

terrorist attack.[215] Based on the post-9/11 state practice examined above, the right to use force in foreign territory in response to terrorist attacks that are not attributable to a state, where such force is necessary due to the host state's complicity or acquiescence in the terrorist activities emanating from its territory, is recognized as meeting the requirements of Article 51 of the UN Charter. The right to target the state itself in response to terrorist attacks that are not attributable to it (given that state's acquiescence in terrorist activities emanating from its territory) asserted during Operation Enduring Freedom is not supported by this post-9/11 state practice. As Operation Enduring Freedom remains the only example of such a broad right of self-defence, it should certainly not be considered to have expanded the rules of attribution to include complicity or acquiescence in terrorism, whether for the purposes of defining an 'armed attack' or for the purposes of state responsibility. The rules of attribution applicable to terrorist attacks therefore remain limited to cases in which non-state actors are *de facto* organs or *de facto* agents of the host state in whose territory defensive force is used.

If the standard of attribution is lowered to include complicity or acquiescence in terrorism in the *jus ad bellum* context, uses of terrorist force could be attributed to complicit or acquiescing states, thereby justifying the use of defensive force directly against those states. The real difficulty with such uses of force (and attempts to justify them) is that targeting a terrorist-harbouring state directly is likely to decrease its counter-terrorism capacity, including its military capacity to effectively assert control over relevant parts of its territory. As a result, where a state's counter-terrorism failures are limited to a failure to prevent (or acquiescence in) terrorism, targeting the territorial state itself will very rarely, if ever, pass the necessity and proportionality thresholds of the *jus ad bellum*. One might therefore legitimately wonder if all the proponents of complicity as a basis of attribution achieve is a more coherent legal explanation of the international community's response to the terrorist attacks of 9/11. Based on the international community's negative reaction to Israel's use of force against both Hezbollah *and Lebanese infrastructure* in the summer of 2006, in response to terrorist attacks by Hezbollah, it is certainly premature to reconceptualize the rules of attribution to legally justify (and explain) the 9/11 related use of force against a terrorist-harbouring state.

It is equally untenable to reconceptualize the rules of attribution for the purposes of state responsibility. Not only is such a reconceptualization not supported by the

---

[215] Trapp (2007), 147. Article 2(4) of the UN Charter prohibits uses of force against the territorial integrity (and political independence) of states. Using force against the base of operations of non-state terrorist actors within another state's territory surely amounts to a violation of that state's territorial integrity. As a matter of logic, a use of defensive force pursuant to Article 51 of the UN Charter should only properly qualify as an exception to the prohibition on the use of force if it excuses the violation of territorial integrity (or political independence). When the state in whose territory defensive force is employed is the aggressor or perpetrator of the armed attack (or the armed attack is attributable to it), the excuse for violating that state's territorial integrity is readily available. Where the conduct is not attributable to the host state, the excuse for the violation of territorial integrity is based on the state's acquiescence in terrorist activities, which itself amounts to a prohibited use of force under the UN Declaration on Friendly Relations, UNGA Resolution 2625 (1970). See Trapp (2007), 145–6; Trapp (2009).

state practice discussed above (were any proposed lowering of the standard of attribution for the purposes of the *jus ad bellum* carried through to the state responsibility context), there is absolutely no reason at all to label complicity a basis of attribution for the purposes of state responsibility. While there was a driving force (albeit a misguided one) behind reading down the rules of attribution in the *jus ad bellum* context—to legally account for and authorize uses of defensive force against terrorist-harbouring states—such a reading down in the state responsibility context does nothing but collapse a primary rule into a secondary rule of state responsibility. States are under customary international law and treaty obligations to refrain from supporting terrorist activities[216] and to prevent such activities within their territories.[217] Complicity in terrorist activities, whether put in evidence through support for or a deliberate failure to prevent terrorism, is in breach of an independent obligation under both customary international law and treaty law. An argument that states should be held directly responsible for positive conduct (the commission of a terrorist act) on the basis of attributability, when all they may be responsible for is an omission (a however deliberate failure to prevent), would render many of the primary rules in the terrorism context redundant.[218] While a wrongdoing state's responsibility is not invoked as often as it might be in the terrorism context, as discussed further in Chapters 4, 5 and 6, holding states responsible as a matter of law for more than they are responsible for as a matter of fact will certainly not encourage more reliance on the regime of state responsibility as a mechanism for re-establishing the primary legal relationship between injured and wrongdoing states.

2.3 Conclusion

A state's 'direct' responsibility for an act of terrorism (as distinguished from responsibility for supporting or failing to prevent acts of terrorism, or for failing to extradite or submit terrorist actors to prosecution) turns on the application of the secondary rules of attribution. But it will be difficult to establish a state's 'direct' responsibility for acts of international terrorism. Part of the reason for this stems from conceptual difficulties in situating terrorism within a legitimate sphere of state activity and qualifying terrorism as falling within the official capacity of state organs. This particular issue, however, is a consequence of the often clandestine nature of terrorism and the evidentiary difficulties that that raises, rather than a consequence of the rules of attribution themselves.

A further difficulty in attributing terrorist conduct to a state is the result of the standard of control set by the ICJ in its application of Article 8 of the ILC Articles on State Responsibility. In particular, the 'effective control' standard responds to concerns in the context of military and paramilitary operations, but fails to consider

---

[216] See Section 2.1.
[217] See Section 3.1.
[218] See further Trapp (2009).

the appropriate standard of control in cases where the breach of international law is inherent in the use of force—as in the terrorism context. A flexible and context-sensitive approach to the application of Article 8 of the ILC Articles on State Responsibility, which incorporates the 'overall control' standard set out in the ICTY's *Tadić* decision, is all that is required to respond to this difficulty. It is rather extreme to propose a complicity-based rule of attribution, or to suggest that attribution should not be the basis of 'direct' state responsibility at all, to respond to a problem that is more than amply addressed through flexibility and a sensitive appreciation of different contexts. Complicity-based rules of attribution are equally unnecessary in the *jus ad bellum* context given the alternative framework available (discussed in Section 2.2.3) for addressing the security concerns of victim states.

Even in the absence of attributability (assuming a sensitive application of the rules), a state's support for terrorism may still amount to a prohibited use of force or an illegal intervention in the affairs of another state. But state responsibility for participation in terrorist activities is rarely invoked formally, whether such responsibility is characterized as 'direct' or 'indirect'. The increasing use of the ICJ in the use of force context,[219] and the potential basis of the Court's jurisdiction under the TSCs for a state's sponsorship of or support for acts of international terrorism (discussed in Section 4.2 below), may well stimulate change in this regard.

---

[219] See Gray (2003).

3

Obligations to prevent and punish acts of international terrorism

A state's active participation in international terrorism undoubtedly undermines international peace and security, and is therefore appropriately viewed through the prism of the UN Charter. The state itself is the subject of the prohibition of state terrorism, imposed on states through the general rules of international law prohibiting the use of force and interventions in the domestic affairs of foreign states. Efforts to suppress international terrorism, however, have equally addressed threats emanating from the terrorist conduct of non-state actors, and obligations to prevent and to extradite or submit cases to prosecution have long been a corner-stone of such efforts.[1] Rather than treating the state itself as the subject of control, the obligation to prevent and the obligation to extradite or submit to prosecution treats the state as the mechanism of control through which individual terrorist behaviour is addressed. This chapter examines both the customary and treaty basis of the obligation to prevent, and the treaty basis of the obligation to extradite or submit to prosecution, with a view to defining the content of these primary obligations, breach of which results in a state's international responsibility.

This chapter also examines the impact of the self-determination debate on the scope of the Terrorism Suppression Conventions. Whether a distinction should be drawn between acts of terrorism and acts of violence committed in furtherance of a struggle for self-determination has long been an issue on the international community's agenda, and has played itself out partly in the negotiation of the TSCs. In particular, a number of the TSCs contain exclusion clauses that treat the proposed distinction as a question of regime interaction between the Terrorism Suppression Conventions and international humanitarian law. But the regime interaction rules adopted in the TSCs, which attempt to give priority to humanitarian law as the applicable law in the context of armed conflicts, do not always apply as intended. This is in part due to the ratification pattern of certain humanitarian law conventions and in part due to the absence of a compulsory regime of criminal law enforcement applicable to non-international armed conflicts. As a result, some states have also made reservations to the TSCs applicable in the self-determination

---

[1] The first effort to formalize the obligation to prevent and to extradite or prosecute acts of international terrorism within a treaty regime was undertaken in the context of the League of Nations, in response to the assassination of King Alexander of Yugoslavia in 1934. See *infra* Chapter 6, notes 142–4 and accompanying text.

context that might further define the scope of the Conventions, depending on the precise effect they are given.

3.1 The obligation to prevent acts of international terrorism

Customary international law has long imposed an obligation on states not to 'allow knowingly [their] territory[ies] to be used for acts contrary to the rights of other States',[2] subject to a due diligence standard of conduct.[3] A state's obligation to prevent international terrorism (as a particular type of harm that might emanate from a state's territory) is a specific instantiation of this general obligation, and the TSC formulation of the obligation drew heavily on customary international law. In drafting the Internationally Protected Persons Convention, the ILC regarded a state's obligation to take all practicable measures to prevent the offence defined therein as a particular example of the well-established principle of international law 'that every state must ensure that its territory is not used for the preparation of offences to be committed in or against other states'.[4] States did not consider themselves to be formulating a new obligation, but rather to be applying existing international law to the specific offences defined in the TSCs. As is the case for the customary international law obligation to prevent, the TSC obligations to prevent international terrorism[5] have a territorial component and are subject to a due diligence standard.[6] Starting with the Internationally Protected Persons Convention, the TSCs require states to prevent preparations for the defined offence *in their*

---

[2] *Corfu Channel (UK v. Albania)*, Merits, 22. See also the ILC's survey of international law in relation to its work of codification, UN Doc. A/CN.4/1/Rev.1 (1949), 56, para 97, referring to 'failures to prevent the use of national territory as a base for acts noxious to the legitimate interests of neighbouring States' as one of the central problems of state responsibility calling for elucidation.

[3] See e.g. H. Lauterpacht (1927), 276; Brownlie (1983), 37–49; Pisillo-Mazzeschi (1992), 34–6; Zegfeld (2002), 181–2; UN Secretariat, 'Force majeure' and 'Fortuitous event' as circumstances precluding wrongfulness, UN Doc. A/CN.4/315 (1978), in which the UN Secretariat surveys state practice, international jurisprudence, and doctrine which applied the due diligence standard to obligations of prevention. See further the *Alabama Claims Case (US/GB)*, 572–3; *Neer Case (US–Mexico General Claims Commission, 1926)*, 61–2; *Saint Albans Raid Case (GB/US)*, 4054; *SS Lotus Case (France v. Turkey)*, Dissenting Opinion of Judge Moore, 88; *Nicaragua (Nicaragua v. US)*, Merits, paras 155–60. Early efforts to codify the international law of state responsibility, which initially focused primarily on responsibility for injuries to aliens, also consistently held the obligation to prevent harm emanating from a state's territory to a due diligence standard of conduct. See League of Nations, Conference for the Codification of International Law, Bases of Discussion for the Conference drawn up by the Preparatory Committee, Vol. III (Responsibility of states for Damage caused in their Territory to the Person or Property of Foreigners), LN Doc. C.75.M.69.1929.V, 515–21, Bases of Discussion No. 16 and 17; Art. 10, Harvard Draft Convention (1929), 187; Art. 3, Roth (1932), 152; Ago (1978).

[4] See Report of the International Law Commission on the work of its twenty-fourth session, UN Doc. A/8710/Rev.1 (1972), 317.

[5] See Art. 9, Hague Convention; Art. 10, Montreal Convention; Art. 4(a), Internationally Protected Persons Convention; Art. 4(a), Hostages Convention; Art. 13, SUA Convention; Art. 15(a), Terrorist Bombing Convention; Art. 18, Terrorism Financing Convention; Art. 7, Nuclear Terrorism Convention. On the obligation of prevention in the Terrorism Financing Convention, see Kantor (2002); Bantekas (2003).

[6] The obligation to prevent terrorism specifically has long been considered subject to a due diligence standard of conduct. See e.g. Lillich and Paxman (1977), 309–10; International Law Association (1984), 7; Condorelli (1989), 240–1; Murphy et al. (1991), 22; Becker (2006), 140–1; Saul (2006), 196.

respective territories.[7] Furthermore, the obligation of prevention set out in each of the TSCs requires only that 'all practicable measures'[8] be taken, implying a due diligence standard of conduct and indicating that the obligation is one of conduct, not of result.

The distinction between obligations of conduct and obligations of result turns on an analysis of primary rules and whether they require absolutely that state conduct produce a certain result (obligation of result), or whether they require only that a state make certain efforts to produce a desired, but uncertain, result (obligation of conduct).[9] The ICJ, in its *Bosnia Genocide Case* decision, drew on the distinction between obligations of conduct and obligations of result to characterize the obligation to prevent genocide as one subject to a due diligence standard.[10] In the Genocide Convention, the obligation to prevent is unqualified, yet the Court still considered it an obligation of conduct. The argument that prevention is subject to a due diligence standard of conduct is therefore even stronger in the case of the TSCs, which do qualify the obligation to prevent with a practicability standard.

A state's compliance with the obligation to prevent its territory from being used for 'acts contrary to the rights of other states' is evaluated in light of what the state knew (or ought to have known) about the threat emanating from its territory, and its genuine capacity to avert the threat. While knowledge and capacity are considered below separately for purposes of analytical clarity, they interact to inform the assessment of whether a state has acted diligently to prevent harm emanating from

---

[7] Art. 4(a), Internationally Protected Persons Convention; Art. 4(a), Hostages Convention; Art. 13, SUA Convention; Art. 15(a), Terrorist Bombing Convention; Art. 18, Terrorism Financing Convention; Art. 7, Nuclear Terrorism Convention. The Hague Convention requires states to take all appropriate measures to restore control of an aircraft to its rightful commander when any offence defined in the Convention has *or is about to* occur. There is no territorial component to this obligation of prevention because of the inherently transnational nature of air travel. Equally, the Montreal Convention requires states to take all practicable measures for the purposes of preventing the defined offences, but that obligation is not limited to the respective territories of the state parties. Given the fact that states will have the capacity to impose safety obligations on flight carriers registered in their jurisdiction, but often operating outside their territory, a strictly territorial obligation of prevention would not have best achieved the objective of safety for civil aviation.

[8] *Supra* note 5. See also the UN Declaration on International Terrorism, UNGA Resolution 49/60 (1994), Annex, which urges states to 'take *appropriate practical measures* to ensure that their respective territories are not used for terrorist installations or training camps, or the preparation or organization of terrorist acts intended to be committed against other States or their citizens'. Emphasis added. On the flexibility inherent in the concept of an 'all practicable measures' standard, see *infra* notes 73–8 and accompanying text.

[9] See Pisillo-Mazzeschi (1992). The distinction Pisillo-Mazzeschi draws is in line with the traditional civil law distinction between obligations of conduct and obligations of result, and is therefore different from the distinction proposed by Special Rapporteur Ago for the ILC draft Articles on State Responsibility. See Ago (1977), 4–20, paras 1–46; Report of the International Law Commission on the work of its twenty-ninth session, UN Doc. A/32/10 (1977), 11–30). Ago's distinction was heavily criticized as confusing and unhelpful (see Combacau (1981), 190–6; Tomuschat (1994), 335), and was rejected by Special Rapporteur Crawford in his Second Report on State Responsibility (Crawford (1999), 38, para 88). The ILC Articles on State Responsibility, as finally adopted, do not distinguish between obligations of conduct and obligations of result.

[10] *Bosnia Genocide Case*, Judgment, para 430. But see Ben-Naftali (2009), 41, arguing that there is an inconsistency between characterizing the obligation to prevent genocide as one of conduct (rather than result) and its scope *ratione temporis*.

its territory. The focus of this section is on the obligation to prevent international terrorism. But as the obligation to prevent terrorism is a particular instantiation of a state's general obligation to prevent its territory from being used for the preparation of offences committed in or against other states, this section will equally consider the general obligation in elucidating the precise nature of the primary rules in the terrorism context.

3.1.1 Knowledge

A state's knowledge or notice of harmful activities emanating from its territory is an important element in assessing whether it has complied with its obligation to diligently prevent international terrorism. An absence of actual knowledge or notice of such activities, however, does not automatically preclude a finding of responsibility. This is particularly true in the post-9/11 terrorism context, in which notice of the threat of international terrorism is built into the system developed around Security Council Resolution 1373 (2001) and the reporting requirements to the Counter-Terrorism Committee created thereby.[11]

Equally, international jurisprudence suggests that reasonably discoverable threats will bear on an assessment of compliance with the obligation to prevent in the same way as actual knowledge. States therefore have an obligation to keep themselves informed, but the obligation is one of conduct, not result. For instance, dissenting opinions in the ICJ's *Corfu Channel* decision evaluated Albania's responsibility in light of whether it could have discovered threats emanating from its territory.[12] Dissenting Judge Azevedo held that, even if it was not possible to prove the knowledge of Albania, one could examine whether Albania could or ought to have had cognizance of the mine-laying in the Channel. Judge Azevedo noted Albania's deserted coastline and held that 'Albania [. . .] failed to place lookout posts at the spots considered most suitable when the coast defences were organized [. . .]. Albania must therefore bear the consequences [. . .]'.[13] Brownlie interprets the effect of the decision as placing Albania under a duty to take *reasonable* care to discover the activities of trespassers.[14] Dissenting Judge Krylov reached the opposite conclusion as to Albania's responsibility based on the insufficiency of time to warn and Albania's lack of technical means to do so. Nevertheless, he concurred with Judge Azevedo that a state is under a continuous duty to inform itself (as best it can) of threats emanating from its territory, but considered Albania's efforts to monitor its coast (and thereby discover potential threats) to be diligent. In particular, Judge Krylov held that he could not find 'in the organization and functioning of the Albanian coastal watch—having regard to

---

[11] *Infra* note 99 and accompanying text.
[12] The majority judgment, having held Albania responsible for a failure to warn, implicitly considered Albania to have the necessary capacity to discover threats emanating from its territory, and was therefore not concerned with its diligence in developing that capacity.
[13] *Corfu Channel (UK v. Albania)*, Merits, Dissenting Opinion of Judge Azevedo, 93.
[14] Brownlie (2008), 441.

the limited resources of that small country—such a lack of diligence as might involve the responsibility of Albania'.[15]

Once a state has knowledge of a threat (or ought to have known of the threat had it been diligent), assessment of its compliance with the obligation to prevent becomes particularized.[16] This is principally the case because an obligation to prevent the occurrence of a particular event is only breached if the particular event occurs.[17] What amounts to diligent prevention will therefore involve an assessment of whether the state (subject to available means discussed below) took specific action to avert the known threat from materializing. International jurisprudence is consistent in its treatment of knowledge as an element which particularizes the assessment of compliance with the obligation to diligently prevent. An early example is the *Alabama Claims Case*: the US claimed that the UK's failure to prevent the construction and arming of war ships intended for participation in the American civil war amounted to a breach of the UK's proclaimed neutrality. The arbitrators concluded that the UK had failed to use due diligence in fulfilling its neutrality obligations, and 'especially that it omitted, notwithstanding the warnings and official representations made by the diplomatic agents of the United States [. . .], to take in due time any effective measures of prevention [. . .]'.[18] While the UK had a general obligation to be vigilant in preventing its territory from being used in a way contrary to its neutrality obligations, and to do what it could to discover any such activities, the UK was held responsible because it failed to take a

---

[15] *Corfu Channel (UK v. Albania)*, Merits, Dissenting Opinion of Judge Krylov, 72. Despite the decision in *Corfu Channel*, there is some disagreement in the literature as to whether the obligation to develop capacity (in reference to the obligation to prevent terrorism specifically) is one of result. See Pisillo-Mazzeschi (1992), 27; Becker (2006), 145–6. Becker argues convincingly that the obligation to develop capacity to discover threats must be an obligation of due diligence, lest failing states or states with limited resources effectively be held to an absolute obligation to prevent acts of international terrorism. Early codification efforts regarding the general obligation to prevent acts contrary to the rights of other states further support this in providing that '[a] State has a duty to maintain governmental organization adequate, under normal conditions, for the performance of its obligations under international law and treaties'. Art. 4, Harvard Draft Convention (1929), 146. The Commentary to the Harvard Draft Convention (1929) noted that, even in abnormal times, a state has a duty to use the means at its disposal for the protection of aliens. Commentary to Art. 4, Harvard Draft Convention (1929), 146. By invoking a state's particular means as a limitation on the obligation to maintain governmental organization adequate for the performance of international obligations (for instance the obligation to prevent harm), the Commentary eschewed any conception of such an obligation as one of result. See D.P. O'Connell (1970), 966–7.

[16] See *Bosnia Genocide Case*, Judgment, para 431. See also Lillich and Paxman (1977), 275, arguing that a state's breach of its obligation to prevent terrorism consists of its 'failure to exercise "due diligence" in curbing the activities *once knowledge of the activities is acquired*'. Emphasis added. See also, in the context of preventing harm within a state's own territory, the European Court of Human Rights' decision in *Kilic v. Turkey* (ECtHR, 2000), holding that a positive obligation to take particular action arises once the authorities '*knew or ought to have known* [. . .] of a real and immediate risk to the life of an identified individual [. . .] and that they failed to take measures within the scope of their powers which, judged reasonably, might have been expected to avoid *that* risk'. Emphasis added.

[17] Art. 14(3), ILC Articles on State Responsibility. See also the extensive review of jurisprudence and doctrine in Ago (1978), 83–5, supporting the proposition that breach of an obligation to prevent a particular type of harm requires both (a) that the harm which it was the purpose of international law to prevent actually occurs, and (b) a lack of diligence on the part of the state under an obligation to prevent.

[18] *Alabama Claims Case (US/GB)*, 654–6.

particular measure—prevent construction of the *Alabama* or its departure for international waters. The assessment of responsibility in the circumstances was informed by the UK's specific knowledge of the ship's construction and the purposes to which the ship would be put.

Similarly, in its *Corfu Channel* decision, after concluding that mines could not have been laid in the Channel without Albania's knowledge,[19] the ICJ held that the resulting obligations for Albania consisted in notifying shipping in general of the existence of the mines, and warning the approaching British warships in particular of the imminent danger.[20] Albania's responsibility in the circumstances, measured in terms of its failure to warn the British warships, resulted from its specific knowledge of the threat (and the actualization of that threat).

With regard to internationally protected persons or embassies, states have a continuous obligation to diligently prevent harm within their territories. Diligent conduct in fulfilling such obligations often involves posting security forces outside embassies and the private dwellings of diplomatic agents. Where there is particular notice of a threat, however, a state's compliance with its prevention obligations is evaluated in light of whether it took action precisely targeted at countering the relevant threat. In the *Tehran Hostages* case, the ICJ was satisfied that the Iranian authorities were amply aware of the attack against the US embassy in Tehran, and its continuing nature.[21] This awareness imbued compliance with the obligation of prevention with a specificity that it would not have had in the absence of notice, and required action designed to counter the particular threat.

Proof to which the element of knowledge is susceptible

Given the absence of a discovery process in international law, there is no reliable means of making factual determinations about a given state agent's knowledge,[22] particularly because evidence (including access to relevant state agents) will be in the control of the respondent state.[23] As a result, requiring proof of subjective knowledge would effectively act as a bar to any finding of responsibility for a failure to prevent. The ICJ's approach to knowledge has consistently been to determine what the state ought to have known, given the facts and circumstances. The Court has sometimes relied on evidence of the actual knowledge of state agents—but

---

[19] *Corfu Channel (UK v. Albania)*, Merits, 22.

[20] *Ibid.* Brownlie explains the ICJ's decision in *Corfu Channel* as based on the violation of a particular duty, with knowledge as a condition of the responsibility. See Brownlie (1983), 43. This formulation implies that the duty to warn exists independently of the obligation to prevent and the knowledge of impending harm. A better formulation might be that the case is based on the violation of the general duty of prevention, and that assessment of compliance is particularized by Albania's knowledge of impending harm.

[21] The ICJ noted a number of appeals for help to the Iranian Foreign Ministry from the US Chargé D'Affaires who was at the Foreign Ministry at the time, and from US governmental officials in Washington DC to the Iranian Chargé D'Affaires there. *Tehran Hostages (US v. Iran)*, Judgment, paras 18 and 68(b).

[22] See Setear (1997), 46–50.

[23] See Gattini (1992), 254; Bedjaoui (2000). See also Verdier (2002), 854.

treated it as evidence of what the state ought to have known, rather than requiring such evidence to satisfy the element of knowledge itself.

In the *Bosnia Genocide Case*, proof that President Milosevic was aware of the danger that genocide might be committed during the course of the military operations in Srebrenica served as the basis for concluding that the FRY ought to have been aware of the serious risk of genocide.[24] President Milosevic's awareness of the risk was inferred from both an objective assessment of what he ought to have known (based on the level of international concern being expressed), and subjective elements related to his conversations with General Mladic. The conclusion that 'it must have been clear that there was a serious risk of genocide in Srebrenica',[25] however, is of the 'ought to have known' variety, which is undoubtedly an objective standard—and is not based solely on an evaluation of what President Milosevic did in fact know. The distinction here is between the standard applicable in proving knowledge, which is objective and does not require proof of subjective knowledge, and the evidence that might be adduced in support of the proposition that a state 'ought to have known' something, which may (but need not) include a particular individual's actual (and subjective) knowledge. In *Corfu Channel*, the ICJ held that mines could not have been laid in the Channel 'without the knowledge of Albania's government'.[26] And while the Court certainly refused to infer knowledge from objective factors like control over territory[27] it relied on other objective factors, unrelated to the actual knowledge of state agents, including the close watch Albania kept over the Channel and the location of look-out posts, to determine that Albania ought to have known that mines were being laid.

The terrorism context is equally susceptible to an analysis of what the state ought to have known, given the particular facts and circumstances.[28] In the Lebanon/ Hezbollah war of 2006,[29] there were difficult questions of fact and law regarding Lebanese notice that its territory would be used as a base for planning and launching terrorist attacks against Israel. The Secretary-General remarked in July 2006 that it was clear that the Lebanese Government had no advance knowledge of the attacks.[30] And in its presentation to the Security Council following the kidnapping of the Israeli soldiers, the Lebanese Government distanced itself from Hezbollah's attacks against Israel, and informed the Council that it had no advance notice of the events and that it did not endorse them.[31] Indeed, before the July 2006 attacks, Hezbollah had not attacked Israeli civilians from Lebanese territory

---

[24] *Bosnia Genocide Case*, Judgment, paras 436–8.

[25] *Ibid*, para 438.

[26] *Corfu Channel (UK v. Albania)*, Merits, 22.

[27] *Ibid*, 18.

[28] To the extent that it is available, however, proof of a particular agent's knowledge or negligence, where that agent was the organ responsible for taking action to prevent an act of terrorism, would certainly go a long way in proving a state's lack of diligence. See Brownlie (2008), 441.

[29] See Section 2.2.3 for an account of the facts leading up to the war.

[30] UN Doc. SG/SM/10570 (2006).

[31] Identical letters dated 13 July 2006 from the Chargé D'Affaires a.i. of the Permanent Mission of Lebanon to the United Nations addressed to the Secretary-General and the President of the Security Council, UN Doc. S/2006/518.

since August 2003.[32] As a result, Lebanon would be in a position to argue that it did not have particular notice of terrorist attacks being planned and organized from its territory. That said, Lebanon was surely on general notice of the danger that its territory might be used to launch attacks against Israel, particularly given that such attacks had been launched in the past (however distant that past). The analysis would therefore turn on what Lebanon ought to have known in the circumstances, which would itself turn in part on Lebanese counter-terrorism capacity, as discussed below.

3.1.2 Capacity

Given that the obligation to prevent is one of due diligence, not of result, it is subject to an 'available means' analysis. As a result, international jurisprudence[33] and doctrine[34] have generally held that capacity (or rather incapacity) is the limit of responsibility. Some commentators have warned against this approach in the terrorism context, not least because terrorist organizations are likely to set up operations in states with limited capacity to oppose them, yet be shielded from foreign interference by the sovereignty, territorial integrity and political independence of their host state.[35] If we accept, however, a right to use defensive force directly against non-state terrorist actors launching an armed attack from foreign territory (given an inability to rely on the host state to prevent its territory from being used as a base of terrorist operations),[36] there is no need to reconceptualize the limits of due diligence and state responsibility to respond to the security interests of victim states.[37]

Unlike knowledge, which particularizes an assessment of compliance with the obligation to prevent, questions of incapacity serve to inform the standard of diligence to which a particular state will be held. Diligence requires using available capacity effectively to respond to known or knowable threats. Without certain types of capacity, states cannot be held responsible for breaching their obligation to diligently prevent harm emanating from their territory. For the purposes of analytical clarity, this section considers capacity under three separate headings: institutional capacity; resource capacity and territorial capacity. They are not three

---

[32] Israel Ministry of Foreign Affairs, 'Hizbullah attacks along Israel's northern border May 2000–June 2006', <http://www.mfa.gov.il/NR/exeres/9EE216D7-82EF-4274-B80D-6BBD1803E8A7, frameless.htm?NRMODE=Published>.

[33] Capacity, or the 'power' to prevent, has long been considered a limitation on a state's responsibility for a failure to prevent. See *The Jamaica Case (Great Britain/US)*, 3990–91. Much more recently, see *Bosnia Genocide Case*, Judgment, para 430. See also *infra* notes 40–3 and accompanying text.

[34] See Garcia-Mora (1962), 63; De Vissher (1970), 308; D.P. O'Connell (1970), 969; Bowett (1972), 20; Report of the International Law Commission on the work of its thirtieth session, UN Doc. A/33/10 (1978), 82–3; Report of the International Law Commission on the work of its fifty-third session, UN Doc. A/56/10 (2001), 155, para 13; Zegfeld (2002), 192.

[35] See Reisman (1999), 50; Byman (2005), 219.

[36] See Section 2.2.3.

[37] See Trapp (2008), 412–13.

different types of capacity, but are rather three different aspects of capacity that overlap and work together to form a state's total capacity to prevent.

(i) Institutional capacity

The first, institutional, aspect of capacity concerns the legal regime (including criminal law enforcement framework) that a state has in place to allow for and support preventive efforts. Of the three aspects of capacity, institutional incapacity is the least likely to inform an assessment of diligent prevention. An early international arbitral decision that addressed the availability of an institutional framework to facilitate prevention was the *Alabama Claims Case*. The arbitral tribunal held that 'the Government of her Britannic Majesty cannot justify itself for a failure of due diligence on the plea of insufficiency of the legal means of action which it possessed'.[38] This is a fairly strict approach to institutional incapacity as a factor in assessing due diligence, but is likely to be applied in the present day terrorism context given the institutional capacity-building activities of the UN and related international organizations and agencies (discussed below in Section 3.1.3). It bears noting, however, that having an institutional capacity to prevent terrorism is very different from having the resources or territorial control necessary to put that institutional capacity to good and 'diligent' use.

(ii) Resource capacity

The second aspect of capacity is resource-based, in particular whether a state has the financial, technical or human resources available to put its institutional capacity to good use. International jurisprudence has generally been sympathetic to the resource incapacity argument as a basis for finding no lack of diligence,[39] and states often invoke limited resources to justify their failures to prevent.

In *Corfu Channel*, the majority opinion was careful to highlight that Albania had the means at its disposal to meet its obligation to warn approaching British warships.[40] Dissenting Judge Krylov, however, held that even if Albania had knowledge of the minefield, the Albanian coastal guard service could not have warned the British ships of that fact on the day because—given the circumstances of the ships' passage—the coastal guards had neither sufficient time nor the necessary technical means for giving such a warning. He also made a point of highlighting the 'limited resources of that small country' in finding no lack of diligence.[41] While the majority and dissent reached different factual conclusions as to Albania's capacity to warn, both judgments illustrate the importance of available

---

[38] *Alabama Claims Case (US/GB)*, 656.
[39] But see an 1875 arbitral award, *Montijo Case (US/Colombia)*, 1444, in which the arbitral tribunal acknowledged that Colombia did not have the resources to fulfil its obligations, but found it responsible even if its absence of capacity was through 'no fault of its own'.
[40] *Corfu Channel (UK v. Albania)*, Merits, 23.
[41] *Corfu Channel (UK v. Albania)*, Merits, Dissenting Opinion of Judge Krylov, 72.

technical resources in assessing whether a state has breached its due diligence obligation.

In its *Tehran Hostages* decision, the ICJ emphasized the availability of resources, in particular the Iranian regime's successes in acting effectively to prevent and put an end to attacks on other embassies, in finding that Iran had violated its due diligence obligation to prevent harm to the US embassy.[42] In *Nicaragua*, the ICJ's consideration of Nicaraguan responsibility for failing to prevent the arms traffic through its territory to El Salvadorian rebels (which the US argued made it susceptible to action in collective self-defence) also touched on the resources issue. The Court reasoned that:

if [. . .] the exceptionally extensive resources deployed by the United States have been powerless to prevent this [arms] traffic from keeping the Salvadorian opposition supplied, this suggests how powerless Nicaragua must be with the much smaller resources at its disposal for subduing this traffic if it takes place on its territory and the authorities endeavour to put a stop to it.[43]

Finally, in its *Bosnia Genocide Case* decision, the ICJ held that the obligation to prevent genocide is one of conduct (not result) requiring states 'to employ all means reasonably available to them, so as to prevent genocide so far as possible'.[44] The Court went on to hold that:

a State's obligation to prevent, and the corresponding duty to act, arise at the instant that the State learns of, or should normally have learned of, the existence of a serious risk that genocide will be committed. From that moment onwards, *if the State has available to it means* likely to have a deterrent effect on those suspected of preparing genocide, or reasonably suspected of harbouring specific intent (*dolus specialis*), it is under a duty to make such use of these means as the circumstances permit.[45]

An example of the role resources might play in assessing compliance with the obligation to prevent resulted from the printing in Western European newspapers of cartoons depicting the Prophet Mohammad. In response, there were demonstrations throughout the Middle East in front of Western European embassies, in particular those of Norway and Denmark, which had first printed the cartoons. In Syria, the demonstrations resulted in significant damage to the Norwegian and Danish embassies in Damascus. Denmark and Norway each condemned Syria's failure to protect the embassies,[46] but Syria informed the Security Council that the embassies were damaged despite its efforts of prevention.[47] In particular, the Syrian Government claimed that the peaceful demonstrations suddenly turned to the use of violence:

---

[42] *Tehran Hostages (US v. Iran)*, Judgment, paras 63–4 and 68.
[43] *Nicaragua (Nicaragua v. US)*, Merits, para 157.
[44] *Bosnia Genocide Case*, Judgment, para 430.
[45] Emphasis added. *Ibid*, para 431.
[46] See CBC, 'Denmark, Norway condemn Syria after embassy attacks', 5 February 2006, <http://www.cbc.ca/world/story/2006/02/04/cartoon-controversy060204.html>.
[47] Letter dated 13 February 2006 from the Permanent Representative of the Syrian Arab Republic to the United Nations addressed to the Secretary-General, UN Doc. A/60/690 (2006), 1–2.

despite the efforts made by the police and security forces, who tried *with available means*, namely tear gas, water hoses and the formation of a human shield, to prevent the demonstrators from approaching the embassies in question, and despite the appeals made by officials and spiritual leaders, some of the demonstrators managed to cause damage to a number of embassies.[48]

The claim was rejected by both Norway and Denmark. By Syria's own admission, it had other resources available that it could have mobilized to prevent (and halt once commenced) the attacks on the embassies. Syria's letter to the Security Council made it clear that the number of security forces and other security measures were not increased (including barricading streets leading to the embassies) until after the peaceful demonstrations outside the embassies had turned violent.[49] The refusal to accept an 'available means'-based excuse for Syria's failure to prevent was undoubtedly intertwined with the fact that the Syrian Government had been on notice of the threat to the Danish and Norwegian embassies[50]—which in itself requires more precise measures to comply with the obligation to prevent.

While assessing a state's available counter-terrorism resources is sometimes straightforward—particularly where a state has put further resources to work in similar situations or after the fact, as was the case in reference to the *Tehran Hostages* case and the Syrian case discussed above—this will often not be the case. States faced with threats to their own security and other important priorities will inevitably divert resources from counter-terrorism to address more pressing concerns. An example best illustrates the point. Pakistan's counter-terrorism efforts are considered, at least by the US, as absolutely essential to the successful execution of the 'war on terror'. But Pakistan has a number of pressing priorities that are undoubtedly a drain on its resources, including its conflict with India over Kashmir. International law, however, has very little to say about how states should prioritize resource allocation[51]—and given competing priorities—the assessment of a state's 'resources capacity' to prevent acts of international terrorism needs to be realistic and context-sensitive.

(iii) Territorial capacity

A deficit of territorial capacity, in the sense of a state's incapacity to extend its control over the entirety of its territory, often results in a state's inability to effectively prevent its territory from being used as a base of terrorist operations.[52]

---

[48] Emphasis added. *Ibid.*

[49] *Ibid*, 2.

[50] Denmark and Norway each condemned Syria's failure to protect their Embassies, particularly in light of the fact that requests for extra security around the Embassies went unheeded, and despite warnings that a major demonstration was brewing. See CBC, *supra* note 46.

[51] The Security Council has generally been silent on the question of *prioritizing* resource allocation, although has urged states, in the non-operative paragraphs of a Chapter VII resolution, to allocate sufficient resources to counter-terrorism. See UNSC Resolution 1922 (2008).

[52] The US identifies a number of countries and regions in which limited governmental control over territory is the result of harsh climates, terrain, and dense forest, resulting in territory being used as a safe haven by terrorists. See US Department of State Country Reports on Terrorism (2008), Chapter 5,

Incapacity to fully control certain territory often results from the territory being placed beyond governmental authority because of its difficult terrain, inhospitable climate, or distance from central government, and has long been considered a factor that weighs against finding a lack of diligence. For instance, in 1963, the British Government maintained a policy of neutrality in the Yemeni civil war by not allowing the territory of South Arabia to be used by either side of the civil conflict as a 'springboard for an attack on the other side'.[53] In response to inquiries regarding its ability to stem gun-running into Yemen, the British Government replied that 'the nature of the country and the ill-defined border between the Yemen and the Federation of South Arabia make it quite impossible to control'.[54] The extensive border between Yemen and Saudi Arabia, and difficulties in policing that border, continues to be identified as a factor contributing to Yemen's safe haven status.[55]

The ICJ has also consistently regarded difficult terrain as an element that weighs against holding a state responsible for failing to prevent. In *Nicaragua*, the Court examined Nicaragua's role in facilitating (or at least failing to prevent) the arms traffic through its territory to El Salvadorian rebels. The Court considered the geographical obstacles and the clandestine nature of arms traffic as factors against finding that Nicaragua failed to diligently prevent the arms traffic.[56] In its *Armed Activities on the Territory of the Congo (DRC v. Uganda)* decision, the ICJ considered the DRC's obligation to prevent its territory from being used as a base of hostile operations by anti-Ugandan rebels. The ICJ noted that the rebel groups were able to operate from the border region unimpeded because of its mountainous terrain, its remoteness from Kinshasa, and the almost complete absence of central government presence or authority in the region during President Mobutu's thirty-two years in office.[57] The ICJ further noted that both anti-DRC and anti-Ugandan rebels operated from the border region and that neither the DRC nor Uganda was in a position to put an end to their activities. The ICJ therefore refused to conclude that the absence of any action by the DRC Government against the rebels in the border area was tantamount to 'tolerating' or 'acquiescing' in their activities.[58] The Court failed to make the basis of its conclusion explicit, but presumably the reasoning is that the DRC had an interest in controlling its border region given insurgent activities launched therefrom, and its failure to do so was not the result of a policy decision to passively support anti-Ugandan rebel groups, but rather as a result of its incapacity. This reasoning is supported by Uganda's own description of

discussing remoteness in the Trans-Sahara, widely spread islands in the Sulu Archipelago, and difficult terrain in the Afghan and Pakistan border regions, as factors that contribute to the emergence of terrorist safe havens.

[53] E. Lauterpacht (1963), 26.
[54] E. Lauterpacht (1964), 187.
[55] See US Department of State Country Reports on Terrorism (2008), Chapter 5.
[56] *Nicaragua (Nicaragua v. US)*, Merits, paras 157 and 230.
[57] These submissions were in fact made on behalf of Uganda to the ICJ, intended not to be a mitigating factor, but proof of a failure to exercise diligence generally. *Armed Activities on the Territory of the Congo (DRC v. Uganda)*, Judgment, para 301.
[58] *Ibid.*

the difficult terrain and distance from central government[59] and the Court's high-lighting that Uganda had also not been able to control attacks from the border region.

If part of a state's territory is subject to a civil armed conflict, that does not, however, relieve a state from taking 'all the political, judicial and other measures at [their] disposal to re-establish [...] control over [their] territory'.[60] But a state's obligation to establish control over its territory is limited by what it *can* do, evaluated on the basis of its financial and military resources, and the opposition it encounters in its efforts to establish control over territory.[61] This is evident in the international community's reaction to the Israel/Hezbollah war of 2006.[62] Lebanon certainly cannot be said to fully control its southern border region with Israel, which is instead controlled principally by Hezbollah. While part of the difficulty results from a complicated political situation, Lebanon's territorial incapacity is also the result of its relatively weak army—facing the most capable non-state armed group in the region.[63] Israel invoked Lebanese responsibility for Hezbollah rockets launched into its territory, on the basis that Lebanon had failed to fully assert its sovereignty over the entirety of its territory.[64] To the extent that Lebanon could be held responsible for its failure to prevent terrorist attacks launched from its territory into Israel, responsibility would likely turn on Lebanon's failure to diligently attempt to extend its territorial capacity,[65] coupled with a general notice that its territory could be used as a base from which Hezbollah might launch terrorist attacks, rather than the absence of territorial capacity itself.

3.1.3 Effect of 9/11 on due diligence obligations as they relate to terrorism

In Section 2.2.3 above, it is argued that there is no need to reconceptualize the law of state responsibility, in particular the rules of attribution, to account for post-9/11 state practice. It is equally true that a reconceptualization is unnecessary in the terrorism prevention context. The 9/11 terrorist attacks and the response thereto,

---

[59] *Supra* note 57.

[60] See, in respect of positive obligations to protect human rights and the lack of territorial control necessary to effectively meet those obligations, *Ilascu v. Moldova and Russia* (ECtHR, 2004), para 340.

[61] *Ibid*, paras 341–4.

[62] See Section 2.2.3 for details regarding the armed conflict.

[63] Ruys (2007), 284. See also Butters, 'Who Will Disarm Hizballah? Not the Lebanese Army', Time, 4 August 2006, <http://www.time.com/time/world/article/0,8599,1223159,00.html>; Council on Foreign Relations Fellow, Steven Cook: 'Hezbollah's militia, estimated at some 3,000 full-time fighters based in Lebanon's southeast, is as strong as the Lebanese army', quoted in Pan (2006).

[64] See Identical letters dated 18 June 2007 from the Chargé D'affaires a.i. of the Permanent Mission of Israel to the United Nations addressed to the Secretary-General and the President of the Security Council, UN Doc. S/2007/368; Interview with Israeli Foreign Minister Livni on IDF Radio, 18 June 2007, <http://www.mfa.gov.il>.

[65] Member states of the UN and the Security Council have consistently underlined the need for Lebanon to extend its exclusive control over all of its territory. UNSC Resolution 1559 (2004), paras 1–3; UNSC Resolution 1583 (2005), paras 3–4; UNSC Resolution 1655 (2006), paras 3, 6 and 8; UNSC Resolution 1680 (2006), preamble; UNSC Resolution 1701 (2006), para 3.

including the Security Council's imposition of counter-terrorism obligations under Chapter VII, have not changed the substance of the obligation to prevent—states are, as before 11 September 2001, under an obligation to diligently prevent international terrorism. There have, however, been three changes to the way that compliance with the obligation is measured and evaluated, which will be dealt with in turn: a shift in the approach to compliance with terrorism prevention obligations; a decrease in the margin of appreciation which states enjoyed in reference to setting their own priorities and determining appropriate measures to meet those priorities; and a *rapprochement* in the relationship between positive obligations of prevention and negative obligations to refrain from acquiescing in terrorism.

(i) Shift in approach to compliance with terrorism-prevention obligations

Before the 9/11 terrorist attacks, states focused their compliance with the Terrorism Suppression Conventions almost exclusively on criminal law enforcement.[66] Reports submitted to the Secretary-General of the UN on measures taken pursuant to the TSCs detailed the adoption of legislation criminalizing relevant terrorist conduct and the negotiation of bilateral or multilateral extradition treaties.[67] While the existence of a criminal law framework providing for the extradition or prosecution of alleged terrorist offenders might be said to prevent terrorist activities in so far as the possibility of criminal sanctions deters such activities, its application to terrorist offence is *post facto* and therefore not strictly preventive.[68] Following 9/11, with the adoption of Security Council Resolution 1373 (2001) and the creation of the Counter-Terrorism Committee ('CTC'), states began to report on measures taken to prevent terrorists from gaining access to funds[69] or from using their territories as a base of operations or indoctrination.[70] The obligation to prevent international terrorism, both under customary international law and the TSCs, was never limited to criminal law enforcement. As such, it is not the case that 9/11 and the adoption of Security Council Resolution 1373 has changed the substance of those obligations. It is more that 9/11 and the adoption of Security Council

---

[66] The TSCs require states to criminalize the defined terrorist conduct and to provide for appropriate penalties. See e.g. Art. 3, Hague Convention; Art. 2, Hostages Convention; Art. 4, Terrorism Financing Convention.

[67] See UNSG Reports on measures to prevent international terrorism, UN Doc. A/36/425 (1981); UN Doc. A/38/355 (1983); UN Doc. A/42/519 (1987); UN Doc. A/44/456 (1989); UN Doc. A/46/346 (1991); UN Doc. A/48/267 (1993); UN Doc. A/49/257 (1994); UN Doc. A/50/372 (1995); UN Doc. A/51/336 (1996); UN Doc. A/52/304 (1997); UN Doc. A/53/314 (1998); UN Doc. A/54/301 (1999); UN Doc. A/55/179 (2000); UN Doc. A/56/160 (2001).

[68] See *Bosnia Genocide Case*, Judgment, para 162, holding that criminalizing and punishing acts of genocide does not fully discharge the obligation to prevent genocide.

[69] See e.g. UNSG Report on measures to prevent international terrorism, UN Doc. A/57/183 (2002), paras 61, 71, 100–2 and 130. State reporting on measures taken to counter terrorist financing increased substantially as more and more states ratified the Terrorism Financing Convention. See UNSG Reports on measures to prevent international terrorism, UN Doc. A/58/116 (2003); UN Doc. A/59/210 (2004); UN Doc. A/60/228 (2005).

[70] For instance, Pakistan reported on increasing its border security with Afghanistan and reforming the *deeni madaris* to ensure that they were not 'indulging in extremism, subversion [or] militancy'. See UNSG Report on measures to prevent international terrorism, UN Doc. A/57/183 (2002), 17.

Resolution 1373 shifted the focus of compliance with the TSCs from criminal law enforcement to actual terrorism prevention.

(ii) Decrease in the margin of appreciation

The Security Council's response to the 9/11 terrorist attacks has decreased the margin of appreciation states have enjoyed both in regard to setting their own domestic priorities and determining the best means of meeting those priorities. Prior to 9/11, states that considered themselves free from terrorists operating within their territory also considered themselves free from an obligation to develop a counter-terrorism capacity. These states did not ratify the Terrorism Suppression Conventions or adopt a terrorism-specific legal framework providing for criminalization, extradition or prosecution.[71] With the adoption of Resolution 1373 and its binding Chapter VII obligations to act in the prevention of terrorism, the Security Council sought to make effective its determination that the threat of terrorism is international in scope. As a result, the discretion afforded states in assessing the risk of terrorists operating from within their territory (and acting accordingly) has effectively been limited.[72]

In addition, states always had a margin of appreciation in determining the measures they deemed necessary to prevent international terrorism. The first TSC negotiated under the auspices of the UN required states to take 'all practicable measures' to prevent preparations in their territory for the commission of international terrorist offences.[73] This language has rightly been described as preserving a state's discretion by subjecting the obligation of prevention to the limitations of national law and the practicalities of any given situation.[74] A proposal to change the language so that states would be required to take 'all measures' to prevent the relevant terrorist offence was rejected during the Hostages Convention negotiations.[75] In particular, the US argued that the requirement that a state take 'all practicable measures' (instead of 'all measures') reflected the diversity in legal systems around the world,[76] and the Canadian representative argued that the 'all

---

[71] See e.g. UNSG Reports on measures to prevent international terrorism, UN Doc. A/42/519 (1986), 7 (the Bahamas); UN Doc. A/49/257 (1994), 18 (San Marino); UN Doc. A/52/304/Corr.1 (1997).

[72] See e.g. Bolivia's report to the SG on Measures to prevent terrorists from acquiring weapons of mass destruction, noting that 'Bolivia considers that although no activities related to terrorism, let alone the use of weapons of mass destruction, have been detected on its territory in the last few years, this possibility should not be ruled out given the implications of terrorism's international scope'. UN Doc. A/60/185 (2005), 3. Prior to 9/11 and the adoption of Chapter VII legislation pursuant to UNSC Resolution 1373, Bolivia's reports to the SG condemned acts of terrorism and supported convening an international conference for the purposes of defining terrorism, but did not address measures taken in the prevention of terrorism. UNSG Reports on measures to prevent international terrorism, UN Doc. A/46/346 (1991), 5; UN Doc. A/48/267 (1993), 4.

[73] Art. 4, Internationally Protected Persons Convention.

[74] UNGA, 28th Session, UN Doc. A/PV.2202 (1973), para 242.

[75] Report of the *Ad Hoc* Committee on the Drafting of an International Convention against the Taking of Hostages, UN Doc. A/33/39 (1978), 33, para 47.

[76] Report of the *Ad Hoc* Committee on the Drafting of an International Convention against the Taking of Hostages, UN Doc. A/32/39 (1977), 68–9, para 4.

practicable measures' language would give state parties necessary latitude regarding the preventive measures they would adopt.[77] The ILC's position is similarly that the 'all practicable measures' language allows state parties to determine for themselves, on the 'basis of their particular experience and requirements', what preventive measures to adopt.[78] All the TSCs use the 'all practicable measures' language, thereby permitting states a margin of appreciation in determining the appropriate preventive measures to adopt.

This margin of appreciation, in determining appropriate measures to prevent terrorism, has also been circumscribed post-9/11. The limitation has resulted from a number of developments. In particular, the CTC's focus on implementing the very specific means of preventing the financing of terrorism set out in the Terrorism Financing Convention (and Security Council Resolution 1373 which reproduces those measures to a large extent) leaves states with very little latitude in determining for themselves the appropriate mechanisms for countering terrorism financing. Similarly, specialized UN agencies like the ICAO and the IMO have defined very specifically the measures that amount to compliance with international terrorism prevention obligations in their spheres of competence, and provide training to governments in relation thereto.[79]

This decrease in the margin of appreciation runs in parallel with a 'capacity-building blitz' the likes of which the international community has not seen before.[80] States are being afforded every opportunity to develop their counter-terrorism capacities in partnership with the Counter-Terrorism Implementation Task Force '-('CTITF').[81] The CTITF was created in July 2005 to co-ordinate the counter-terrorism support provided by a range of UN agencies and subsidiary bodies,[82] including that of the CTC and relevant regional organizations,[83] the UN Office on Drugs and Crime,[84] and the Financial Action Task Force.[85] The

---

[77] *Ibid*, 74, para 3.

[78] Report of the International Law Commission on the work of its twenty-fourth session, UN Doc. A/8710/Rev.1 (1972), 317.

[79] See UNSG Report on measures to prevent international terrorism, UN Doc. A/60/228 (2005), 15–17. See further Joyner and Friedlander (2008), 850, on the International Air Transportation Association's development of industry policies and procedures to combat acts of international terrorism against civil aviation.

[80] See in general Ward (2003).

[81] See in particular UNSC Resolution 1805 (2008).

[82] See <http://www.un.org/terrorism/cttaskforce.shtml>.

[83] The CTC facilitates the provision of technical assistance to member states by disseminating best practices; identifying existing technical, financial, regulatory and legislative assistance programmes; and promoting synergies between the assistance programmes of international, regional and sub-regional organizations. See <http://www.un.org/en/sc/ctc/>.

[84] The UN Office on Drugs and Crime offers assistance to requesting states for the ratification and legislative incorporation of the Terrorism Suppression Conventions. See UNSG Report on strengthening international cooperation and technical assistance in preventing and combating terrorism, UN Doc. A/60/164 (2005), 57, para 15.

[85] The Financial Action Task Force is an inter-governmental body whose purpose is the development and promotion of national and international policies to combat money laundering and terrorist financing, and it has produced Special Recommendations on Terrorist Financing, including ;interpretative notes and best practices. See <http://www.fatf-gafi.org/document/9/0,2340, en_32250379_32236920_ 34032073_1_1_1_1,00.html>. See also the Report of the High Level Panel

Commission on Crime Prevention and Criminal Justice equally works to develop counter-terrorism capacity among member states by focusing on the modernization of criminal justice processes, the strengthening of judicial integrity and the improvement of the treatment of witnesses—which are considered essential elements of a rule of law society committed to eradicating terrorism.[86] By defining what amounts to diligent measures of prevention, and contributing significantly to the feasibility of domestic implementation of such measures through capacity-building initiatives, the UN and related agencies have effectively limited the discretion that states enjoyed in deciding for themselves what preventive measures to adopt.

This decrease in the margin of appreciation will have a similar effect on an evaluation of compliance with the obligation to diligently prevent terrorism as notice of a specific terrorist threat. Where there is notice of a particular threat, only the adoption of a defined set of measures will amount to diligent preventive conduct.[87] The increased specificity with which the obligation of prevention is imbued post-9/11, in combination with the UN capacity-building programmes, heightens the standard of conduct to which states are held. Whereas states had a margin of appreciation in determining appropriate prevention measures before 9/11, they are now more likely to be required to account for having failed to take the precise measures called for by the CTC and relevant capacity-building partners. That said, most of the UN capacity-building aid relates to developing an institutional capacity to prevent international terrorism. Small states with limited resources will still have difficulty in putting institutional capacity to good use given a lack of human and financial resources.[88] In particular, these states have to carefully prioritize the use of their limited resources, perhaps allocating resources to threats they face more acutely than that of terrorism—like environmental degradation or drug trafficking. In assessing a state's compliance with its due diligence obligations, greater and greater sensitivity will therefore need to be paid to available material resources and a state's competing priorities. As such, despite warnings to the contrary,[89] the increasingly high standard imposed by counter-terrorism obligations will lead to a reinforcement of 'capacity as the limit of responsibility'.

---

on Threats, Challenges and Change, A more secure world: our shared responsibility, UN Doc. A/59/565 (2004), para 150, urging states to 'adopt the eight Special Recommendations on Terrorist Financing issued by the Organization for Economic Cooperation and Development (OECD)-supported Financial Action Task Force on Money-Laundering and the measures recommended in its various best practices papers'.

[86] See UNSG Report on strengthening international cooperation and technical assistance in preventing and combating terrorism, UN Doc. A/60/164 (2005), 6, para 16.

[87] See Section 3.1.1.

[88] See for instance the High Level Panel Report noting that '[b]ecause United Nations-facilitated assistance is limited to technical support, States seeking operational support for counter-terrorism activities have no alternative but to seek bilateral assistance' and suggesting that a 'United Nations capacity to facilitate this assistance would in some instances ease domestic political constraints, and this can be achieved by providing for the Counter-Terrorism Executive Directorate to act as a clearing house for State-to-State provision of military, police and border control assistance for the development of domestic counterterrorism capacities'. Report of the High Level Panel on Threats, Challenges and Change, A more secure world: our shared responsibility, UN Doc. A/59/565 (2004), para 154.

[89] *Supra* note 35 and accompanying text.

(iii) Rapprochement *between the obligation to prevent and the obligation to refrain*

The distinction before 9/11

States are under both a positive obligation to prevent international terrorism and a negative obligation to 'refrain from [. . .] acquiescing in organized activities within its territory directed toward the commission of [terrorist] acts'.[90] There are two generally agreed distinctions between the positive obligation to prevent and the negative obligation to refrain from acquiescing. The first is that only positive obligations are subject to a due diligence standard of conduct. Obligations to refrain are obligations of result.[91] A state must do more than use its best efforts to refrain from acquiescing in terrorism. It must refrain from acquiescing in terrorism full stop. The distinction may be clear in theory, but is less clear in practice. First, whereas a breach of the obligation to refrain from acquiescing in terrorism will always (subject to comments below) amount to a breach of the obligation to prevent international terrorism,[92] the reverse is not always true. Courts must balance the type and degree of preventive action a state takes against its awareness of the terrorist threat and its capacity to prevent. A state may have taken some—but not enough—preventive measures, based on its appreciation of the risk involved and its capacity to act. As long as a state's efforts are not a colourable attempt to be seen to be complying with its obligation to prevent acts of international terrorism (as a cover for its acquiescence therein),[93] a state's failure to exercise due diligence will not always amount to acquiescence. But where there is knowledge of a terrorist threat, and a capacity to act to counter the threat, a state's failure to take any (rather than some, but not enough) measures to prevent international terrorism edges closer to its acquiescence therein.[94] The distinction between prevention and acquiescence becomes even more difficult to maintain in practice

---

[90] UN Declaration on Friendly Relations, UNGA Resolution 2625 (1970). The ICJ has held the obligation to refrain from acquiescing, as set forth in the UN Declaration on Friendly Relations, to be customary international law. *Armed Activities on the Territory of the Congo (DRC v. Uganda)*, Judgment, paras 162 and 300. The obligation not to acquiesce is also the subject of a Chapter VII obligation in that UNSC Resolution 1373 (2001) '[d]ecides that all States shall [. . .] [r]efrain from providing any form of support, active or *passive*, to entities or persons involved in terrorist acts, including by suppressing recruitment of members of terrorist groups and eliminating the supply of weapons to terrorists'. Emphasis added.

[91] See Reuter (1958), 140; Ago (1978); Pisillo-Mazzeschi (1992); Becker (2006).

[92] See for instance the ICJ's assessment of Uganda's failure to meet its obligation to prevent its military from plundering DRC resources. The ICJ noted that Ugandan military officials facilitated the very activities Uganda was legally bound to prevent. *Armed Activities on the Territory of the Congo (DRC v. Uganda)*, Judgment, para 248.

[93] The ICJ's review of Uganda's failure to prevent plundering of DRC resources highlighted a report charging Uganda with colourable attempts to be seen to be complying with obligations of prevention. *Armed Activities on the Territory of the Congo (DRC v. Uganda)*, Judgment, para 248.

[94] In its Judgment in the *Bosnia Genocide Case*, Judgment, paras 418–21 and 432, the ICJ maintained that there is a clear distinction between complicity in genocide and a failure to prevent genocide, because complicity requires full knowledge of the facts and requires some positive act (like aid or assistance), while a state might be held responsible for a failure to prevent on the basis of what it ought to have known and requires only an omission (rather than a positive act). See Ben-Naftali

when we consider that the evidence relevant to evaluating compliance with both is the same. Due diligence in preventing international terrorism, including in preventing one's territory from being used as a base of operations, amounts to evidence that a state is not acquiescing in terrorism.[95] Even the ICJ has given in to the confusion occasionally. In its decision in *Armed Activities on the Territory of the Congo (DRC v. Uganda)*, the Court blurred the distinction between the obligation to prevent territory from being used as a base of hostile operations against a foreign state and the obligation not to acquiesce in or tolerate such activity. In particular, the Court characterized the issue as whether the DRC had 'breached its duty of vigilance by tolerating anti-Ugandan rebels on its territory'.[96]

The second distinction between the obligation to prevent and the obligation to refrain from acquiescing is that the latter is not one which depends on the materialization of a terrorist threat. An obligation to prevent the occurrence of a particular event is only breached if the particular event occurs—and only then if preventive efforts were not diligent.[97] The actualization of a terrorist threat is not, however, a condition for breach of the prohibition of acquiescing in terrorism.[98] This distinction is important in determining the obligations that a state may have breached. While a failure to prevent might be considered a lesser and included 'offence' of acquiescence, this will not always be the case. A state that acquiesces in terrorists operating from its territory cannot also be held to have breached its obligation of prevention unless the terrorist activities acquiesced in result in a terrorist attack causing harm to a foreign state or citizens.

The distinction after 9/11
Knowledge and capacity are elements in evaluating a state's compliance with its obligation to diligently prevent terrorism, and this evaluation has generally been based on a state's particular circumstances. But Security Council Chapter VII resolutions and media exposure have built a certain amount of notice regarding the terrorist threat into the system, making states' claims that terrorism is not a threat within their borders less sustainable.[99] Additionally, the efforts of the CTITF, the CTC, and related UN agencies to develop institutional capacity have made it more difficult for states to legitimately claim that they do not have the relevant counter-terrorism institutional infrastructure in place. The notice of the terrorist threat and the availability of capacity-building aid serve both to increase the standard of diligence required of states, and to decrease the relevance of factors that militate

---

(2009), 41, for a critique of the very fine distinction the Court is drawing. 'Acquiescence', however, does not suggest a need for positive conduct.

[95] See for example Sri Lanka's comments before the Sixth Committee that '[t]he duty not to acquiesce in [terrorist] activities meant that a State should take positive steps to prevent even the commission of acts which were preparatory to the commission of terrorist acts in another State'. UNGA, Sixth Committee, UN Doc. A/C.6/51/SR.11 (1996), para 8.

[96] *Armed Activities on the Territory of the Congo (DRC v. Uganda)*, Judgment, para 300.

[97] Art. 14(3), ILC Articles on State Responsibility; Ago (1978), 83–5.

[98] Ago (1978), 36.

[99] See Becker (2006), 135.

against finding responsibility for a breach of the obligation of prevention. The result is a *rapprochement* between a breach of the obligation to prevent international terrorism and the obligation to refrain from acquiescing therein. Assuming that a state has the financial and human resources to diligently prevent international terrorism, a failure to do so looks very much like a deliberate choice, one that implies acquiescence in terrorist activities.[100] Such a *rapprochement* might affect the circumstances under which a state can be held responsible for a breach of its obligation to prevent international terrorism. While breach of an obligation to prevent terrorism is only occasioned by the materialization of the terrorist threat to be prevented, the obligation to abstain from acquiescing is violated irrespective of whether terrorist acts result from the host state's acquiescence. As a failure to exercise due diligence looks more and more like a breach of the prohibition of acquiescence, materialization of terrorist threats will become less and less necessary for the purposes of establishing a state's responsibility.

3.2 The obligation to extradite or submit for prosecution

The difficulty in bringing international terrorists to justice, given their transnational existence and the limits of states' jurisdiction, has long been an issue on the international community's agenda. The issue was first addressed in a multilateral setting under the auspices of the League of Nations,[101] in response to which the League adopted a terrorism suppression convention that included a somewhat ineffective obligation to extradite or prosecute.[102] Initial proposals during negotiation of the League of Nations Terrorism Convention were to make the 'extradite or prosecute' obligation mandatory and without exception, subject to the possibility of prosecution before an international criminal court created for that purpose. Such proposals were not successful, primarily because states wanted to retain the flexibility to refuse extradition on the basis of the political offence exception.[103] Extradition was therefore 'subject to any conditions and limitations recognized by the law

---

[100] This is an assumption that *should not* be made lightly. See the High Level Panel concluding that '[n]on-compliance [with terrorism prevention obligations] can be a matter of insufficient will but is more frequently a function of lack of capacity'. Report of the High Level Panel on Threats, Challenges and Change, A more secure world: our shared responsibility, UN Doc. A/59/565 (2004), para 155.

[101] See Section 6.4.1.

[102] See Arts. 8 and 9, League of Nations Convention for the Prevention and Punishment of Terrorism, adopted 16 November 1937 (never entered into force), LN Doc. C.546(I).M.383 (I).1937.V, in League of Nations Official Journal (1938), 19 [hereinafter 'League of Nations Terrorism Convention'].

[103] See League of Nations, Committee for the International Repression of Terrorism, Report to the Council adopted by the Committee on 15th January 1936, LN Doc. A.7.1936.V, Appendix III: Replies of Governments received after the First Session of the Committee (the Netherlands); League of Nations, International Repression of Terrorism, Observations by Governments on Draft Convention for the Prevention and Punishment of Terrorism; Draft Convention for the Creation of an International Criminal Court, Series I, LN Doc. A.24.1936.V (Belgium, UK, Norway, the Netherlands). See *infra* note 123 below, in reference to the availability of the political offence exception under the TSCs.

or the practice of the country to which application is made'.[104] The Convention also recognized the possibility of impunity in that it contemplated situations in which a state could not extradite a foreigner, but could not prosecute because it did not have domestic enforcement jurisdiction over offences committed abroad by foreigners.[105] In part due to the political situation in Europe in the late 1930s, the League of Nations Terrorism Convention did not receive sufficient ratifications and never entered into force.[106] This first attempt to address the difficulties in bringing international terrorists to justice has been improved upon, as the 'extradite or submit for prosecution' obligation in the TSCs is supported by an obligation to establish universal jurisdiction over defined offences.[107] But as examined below, the obligation to extradite or submit to prosecution in the TSCs is qualified by respect for a sphere of sovereign authority in regard to a state's domestic criminal regulation, which in turn affects the extent to which the TSCs ensure that there is no impunity for terrorist offences.

Each of the TSCs imposes the following obligation on states:

The State Party in the territory of which the alleged offender is found shall, if it does not extradite him, be obliged, without exception whatsoever and whether or not the offence was committed in its territory, to submit the case to its competent authorities for the purpose of prosecution [. . .].[108]

---

[104] Art. 8(4), League of Nations Terrorism Convention. See also Saul (2006), 86.

[105] Art. 10, League of Nations Terrorism Convention. See Poland's comments during negotiation of the Convention, setting out clearly the potential 'loop-holes which would make it possible for acts of terrorism to go unpunished, contrary to the intention of the Convention'. League of Nations, International Repression of Terrorism, Observations by Governments on Draft Convention for the Prevention and Punishment of Terrorism; Draft Convention for the Creation of an International Criminal Court, Series II, LN Doc. A.24(a).1936.V.

[106] Lambert (1990), 29.

[107] The Terrorism Suppression Conventions support the obligation to submit to prosecution (in default of extradition) by requiring states to establish prescriptive jurisdiction over relevant terrorist crimes—even in the absence of any other jurisdictional nexus—so that when an alleged offender is in a state's territory, but it has no other connection to the offender, victims, or offence, that state is nevertheless in a position to prosecute. The prescriptive jurisdiction states are required to establish under the TSCs and treaties like it has been qualified as 'universal jurisdiction' by the ILC (Report of the ILC on the work of its forty-eighth session, Draft Code of Offences against the Peace and Security of Mankind, UN Doc. A/51/10 (1996), Commentary to Articles 8 and 9) and in the literature (see O'Keefe (2004); Kolb (2004), 253). But Judges Higgins, Kooijmans and Buergenthal, in their Joint Separate Opinion appended to the *Arrest Warrant Case (DRC v. Belgium)*, Judgment, para 42, note that the jurisdiction states are required to establish under conventions like the TSCs (in support of the *aut dedere aut judicare* obligation) is not universal jurisdiction properly so called (which applies to pirates), but rather the 'jurisdiction to establish a territorial jurisdiction over persons for extraterritorial events'. See also Shaw (2008), 1160; Williams (1988), 91; Cassese (1989), 593; Guillaume (1989a), 350 (all qualifying the jurisdiction that states are required to establish in order to give effect to an *aut dedere aut judicare* obligation as something less than pure universal jurisdiction). But this position rather confuses the basis of prescriptive jurisdiction (which is universal in that no other connection to the crime is required, and the crime is of concern to the international community) and the condition for its exercise pursuant to an *aut dedere aut judicare* obligation (which is the existence of enforcement jurisdiction over the alleged offender). As a result, the prescriptive jurisdiction states are required to establish under the TSCs will be referred to in this book as universal jurisdiction, pure and simple.

[108] See Art. 7, Hague Convention; Art. 7, Montreal Convention; Art. 7, Internationally Protected Persons Convention; Art. 8, Hostages Convention; Art. 10, SUA Convention; Art. 8, Terrorist Bombing Convention; Art. 10, Terrorism Financing Convention; Art. 11, Nuclear Terrorism Convention. The

There is continuing debate whether there is an *aut dedere aut judicare* obligation under customary international law,[109] particularly as regards terrorist offences,[110] but no settlement of the issue.[111] This section first examines the substance of the *aut dedere aut judicare* obligation under the TSCs, before considering the impact of state immunity (if any) on performance of that obligation.

3.2.1 The substance of the *aut dedere aut judicare* obligation

While the *aut dedere aut judicare* obligation has been interpreted by the ILC's Special Rapporteur on the obligation to extradite or prosecute as an 'either/or' obligation[112] (what might be described more technically as a disjunctive compound obligation), it is in fact a conditional obligation. An 'either/or' obligation would mean that if a state does not extradite, it is under an obligation to submit to prosecution, and if it does not submit to prosecution, the state is under an

obligation is commonly shorthanded as 'extradite or prosecute' or in Latin as *aut dedere aut judicare*. While the English shorthand does not quite capture the obligation as framed in the TSCs, which do not require prosecution, but rather submission to competent authorities for the purposes of prosecution, the term 'judicare' in Latin may be sufficiently broad to cover any inquiry for the purposes of determining whether to submit to prosecution. See Bassiouni and Wise (1995), 4. This book will either describe the obligation set forth in the TSCs as an obligation to 'extradite or submit to prosecution', or adopt the Latin formulation (*aut dedere aut judicare*) which is broad enough to encompass the obligation as framed in the TSCs.

[109] For the general conclusion that *aut dedere aut judicare* is not a customary international law obligation, see *Arrest Warrant Case (DRC v. Belgium)*, Judgment, Separate Opinion of President Guillaume, para 12; ILC, Comments and information received from Governments on the obligation to extradite or prosecute (*aut dedere aut judicare*), UN Doc. A/CN.4/612 (2009), paras 31–3 (Belgium argued that the obligation to extradite or prosecute is not customary, except in reference to genocide, crimes against humanity and war crimes). The customary status of the obligation to extradite or prosecute, at least in reference to crimes against humanity, has been put to the ICJ in Belgium's Application in *Questions relating to the Obligation to Prosecute or Extradite (Belgium v. Senegal)*, but has yet to be decided by the Court. See *Questions relating to the Obligation to Prosecute or Extradite (Belgium v. Senegal)*, Provisional Measures.

[110] Taking the position that there is no customary international law *aut dedere aut judicare* obligation in reference to terrorist crimes, see Murphy (1980), 27–8; Joyner (2003), 499–500; *Lockerbie Case (Libya v. UK)*, Provisional Measures, Joint Declaration by Judges Evensen, Tarassov, Guillaume and Aguilar Mawdsley, 24. See further United Nations Global Counter-Terrorism Strategy, UNGA Resolution 60/288 (2006), Annex, in which member states of the UN resolved to (i) deny safe haven to terrorists on the basis of the principle of extradite or prosecute, (ii) ensure the apprehension and prosecution or extradition of perpetrators of terrorist acts and (iii) endeavour to conclude and implement *to that effect* extradition agreements. The implication of states agreeing that they will *endeavour* to conclude extradition treaties, in order to give effect to their resolution to ensure the apprehension and extradition or prosecution of terrorists, is that there is no obligation to extradite or prosecute in the absence of specific treaty commitments. For the opposite view, see Bassiouni (1981), 2; Perera (2004), 569; *Lockerbie Case (Libya v. UK)*, Provisional Measures, Dissenting Opinion of Judge Weeramantry, 69; UNGA, Sixth Committee, UN Doc. A/C.6/62/SR.22, para 33 (Sweden).

[111] See Galicki (2006), 12–13, paras 40–2; Galicki (2007), 8, paras 25–8; Galicki (2008), 20–1, para 98. See also UNGA, Sixth Committee, UN Doc. A/C.6/62/SR.22 (2007), para 90 (US); ILC, Comments and information received from Governments on the obligation to extradite or prosecute (*aut dedere aut judicare*), UN Doc. A/CN.4/579/Add.2 (2007), para 5 (US); UN Doc. A/CN.4/599 (2008), 14–15, paras 47–55 (Russian Federation).

[112] See Galicki (2006), para 49.

obligation to extradite.[113] But the relevant *aut dedere aut judicare* provisions in the TSCs only frame 'submit to prosecution' in the language of obligation. As explained further below, extradition under the TSCs is not an obligation—it is an option, failing exercise of which, a state is required to submit the case to prosecution.[114] A state's obligation to submit to prosecution (which is triggered by the presence of an alleged offender in its territory) is therefore conditional on non-extradition.

Where an extradition request is made, there is nothing in the formulation of the *aut dedere aut judicare* obligation in the TSCs that requires the requested state to accede thereto.[115] In fact, efforts to limit the discretionary nature of extradition were rejected during negotiation of the Hague Convention (the language of which is copied, virtually verbatim, in subsequent TSCs).[116] For instance, a state for which extradition is conditional on the existence of a treaty 'may *at its option* consider the [relevant TSC] as the legal basis for extradition'.[117] There is nothing in the language of the TSCs that limits a state's discretion in this regard. As most states do indeed condition extradition on the existence of a treaty, acceding to an extradition request will often be discretionary under the TSCs in the absence of any such treaty. Extradition is further subject to the conditions provided for by the law of the requested state.[118] Such conditions might include the absence of any immunity for the relevant conduct,[119] a requirement that the alleged offender be a non-national of the requested state,[120] and should at least include some degree of certainty that the requesting state will not torture the alleged offender.[121] The

---

[113] See Harrington (2009).

[114] See *Arrest Warrant Case (DRC v. Belgium)*, Judgment, Joint Separate Opinion of Judges Higgins, Kooijmans and Buergenthal, para 30, in reference to the version of the *aut dedere aut judicare* obligation found in the Geneva Conventions: 'But the obligation to prosecute is primary, making it even stronger'. See further Cheng (1988), 35; Kolb (2004), 257.

[115] See *Lockerbie Case (Libya v. UK)*, Provisional Measures, Joint Declaration of Judges Evensen, Tarassov, Guillaume and Aguilar Mawdsley, para 3.

[116] See, in reference to the Hague Convention, Mankiewicz (1971), 206; Cheng (1988), 33–41.

[117] See Art. 8(2), Hague Convention; Art. 8(2), Montreal Convention; Art. 8(2), Internationally Protected Persons Convention; Art. 10(2), Hostages Convention; Art. 11(2), SUA Convention; Art. 9(2), Terrorist Bombing Convention; Art. 11(2), Terrorism Financing Convention; Art. 13(2), Nuclear Terrorism Convention.

[118] See Arts. 8(2) and 8(3), Hague Convention; Arts. 8(2) and 8(3), Montreal Convention; Arts. 8(2) and 8(3), Internationally Protected Persons Convention; Arts. 10(2) and 10(3), Hostages Convention; Arts. 11(2) and 11(3), SUA Convention; Arts. 9(2) and 9(3), Terrorist Bombing Convention; Arts. 11(2) and 11 (3), Terrorism Financing Convention; Arts. 13(2) and 13(3), Nuclear Terrorism Convention.

[119] See Section 3.2.2.

[120] This restriction was of relevance in the *Lockerbie Case* discussed below and is often invoked as a basis for refusing to extradite persons accused of terrorist crimes. For instance, a US–Yemeni citizen, prosecuted in Yemen for his role in bombing the French tanker 'Limburg' off the coast of Yemen in October 2002 (see Keesing's, Vol. 48, October 2002, 45070 for details of the bombing) was also charged with terrorism-related offences in the US, but could not be extradited to the US because Yemeni law forbids extradition of nationals. Keesing's, Vol. 54, May 2008, 48611.

[121] States are prohibited from expelling, returning or extraditing ('refouler') a person to another state where there are substantial grounds for believing that he would be in danger of being subjected to torture. Art. 3, Convention against Torture and other Cruel, Inhuman or Degrading Treatment or Punishment, 10 December 1984, 1465 UNTS [hereinafter the 'Torture Convention']; Art. 33(1), Refugee Convention (considered to be a rule of customary international law by the UNHCR, *Advisory Opinion on the Extraterritorial Application of Non-Refoulement Obligations under the 1951 Convention relating to the Status of Refugees and its 1967 Protocol*, para 15); Art. 7, International Covenant on Civil

TSCs negotiated after 1997 further support the discretion to extradite by stipulating that:

[n]othing in this Convention shall be interpreted as imposing an obligation to [. . .] extradite [. . .] if the requested State Party has substantial grounds for believing that the request for extradition [. . .] has been made for the purposes of prosecuting or punishing a person on account of that person's race, religion, nationality, ethnic origin or political opinion or that compliance with the request would cause prejudice to that person's position for any of these reasons.[122]

In any event, a restriction on a state's discretion to refuse extradition cannot be presumed absent express language in the relevant Convention.[123] It would therefore be incorrect to characterize the *aut dedere aut judicare* formulation in the TSCs as placing a state under an *obligation* to extradite. A requested state *may* extradite, but is never required to do so, and the terms of the TSCs recognize the full scope of a requested state's discretion. But where a state refuses to extradite, for whatever reason, it is thereby placed in the same position as a custodial state to which no extradition request has been made—it is under an obligation to submit the case to its competent authorities for prosecution.

Notwithstanding the above, the 'either/or' formulation of the *aut dedere aut judicare* obligation has been put to the ICJ in an application filed by Belgium

---

and Political Rights, 19 December 1996, 999 UNTS 171 (as interpreted by the UN Office of the High Commissioner for Human Rights, General Comment No. 20, para 9).

[122]   See Art. 12, Terrorist Bombing Convention; Art. 15, Terrorism Financing Convention; Art. 16, Nuclear Terrorism Convention; Art. 11*ter*, 2005 Protocol to the SUA Convention; Art. 8*ter*, 2010 Protocol to the Hague Convention; Art. 8*ter*, Beijing Convention. Starting from 2005, the relevant provisions added 'gender' to the list of prohibited purposes.

[123]   One of the conditions provided for by domestic law to which extradition is often subject, of particular relevance in the terrorism context, is the political offence exception. Only the Terrorist Bombing Convention, Terrorism Financing Convention, Nuclear Terrorism Convention, 2005 Protocol to the SUA Convention, and 2010 Protocol to the Hague Convention and Beijing Convention (both adopted on 10 September 2010 and not yet in force) expressly prohibit a refusal to extradite 'on the sole ground that it concerns a political offence', but do not otherwise limit a state's discretion in refusing extradition. There is nothing in the language of the other TSCs to suggest that states should be limited in their invocation of the political offence exception as a basis for refusing to extradite. Indeed, the ICAO Legal Committee, in considering potential amendments to the Hague and Montreal Conventions, noted that some of the other TSCs contain provisions that prohibit invocation of the political offence exception, and proposed that an explicit provision to that effect should be included in any amendment to the ICAO TSCs. See ICAO Assembly, 36th Session, Legal Committee, Acts or Offences of Concern to the International Aviation Community and Not Covered by Existing Air Law Instruments, ICAO Doc. A36-WP/12, LE/4 (2007), para 2.1.3.3. This proposal, which has in fact been adopted in the 2010 Protocol to the Hague Convention and Beijing Convention, suggests that the availability of the political offence exception was not limited in any way by the *aut dedere aut judicare* obligation as framed in the Montreal and Hague Conventions (which served as the model for subsequent TSCs). During negotiations of the draft comprehensive terrorism suppression convention, Sweden (on behalf of the Nordic countries) noted that 'any prohibition against applying national law to extradition, such as prohibition of the political offence exception, a common feature in recent anti-terrorist instruments, *must be clearly expressed* in the instrument and could not be deduced from the general nature of the obligation'. Emphasis added. UNGA, Sixth Committee, UN Doc. A/C.6/62/SR.22 (2007).

against Senegal. Belgium's Application to the Court invokes (in part) Senegal's responsibility for a breach of its *aut dedere aut judicare* obligation under the Torture Convention.[124] Belgium made a request to Senegal for the extradition of former Chadian President Hissène Habré, who has been indicted in Belgium for torture and crimes against humanity he allegedly committed in Chad during the term of his presidency. Belgium has argued that its request for Mr Habré's extradition 'confers a specific right upon [Belgium] to see Senegal prosecute Mr Habré or, failing that, to obtain his extradition in accordance with Article 7 of the [Torture] Convention'.[125] In framing the *aut dedere aut judicare* obligation in these terms, Belgium is effectively arguing that it is a disjunctive compound obligation, emphasizing the second part of the disjunction: if Senegal does not prosecute, it is under an obligation to extradite.[126] Senegal, on the other hand, argues that the *aut dedere aut judicare* obligation to which it is subject can only confer a right on other state parties to demand extradition (to be distinguished from a right to have their request acceded to)—and that the right to demand extradition cannot prevail over the right of a state that takes on its obligation to hold a trial.[127] The Court has yet to decide the matter, but considered Belgium's interpretation of the *aut dedere aut judicare* obligation as 'plausible' at the Provisional Measures stage of the proceedings.[128] The Committee against Torture ('CAT') has similarly held, in response to an individual complaint filed against Senegal in relation to Habré's prosecution, that Senegal's refusal to extradite *to Belgium*, in a situation where it had decided not to prosecute Habré, amounted to a breach of the *aut dedere aut judicare* obligation under the Torture Convention.[129] Neither the ICJ nor CAT tie their conclusion to the specific facts of the case—but an interpretation of the Torture Convention which imposes an obligation to extradite to a particular state (or at all) is not convincing. Extradition under the Torture Convention, like under the TSCs, is subject to the conditions provided by the law of the requested state and to general international law.[130] As a result, extradition to a particular state may well be

---

[124] *Questions relating to the Obligation to Prosecute or Extradite (Belgium v. Senegal)*, Application, paras 7–8. The *aut dedere aut judicare* obligation in the Torture Convention is framed in similar terms to that in the TSCs.

[125] *Questions relating to the Obligation to Prosecute or Extradite (Belgium v. Senegal)*, Provisional Measures, para 58.

[126] See Harrington (2009).

[127] *Questions relating to the Obligation to Prosecute or Extradite (Belgium v. Senegal)*, Provisional Measures, para 59.

[128] *Ibid*, para 60. The Court did not make it clear whether it considered Belgium's claim to have a 'specific right' to see Senegal prosecute Mr Habré, to obtain his extradition, or both, to be a plausible interpretation of the Torture Convention. But Belgium almost certainly does not have a 'right' to Habré's extradition (as Senegal cannot be said to be under an obligation to extradite him), and it is not clear why Belgium would have any specific right to see Habré prosecuted—which is an obligation *erga omnes* and in which Belgium would have the same interest as other states party to the Torture Convention. As the Court's decision is only a *prima facie* determination of the existence of a dispute between the parties, it may well revisit the plausibility of Belgium's interpretation.

[129] *Guengueng et al. v. Senegal* (Committee against Torture, 2001), para 9.9.

[130] See Art. 8, Torture Convention; Arts. 8(2) and 8(3), Hague Convention; Arts. 8(2) and 8(3), Montreal Convention; Arts. 8(2) and 8(3), Internationally Protected Persons Convention; Hostages Convention, Arts. 10(2) and 10(3); Arts. 11(2) and 11(3), SUA Convention; Arts. 9(2) and 9(3),

precluded by the requested state's national law or indeed by the *jus cogens* norm of non-refoulement—and such a result is contemplated by the way in which the *aut dedere aut judicare* obligation is framed. Given the discretion built into the extradition provisions of the Torture Convention (and the TSCs), states cannot be said to be under an obligation to extradite. This is particularly true given that the capacity to extradite will often depend on matters beyond the custodial state's control—including whether there is any extradition request to accede to or whether requesting states are states that will not engage in torture. If Senegal refuses to prosecute Habré, it is not thereby under an *obligation* to extradite him to Belgium—even though extraditing Habré to Belgium (given it is the only extradition request that has been made) will be the only way for Senegal to comply with its *aut dedere aut judicare* obligation under the Torture Convention.

States that cannot (or will not) extradite to requesting states, but fail to *effectively* submit a case for prosecution, will therefore be in breach of their *aut dedere aut judicare* obligation. CAT held that if there was insufficient evidence to prosecute, a refusal to do so (even in the absence of an extradition request to which the requesting state accedes) would not amount to a breach of the *aut dedere aut judicare* obligation.[131] While the decision does not suggest that if there *is* sufficient evidence, a refusal to prosecute *will* amount to a breach of the *aut dedere aut judicare* obligation, it does suggest that a decision not to prosecute must be justifiable on objective grounds.[132] The obligation to extradite or submit to prosecution must also be interpreted as subject to a good faith test of effective compliance.[133] This was one of the issues raised in the *Lockerbie Case*. Libya had no extradition treaties with the US or UK, was prohibited under its domestic law from extraditing absent such a treaty, and its domestic law precluded the extradition of Libyan nationals. As a result, Libya would not extradite the two accused to the US or the UK.[134] Nor was it required to do so under the Montreal Convention. But the US and UK did not consider Libya to have a right to prosecute under the Montreal Convention on the basis of its alleged complicity in the very act it

---

Terrorist Bombing Convention; Arts. 11(2) and 11(3), Terrorism Financing Convention; Arts. 13(2) and 3(3), Nuclear Terrorism Convention.

[131] *Guengueng et al. v. Senegal* (Committee against Torture, 2001), para 9.8.

[132] This seems to have been the position taken by the Dutch courts in reference to a suit against the Dutch Public Prosecutor claiming a failure to abide by the *aut dedere aut judicare* obligation under the Torture Convention (in this case, a failure to extradite or prosecute General Pinochet who was visiting Amsterdam). The Courts held that the Dutch Public Prosecutor was within his rights to refuse to prosecute given that (i) Pinochet might be entitled to immunity, and (ii) any evidence that might form the basis of a prosecution would be in Chile, and the Netherlands had no cooperative arrangements with Chile in reference to criminal proceedings. See *Chili Komitee Nederland (CKN, Dutch branch of the Chile Committee) v. Public Prosecutor*, the Netherlands (Court of Appeal of Amsterdam, 4 January 1995), 28 Netherlands Yearbook of International Law (1997) 363.

[133] The obligation to exercise a right in good faith is related to the doctrine of 'abus de droit' in international law. See Cheng (1953). See also Politis (1925); Kiss (1953), 193–6; Ago (1970), paras 48–9. On the principle of good faith generally in international law, see Goodwin-Gill (2004); Kolb (2006).

[134] *Lockerbie Case (Libya v. UK)*, Application, 3–5.

proposed to prosecute.[135] To allow for such a right, at the complicit state's option, was considered to undermine the very purpose of the Montreal Convention— which was to ensure the effective prosecution of acts of international terrorism against civil aviation.[136] The *Lockerbie Case* was settled before the merits phase of the proceedings. But had the Court accepted that the right to opt for submitting a case to prosecution (over extradition) under the TSCs cannot be exercised if it would amount to a colourable attempt to shield an accused from genuine criminal responsibility,[137] *and* that Libya's *bona fide* was subject to doubt, there would have been very little that Libya could have done, short of changing its domestic law applicable to extradition, to meet its *aut dedere aut judicare* obligation under the Montreal Convention. Given that the good faith issue only arises incidentally when a significantly more serious breach of international law is alleged, in particular sponsorship or support for international terrorism, the state responsibility issue that really needed resolution was Libya's responsibility for the Lockerbie bombing. Absent a determination of Libya's responsibility for the act of terrorism itself, there could be nothing objectionable in its opting to prosecute its nationals.

The issue of effective prosecution is also raised in a somewhat different form in the ongoing *Belgium v. Senegal* proceedings. Senegal claims that it cannot extradite to Belgium[138] and that it intends to submit Mr Habré's case to its prosecutorial authorities on receipt of €27.4 million in international funding for all the costs of a trial.[139] The obligation to submit to prosecution, however, is an obligation of

---

[135] *Lockerbie Case (Libya v. UK)*, Provisional Measures, Oral Proceedings, CR 1992/3 (1991), 22; *Lockerbie Case (Libya v. US)*, Provisional Measures, Oral Proceedings, CR 1992/4 (1991), 62.

[136] Some commentators have argued that the Security Council's adoption of Resolution 748 (1992) in support of the US and UK's demand that Libya surrender the two accused parties for trial suggests that the Council did not consider the Montreal Convention, and its *aut dedere aut judicare* obligation, to be workable in circumstances of alleged custodial state complicity. See Plachta (2001), 129; Joyner and Rothbaum (1992), 254; Morris (2004), 65.

[137] That the obligation to submit to prosecution must be exercised in good faith, as a genuine effort to bring alleged terrorists to justice (rather than in a colourable attempt to shield them from responsibility) is implicit in the general purpose of the TSCs—to ensure that there is no impunity (or safe havens) for terrorist crimes (see UNSG Report on measures to prevent international terrorism, UN Doc. A/51/336 (1996), para 17).

[138] Senegalese courts have considered Belgium's extradition request, but have held that they lack jurisdiction to rule on Belgium's request in virtue of Habré's state immunity, resulting from his former head of state status. See *Guengueng et al. v. Senegal* (Committee against Torture, 2001), para 9.4. On immunity as a procedural bar to prosecution, see Section 3.2.2.

[139] Human Rights Watch, 'AU: Push Senegal to Try Habré', 29 June 2009, <http://www.hrw.org/en/news/2009/06/29/au-push-senegal-try-habr>. Senegal first indicted Mr Habré in 2000, but apparent political intervention (see Keesing's, Vol. 46, July 2000, 43660) and Senegal's failure to establish jurisdiction over extra-territorial torture, in breach of its obligations under the Torture Convention (*Guengueng et al. v. Senegal* (Committee against Torture, 2001), paras 3.2–3.7), resulted in Senegalese courts holding that they had no jurisdiction to try the case. Following a decision by the African Union that Habré should be prosecuted in Senegal 'on behalf of Africa' (Human Rights Watch, 'AU: Push Senegal to Try Habré', 29 June 2009), Senegal amended its domestic legislation (retroactively) to provide for universal jurisdiction over crimes against humanity committed abroad (Keesing's, Vol. 54, April 2008, 48511), and now claims it is prepared to prosecute if it receives international assistance in paying for the trial.

result, not due diligence,[140] and financial difficulty in meeting an obligation of result will not generally amount to a circumstance precluding wrongfulness.[141]

In the final analysis, the *aut dedere aut judicare* obligation in the TSCs requires states to submit a case to their competent authorities for prosecution in default of a decision to extradite to a requesting state, and competent authorities must take their decision in the same manner as in the case of any other offence of a grave nature. At the very least, this will require a good faith intention to effectively implement the criminal law enforcement obligations of the TSCs. CAT jurisprudence and general principles of international law further suggest that a refusal to prosecute must be justifiable on the basis of objective reasons (for instance, insufficient evidence or the applicability of immunity, as discussed below). Insufficiency of evidence will be particularly relevant in the terrorism context given the nature of the conduct and the secrecy with which it is generally carried out. And as acts of terrorism are often planned and prepared for in a state other than that in which they are carried out, there may equally be difficulties in securing foreign state assistance in gathering evidence.[142] By framing the obligation in terms of the general practice of the custodial state, there is certainly room for competent authorities to refuse to prosecute in a way that is compliant with the *aut dedere aut*

---

[140] See Section 3.1.2 above, discussing resource incapacity in reference to obligations of diligent prevention.

[141] But see *Gabčíkovo–Nagymaros (Hungary v. Slovakia)*, Judgment, para 102, noting that states recognize that financial difficulties might preclude the wrongfulness of non-performance by a party of its treaty obligations. While this may be the case in respect of obligations of due diligence (see Section 3.1.2), it will not generally be the case in respect of obligations of result. In respect of obligations of result, financial difficulties will not amount to *force majeur* (see *Sempra Energy International v. Argentine Republic* (ICSID, 2007), para 246, in reference to the Argentinean economic crisis; see also *Serbian Loans (France v. Serbia)*, Judgment, 39–40; *Brazilian Loans (France v. Brazil)*, Judgment, para 271, both in reference to the payment of debts), nor will they meet the conditions of distress. Finally, financial difficulties (even those amounting to impending economic collapse) will not meet the conditions for necessity as a circumstance precluding wrongfulness given that breaching a particular obligation (owing to how expensive meeting the obligation is) will rarely be the *only way* to safeguard an essential interest. See *CMS Gas v. Argentina*, (ICSID, 2005), para 324 (also in reference to the Argentinean economic crisis). In arriving at its conclusion, the ICSID Tribunal relied on the Commentary to Article 25 of the ILC Articles on State Responsibility to the effect that the plea of necessity is 'excluded if there are other (otherwise lawful) means available, *even if they may be more costly or less convenient*' (emphasis added).

[142] The TSCs require state parties to afford one another assistance in connection with investigations or criminal or extradition proceedings in respect of offences defined under the Conventions, including assistance in obtaining evidence necessary for any such proceedings, *but* the obligation is subject to mutual legal assistance treaty arrangements or domestic legal restrictions. See Art. 10, Hague Convention; Art. 10, Montreal Convention; Art. 10, Internationally Protected Persons Convention; Art. 11, Hostages Convention; Art. 12, SUA Convention; Art. 10, Terrorist Bombing Convention; Art. 12, Terrorism Financing Convention; Art. 14, Nuclear Terrorism Convention; Art. 10, Beijing Convention (not yet in force). See further *The Chili Komitee Nederland (CKN, Dutch branch of the Chile Committee) v. Public Prosecutor*, the Netherlands (Court of Appeal of Amsterdam, 1995), reported in 28 Netherlands Yearbook of International Law (1997) 363, 364 (in which the Court of Appeal upheld the Public Prosecutor's decision not to prosecute former President Pinochet of Chile for torture, as such a prosecution would be 'illusory' because virtually all evidence would be in Chile and the Netherlands did not have a treaty with Chile requiring mutual criminal assistance. The provision for mutual criminal assistance in the Torture Convention, like those in the TSCs, is subject to conditions in any treaties between state parties).

judicare obligation.[143] Given that states are under no obligation to grant a request for extradition under the TSCs, the freedom afforded states in prosecutorial decisions potentially undermines the 'no impunity' objective of the *aut dedere aut judicare* obligation.[144]

3.2.2 Immunity of state officials from foreign criminal proceedings

A further factor that might limit the effectiveness of the *aut dedere aut judicare* obligation in the TSCs is the potential applicability of state immunity from prosecutions, considered below. A state's obligation to submit a case to its competent authorities for the purposes of prosecution under the TSCs is 'without exception whatsoever'.[145] The phrase was first agreed to during negotiation of the Hague Convention as a compromise, to replace proposed language 'whatever the motive for the offence'.[146] Given the identity of hijackers in the 1970s (principally dissident non-state actors),[147] both phrases contemplated refusals to prosecute non-state actors on the basis of the political character of their offence. All subsequently negotiated TSCs adopted the compromise language 'without exception whatsoever' in framing the obligation to submit a case to prosecution. The TSCs do not make any reference to state immunity and therefore do not address whether 'without exception' is intended to qualify the international law of state immunity that might otherwise apply to prosecutions. But given the focus on non-state actors committing political offences during negotiation of the Hague Convention, it is clear that states did not initially contemplate the possibility of prosecuting persons acting on behalf of a state. To the extent that silence on the question of state immunity is interpreted as non-regulation,[148] the *aut dedere aut judicare* obligation in the TSCs should be interpreted consistently with general international law,[149] including the law of state immunity where (and only where) it imposes an obligation on a state not to exercise its adjudicative and enforcement jurisdiction.[150] As a result, one reason a state's prosecutorial authorities might

---

[143] See Kolb (2004), 261.

[144] See Cheng (1988), 37.

[145] See Art. 7, Hague Convention; Art. 7, Montreal Convention; Art. 7, Internationally Protected Persons Convention; Art. 8, Hostages Convention; Art. 10, SUA Convention; Art. 8, Terrorist Bombing Convention; Art. 10, Terrorism Financing Convention; Art. 11, Nuclear Terrorism Convention.

[146] See ICAO, International Conference on Private Air Law (1970–1971), Sixteenth Meeting of the Commission of the Whole (11 December 1970), paras 4–10, 21; ICAO, International Conference on Private Air Law (1970–1971), Tenth Plenary Meeting (14 December 1970), paras 7–21 and 47.

[147] See A.E. Evans (1978).

[148] On whether state parties to the TSCs have impliedly waived state immunity in reference to crimes defined in the Conventions, on the basis of the treaty interpretation principle of effectiveness, see Section 3.2.1.

[149] See Orakhelashvili (2008), 375–6.

[150] See Draft Declaration on Rights and Duties of States, UNGA Resolution 375 (1949), Annex, Art. 2: 'Every State has the right to exercise jurisdiction over its territory and over all persons and things therein, subject to the immunities recognized by international law'. See further Sinclair (1980), 199: 'immunity can be defined jurisprudentially as the correlative of a duty imposed upon the territorial State to refrain from exercising its jurisdiction over a foreign State'.

refuse to prosecute or a Court may refuse to proceed with the prosecution[151] is that the relevant actor is either: (i) absolutely immune from the criminal jurisdiction of the custodial and forum state (immunity *ratione personae*);[152] or (ii) the actor is an official of a foreign state, carried out the acts in question in his official capacity, and the custodial state is bound to recognize that the acts are not subject to its criminal jurisdiction on the basis of the foreign state's immunity (immunity *ratione materiae*),[153] each as discussed more fully below. Immunity is therefore relevant to the question of state responsibility for breach of the TSCs in so far as it might qualify the obligation to submit a case to competent authorities for prosecution. To the extent that international law *requires* a prosecuting state to give effect to the immunity of the accused,[154] refusing to prosecute that offender (even in the absence of extradition) cannot be in breach of the *aut dedere aut judicare* obligation.[155]

The issue of immunity from criminal jurisdiction assumes that the custodial state has established its jurisdiction over the relevant terrorist offence[156] (as required by the TSCs) and arises only in the context of a custodial state's obligation to submit a case involving a *foreign national* to its competent authorities for the purposes of prosecution. Domestic public law that precludes the prosecution of a state's own nationals (perhaps because of their status, for instance head of state or other members of the executive branch) will not be examined in this section. The point should be made, however, that where the custodial state (being also the state of nationality) cannot extradite, such a domestic law may well put the state in breach of its *aut dedere aut judicare* obligations under the TSCs.[157] If a head of state or other high ranking official is immune from prosecution in his own state for an

---

[151] Prosecutorial authorities and national courts must consider the question of immunity 'as a preliminary issue to be expeditiously decided in *limine litis*'. See *Differences Relating to Immunity*, Advisory Opinion, para 67. See also Fox (2008), 29.

[152] See generally Kolodkin (2008), 37–8; ILC, Memorandum by the Secretariat on immunity of State officials from foreign criminal jurisdiction, UN Doc. A/CN.4/596 (2008), paras 94–153, for a discussion of immunity *ratione personae*.

[153] See generally Kolodkin (2008), 37–8; ILC, Memorandum by the Secretariat on immunity of State officials from foreign criminal jurisdiction, UN Doc. A/CN.4/596 (2008), paras 154–212 for a discussion of immunity *ratione materiae*. See also *Certain Questions Concerning Mutual Assistance in Criminal Matters (Djibouti v. France)*, Judgment, para 170.

[154] There is some debate in the literature as to whether foreign state immunity is opposable against domestic courts as a matter of right (to the extent of the accepted scope of that immunity at international law), or whether it is accorded at the discretion of the forum court. *Infra* note 174. The better view is that states are required, as a matter of international law, to hold foreign states immune from the jurisdiction of their domestic courts.

[155] As states are not under an *obligation* to extradite foreign nationals under the TSCs, and can refuse to extradite on the basis of domestic law (including the law of state immunity as incorporated), this section will not examine immunity as it applies to extradition requests. The analysis applicable to the question of prosecution, however, applied *mutatis mutandis* to questions of extradition, as requested states will not extradite if the accused is immune from prosecution. In any event, extradition (other than to the state of nationality of the accused) is to no effect, as any requesting states would equally be barred from prosecuting on the basis of the accused's immunity (assuming the state of nationality asserts immunity in respect of any such foreign prosecution).

[156] See *Arrest Warrant Case (DRC v. Belgium)*, Judgment, para 46. See also *Arrest Warrant Case (DRC v. Belgium)*, Judgment, Joint Separate Opinion of Judges Higgins, Kooijmans and Buergenthal, para 3.

[157] See Cassese (2003), 273–4.

act of terrorism committed abroad,[158] and cannot be extradited in virtue of his nationality, it is likely to be the more serious breach of international law—in particular the sponsorship of an act of international terrorism—that attracts attention and pressure for resolution.

(i) *Immunity* ratione personae *and* ratione materiae

Immunity *ratione personae* is absolute but temporally limited. It is absolute in the sense that it extends to acts performed by a state official in both an official and a private capacity, both before and while occupying his post, and temporally limited in that it begins when a state official takes up a post to which immunity *ratione personae* attaches, and ends when that official ceases to serve in that post.[159] It is widely accepted that immunity *ratione personae* attaches to the post of head of state[160] and head of government.[161] Slightly more controversial is the ICJ's extension of immunity *ratione personae* to ministers of foreign affairs based on a functional analysis,[162] and the English courts' extension of that extension to ministers of defence and ministers for commerce and international trade.[163]

For as long as absolute immunity attaches to a particular person in virtue of his position, there is no question of determining whether an act of terrorism carried out by such person is 'official' or 'private'—immunity attaches irrespective of the character of the conduct.[164] Were an acting head of state or head of government (and perhaps a minister of foreign affairs or a minister of defence) alleged to be responsible for an act of terrorism falling within the scope of one of the TSCs, a foreign custodial state could not be held to be in breach of its *aut dedere aut judicare*

---

[158] The TSCs do not apply to acts of terrorism committed within a single state if the terrorist actor and victims of the terrorist act are nationals of that state and the alleged offender is found in the territory of that state. *Supra* Chapter 1, notes 109–11, and accompanying text.

[159] See Fox (2008), 666; Kolodkin (2008), para 79. The ICJ has described the immunity as 'full immunity from criminal jurisdiction and inviolability'. *Certain Questions Concerning Mutual Assistance in Criminal Matters (Djibouti v. France)*, Judgment, para 170; *Arrest Warrant Case (DRC v. Belgium)*, Judgment, para 54. See also *Affaire Gaddafi,* France (Cassation Criminelle, 13 March 2001), 125 International Law Reports 456; *Mugabe Case*, England (Magistrates' Court, 14 January 2004), reported in Warbrick (2004), 770.

[160] See e.g. *Affaire Gaddafi,* France (Cassation Criminelle, 2001); *Mugabe Case*, England (Magistrates' Court, 2004); *Regina v. Bartle and the Commissioner of Police for the Metropolis and Others Ex Parte Pinochet ('Pinochet (no. 3)')*, UK (House of Lords, 24 March 1999), [2000] 1 AC 147.

[161] See e.g. *Arrest Warrant Case (DRC v. Belgium)*, Judgment, para 51; *H.S.A. et al. v. S.A. et al.*, Belgium (Cour de Cassation, 12 February 2003), 42 International Legal Materials (2003), 596.

[162] The Court based its reasoning on whether the immunity was necessary for the effective performance of the minister's official functions on behalf of the state he represented. See *Arrest Warrant Case (DRC v. Belgium)*, Judgment, paras 53–4. But see *Arrest Warrant Case (DRC v. Belgium)*, Judgment, Dissenting Opinion of Judge *ad hoc* Van den Wyngaert, paras 10–21, holding that there is no rule of international law extending immunity *ratione personae* to ministers of foreign affairs (even though comity and political wisdom might dictate such a result). See further *Arrest Warrant Case (DRC v. Belgium)*, Judgment, Dissenting Opinion of Judge Al-Khasawneh, para 4; Kamto (2002); Wouters (2003).

[163] See *Re General Shaul Mofaz*, England (Magistrates' Court, 12 February 2004), reported in Warbrick (2004) 771; *Re Bo Xilai*, England (Magistrates' Court, 8 November 2005), 128 International Law Reports 713.

[164] See *Arrest Warrant Case (DRC v. Belgium)*, Judgment, para 55.

obligation if it refused to prosecute (or extradite) the accused on the basis of his absolute immunity from its criminal jurisdiction. The International Court of Justice has said as much in reference to Belgium's proposed prosecution of the Congolese minister of foreign affairs for war crimes and crimes against humanity:

Thus, although various international conventions on the prevention and punishment of certain serious crimes impose on States obligations of prosecution or extradition, thereby requiring them to extend their criminal jurisdiction, such extension of jurisdiction in no way affects immunities under customary international law [. . .]. These remain opposable before the courts of a foreign State, even where those courts exercise such a jurisdiction under these conventions.[165]

State immunity *ratione materiae*, however, is more complicated, particularly in its application to the prosecution of offences defined under international law and in international conventions. Immunity *ratione materiae* attaches to the conduct of state officials acting in their official capacity. There is general consensus that the conduct of *de jure* organs[166] and persons empowered by domestic law to exercise elements of governmental authority,[167] each as acting in exercise of official functions, should be covered by immunity *ratione materiae*. And while there is some suggestion in the literature[168] and domestic jurisprudence[169] that immunity *ratione materiae* should be determined in reference to the principles of attribution in the international law of state responsibility, there is no state practice of a state claiming immunity for the conduct of non-state actors that it instructed or controlled, whose conduct would be attributable to the state.[170] This is no doubt because claiming such immunity would amount to an admission of attributability[171] and the very

---

[165] *Arrest Warrant Case (DRC v. Belgium)*, Judgment, para 59.

[166] See Art. 4, ILC Articles on State Responsibility. See also Lord Browne-Wilkinson's speech in *Pinochet (no. 3)*, UK (House of Lords, 1999): '[i]mmunity *ratione materiae* applies not only to ex-heads of state and ex-ambassadors but to all state officials who have been involved in carrying out the functions of the state'.

[167] See Art. 5, ILC Articles on State Responsibility. Persons empowered to exercise elements of governmental authority need not be *de jure* organs, since states are entitled to organise their internal affairs as they see fit. See *Blaškić* (ICTY-95-14-A), para 41.

[168] See e.g. Whomersley (1992), 857; Tomonori (2001), 275; Kolodkin (2008), para 108.

[169] See e.g. Lord Hoffmann's speech in *Jones v. Saudi Arabia*, UK (House of Lords, 14 June 2006), [2006] UKHL 26, para 74: 'It has now been generally assumed that the circumstances in which a state will be liable for the act of an official in international law mirror the circumstances in which the official will be immune in foreign domestic law. There is a logic in this assumption: if there is a remedy against the state before an international tribunal, there should not also be a remedy against the official himself in a domestic tribunal. The cases and other materials on state liability make it clear that the state is liable for acts done under colour of public authority, whether or not they are actually authorized or lawful under domestic or international law'. It bears noting that the *Jones v. Saudi Arabia* case was not a criminal, but a civil proceeding. As a result, the concurrence of state responsibility and individual civil responsibility for the same conduct could result in doubling up on reparations, which appears to be one of the driving forces behind Lord Hoffmann's suggestion that attribution should be co-extensive with immunity *ratione materiae*. The same concern would not apply to concurrent state responsibility and individual criminal responsibility.

[170] Art. 8, ILC Articles on State Responsibility. See also Section 2.2.1.

[171] The ICJ's statement in *Certain Questions of Mutual Assistance in Criminal Matters (Djibouti v. France)*, Judgment, para 196 ('[T]he State notifying a foreign court that judicial process should not

point of using non-state actors (at least in the international terrorism context) will be an attempt to secure plausible deniability.[172] Beyond cases of non-state actors, the extent to which state immunity should be co-extensive with state responsibility is unsettled, as examined below.

(ii) The relationship between immunity ratione materiae and attribution

Immunity *ratione materiae* is often treated as derivative of the state's immunity because any proceeding against a state official acting in his official capacity is considered to be a proceeding against the state itself.[173] On the basis of their sovereign equality, states are immune from foreign domestic adjudicative and enforcement jurisdiction,[174] at least in so far as the proceedings touch on their exercise of sovereign authority.[175] As a result, state officials acting in their official capacity are immune from the jurisdiction of foreign courts in order to ensure that proceedings against officials are not used as an indirect means of accomplishing that which cannot be accomplished directly.[176] If proceeding against an individual is to be the equivalent of proceeding against the state itself (thereby engaging the state's immunity from which the individual state official benefits), then attribution must be a necessary condition of immunity. The question remains, however, whether attribution is a sufficient condition for immunity. To the extent that it is so, state

proceed, for reasons of immunity, against its State organs, is assuming responsibility for any internationally wrongful act in issue committed by such organs') should apply in principle to the conduct of non-state actors.

[172] See Section 2.2.2.

[173] See *Certain Questions of Mutual Assistance in Criminal Matters (Djibouti v. France)*, Judgment, paras 187–8. See also *Propend Finance v. Sing*, England (Court of Appeal, 17 April 1997), 111 International Law Reports 611, 669, holding that immunity affords individual officials of a foreign state 'protection under the same cloak as protects the state itself'.

[174] This principle has long been recognized in international law. See e.g. *The Parlement Belge*, England (Probate, Divorce and Admiralty Division), [1880] 5 PD 197, 217. See also Sucharitkul (1976), 117. More recently, see *Pinochet (no. 3)*, UK (House of Lords, 1999), 201 (per Lord Browne-Wilkinson), 268–9 (per Lord Millett). Some theorists have argued that state immunity is not a consequential right of sovereignty, characterizing immunity instead as a self-imposed limitation on the forum state's territorial jurisdiction (such territorial jurisdiction being the dominant principle of international law in this regard). See Sinclair (1980), 215; Caplan (2003). But see Fox (2008), 18–23, arguing convincingly that the weight of practice suggests that states do not consider immunity to be a discretionary limitation that they self-apply to their adjudicative and enforcement jurisdiction. Instead, states consider immunity to be a binding limitation on jurisdiction as a matter of international law.

[175] The doctrine of restrictive immunity (which limits immunity to a state's exercise of its sovereign power—*jure imperii*) is a relatively new development in international law. While accepted by a large segment of the international community (see Fox (2008), 415), the doctrine is not universally accepted (see Brownlie (2008), 330). As the conduct that falls outside the scope of *jure imperii* (and outside the scope of immunity) is often defined in reference to commercial transactions, and is therefore irrelevant in regard to terrorist conduct, whether immunity is absolute or restrictive is not strictly relevant for present purposes.

[176] See *Propend Finance v. Sing*, England (Court of Appeal, 1997), 669, holding that any applicable immunity regarding sovereign functions would be rendered illusory if 'officers . . . could be sued as individuals for matters of State conduct regarding which the State they were serving had immunity'.

responsibility and state immunity will be co-extensive, and there will be no possibility of concurrent responsibility.

A principle which suggests that attribution is a sufficient condition for immunity, advanced in connection with immunity *ratione materiae*, was first articulated in reference to the McLeod incident in 1840:[177]

an individual forming part of a public force, and acting under the authority of his Government, is not to be held answerable, as a private trespasser or malefactor [...]. [T]he act becomes one for which the State to which he belongs is [...] alone responsible [...].[178]

This principle (the 'McLeod principle') is one of non-concurrence of responsibility[179] to the effect that when a state is responsible for conduct, the individual acting on behalf of the state will not be. The principle certainly explains immunity *ratione materiae* in the context of civil proceedings, given that a damages award against an individual official may well duplicate reparations owed by the responsible state, and proceeding against a state official is a colourable attempt to circumvent the immunity of the state in domestic fora. It is not clear, however, whether (and to what extent) the principle should reflect application of immunity *ratione materiae* in domestic criminal proceedings given the different purposes of criminal and delictual responsibility—particularly in the present day context discussed further below. That said, the principle was first formulated in reference to criminal proceedings, and is today reframed as a substantive defence to criminal charges that a state official is entitled to invoke in foreign domestic proceedings,[180]

---

[177] During the Mackenzie Rebellion against the British in Upper Canada (present day Ontario), Canadian rebels occupied an island in the Niagara river on which they were supplied and reinforced by Americans (using the 'Caroline' steamboat) who sympathized with their cause. In order to prevent the 'Caroline' being used to reinforce the Canadian rebels, British soldiers crossed into American territory and destroyed the 'Caroline', setting it alight and adrift to crash over Niagara Falls. Some years after the destruction of the steamboat, a British national named McLeod, while visiting New York, boasted of having participated in the raid on the 'Caroline'. He was arrested and charged with arson and murder. The US and British Governments, following a series of diplomatic exchanges, agreed to a statement of principle that should have resulted in McLeod not being prosecuted (*infra* note 178 below and accompanying text). See also Jennings (1938). McLeod was nevertheless prosecuted because it was not for the US federal government to make binding promises as to the exercise of prosecutorial discretion in New York state. See *The People v. McLeod*, 1 Hill (N.Y.) 377 (1841) and 3 Hill (N.Y.) 635 (1841).

[178] British and Foreign State Papers, Volume 29, 1139. See also JB Moore, 'International Arbitrations', Vol. III, 1898, 2419. See *Arrest Warrant Case (DRC v. Belgium)*, Judgment, para 60 (in which the Court clearly held that immunity is a procedural bar to a state's exercise of its enforcement jurisdiction, and that immunity has no bearing on the applicability of a state's exercise of its prescriptive jurisdiction to a particular act); Kolodkin (2008), paras 64–6.

[179] On concurrent responsibility, see Section 1.2.

[180] See Cassese (2002), 862–3; Akande (2009). Fox also characterizes the McLeod principle as one that gives rise to a plea of 'non-answerability' for the state official in domestic proceedings. She does so on the basis of either an 'exclusive State responsibility' model (but does not explain the mechanism for giving effect to a state's exclusive responsibility as a matter of international law in domestic criminal proceedings outside the application of the rules on state immunity) or an 'act of State' model (but acknowledges that this may not be a satisfactory explanation for the McLeod principle because the state can waive immunity and consent to the criminal proceedings against its official). See Fox (2008), 96–7.

sometimes based on the non-attributability of the conduct to the individual.[181] But this characterization of the principle rather confuses the issue. There is no known rule of customary international law that requires states to create a substantive defence, as a matter of domestic *criminal* law, to the effect that conduct carried out on behalf of a state is not personally attributable to the physical person who carried it out. While a defence based on principles of agency (and therefore non-attributability for the purposes of personal responsibility) is widely recognized in reference to domestic civil proceedings, agency is not (absent extreme circumstances more aptly characterized as duress) a substantive defence to criminal charges.[182] Furthermore, the exclusive responsibility of the state espoused in reference to McLeod's prosecution could easily be waived by the responsible state, and substantive defences under domestic criminal law cannot be waived by persons other than the defendant.

The better explanation is that the McLeod principle is simply a reformulation of immunity *ratione materiae*[183] or perhaps a description of the consequences of that immunity, and is therefore subject to the same exceptions as the immunity itself. It is not a source of immunity (the source of the official's immunity being that of the state), nor a defence to criminal charges over which a forum state is otherwise validly exercising jurisdiction, because questions of immunity go to whether the forum state has jurisdiction, and do not affect questions of substantive law.[184]

Exceptions to the application of immunity *ratione materiae* and the exclusive responsibility of the state in reference to criminal conduct are products of devel-

---

[181] See *Blaškić* (ICTY-95-14-A), para 38: 'State officials cannot suffer the consequences of wrongful acts which are not attributable to them personally but to the State on whose behalf they act: they enjoy so-called "functional immunity"'. The Appeals Chamber relied on the McLeod principle as a *source* of this immunity, supporting its decision with references to France's position regarding the Rainbow Warrior incident (discussed below) and the Israeli Supreme Court's decision in *Eichmann*. In both those cases, however, an absolute principle of non-concurrence of responsibility was not applied to domestic criminal proceedings. The principle (also framed in terms of non-attributability) was equally referenced by Counsel for Djibouti, and accepted by Counsel for France (Alain Pellet) in their oral pleadings for *Certain Questions of Mutual Assistance in Criminal Matters (Djibouti v. France)*, Judgment, Oral Proceedings, CR 2008/5, para 75. In its Judgment, the ICJ noted the principle of law, but took no position on it because Djibouti had not clearly articulated its submissions to the ICJ in terms of immunity and had not invoked the immunity before the French courts. *Certain Questions of Mutual Assistance in Criminal Matters (Djibouti v. France)*, Judgment, paras 187–96.

[182] See D'Amato (2008), 288, noting that superior orders are not treated as a defence in domestic criminal proceedings, but rather as an admission of guilt that might be taken into account in mitigation of sentence. This is consistent with the approach the NZ court took in reference to the 'Rainbow Warrior' bombing discussed below, *infra* note 198 and accompanying text.

[183] See for instance Lord Hoffmann's speech in *Jones v. Saudi Arabia*, UK (House of Lords, 2006), para 68: 'it is a little artificial to say that the acts of officials are "not attributable to them personally" and [. . .] this usage can lead to confusion', suggesting instead that the issue be characterized in terms of immunity and exceptions thereto. He notes, however, that 'this is a difference in the form of expression and not the substance of the rule'. *Ibid*.

[184] See *Arrest Warrant Case (DRC v. Belgium)*, Judgment, para 60 (in which the Court clearly held that immunity is a procedural bar to a state's exercise of its enforcement jurisdiction, and that immunity has no bearing on the applicability of a state's exercise of its prescriptive jurisdiction to a particular act); Kolodkin (2008), paras 64–6.

opments in international criminal law. The Caroline incident (which precipitated McLeod's arrest) has long been characterized as a use of force in exercise of the right of self-defence,[185] but international law did not, at the time, restrict means and methods of warfare, nor did it impose obligations on individual soldiers to act in accordance with international standards. The exclusivity of state responsibility espoused in reference to McLeod's prosecution reflects this context. In 1840, states were the only subjects of international law. States had not yet agreed among themselves that certain conduct was to be prohibited absolutely as a matter of international law, and that individual criminal responsibility would attach to such conduct.

The international legal context has changed dramatically since the time of McLeod's prosecution. The Nuremberg Principles[186] clearly recognize individual criminal responsibility of state officials for 'crimes under international law'[187] for which the state will also be responsible.[188] Equally, the official nature of an act (including its having been committed under the orders of a superior or government) is no longer an acceptable substantive defence to the charge of having committed an international crime.[189] The ILC noted (in commentaries to its Draft Code of Offences against the Peace and Security of Mankind) that it would be paradoxical if the substantive defence of official conduct were eliminated, only to allow the official nature of conduct to amount to a procedural defence (in the form of immunities).[190] To this effect, jurisprudence suggests a developing

[185] See e.g. Jennings (1938), 92; Brierly (1963), 405–6; Schachter (1984), 1635; Dinstein (2005), 248–50; Moir (2010), 12.

[186] See Principle IV: 'The fact that a person acted pursuant to order of his Government or of a superior does not relieve him from responsibility under international law, provided a moral choice was in fact possible to him'. Principles of International Law Recognized in the Charter of the Nüremberg Tribunal and in the Judgment of the Tribunal, [1950] Yearbook of the International Law Commission, Volume II, 191.

[187] Crimes under international law, or international crimes, are generally restricted to genocide, war crimes and crimes against humanity. These crimes are sometimes referred to as 'core crimes', to be distinguished from 'treaty crimes' like terrorism. Indeed, delegates to the *Ad Hoc* Committee and the Preparatory Committee on the establishment of an International Criminal Court expressed concern that terrorist crimes were of a lesser magnitude than the 'core crimes' of genocide, crimes against humanity and war crimes, and that they should be excluded from the ICC's jurisdiction on that basis. See e.g. Reports of the *Ad Hoc* Committee on the establishment of an International Criminal Court, UN Doc. A/50/22 (1995), para 55; UN Doc. A/51/22 (1996), para 107. One of the difficulties with the crime of 'terrorism' becoming an international crime for which there is individual criminal responsibility as a matter of customary international law is the lack of a definition of terrorism generally. See Kolb (2004), 276–7.

[188] In reference to war crimes, see e.g. Art. 29, Geneva Convention Relative to the Treatment of Prisoners of War of 12 August 1949, 75 UNTS 135 [hereinafter 'GC III'], which stipulates that 'the Party to the conflict in whose hands protected persons may be is responsible for the treatment accorded to them by its agents, irrespective of any individual responsibility which may be incurred'.

[189] See Art. 33, Rome Statute of the International Criminal Court, 17 July 1998, A/CONF.183/9, <http://www.icc-cpi.int/library/about/officialjournal/Rome_Statute_English.pdf> [hereinafter 'Rome Statute'].

[190] See Report of the International Law Commission on the work of its forty-eighth session, UN Doc. A/51/10 (1996), 41. The commentary is in reference to core international crimes, as terrorism was not included in the draft adopted on second reading in 1996. See further Section 6.4.

exception to immunity *ratione materiae* for crimes under international law.[191] The existence of such an exception has not yet fully crystallized, partly because there is no settled view on the principled basis of the exception to immunity,[192] but more particularly because the ICJ's dictum in the *Arrest Warrant Case* might be read as suggesting that there is no exception to immunity *ratione materiae* for crimes under international law.[193] Nonetheless, a great deal of academic authority supports the exception.[194] Given, however, the distinction between crimes under international law (to which an exception to immunity *ratione materiae* is likely developing) and terrorism,[195] it remains to consider whether the movement away from the exclusive responsibility of states (first espoused in reference to the McLeod prosecution) applies to acts of terrorism carried out on behalf of a state.

[191] See e.g. *Blaškić* (ICTY-95-14-A), para 41, holding that there is an exception to immunity *ratione materiae* in criminal proceedings for crimes under international law. In reference to an exception to state immunity for civil proceedings regarding liability for the commission of international crimes, see *Ferrini v. Federal Republic of Germany*, Italy (Court of Cassation, 2004), as described in Focarelli (2005). But see Germany's application before the ICJ (*Jurisdictional Immunities of the State (Germany v. Italy)*) challenging the exception to state immunity as applied in the *Ferrini* case, at least in so far as it relates to civil proceedings directly against the state of Germany. Germany's application to the ICJ highlights that the Italian courts acknowledge the exception to immunity they apply does not exist as a matter of positive international law, but is rather an exception 'in formation'. *Jurisdictional Immunities of the State (Germany v. Italy)*, Application, 11, para 13.

[192] Some commentators have justified an exception to immunity *ratione materiae* based on the *jus cogens* nature of the crimes in respect of which an exception to immunity might operate. See e.g. Bianchi (1999), 265; Kamto (2002), 526–9. See also *Arrest Warrant Case (DRC v. Belgium)*, Dissenting Opinion of Judge Al-Khasawneh, para 7; *Pinochet (no. 3)*, UK (House of Lords, 1999), 278 (per Lord Millet). In respect of the potential conflict between *jus cogens* prohibitions and immunity *ratione materiae*, the ICJ held in its decisions in *Armed Activities on the Territory of the Congo (DRC v. Rwanda)* (New Application: 2002), Jurisdiction and Admissibility, paras 64–7, that jurisdictional questions cannot be in conflict with substantive *jus cogens* norms. Supporting this position in reference to immunity (as a jurisdictional question), see *Jones v. Saudi Arabia*, UK (House of Lords, 2006), para 71 (per Lord Hoffmann); Fox (2008), 151–2.

[193] The Court held that 'a court of one State may try a former Minister for Foreign Affairs of another State in respect of acts committed prior or subsequent to his or her period of office, as well as in respect of acts committed during that period of office *in a private capacity*'. Emphasis added. *Arrest Warrant Case (DRC v. Belgium)*, Judgment, para 61. The dictum has been heavily criticized because it can be interpreted as suggesting that state officials remain immune *ratione materiae* for crimes under international law (in disregard of the developing system of international law aimed at ensuring that there is no impunity for such crimes), and because, to the extent that the judgment admits the possibility of prosecution for international crimes, it must have qualified them as 'private' for the purposes of immunity (thereby permitting prosecution, but effectively undermining any possibility of holding a state responsible for such crimes because private conduct is not attributable to a state). See e.g. Wouters (2003), 267; Casesse (2002), 866–70; Sassòli (2002), 800; Spinedi (2002), 899; Wirth (2002); Bianchi (2009), 19.

[194] See e.g. Watts (1994), 82; Bianchi (1999); Dominicé (1999a); Casesse (2002); Report of the Committee of Eminent African Jurists on the case of Hissène Habré, submitted to the Summit of the African Union (July 2006), available at <http://www.hrw.org/justice/habre/CEJA_Repor0506.pdf>, para 13 (in their Report on the case of Hissène Habré submitted to the Summit of the African Union). See also *Arrest Warrant Case (DRC v. Belgium)*, Judgment, Dissenting Opinion of Judge ad hoc Van den Wyngaert, para 31.

[195] *Supra* note 187.

(iii) An exception to immunity ratione materiae *for acts of international terrorism*

More than a century after its initial formulation, the McLeod principle was relied on by France in the Rainbow Warrior incident.[196] On the arrest of its agents in New Zealand for manslaughter, France insisted that its international responsibility for destroying the Greenpeace ship was exclusive, and should absorb (or displace) the criminal responsibility of its agents for manslaughter.[197] But the two agents pleaded guilty to the charges, and the fact that they acted on orders from the French Government was only taken into account in sentencing.[198] The New Zealand court, having acknowledged the official capacity in which the French agents acted, did not consider whether principles of immunity *ratione materiae* affected its adjudicative jurisdiction, although it bears noting that France did not formally invoke immunity before the court. Following the conviction of the French agents, France continued to protest their detention, and the Secretary-General was asked to resolve the dispute between France and New Zealand (as to the disposition of the agents and any compensation to be paid by France) in an 'equitable and principled manner'. The Secretary-General did not allow for France's responsibility to absorb or displace the individual criminal responsibility of its agents. Instead, the Secretary-General ruled that the agents should serve a three-year sentence in a French military facility on a remote island outside of Europe *and* that France should pay appropriate compensation in discharge of its responsibility.[199] In confirming the individual criminal responsibility of the French agents and holding France responsible for the bombing of the 'Rainbow Warrior', the Secretary-General's Ruling supports the possibility of concurrent responsibility for an official act of international terrorism.

Even accepting that the Secretary-General was not necessarily guided by international law[200] (though there is nothing in the Ruling to suggest that he disregarded legal principles in reaching his decision), the Secretary-General's Ruling certainly calls into question the validity of the McLeod 'non-concurrence of responsibility' principle in reference to terrorist offences. Indeed, it has long been

---

[196] For the facts of the Rainbow Warrior incident, see Section 2.2.1.

[197] In its submissions to the Secretary General, France argued that the detention of its agents in New Zealand was unjustified 'taking into account in particular the fact that they acted under military orders and that France [was] ready to give an apology and to pay compensation to New Zealand for the damage suffered'. France further argued that 'for reasons of law and in order to restore the traditional friendly relations between the two countries, it behoves the New Zealand Government to release the two offenders' and expressly invoked the McLeod precedent in support of its legal argument. See *UNSG Rainbow Warrior Ruling* (1986), 213, 211. See also Memorandum of the Government of the French Republic to the Secretary General of the United Nations, Rainbow Warrior, 74 International Law Reports 264.

[198] *R. v. Mafart and Prieur*, New Zealand (High Court, 22 November 1985), 74 International Law Reports 243, 250–1.

[199] See *UNSG Rainbow Warrior Ruling* (1986).

[200] See Pugh (1987), 656. See also Merrills (2005), 109, classifying the Rainbow Warrior proceedings as conciliation, rather than an arbitration.

accepted that a forum state need not give effect to immunity *ratione materiae* in the event of espionage, sabotage, or unauthorized incursions by an organ of a foreign state in the territory of that forum state,[201] which supports the Secretary-General's Ruling in the Rainbow Warrior case. In principle, such an exception to immunity recognizes that the forum state should have a monopoly over the exercise of sovereign public authority within its territory, and therefore need not recognize the sovereign nature of acts by foreign states carried out in its territory without its consent.[202]

In addition to the Rainbow Warrior precedent, there is a strong argument to be made that acts of terrorism as defined in the TSCs carried out by or on behalf of states should qualify as an exception to immunity *ratione materiae* in reference to the criminal prosecution of individual state actors. The argument is derived from a purposive interpretation of the TSCs. In particular, it is possible to argue that in ratifying the TSCs, state parties have impliedly waived immunity *ratione materiae* in reference to the prosecution of their officials for acts of terrorism defined under the Conventions. To the extent that this exception to state immunity is built into the TSCs themselves, a refusal to prosecute on the basis of the relevant actor's immunity *ratione materiae* will amount to a breach of the *aut dedere aut judicare* obligations thereunder. An exception to immunity derived from the TSCs would also sever the relationship between immunity and state responsibility suggested by the McLeod principle, such that concurrent responsibility for acts of international terrorism covered by the TSCs would be possible.[203]

This exception to immunity *ratione materiae* would arise under the TSCs because they impose an *aut dedere aut judicare* obligation, coupled with an obligation to establish universal jurisdiction over defined offences, and draws on the purposive interpretation of the Torture Convention in the reasoning of the House of Lords in *Pinochet (No. 3)* (as clarified in *Jones v. Saudi Arabia*). In *Pinochet (No. 3)*, Lord Browne-Wilkinson held that, if immunity *ratione materiae* applied to official acts of torture (and by definition, all acts of torture under the Torture Convention are official):

---

[201] See Fox (2008), 96; *Certain Questions of Mutual Assistance in Criminal Matters (Djibouti v. France)*, Judgment, Oral Proceedings, CR 2008/3, 11. See also discussion (in Section 6.2) of a German court's conviction of a Libyan secret service agent for the La Belle disco bombing and France's conviction (in *absentia*) of Libyan officials for the bombing of UTA Flight 722.

[202] Whether states are bound to give effect, *proprio motu*, to immunity *ratione materiae* is an unsettled question (see ILC, Memorandum by the Secretariat on immunity of state officials from foreign criminal jurisdiction, UN Doc. A/CN.4/596 (2008), paras 215–18). But, even if so bound, there is no such obligation on a forum state in reference to secret conduct carried out in its territory to which it had not given prior consent.

[203] In holding that Pinochet was not immune from prosecution (or extradition), this is precisely what the House of Lords did in reference to torture in its *Pinochet (no. 3)* decision. Pinochet could be held criminally responsible for torture, and a policy of torture sanctioned by a head of state would certainly give rise to state responsibility for torture (which responsibility could be invoked by either the state of nationality of any non-Chilean victims on the basis of diplomatic protection, or on the basis of Article 48 of the ILC Articles on State Responsibility, in virtue of the *erga omnes* (and *jus cogens*) nature of the prohibition).

the whole elaborate structure of universal jurisdiction over torture committed by officials is rendered abortive and one of the main objectives of the Torture Convention—to provide a system under which there is no safe haven for torturers—will have been frustrated. In my judgment all these factors together demonstrate that the notion of continued immunity for ex-heads of state is inconsistent with the provisions of the Torture Convention.[204]

A purposive interpretation suggests that state parties to the Torture Convention must have implicitly waived state immunity in regard to the prosecution of their officials in foreign jurisdictions, lest the 'no-impunity'-related obligations under the Convention be without effect.[205] This interpretation of the Torture Convention was paraphrased by Lord Bingham in *Jones v. Saudi Arabia* as follows: 'International law could not without absurdity require criminal jurisdiction to be assumed and exercised where the Torture Convention conditions were satisfied and, at the same time, require immunity to be granted to those properly charged'.[206]

The Lords' interpretation of the Torture Convention relied in part on the definition of the crime of torture, which requires that the act be performed in an official capacity (thereby triggering immunity *ratione materiae*), but also on the universality of the *aut dedere aut judicare* obligation and the creation of a treaty-based system of universal jurisdiction, to support the implicit waiver of immunity argument.[207] The TSCs do not restrict the definition of offences to those carried out by state officials acting in their official capacity. Instead, they define offences in more neutral terms as acts that might be committed by 'any person'.[208] That said, in reference to proposals during the negotiation of the SUA Convention to expressly include persons acting on behalf of a state in the term 'any person', states expressed the view that the existing language was broad enough to include criminal responsibility for acts carried out on behalf of governments.[209] And the TSCs, like

---

[204]   *Pinochet (no. 3)*, UK (House of Lords, 1999), 205 (per Lord Browne-Wilkinson).
[205]   The principle of effectiveness is an important tool of treaty interpretation, and often relied on by Courts to read implicit rights or obligations into a treaty text. *Infra* Chapter 4, note 55. But see Orakhelashvili (2008), 396, arguing that the principle of effectiveness should not be given so large a scope (including broad teleological approaches that result in reading unexpressed matters into a treaty) as to undermine good faith textual interpretation.
[206]   *Jones v. Saudi Arabia*, UK (House of Lords, 2006), para 19 (per Lord Bingham). See also Akande (2004), 413–15, arguing that there is an exception to immunity *ratione materiae* in respect of all crimes subject to universal jurisdiction because immunity and universal jurisdiction cannot logically co-exist.
[207]   See e.g. Lord Phillips' speech, *Pinochet (no. 3)*, UK (House of Lords, 1999), 289, in which he suggests that 'state immunity *ratione materiae* cannot co-exist with [international crimes and extra-territorial jurisdiction in relation to them]' and that 'once extraterritorial jurisdiction is established, it makes no sense to exclude from it acts done in an official capacity'. See also *Jones v. Saudi Arabia*, UK (House of Lords, 2006), para 19 (per Lord Bingham), to the same effect.
[208]   See Art. 1 of the Hague Convention, Montreal Convention, Internationally Protected Persons Convention, Hostages Convention, SUA Convention, Terrorist Bombing Convention, Nuclear Terrorism Convention.
[209]   IMO, Report of the *Ad Hoc* Preparatory Committee on the Suppression of Unlawful Acts against the Safety of Maritime Navigation, 2nd Session, 18–22 May 1987, IMO Doc. PCUA 2/5 (1987), para 66.

the Torture Convention in respect of torture, are intended to ensure that there is no 'safe haven' for terrorists through imposition of an *aut dedere aut judicare* obligation and an obligation to establish universal jurisdiction over defined offences.[210] Immunity *ratione materiae* for acts of terrorism would frustrate that objective, at least as it applies to official acts of terrorism, which states considered to be covered by the provisions regarding criminal responsibility.[211] The *Pinochet* analysis therefore suggests that states should be considered to have impliedly waived immunity *ratione materiae* in respect of offences defined in the Terrorism Suppression Conventions. The applicability of the *Pinochet* analysis to the terrorism suppression context is further supported by a unique feature of some of the TSCs: they exclude military conduct from the scope of the Conventions.[212] That the Conventions contemplate the individual criminal responsibility of *some* state officials is implied by their exclusion of criminal responsibility for others—further suggesting that states implicitly waived immunity for the conduct of state officials (for instance secret service agents) falling within the scope of the TSCs that meets the elements of the offences defined therein.

Any waiver of immunity based on a *Pinochet* analysis, however, would be *inter partes*, and states not party to a particular TSC could not be held to have implicitly waived the immunity *ratione materiae* of their state officials for offences defined therein should they decide to invoke that immunity. But as between state parties to the TSCs, a state's refusal to prosecute on the basis of immunity *ratione materiae* will be in breach of its TSC *aut dedere aut judicare* obligations because such immunity does not apply, based on its implied waiver. In cases where the state on whose behalf an alleged terrorist acted is not a party to a relevant TSC, the general exception to the obligation to give effect to immunity *ratione materiae* (in cases of unauthorized incursions by an organ of one state into the territory of another, like that in the Rainbow Warrior case)[213] would still apply. Because there is no *obligation* in such cases to recognize or give effect to immunity *ratione materiae*, the *aut dedere aut judicare* obligation is unqualified by any inconsistent immunity obligations. As long as the custodial state is a party to the relevant TSC—it will be in breach of its *aut dedere aut judicare* obligation to refuse to submit to prosecution (in default of extradition) on the basis of immunity. In either case, the McLeod principle of non-concurrence of responsibility is inapplicable in the terrorism context.

---

[210] See UNSG Report on measures to prevent international terrorism, UN Doc. A/51/336 (1996), para 17.

[211] *Supra* note 209. The criminal responsibility of state officials for acts meeting the elements of crimes offences defined in the TSCs, however, is only imposable to the extent that the relevant act falls within the scope of the TSC. See Section 4.2.2 discussing the exclusion of military activities from the scope of some of the TSCs.

[212] See Section 4.2.2 for a discussion of the exclusion clauses in the Hostages Convention, Terrorism Bombing Convention and Nuclear Terrorism Convention.

[213] *Supra* note 201 and accompanying text.

3.3 The self-determination debate and the scope of the TSCs

It is often argued that the international community circumvented the self-determination deadlock on defining terrorism by adopting the TSCs. In particular, some commentators have suggested that states were able to agree on the prohibition of certain manifestations of terrorist conduct, even though they could not agree on whether or not to distinguish between acts committed in furtherance of self-determination and acts of terrorism as a general matter of international law.[214] This is not strictly accurate. Whether or not acts committed in furtherance of a people's right of self-determination should be distinguished from acts of terrorism covered by some of the TSCs—particularly those negotiated under the auspices of the United Nations—was a matter of fierce debate. While this debate has not been settled one way or the other (and is still a matter for negotiation in reference to the draft comprehensive terrorism suppression convention), it left its footprint on the final negotiated texts in at least two different ways. Notably, the debate did not result in any distinction being drawn between acts of terrorism and self-determination as a matter of *definition* of the acts of terrorism covered by the TSCs. Rather, the debate affected the negotiation of exclusion clauses in the Hostages Convention, Terrorist Bombing Convention and Nuclear Terrorism Convention, each approaching the self-determination issue from the perspective of regime interaction, defining the spheres of application of the terrorism suppression regime and international humanitarian law. The application of these exclusion clauses is important for determining whether states are under an obligation to extradite or submit for prosecution (as there is no alternative obligation under customary international law[215] and alternative treaty-based obligations will not necessarily apply). The scope of the exclusion clauses may also affect the potential jurisdiction of the ICJ to settle disputes (pursuant to the compromissory clauses in the TSCs) regarding breach of the *aut dedere aut judicare* obligation and the obligation to prevent under those TSCs.

Both the proponents and opponents of distinguishing between acts of terrorism and acts carried out in furtherance of a people's right of self-determination claim victory in reference to the scope of the negotiated exclusion clauses. As a result of that ambiguity, the second way in which the debate on self-determination has left its footprint on the TSCs is through the adoption of reservations. A number of states have made reservations to the Hostages Convention, Terrorist Bombing Convention and Terrorism Financing Convention that purport to exclude acts committed in furtherance of a people's right of self-determination from the scope of those TSCs. The potential effect of these reservations (particularly in cases where the negotiated exclusion clauses do not operate as they should in reference to the

---

[214] See Lambert (1990), 50; Higgins (1997), 14; Cassese (2003), 123; Kolb (2004), 229. See also UNGA, Sixth Committee, UN Doc. A/C.6/54/SR.34 (1999), para 46 (Canada); UNGA, Sixth Committee, UN Doc. A/C.6/54/SR.35 (1999), para 9 (US).

[215] *Supra* notes 109–11 and accompanying text.

interaction between the TSCs and humanitarian law) will determine the scope of the TSCs and through them the scope of the obligations to criminalize, prevent, and extradite or submit to prosecution, breach of which will result in a state's international responsibility. The reservations may also affect the potential jurisdiction of the ICJ to settle disputes regarding breach of the *aut dedere aut judicare* obligation and the obligation to prevent under the TSCs to which they apply.

Given that decolonization is virtually complete, the impact of the self-determination debate on the scope of the TSCs should not be exaggerated. That said, the issue remains live in relation to the Israeli/Palestinian conflict,[216] and is certainly relevant as regards relations between Pakistan and India in so far as the disputed status of Kashmir is concerned.[217] Several non-state actor groups in these conflicts, including Hamas and Hezbollah, are considered to be freedom fighters by states like the Sudan, Syria and Iran.[218] As significant acts of violence (and concomitant failures to prevent and punish) are associated with these conflicts, the extent of the applicability of the TSCs to acts committed in furtherance of a struggle for self-determination remains an important issue.

3.3.1 Exclusion of acts committed in furtherance of a people's right of self-determination from the scope of the TSCs

Whether a state could argue that a TSC does not apply to acts committed in furtherance of a people's right of self-determination, and that the obligations to criminalize, prevent, and extradite or submit for prosecution are therefore inapplicable in respect of a particular terrorist act, will depend in large measure on the TSC being invoked and the interpretation of its exclusion clause. What is absolutely clear is that the applicability of the TSCs to acts committed in furtherance of a struggle for self-determination is not dealt with as a matter of the definition of the relevant terrorist offence. Offences are defined generally without reference to self-determination, and potential exclusion from the scope of a TSC is addressed through regime interaction clauses or reservations that bear on the applicability of the terrorism suppression regime to the particular act.

The TSCs negotiated under the auspices of the ICAO were generally exempt from debate regarding whether they should exclude acts committed in furtherance of a people's right of self-determination.[219] This is in large part because they were

---

[216] See Greenwood (1989), 194, arguing that Article 1(4) of API, which extends the definition of armed conflict to conflicts in which a people is fighting in exercise of its right of self-determination, was aimed at the occupation by Israel of Palestinian territories, in particular the West Bank and Gaza.

[217] See e.g. the dispute between Pakistan and India brought before the ICAO, related to a hijacking by Kashmiri militants, discussed in Section 5.2.3(iii); and India's accusation that Pakistan agencies supported the Kashmiri militant group Lashkar-e-Taiba in its terrorist attacks on Mumbai in November 2008 (BBC, 'Kashmiri views on militant group', 11 December 2008, <http://news.bbc.co.uk/2/hi/south_asia/7778326.stm>; BBC, 'Singh accuses Pakistan on Mumbai', 6 January 2009, <http://news.bbc.co.uk/2/hi/south_asia/7812890.stm>).

[218] See US Department of State Country Reports on Terrorism (2008).

[219] See generally ICAO, International Conference on Private Air Law (1961–63); ICAO, International Conference on Private Air Law (1970–71). Long after their entry into force, Qatar appealed for

adopted before the issue of terrorism was placed on the United Nation's agenda.[220] As a result, there is nothing in the Hague or Montreal Conventions to suggest that acts committed in furtherance of a people's right of self-determination should be excluded from their scope. The SUA Convention, like its ICAO counterparts, was not negotiated within the General Assembly's intensely political setting. As it was modelled on the ICAO Conventions, the SUA Convention does not contain anything in its preamble or otherwise that reaffirms the right of self-determination or suggests any scope for exclusion in reference to activities carried out in furtherance of that right. The Protocol to the IMO TSCs adopted in 2005 and the Protocol and Amendment to the ICAO TSCs adopted in 2010, however, all contain exclusion clauses identical to that contained in the Terrorist Bombing Convention and Nuclear Terrorism Convention,[221] and will therefore be subject to the same analysis as the Terrorist Bombing Convention in regard to their applicability to acts committed in furtherance of a struggle for self-determination. While the applicability of the Terrorist Bombing Convention to the self-determination context was the subject of some debate during negotiation of that Convention, the same is not true of the TSCs adopted under the auspices of the IMO in 2005 and the ICAO in 2010. Incorporation of the Terrorist Bombing Convention exclusion clause in these Conventions is largely the product of a desire for consistency in the TSCs and is aimed at addressing their applicability to acts committed by state military forces.[222] Nevertheless, as examined below, the exclusion clause is drafted in such a way as to have some

---

the renegotiation of the Terrorism Suppression Conventions adopted under the auspices of the ICAO, to provide that hijackers should be exempt from prosecution when the hijacked aircraft belongs to or is leased to colonial occupation authorities, or the hijacker is a national of an occupied or colonized country that has claimed and not been granted its right to independence or self-determination. UNSG Report on measures to prevent international terrorism, UN Doc. A/36/425 (1981), para 4. No action was taken on the basis of Qatar's proposal.

[220] Once terrorism was placed on the General Assembly's agenda (in 1972, *supra* Chapter 1, note 78), the distinction to be drawn (if any) between acts of terrorism and acts committed in furtherance of a struggle for self-determination dominated the 'terrorism' debate. The General Assembly's first resolution on terrorism (UNGA Resolution 3034 (1972)) *expressed concern* (in the place of condemnation) over increasing acts of violence; reaffirmed the inalienable right of peoples to self-determination, and condemned 'terrorist acts by colonial, racist and alien regimes' in denying peoples their right to self-determination. The General Assembly adopted resolutions reaffirming the right of self-determination, without unequivocally condemning acts of terrorism committed by non-state actors, until 1983. See e.g. UNGA Resolution 32/147 (1977); UNGA Resolution 34/145 (1979); UNGA Resolution 36/109 (1981); UNGA Resolution 38/130 (1983). In 1985, the General Assembly adopted Resolution 40/61, in which it reaffirmed the inalienable right to self-determination and independence of all peoples under colonial and racist regimes and other forms of alien domination, and upheld the legitimacy of their struggle (preamble), but 'unequivocally condemn[ed] as criminal all acts methods and practices of terrorism *wherever and by whomever committed,* including those which jeopardize friendly relations between states'. Emphasis added. UNGA Resolution 40/61 (1985). It took another ten years, however, before the General Assembly would separate its condemnation of international terrorism from issues of self-determination. See UN Declaration on International Terrorism, UNGA Resolution 49/60 (1994), Annex; Supplement to the UN Declaration on International Terrorism, UNGA Resolution 51/210 (1996), Annex.

[221] See Art. 3, 2005 Protocol to the SUA Convention; Art. VI, 2010 Protocol to the Hague Convention; Art. 6, Beijing Convention.

[222] See generally IMO, Report of the Legal Committee on the work of its ninetieth session, IMO Doc. LEG 90/15 (2005); ICAO Legal Committee, 34th Session, Draft report on the work of the Legal Committee during its 34th session, ICAO Doc. LC/34-WP/4-1 (2009), paras 2.71–2.8.

consequences in regard to the applicability of the Conventions to acts committed in furtherance of a struggle for self-determination.

The 2005 Protocol to the SUA Convention entered into force in July 2010, at which point it had thirteen state parties.[223] As a result, the SUA Convention, unaffected by the exclusion clause in the 2005 Protocol, remains in force for the state parties that have not yet ratified the Protocol.[224] The 2010 Protocol to the Hague Convention and the Beijing Convention were both adopted on 10 September 2010 and each requires twenty-two ratifications before entering into force.[225] Until they enter into force, the Hague Convention, Montreal Convention and 1988 Protocol to the Montreal Convention are silent on the issue of self-determination.

Internationally Protected Persons Convention

During negotiation of the Internationally Protected Persons Convention, several states proposed that acts carried out in furtherance of a people's right of self-determination be excluded from the scope of the Convention.[226] Western states argued that offences against internationally protected persons should be criminalized without exception.[227] The compromise position adopted was to require the criminalization of violence against internationally protected persons without exception, but to annex the Internationally Protected Persons Convention to a General Assembly resolution which provides that 'the provisions of the annexed Convention could not in any way prejudice the exercise of the legitimate right to self-determination and independence by peoples struggling against colonialism, alien domination, foreign occupation, racial discrimination and apartheid'.[228] A state that is sympathetic to a particular group of non-state actors, and in whose territory those non-state actors have taken refuge, might refuse to extradite or submit for prosecution on the basis that the Internationally Protected Persons Convention does not apply to acts carried out in furtherance of a people's right of self-determination in virtue of the GA Resolution to which the Convention is annexed. The terms of a treaty need to be interpreted in their context, which includes instruments made in connection with the conclusion of the treaty.[229] Any interpretation excluding acts committed in furtherance of a struggle for self-determination would involve arguing that the criminalization of such conduct, and an obligation to ensure that persons committing defined offences are held to account (through application of the *aut dedere aut judicare* obligation), 'prejudice[s] the exercise

---

[223] See <http://www.imo.org/About/Conventions/StatusOfConventions/Pages/Default.aspx>.

[224] At the time of writing, 140 states were party to the SUA Convention, but not party to the 2005 Protocol to the SUA Convention.

[225] Art. XXII, 2010 Protocol to the Hague Convention; Art. 22, Beijing Convention.

[226] See generally ILC, Question of the protection and inviolability of diplomatic agents and other persons entitled to special protection under international law, UN Doc. A/CN.4/253 and Add.l (1972).

[227] *Ibid.*

[228] UNGA Resolution 3166 (1973).

[229] Art. 31(2)(b), Vienna Convention on the Law of Treaties, 22 May 1969, 1155 UNTS 331 [hereinafter 'VCLT'].

of the legitimate right to self-determination,' contrary to General Assembly Resolution 3166 (1973). Were the question ever put to the ICJ, it would certainly be open to the Court to hold that prohibiting offences against internationally protected persons does not 'prejudice' the exercise of the right to self-determination, but rather sets limits on the means of its exercise. Such an interpretation would be consistent with the approach taken during the negotiation of API to conflicts in which a people is fighting in exercise of their right of self-determination, which extended both the benefits *and the obligations* of the laws of Geneva to freedom fighters.[230] As internationally protected persons would in almost all cases amount to civilians from the perspective of humanitarian law, targeting them would be prohibited in an armed conflict in which a people is fighting in exercise of its right of self-determination as well. While the question should be dealt with as a matter of humanitarian law, the Internationally Protected Persons Convention does not address the self-determination issue as a question of regime interaction. As a result, an injured state would be able to invoke the Convention as a basis for a state's responsibility in reference to a failure to prevent or a breach of the *aut dedere aut judicare* obligation (whether through diplomatic channels or by submitting an Application to the ICJ), even if the relevant offence was committed during an armed conflict fought in furtherance of a people's right of self-determination.

Hostages Convention

During the negotiation of the Hostages Convention, a number of NAM delegates proposed that the definition of the offence 'taking of hostages' exclude 'any acts carried out in the process of national liberation against colonial rule, racist and foreign regimes, by liberation movements recognized by the United Nations'.[231] While the proposal was initially in reference to the definition of the terrorist offence covered by the Hostages Convention, it focused attention on the question of regime interaction. In particular, Western states began to express concern about the relationship between the proposed carve-out for national liberation movements on the one hand and the recently adopted API on the other.[232] API extended the

---

[230] See discussion of API below in reference to its relationship with the Hostages Convention.

[231] Report of the *Ad Hoc* Committee on the drafting of an International Convention against the Taking of Hostages, Proposal by Lesotho, Tanzania, Algeria, Egypt, Libya and Nigeria, UN Doc. A/AC.188/L.5 (1978), para 11. See also Tanzania's comment '[t]he oppressed peoples and colonial peoples who were held in perpetual bondage could not be stopped from taking their oppressors hostage, if that became inevitable'. Report of the *Ad Hoc* Committee on the drafting of an International Convention against the Taking of Hostages, UN Doc. A/32/39 (1977), Annex, paras 28–9. See further Report of the *Ad Hoc* Committee on the drafting of an International Convention against the Taking of Hostages, UN Doc. A/33/39 (1978), para 58.

[232] See summary record of the 12th meeting of the *Ad Hoc* Committee on the drafting of an International Convention against the Taking of Hostages, UN Doc. A/AC.188/SR.12 (1978), para 4 (UK), para 11 (US); summary record of the 13th meeting of the *Ad Hoc* Committee on the drafting of an International Convention against the Taking of Hostages, UN Doc. A/AC.188/SR.13 (1978), para 9 (Germany); summary record of the 27th meeting of the *Ad Hoc* Committee on the drafting of an International Convention against the Taking of Hostages, UN Doc. A/AC.188/SR.27 (1978), paras 1–5 (France), paras 9–11 (Canada).

scope of application of Common Article 2 of the 1949 Geneva Conventions to armed conflicts in which peoples are fighting in exercise of their right of self-determination.[233] In so doing, subject to a declaration by the authority representing a people,[234] API imposed the full range of obligations applicable in international armed conflicts on freedom fighters (including the obligation, under GCIV and API, not to take hostages).[235] The Western response, emphasizing as it did that relevant states had already accepted (in agreeing to Article 1(4) API) that liberation movements were prohibited from taking hostages during armed conflicts,[236] stressed that the Hostages Convention should not be used as an opportunity to renegotiate settled obligations.

During the negotiation, NAM delegates slowly abandoned efforts to legitimize acts of hostage-taking committed in furtherance of a struggle for self-determination, and ceased regarding the self-determination question as one bearing on the definition of the terrorist offence. Instead, acknowledging that hostage-takings were prohibited as a matter of humanitarian law,[237] NAM's principal negotiating objective became to ensure that hostage-takings committed in furtherance of a people's right of self-determination were qualified as war crimes and not as acts falling within the scope of the Hostages Convention.[238]

Compromise on the self-determination issue therefore took the form of an exclusion clause that reflects the focus on the potential interaction between the Hostages Convention and the 1949 Geneva Conventions and Additional Protocols. Article 12 reads as follows:

In so far as the Geneva Conventions of 1949 for the protection of war victims or the Protocols Additional to those Conventions are applicable to a particular act of hostage-taking, and in so far as States Parties to this Convention are bound under those conventions to prosecute or hand over the hostage-taker, the present Conventions shall not apply to an act of hostage-taking committed in the course of armed conflicts as defined in the Geneva Conventions of 1949 and the Protocols thereto, including armed conflicts mentioned in Article 1, paragraph 4, of Additional Protocol I of 1977, *in which peoples are fighting against colonial domination and alien occupation and against racist regimes in the exercise of their right of self-determination* [...].[239]

---

[233] Art. 1(4), API.

[234] See Art. 96(3), API.

[235] Art. 34, Geneva Convention Relative to the Protection of Civilian Persons in Time of War of 12 August 1949, 7 UNTS 31 [hereinafter 'GCIV']; Art. 73(2)(c), API.

[236] See summary record of the 3rd meeting of the *Ad Hoc* Committee on the drafting of an International Convention against the Taking of Hostages, UN Doc. A/AC.188/SR.3 (1978), para 25; summary record of the 12th meeting of the *Ad Hoc* Committee on the drafting of an International Convention against the Taking of Hostages, UN Doc. A/AC.188/SR.12 (1978), paras 4 and 11; summary record of the 28th meeting of the *Ad Hoc* Committee on the drafting of an International Convention against the Taking of Hostages, UN Doc. A/AC.188/SR.28 (1978), para 10; Report of the *Ad Hoc* Committee established by General Assembly resolution 51/210 of 17 December 1996, U.N. Doc. A/52/37 (1996), paras 38–56.

[237] See Verwey (1981).

[238] Despite the shift in NAM's objective, from legitimizing hostage-taking in the context of struggles for self-determination to shifting the source of condemnation, some commentators have nevertheless interpreted Article 12 of the Hostages Convention as legitimizing hostage-takings committed in furtherance of a struggle for self-determination. See Wardlaw (1982), 113; Aston (1982), 156.

[239] Emphasis added. Art. 12, Hostages Convention. See Verwey (1981), 76, for further discussion of Article 12 of the Hostages Convention.

Exclusion under Article 12 is subject to three separate, but cumulative, conditions: (i) the hostage-taking must have occurred in the course of an armed conflict as defined under the Geneva Conventions and Additional Protocols; (ii) the Geneva Conventions or Additional Protocols must be applicable to the particular act of hostage-taking; and (iii) the state party to the Hostages Convention with custody of the hostage-taker must be under an alternative obligation, pursuant to the Geneva Conventions or Additional Protocols, to prosecute or hand over the hostage-taker.[240] As to the first condition, the reference to Article 1(4) API and armed conflicts in which peoples are fighting in the exercise of their right of self-determination adds nothing to the scope of the exclusion clause. The 1949 Geneva Conventions define 'armed conflict' as international armed conflicts (in Common Article 2)[241] and armed conflicts not of an international character (in Common Article 3).[242] Together, Common Articles 2 and 3 of the 1949 Geneva Conventions cover the field of potential armed conflicts—and would therefore have covered conflicts in which peoples are fighting in exercise of their right of self-determination whether or not Article 1(4) API was expressly incorporated.[243]

As to the second and third conditions for exclusion under Article 12 of the Hostages Convention, their satisfaction will depend on the type of conflict (international or non-international), the identity of the hostage and circumstances of the hostage-taking, and whether the relevant state party to the Hostages Convention is also a party to API.[244] In a number of relevant cases of concern to the Non-Aligned Movement (i.e. those in which peoples are fighting in exercise of their right of

---

[240] This section will not consider the applicability of the Protocol Additional to the Geneva Conventions of 12 August 1949, and Relating to the Protection of Victims of Non-International Armed Conflicts, 8 June 1977, 1125 UNTS 609 [hereinafter 'APII'] to acts of hostage-taking because APII, applying as it does to non-international armed conflicts, is not subject to the grave breaches regime of the Geneva Conventions and acts falling within its scope can therefore never satisfy the third condition for exclusion under the Hostages Convention. For a discussion of the grave breaches regime and the third condition for exclusion from the Hostages Convention, see *infra* note 250 and accompanying text.

[241] An international armed conflict exists as soon as there is a resort to armed force between states (ICRC (2008); *Tadić* (ICTY-94-1-A), Interlocutory Appeal on Jurisdiction, para 70). Such conflicts are generally considered to exist irrespective of the intensity of the confrontation (Pictet (1952), 32), but some states suggest that something more than a border incident is required. See UK Ministry of Defence (2004), para 3.3.1. See also Greenwood (2008), para 202. There is an argument to be made that an international armed conflict also exists when one state uses force in the territory of another state without that state's consent, even if there is no clash between the armed forces of the two states. See Sassòli (2006), 5; Milanovic (2010). But see Gasser (1983); Jinks (2005), 189; Lubell (2010), 96, 104; Kress (2010), 253–5.

[242] A non-international armed conflict requires a protracted armed confrontation amounting to something more than isolated acts of violence, in order to distinguish it from riots and other internal disturbances. See ICRC (2008); *Tadić* (ICTY-94-1-A), Interlocutory Appeal on Jurisdiction, para 70; *Akayesu* (ICTR-96-4-T), para 619; Moir (2002), 43.

[243] The point of Article 1(4) of API is to upgrade a conflict in which a people is fighting in exercise of their right of self-determination from a Common Article 3 conflict to a Common Article 2 conflict, but whether Article 1(4) applies or not, such conflicts would nevertheless have amounted to 'armed conflicts' as defined under the Geneva Conventions.

[244] The Geneva Conventions are universally ratified (with the possible exception of entities whose statehood is still in question, for instance Kosovo), and state party status will therefore be assumed for the purposes of the present analysis. See <http://www.icrc.org/ihl.nsf/CONVPRES?OpenView>.

self-determination), an act of hostage-taking will not meet the second and/or third condition for exclusion, and will therefore be covered by the Hostages Convention.

The first scenario to be considered assumes a state party to the Hostages Convention is only party to the Geneva Conventions, and not to API. In international armed conflicts (those covered by Common Article 2 of the 1949 Geneva Conventions), only the taking of civilian hostages is expressly prohibited[245] and subject to a prosecute or hand over obligation.[246] But international armed conflicts will not generally include conflicts in which peoples are fighting in exercise of their right of self-determination. Classically, international armed conflicts are between states.[247] Non-state actors acting on behalf of (as distinguished from being assisted by) a third party state will, however, generally not be fighting in the exercise of their right of self-determination.[248] Thus, although any taking of civilian hostages committed during the course of an international armed conflict will be excluded from the scope of the Hostages Convention under Article 12, conflicts in which peoples are fighting in exercise of their right of self-determination will not generally qualify as international armed conflicts under the Geneva Conventions and will therefore not benefit from this exclusion.

In Common Article 3 non-international armed conflicts (which may well include conflicts in which a people is fighting in exercise of their right of self-determination), only hostage-taking of '[p]ersons taking no active part in the hostilities, including members of armed forces who have laid down their arms and those placed hors de combat by sickness, wounds, detention, or any other cause' is prohibited.[249] Any such hostage-taking, however, would not meet the third condition for exclusion under Article 12 of the Hostages Convention. The grave breaches regime of the Geneva Conventions, and the concomitant obligation to prosecute or hand over, only applies to international armed conflicts.[250] The

---

[245] Art. 34, GCIV.

[246] Art. 146, GCIV.

[247] Common Art. 2, 1949 Geneva Conventions. International armed conflicts include those in which non-state actors are *de facto* agents of a third party state (and they act on behalf of that third party state in the conflict). The standard of attribution for the purposes of determining whether a conflict is international is 'overall control' rather than 'effective control'. See *Tadić* (ICTY-94-1-A), para 84.

[248] There are possible exceptions to this statement, which will be rare—for instance where the third party state's objectives are the self-determination of the non-state actors acting on its behalf (including where exercise of the right of self-determination is to take the form of incorporation into that third state). See UNGA Resolution 1541 (1960), Principle 6.

[249] Common Art. 3, 1949 Geneva Conventions. Taking active combatants hostage is not prohibited under the Geneva Conventions. Any such hostage-taking, whether committed in the course of a struggle for self-determination or not, would *not* be covered by the Geneva Conventions and would therefore not meet the second of the three cumulative conditions for exclusion under Article 12 of the Hostages Convention. Taking active combatants hostage therefore falls within the scope of the Hostages Convention. See *infra* note 254 in reference to taking active combatants hostage in armed conflicts to which API applies.

[250] See *Tadić* (ICTY-94-1-A), Interlocutory Appeal on Jurisdiction, paras 71 and 78. See also Moir (2009). While some commentators have argued that the grave breaches regime, and the obligation to prosecute or hand over, might apply to internal armed conflicts as a matter of customary international law (see in particular Meron (1996), 242), this is irrelevant for the purposes of the scope of Article 12, as an act of hostage-taking is only excluded from the scope of the Hostages Convention if it is subject to a prosecute or hand over obligation *under* the Geneva Conventions and Protocols thereto.

criminal law enforcement obligations of the Geneva Conventions simply do not apply to non-international armed conflicts, resulting in the inapplicability of the Article 12 exclusion clause to any hostage-taking committed during the course of such conflicts.

If state parties to the Hostages Convention are also party to API, the analysis changes somewhat. First, subject to reservations, state parties to API are bound by the Article 1(4) API expanded definition of international armed conflict, which incorporates self-determination conflicts within the scope of Common Article 2 of the 1949 Geneva Conventions.[251] As a result, such conflicts are internationalized for legal purposes and fall within the grave breaches regime of the Geneva Conventions and Additional Protocols.[252] To the extent that a hostage-taking committed during the course of such a conflict amounts to a grave breach of the Geneva Conventions or Additional Protocols, it would be subject to a prosecute or hand over obligation and thereby satisfy the third condition for exclusion under Article 12 of the Hostages Convention. As noted above, GCIV prohibits the taking of civilian hostages—which is subject to a prosecute or hand over obligation.[253] API also defines the capture of an adversary through resort to perfidy (prohibited under Article 37 API) and making a person *hors de combat* the object of attack (prohibited under Article 41 API) as grave breaches, thereby subjecting such crimes to the prosecute or hand over regime of the Geneva Conventions.[254] As a result, if an active combatant is perfidiously taken hostage or a civilian or person *hors de combat* is taken hostage, each in the context of an international armed conflict (which, under API, includes conflicts in which a people is fighting in exercise of their right of self-determination), the hostage-taking meets all three conditions of Article 12 of

---

[251] Some states have made reservations to API to the effect that they are not bound by declarations made by an authority representing a people under Article 96(3) of API, in which such authority undertakes unilaterally to apply API to its conflict with a state party, unless that state has 'expressly recognized that it has been made by a body which is genuinely an authority representing a people engaged in an armed conflict of the type to which Article 1, paragraph 4, applies'. See e.g. the UK's reservation to API, <http://www.icrc.org/ihl.nsf/NORM/0A9E03F0-F2EE757CC1256402003FB6D2?OpenDocument>.

[252] Purely internal armed conflicts from a factual perspective, for instance those in which there is no foreign element whatsoever, even if legally qualified as international under Article 1(4) of API, still fall outside the scope of the Hostages Convention. This is because the Hostages Convention does not apply where the offence is committed within a single state, the hostage and the alleged offender are nationals of that state and the alleged offender is found in the territory of that state. Art. 13, Hostages Convention.

[253] *Supra* note 245. Article 75(2)(c) of API expands the scope of the prohibition such that it is prohibited to take as a hostage any 'persons who are in the power of a Party to the conflict and who do not benefit from more favourable treatment under the [Geneva] Conventions or [...] Protocol I', which would potentially include (i) prisoners of war under the Geneva Convention Relative to the Treatment of Prisoners of War of 12 August 1949, 75 UNTS 135 [hereinafter 'GCIII'] and (ii) wounded, sick or shipwrecked combatants under the Geneva Convention for the Amelioration of the Condition of the Wounded and Sick in Armed Forces in the Field of 12 August 1949, 75 UNTS 31 [hereinafter 'GCI'] and the Geneva Convention for the Amelioration of the Conditions of Wounded, Sick and Shipwrecked Members of Armed Forces at Sea of 12 August 1949, 75 UNTS 85 [hereinafter 'GCII']. But a violation of the expanded prohibition of hostage-taking under Article 75(2)(c) of API does not amount to a grave breach of the four Geneva Conventions or API, and is therefore not subject to a prosecute or hand over obligation (Art. 85, API).

[254] Art. 85, API.

the Hostages Convention and is therefore excluded from the scope of that Convention (although remains subject to the prosecute or hand over obligation under the Geneva Conventions and API). The difficulty is that many state parties to non-international armed conflicts in which a people is fighting in exercise of their right of self-determination are not state parties to API.[255] As international armed conflicts (between states) are largely irrelevant in the context of self-determination, and the prosecute or hand over obligation only applies to non-international armed conflicts if a relevant state is party to API, the hostage-takings described above will generally fall within the scope of the Hostages Convention. In all other cases not referenced above (i.e. the non-perfidious hostage-taking of an active combatant), the hostage-taking will also fall within the scope of the Hostages Convention and be subject to its obligations to criminalize, prevent and extradite or submit for prosecution.

The complicated regime interaction discussed above (and the even more complicated application of IHL on which the rules relating to that regime interaction depend) is well illustrated by Hezbollah's capture of two Israeli IDF soldiers, Ehud Goldwasserand Eldad Regev, on 12 July 2006. Hezbollah refused to release the soldiers until Israel released a number of Palestinian, Lebanese and other Arab prisoners held in Israeli jails.[256] The capture of the soldiers therefore meets the elements of the offence defined in Article 1 of the Hostages Convention, which requires that detention (or continued detention) be for the purposes of compelling a state or international organization to do or abstain from doing something. As the capture of the soldiers precipitated an armed conflict between Hezbollah and Israel, and there are at least some states that qualify Hezbollah members as freedom fighters,[257] the issue of exclusion from the scope of the Hostages Convention under Article 12 is raised. Regarding the first condition for exclusion, it is far from certain that the conflict between Hezbollah and Israel was an international armed conflict as understood under the Geneva Conventions[258] *at the time of the capture* of the two IDF soldiers.[259] On the day in question, Hezbollah fighters fired rockets across the Israeli border at villages and army posts. At the same time, they crossed the Lebanese border into Israel and attacked an Israeli army patrol directly. They killed three Israeli soldiers in the attack, and took the two above-mentioned soldiers captive. At this point, there is no international armed conflict as there is no

---

[255] A number of states which have non-international armed conflicts in their territory, in which a plausible argument might be made that a people are fighting in exercise of their right of self-determination, are not party to API, including: Pakistan, the Philippines, Israel, India and Turkey.

[256] Keesing's, Vol. 52, July 2006, 47389.

[257] The US Department of State Country Reports on Terrorism (2008) notes that Syria and Lebanon qualify Hezbollah as freedom fighters.

[258] The Additional Protocols do not apply because Israel is not a state party. Given that the grave breaches regime of the Geneva Conventions (and the prosecute or hand over obligation) does not apply to non-international armed conflicts in the absence of API party status, the capture of the two IDF soldiers can only be excluded from the scope of the Hostages Convention if committed in the course of an international armed conflict between two states.

[259] In order for the Article 12 exclusion clause to be engaged, the hostage-taking must have been committed *in the course* of an armed conflict.

confrontation between states (whether directly between their armed forces or through the attributable conduct of non-state actors) and there is no use of armed force by one state in the territory of another.[260] Soon after the Hezbollah attacks in Israel, Israeli soldiers crossed into Lebanese territory in pursuit of the Hezbollah fighters and their captured IDF soldiers, where they used armed force.[261] It is at this point that an international armed conflict *might* be said to begin.[262] Accepting this to be the case, the capture of the two IDF soldiers in Israeli territory precipitated the international armed conflict in that it was one of the catalysts for Israel's crossing into Lebanon—but at the time of capture, no international armed conflict existed. Even assuming an international armed conflict is evaluated more generally, on the day in question (rather than at the precise time the relevant offence was committed), the Geneva Conventions only prohibit the taking of civilian hostages during an international armed conflict.[263] The two Israeli soldiers were clearly not civilians. As a result, the grave breaches regime of the 1949 Geneva Conventions would not apply to the capture of the two IDF soldiers, and the act of hostage-taking would not be excluded from the scope of the Hostages Convention (having failed to meet the third condition for exclusion).

As to the effect of Article 12 on the substantive obligations to which states are subject, the heavily negotiated exclusion clause in the Hostages Convention does not eliminate the obligation to prevent hostage-takings or bring hostage-takers to justice. The obligation to prevent acts of international terrorism is an obligation under customary international law and is unaffected by the exclusion of a particular act of hostage-taking from the scope of the Hostages Convention. In addition, acts of hostage-taking are only excluded from the scope of the Hostages Convention to the extent that the Geneva Conventions or Additional Protocols are applicable thereto. As the Geneva Conventions and Additional Protocols require states to 'respect and ensure respect'[264] for the IHL rules they set out, states will be under an obligation to prevent acts of hostage-taking under Geneva Law whenever they do not have an obligation to do so under the Hostages Convention. Finally, exclusion from the Hostages Convention only shifts the source of a state's *aut dedere aut judicare* obligation. To the extent that a state is under an obligation to prosecute or hand over a hostage-taker under the 1949 Geneva Conventions or Additional Protocols, it will not also have an obligation to do so under the Hostages Convention. As such, no instance of hostage-taking is exempt from criminal law

---

[260] That Hezbollah's attacks may have resulted in a state of non-international armed conflict existing between Israel and non-state actors acting within its territory is irrelevant for the purposes of exclusion under Article 12 of the Hostages Convention. *Supra* note 258.

[261] Keesing's, Vol. 52, July 2006, 47389.

[262] *Supra* note 241.

[263] API prohibits the perfidious capture of active combatants, but is inapplicable because Israel is not a party thereto. In any event, there is no evidence to suggest that Hezbollah captured the Israeli IDF soldiers by feigning a protected status, misusing a protected emblem, or other perfidious conduct.

[264] Art. 1, GC I-IV; Art. 1, API. The obligation to 'ensure respect' has been interpreted as an obligation to prevent breaches.

enforcement obligations bearing on states,[265] breach of which could form the basis of a state's international responsibility. The real effect of the exclusion clause in the Hostages Convention as it applies to self-determination conflicts therefore bears on the question of regime interaction, in particular characterization of conduct as a war crime instead of an act of terrorism, and on the ICJ's jurisdiction to settle a dispute regarding the breach of an *aut dedere aut judicare* obligation. The Geneva Conventions do not have a compromissory clause conferring jurisdiction on the ICJ over disputes, whereas the Hostages Convention (and indeed all other TSCs) do have a compromissory clause.[266] As a result, if an act of hostage-taking is excluded from the scope of the Hostages Convention because it is covered by the Geneva Conventions, the Court is unlikely to have jurisdiction (in the absence of an applicable Article 36(2) declaration under the ICJ Statute) to decide disputes relating to a failure to prevent an act of hostage-taking or to extradite or submit the hostage-taker to prosecution.

Terrorist Bombing Convention

Proposals were made to expressly exclude acts committed in furtherance of a people's right of self-determination from the scope of the Terrorist Bombing Convention.[267] Under pressure from Western states, which argued that the text was a carefully balanced compromise[268] and that the urgency of the need to address terrorist bombings required immediate action,[269] the Terrorist Bombing Convention was adopted without reflecting such proposals. The Terrorist Bombing Convention does however exclude the activities of armed forces during an armed conflict (as such terms are understood in IHL)[270] from the scope of the Convention. The exclusion clause in Article 19(2) of the Terrorist Bombing Convention, reads as follows:

The activities of armed forces during an armed conflict, as those terms are understood under international humanitarian law, which are governed by that law, are not governed by this Convention, and the activities undertaken by military forces of a State in the exercise of their

---

[265] Sofaer (1986), 916. But see International Law Association (1984a), 129, suggesting that uncertainty as to the applicable regime in the self-determination context (Geneva Conventions or the Hostages Convention) may result in impunity for the hostage taker. See also Chadwick (1996), 107–8.

[266] See Section 4.4.

[267] See UNGA, Sixth Committee, Report of the working group on measure to eliminate international terrorism, UN Doc. A/C.6/52/L.3 (1997), Annex II.

[268] Negotiation of the Terrorist Bombing Convention also focused on whether the conduct of state military forces should be excluded from the scope of the convention. *Infra* Chapter 4, note 87 and accompanying text.

[269] UNGA, Sixth Committee, UN Doc. A/C.6/52/SR.33 (1997), para 4 (Australia), para 16 (Italy), para 18 (US).

[270] Unlike Article 12 of the Hostages Convention, which defines terms in reference to the Geneva Conventions and Additional Protocols, the Terrorist Bombing Convention defines 'armed conflict' and 'armed forces' in reference to international humanitarian law in general—thereby incorporating (for definitional purposes) customary international humanitarian law into the Terrorist Bombing Convention.

official duties, inasmuch as they are governed by other rules of international law, are not governed by this Convention.[271]

The Organization of the Islamic Conference ('OIC'), in negotiating the draft comprehensive terrorism suppression convention, has proposed that, *if* the language of Article 19(2) of the Terrorist Bombing Convention is included in the comprehensive convention, the phrase 'activities of armed forces during an armed conflict' be replaced by 'the activities of the parties during an armed conflict, including in situations of foreign occupation'.[272] The purpose of this proposal is apparently to clarify the applicability of the exclusion clause to the conduct of a people fighting in exercise of their right of self-determination, and its implication is two-fold: first, that concerned states are not confident that the term 'armed forces' includes a people fighting in exercise of their right of self-determination; and second that situations of occupation (against which peoples are fighting in exercise of their right of self-determination) do not amount to an 'armed conflict' benefitting from exclusion. Nevertheless, several states made statements in explanation of their vote on the adoption of the Terrorist Bombing Convention to the effect that they did not consider the Convention to require the criminalization of acts committed in furtherance of a struggle for self-determination.[273]

In regard to the proposed replacement of the term 'armed forces' with 'parties to a conflict', the OIC's concern is not entirely misplaced. Early definitions of 'armed forces' were restricted to the forces of a state, therefore excluding freedom fighters fighting *against* the state.[274] In its recent study of customary IHL, however, the International Committee of the Red Cross ('ICRC') has treated the expanded definition of 'armed forces' in Article 43 API, which includes 'organized armed forces, groups and units which are under a command responsible to [a party to the conflict] for the conduct of its subordinates',[275] as having reached customary status.[276] The definition is not dependent on state organ or agent status and

---

[271] For a discussion on the applicability of the Terrorist Bombing Convention to bombings carried out by organs of a state (including its military forces), see Section 4.2.2.

[272] See Report of the *Ad Hoc* Committee established by General Assembly Resolution 51/210 of 17 December 1996, UN Doc. A/57/37 (2002), Annex IV, Text proposed by the Member States of the Organization of the Islamic Conference. See also Hmoud (2006), 1037.

[273] See e.g. statements made by Pakistan, Iran, Iraq, Syria, and Libya before the Sixth Committee vote on the Terrorist Bombing Convention. UNGA, Sixth Committee, UN Doc. A/C.6/52/SR.33 (1997), paras 46–69. See also the Jamaican delegate's statement before the Sixth Committee vote on the Terrorist Bombing Convention, noting that the two different interpretations states had given Article 19(2) of the Terrorist Bombing Convention (one excluding acts committed in the struggle for self-determination from the scope of the Convention, the other considering there to be no exceptions to the prohibition on terrorist bombings) did not bode well for legal certainty. UNGA, Sixth Committee, UN Doc. A/C.6/52/SR.33 (1997), para 81.

[274] See Pictet (1958), 35; ICRC (1960), 51.

[275] Art. 43(1), API. The principal effect of the expanded definition of 'armed forces' was on combatant status, and therefore entitlement to prisoner of war treatment. On the compromise reached in regard to these issues during the negotiation of Protocol I, see Greenwood (2007), 216–18.

[276] ICRC (2005), Vol. I, Rule 4, 14–17. See also ICRC (2005), Vol. II, 86–100. Article 43 of API goes on to stipulate that '[s]uch armed forces shall be subject to an internal disciplinary system which, inter alia, shall enforce compliance with the rules of international law applicable in armed conflict'. Article 44(3) of API further provides that '[w]hile all combatants are obliged to comply with the rules

applies to non-state armed groups (including peoples exercising their right of self-determination) as long as they are organized and operate on the basis of command responsibility. The real aim of the OIC's proposal—in suggesting that the term 'armed forces' be replaced with 'parties' during an armed conflict—is therefore the exclusion of acts of terrorism carried out by unorganized groups that operate without any formal hierarchy. While the proposal is restricted to groups genuinely fighting in exercise of a right of self-determination, the worry of Western states is that the phrase 'parties' will capture many terrorist organizations operating in the twenty-first century, whose organizational structure is fluid rather than hierarchical.[277] The proposal is still being negotiated in reference to the draft comprehensive terrorism suppression convention, and failure to agree on the precise language of the exclusion clause is one of the reasons for the protracted negotiations.[278] As it stands in reference to the Terrorist Bombing Convention, however, terrorist bombings carried out by members of a loosely affiliated organization, even if fighting in exercise of a right of self-determination, do not fall within the scope of Article 19(2) and will therefore be covered by the Terrorist Bombing Convention.

The OIC's concern that the term 'armed conflict' may not cover situations of occupation is indeed a valid cause for concern if their aim is to ensure that peoples fighting in exercise of their right of self-determination are not covered by the Terrorist Bombing Convention. Situations of occupation to which IHL applies arise only in the context of international armed conflicts,[279] where one state party has established control over all or part of the territory of another state party, and is in a position to exercise that control. As international armed conflicts (between states) are unlikely to be relevant conflicts in the context of self-determination,[280] the OIC's proposal attempts to extend the scope of exclusion to situations of occupation in non-international armed conflicts, because such occupations do not themselves qualify as armed conflicts absent a certain threshold of violence.[281] Effectively, the proposal aims to ensure that acts of violence committed in the context of the Israeli occupation of Palestinian Territories[282] are excluded from the scope of the draft comprehensive terrorism suppression convention—and thereby suggests that the OIC does not consider such acts to be excluded from the scope of

---

of international law applicable in armed conflict, violations of these rules shall not deprive a combatant of his right to be a combatant or, if he falls into the power of an adverse Party, of his right to be a prisoner of war'. Article 44(3) of API strongly suggests that the mention of compliance with international humanitarian law in the Article 43 of API definition of 'armed forces' is not an element of that definition, but rather a statement of the obligations by which such armed forces are bound.

[277] Hoffman (2006), 271.

[278] See Reports of the *Ad Hoc* Committee established by General Assembly Resolution 51/210 of 17 December 1996, UN Doc. A/58/37 (2003), Annex II, para 5; UN Doc. A/64/37 (2009), Annex II, para 5; UN Doc. A/65/37 (2010), Annex II, para 5.

[279] See Art. 2, GCIV.

[280] See discussion in reference to the Hostages Convention, *supra* notes 247–8 and accompanying text.

[281] *Ibid*.

[282] On the characterization of Gaza as occupied territory, see Darcy and Reynolds (2010).

the Terrorist Bombing Convention under Article 19(2) as presently drafted. The OIC is correct in so far as a situation of occupation that continues after the end of an international armed conflict in which there is only sporadic violence (even if in furtherance of a people's right of self-determination) would not amount to an 'armed conflict' and would therefore not be excluded from the scope of the Terrorist Bombing Convention.

As to the effect of Article 19 on the substantive obligations to which states are subject, the heavily negotiated exclusion clause in the Terrorist Bombing Convention does not eliminate a state's obligation to prevent its territory from being used as a base from which cross-border bombings are launched. A state's obligation to prevent harm emanating from its territory (including terrorist bombings meeting the elements of the offences defined in the Terrorist Bombing Convention) is an obligation under customary international law and is unaffected by the exclusion of a particular bombing from the scope of the Terrorist Bombing Convention.

The exclusion clause will, however, have an effect on whether a state is under a substantive obligation to extradite or submit to prosecution a bombing that meets the elements of the Terrorist Bombing Convention.[283] If such a bombing is committed in the course of an armed conflict by an organized group subject to command responsibility, it will not be subject to the *aut dedere aut judicare* obligation in the Terrorist Bombing Convention. Bombings that are excluded from the scope of the Terrorist Bombing Convention will not be subject to a prosecute or hand over obligation under the Geneva Conventions or API if in compliance with the laws of war (for instance, if the bombing is justified by military necessity[284] and only targets objects that make an effective contribution to military action, or any incidental loss of civilian life is not excessive in relation to the concrete and direct military advantage anticipated from the bombing).[285] As discussed below, there is a lot of sense in ensuring that bombings committed during an armed conflict in compliance with the laws of war, even if committed by non-state actors, are not subject to prosecution. *But*, bombings that *are in breach* of humanitarian law standards carried out by an organized armed group subject to command responsibility and fighting in exercise of its right of self-determination will not be subject to a prosecute or hand over obligation under Geneva Law if relevant states have not ratified API.[286] As any such bombings would also fall

---

[283] The Terrorist Bombing Convention requires states to criminalize the following offence: 'unlawfully and intentionally delivering, placing, discharging or detonating an explosive or other lethal device in, into or against a place of public use, a State or government facility, a public transportation system or an infrastructure facility, with the intent to cause death or serious bodily injury, or with the intent to cause extensive destruction of such a place, facility or system, where such destruction results in or is likely to result in major economic loss'. Art. 2(1), Terrorist Bombing Convention.

[284] Art. 147, GCIV.

[285] Arts. 50(4), 52(2), and 85(3)(b), API.

[286] While there is increasing evidence that states claim a right to prosecute breaches of IHL committed during non-international armed conflicts (see Graditzky (1998)), there is as of yet no customary international law obligation to prosecute breaches of IHL committed in the context of non-international armed conflicts. See *Tadić* (ICTY-94-1-A), Interlocutory Appeal on Jurisdiction, para 48; Zegfeld (2002), 175; Moir (2002), 235; Moir (2009). The obligation to prosecute or hand over in the Geneva Conventions and API will therefore only apply in the context of armed conflicts in which a

outside the scope of the Terrorist Bombing Convention (as discussed above), they would therefore not be subject to any *aut dedere aut judicare* obligation.

In addition to affecting the substantive obligations to which states are subject, exclusion from the Terrorist Bombing Convention will affect whether the ICJ has jurisdiction to decide disputes in reference to a failure to prevent terrorist bombings. Unless relevant state parties have made an Article 36(2) declaration under the ICJ Statute,[287] the only basis of jurisdiction in reference to a dispute regarding breach of the obligation to prevent terrorism will be the TSCs. With respect to disputes regarding breach of an *aut dedere aut judicare* obligation, exclusion from the scope of the Terrorist Bombing Convention will also have an impact on whether the ICJ has jurisdiction with respect thereto. Even if a bombing is subject to an alternative prosecute or hand over obligation under the Geneva Conventions or API, none of those Conventions have compromissory clauses conferring jurisdiction on the ICJ. As a result, absent an Article 36(2) declaration under the ICJ Statute, breach of an *aut dedere aut judicare* obligation in respect of bombings will only be subject to the Court's jurisdiction to the extent that it falls within the scope of the Terrorist Bombing Convention.

Unlike the Hostages Convention—which operates on the basis that all acts of hostage-taking (whether committed in times of peace or war, and by whoever committed) must be criminalized and subject to an *aut dedere aut judicare* obligation—Article 19 of the Terrorist Bombing Convention does not condition exclusion on the applicability of an alternative criminal law enforcement regime. This is because the Terrorist Bombing Convention attempts to respect the balance achieved by IHL in determining that some bombings will be unlawful, while others will be lawful (if regrettable) acts of war. The shift achieved by API is that certain acts of violence carried out in the context of a struggle for self-determination that might have been characterized as terrorist are, under API, assessed pursuant to a war paradigm. Had exclusion under Article 19 of the Terrorist Bombing Convention been conditioned on the applicability of an alternative criminal law enforcement framework (like under Article 12 of the Hostages Convention), bombings that would be legitimate in an armed conflict as a matter of IHL would nevertheless be unlawful under the terrorism suppression regime (precisely because they were not unlawful—and thereby not subject to an alternative *aut dedere aut judicare* obligation—under IHL).

But certain acts of war that fall outside the scope of the Terrorist Bombing Convention in virtue of Article 19 may not be subject to any prosecute or hand over obligation, despite being in breach of international humanitarian law standards. This results from the uneven ratification of API and the fact that it is not yet settled whether the obligation to prosecute or hand over persons alleged to have committed breaches of humanitarian law in non-international armed conflicts is

---

people is fighting in exercise of their right of self-determination to the extent that relevant states are party to API and accept the expanded legal definition of international armed conflict in Article 1(4) of API.

[287] See Section 4.1.

customary. There may therefore be gaps in coverage such that some bombings that are unlawful under international law will not be subject to any international criminal law enforcement regime. As a result, the scope of Article 19 and its interaction with state party status to API will be very important in determining whether a state has any *aut dedere aut judicare* obligation in reference to a particular bombing.

Terrorism Financing Convention

There were suggestions during the negotiation of the Terrorism Financing Convention that the Convention must define terrorism by differentiating it from conduct undertaken in furtherance of a legitimate struggle for self-determination.[288] Such proposals were not, however, adopted. Article 2(1) of the Terrorism Financing Convention defines acts of terrorism (the financing of which is to be criminalized, prevented and subject to an *aut dedere aut judicare* obligation pursuant to the Convention) as:

(a) [a]n act which constitutes an offence within the scope of and as defined in one of the treaties listed in the annex; and (b) [a]ny other act intended to cause death or serious bodily injury to a civilian, or to any other person not taking an active part in the hostilities of a situation of armed conflict, when the purposes of such act, by its nature or context, is to intimidate a population, or to compel a government or an international organization to do or abstain from doing any act.[289]

There is no general clause excluding matters from the scope of the Terrorism Financing Convention, and the catch-all definition of terrorism set out in Article 2(1)(b) applies in any case where a relevant act does not fall within the scope of the TSCs listed in the annex. As a result, the financing of any act of violence meeting the elements of Article 2(1)(b) falls within the scope of the Terrorism Financing Convention, whether or not that act of violence is committed in furtherance of a people's struggle for self-determination. Even if conduct undertaken in furtherance of a struggle for self-determination were excluded from the scope of the definition of terrorism under Article 2(1)(a) of the Terrorism Financing Convention (because it is excluded from the scope of the Hostages Convention or the Terrorist Bombing Convention), it will still fall within the scope of the catch-all definition of terrorism (to which no exclusions apply) under Article 2(1)(b). Subject to the discussion on reservations below, states are therefore under an obligation to criminalize, prevent, and extradite or submit to prosecution the financing of acts falling within the definition of Article 2(1)(b), regardless of whether the alleged terrorist acted in furtherance of a right of self-determination, and an injured state could submit an application to the ICJ on the basis of the Convention's compromissory clause in reference to state responsibility for breach of those obligations.

---

[288] See e.g. UNGA, Sixth Committee, UN Doc. A/C.6/54/SR.34 (1999), para 30 (Pakistan).
[289] Art. 2, Terrorism Financing Convention.

Nuclear Terrorism Convention, 2005 Protocol to the SUA Convention, 2010 Protocol to the Hague Convention and Beijing Convention

There was a marked absence of any discussion on self-determination during the negotiation of the Nuclear Terrorism Convention, the 2005 Protocol to the SUA Convention, the 2010 Protocol to the Hague Convention or the Beijing Convention (the latter two adopted on 10 September 2010 and not yet in force).[290] In reference to the four Conventions, most proposals submitted by delegations touched on whether acts by states should fall within the scope of the Convention,[291] and the compromise finally reached included language from the exclusion clause set out in Article 19(2) of the Terrorist Bombing Convention.[292] As a result, interpretation of the exclusion clause in these Conventions is subject to the same analysis as set out above in regard to the Terrorist Bombing Convention, and acts in furtherance of a struggle for self-determination, to the extent committed in the course of an armed conflict by an organized group subject to command responsibility, are excluded from the scope of the Nuclear Terrorism Convention, 2005 Protocol to the SUA Convention and the 2010 Protocol to the Hague Convention and Beijing Convention (should they enter into force).

3.3.2 Reservations to the TSCs

Acts meeting the elements of defined terrorist offences committed by national liberation movements outside the context of an armed conflict will never be excluded from the scope of relevant TSCs. Nor should they be. There is absolutely no principled reason to distinguish such acts from other politically motivated acts of violence committed in times of peace that fall within the scope of the terrorism suppression regime.[293] This is because the right of self-determination must be

---

[290] Only Syria proposed that the Nuclear Terrorism Convention not apply to the activities of peoples struggling against a colonial power, foreign occupation, and racist regimes in the exercise of the right to self-determination. The Syrian proposal was not addressed by any other delegates. See Report of the *Ad Hoc* Committee established by General Assembly Resolution 51/210 of 17 December 1996, UN Doc. A/53/37 (1998), Annex II, Written amendments and proposals submitted by delegations, 26. There were no proposals regarding self-determination during the negotiation of the new IMO and ICAO TSCs. See generally IMO, Report of the Legal Committee on the work of its ninetieth session, IMO Doc. LEG 90/15 (2005); ICAO Assembly, 36th Session, Legal Committee, Acts or offences of concern to the international aviation community and not covered by existing air law instruments, ICAO Doc. A36-WP/12, LE/4 (2007); ICAO Legal Committee, 34th Session, Montreal Convention of 1971 as amended by the Airports Protocol of 1988 with amendments proposed by the Legal Committee, ICAO Doc. LC/34-WP/2-5 (2009); ICAO Legal Committee, 34th Session, Draft report on the work of the legal committee during its 34th session, ICAO Doc. LC/34-WP/4-1 (2009).

[291] See Section 4.2.2 for a discussion of the application of the exclusion clause to acts of state.

[292] Each of the Nuclear Terrorism Convention, 2010 Protocol to the Hague Convention and the Beijing Convention contain an additional sub-paragraph in their exclusion clauses that reads: 'The provisions [of the present article] shall not be interpreted as condoning or making lawful otherwise unlawful acts, or precluding prosecution under other laws'. Art. 4(2), Nuclear Terrorism Convention; Art. VI, 2010 Protocol to the Hague Convention; Art. 6(3), Beijing Convention.

[293] But see Klabbers (2003).

distinguished from the methods and means of giving effect to that right. Requiring that the right of self-determination be exercised, in times of peace, in the same manner as other political rights are exercised (i.e. peacefully) simply does not amount to an impermissible limitation on the right itself. Where acts are committed in the context of an armed conflict, however, their exclusion from the scope of a particular TSC will depend on the negotiated principles of regime interaction applicable thereto—which will in turn often depend on the pattern of ratification of API. Because the TSC negotiations (on the basis of consensus) have not always yielded regime interaction principles that are acceptable to NAM states, a number of them have made declarations and reservations to the TSCs that purport to carve out acts committed in furtherance of a people's right of self-determination from the scope of those Conventions, and therefore from the general obligations to criminalize, prevent and extradite or submit to prosecution defined therein. As noted above in reference to the application of the TSC exclusion clauses, excluding conduct committed in exercise of a people's right of self-determination from the scope of the TSCs will not necessarily have an impact on the substantive obligations to which the reserving state is subject. A state's obligation to prevent harm emanating from its territory is an obligation of customary international law, and, in the circumstances discussed above, an obligation to extradite or submit to prosecution will exist under the Geneva Conventions and API irrespective of the cause for which individual actors fight. But for acts of terrorism that are not committed in the context of an armed conflict (and are therefore not covered by Geneva Law), but nevertheless are considered to be in exercise of a people's right of self-determination, the reservations discussed in this section may well liberate states from any criminal law enforcement obligations in reference to such conduct.

On its accession to the Internationally Protected Persons Convention, Burundi made the following reservation:

In respect of cases where the alleged offenders belong to a national liberation movement recognized by Burundi or by an international organization of which Burundi is a member, and their actions are part of their struggle for liberation, the Government of the Republic of Burundi reserves the right not to apply to them the provisions of article 2, paragraph 2 [criminalize defined offences], and article 6, paragraph 1 [apprehend for the purposes of extradition or prosecution].[294]

Lebanon declared that the provisions of the Hostages Convention 'shall not affect the Lebanese Republic's stance of supporting the right of States and peoples to oppose and resist foreign occupation of their territories'.[295] Pakistan, in relation to the Terrorist Bombing Convention declared that:

---

[294] France, Germany, Israel, Italy and the UK objected to the reservation, all but France qualifying the reservation as incompatible with the object and purpose of the Convention. Israel, Italy and the UK did not consider Burundi to have validly acceded to the Convention until it withdrew its reservation. <http://treaties.un.org/pages/ViewDetails.aspx?src=TREATY&mtdsg_no=XVIII-7&chapter=18&lang=en#13>.

[295] <http://treaties.un.org/pages/ViewDetails.aspx?src=TREATY&mtdsg_no=XVIII-5&chapter=18&lang=en>. Lebanon's declaration might be interpreted as a reservation in so far as it purports to exclude

nothing in this Convention shall be applicable to struggles, including armed struggle, for the realization of the right of self-determination launched against any alien or foreign occupation or domination, in accordance with the rules of international law. This interpretation is consistent with Article 53 of the Vienna Convention on the Law of Treaties 1969 which provides that an agreement or treaty concluded in conflict with an existing *jus cogens* or peremptory norm of international law is void and [. . .] the right of self-determination is universally recognized as *a jus cogens.*[296]

Pakistan's contention that an obligation to criminalize and extradite or submit to prosecution is in conflict with the *jus cogens* norm of self-determination is debatable, as the obligations under the TSCs suggest only a limitation on the means of exercising the right, rather than a limitation on the right itself. Nevertheless, Pakistan's reservation purports to do what the Non-Aligned Movement could not achieve in negotiating Article 19(2) of the Terrorist Bombing Convention— that is, to exclude any bombing committed in furtherance of a people's right of self-determination from the scope of the Terrorist Bombing Convention. In a similar vein, Egypt, Jordan and Syria have declared that they do not consider acts of armed resistance in exercise of the right of self-determination as terrorist acts within the meaning of Article 2(1) of the Terrorism Financing Convention.[297] As states are only required to criminalize, prevent, extradite or submit for prosecution the financing of terrorist offences defined in Article 2(1), the Egyptian, Jordanian and Syrian declarations effectively purport to carve out the financing of national liberation movements from their obligations under the Terrorism Financing Convention.

The potential effect of these reservations and declarations is best considered through a hypothetical. Consider the Israel/Hezbollah war of 2006 during which

---

the legal effect of certain provisions of the treaty to peoples resisting foreign occupation. See Aust (2006), 104. In reference to a very similar declaration made by Iran on ratification of the Hostages Convention (to the effect that Iran 'believes that fighting terrorism should not affect the legitimate struggle of peoples under colonial domination and foreign occupation in the exercise of their right of self-determination'), Portugal, Canada, Germany, Italy, the Netherlands and Spain all considered that it attempted to limit the scope of the Convention (i.e. to exclude acts committed in furtherance of a struggle for self-determination). As a result, all considered the declaration to be without legal effect, even though they did not consider it to affect the entry into force of the Convention as between Iran and the objecting state. Portugal, Germany, the Netherlands and Spain qualified the attempt to limit the scope of the Convention as incompatible with object and purpose. France, the US, Austria, and Japan also considered the reservation to be without legal effect (and the Convention to be in force as between Iran and the objecting state), but without specifying whether they considered the declaration to modify or limit the scope of the Convention or to be incompatible with object and purpose.

[296] <http://treaties.un.org/pages/ViewDetails.aspx?src=TREATY&mtdsg_no=XVIII-9&chapter=18 &lang=en>. Australia, Austria, Canada, Denmark, Finland, Germany, India, Ireland, Italy, the Netherlands, New Zealand, Norway, Spain, Sweden, the UK, and the US all objected to the reservation as contrary to object and purpose, but stipulated that the objection would not preclude the entry into force of the Convention as between the objecting and reserving states. France objected to Pakistan's reservation without qualifying it as one that was incompatible with object and purpose; and Israel and Japan objected to the reservation as incompatible with object and purpose, but without stipulating that their objections did not preclude the entry into force of the treaty as between objecting and reserving states.

[297] <http://treaties.un.org/pages/ViewDetails.aspx?src=TREATY&mtdsg_no=XVIII-11&chapter= 18&lang=en>.

Israel launched armed attacks against Hezbollah strongholds in Lebanon in response (in part) to Hezbollah's having taken two Israeli soldiers hostage.[298] For the purposes of the hypothetical, assume that Israel, Lebanon and Syria are state parties to the Hostages Convention and the Terrorism Financing Convention[299] and that those treaties are applicable in their mutual relations.[300] As noted above, the hostage-takings were not committed during the course of an armed conflict (international or otherwise), and therefore the exclusion clause of the Hostages Convention is inapplicable. Lebanon might incur responsibility to Israel in relation to the hostage-takings because, as a party to the Hostages Convention, Lebanon is under an obligation to prevent its territory from being used as a base of operations from which hostage-takings are conducted, and to extradite or submit for prosecution those who are responsible for such hostage-takings.[301] Syria could equally incur responsibility to Israel for its role in Hezbollah's activities because, as a party to the Terrorism Financing Convention, it would be under an obligation to prevent the financing of terrorism (which might include, on the basis of a *Bosnia Genocide Case* analysis, an obligation to itself refrain from financing acts of terrorism carried out by non-state actors).[302] But the applicability of the TSC obligations to prevent hostage-taking and to refrain from financing such activities may be affected by the reservations noted above.

Israel objected to Lebanon's declaration to the Hostages Convention as incompatible with object and purpose.[303] Twenty states objected to Syria's reservation to the Terrorism Financing Convention as incompatible with object and purpose, nineteen of them stipulating that their objection did not preclude the entry into force of the Convention as between the objecting state and Syria.[304] International law is as of yet unclear on whether determinations of incompatibility with object

---

[298] See Sections 2.2.3 and 3.3.1, 'Hostages Convention', for details of the hostage-taking and ensuing armed conflict with Hezbollah in Lebanese territory.

[299] Israel signed the Hostages Convention, but has not ratified it, and Syria is not a party to the Hostages Convention. Although a party to the Terrorism Financing Convention, Syria has excluded the Hostages Convention from the list of TSCs in the annex under Article 2(1)(a). <http://treaties.un .org/pages/Treaties.aspx?id=18&subid=A&lang=en>.

[300] For the purposes of the hypothetical, Syria's reservation to the Terrorism Financing Convention (that '[t]he accession of the Syrian Arab Republic to this Convention shall in no way imply its recognition of Israel or entail its entry into any dealings with Israel in the matters governed by the provisions thereof') will not be given any effect.

[301] Lebanon would equally be under a customary international law obligation to prevent its territory from being used as a base of terrorist operations (see Section 3.1), but would not be under any customary international law obligation to extradite or submit to prosecution (*supra* notes 109–11 and accompanying text).

[302] See Section 4.2.1. It has been alleged that Syria financially supports Hezbollah. See Byman (2005), 135.

[303] <http://treaties.un.org/pages/ViewDetails.aspx?src=TREATY&mtdsg_no=XVIII-5&chapter= 18&lang=en#EndDec>.

[304] Austria, Belgium, Canada, Denmark, Estonia, Finland, France, Germany, Hungary, Italy, Japan, Latvia, the Netherlands, Norway, Poland, Portugal, Spain, Sweden, the UK and the US objected to Syria's reservation as incompatible with object and purpose. Of the objecting states, only Japan failed to stipulate that the objection did not preclude the entry into force of the Terrorism Financing Convention. <http://treaties.un.org/pages/ViewDetails.aspx?src=TREATY&mtdsg_no= XVIII-11&chapter=18&lang=en>.

and purpose are subjective (and, if so, how many objections to a reservation as incompatible with object and purpose is sufficient for the purposes of giving effect to that incompatibility),[305] or whether the matter is for objective determination, for instance by the ICJ,[306] without reference to the position of objecting states.

Even if the reservations discussed above are incompatible with object and purpose based purely on the determination of objecting states, the precise effect of such incompatibility is not settled. While the Special Rapporteur on Reservations to Treaties has concluded that incompatibility with object and purpose results in the invalidity of a reservation,[307] the ILC has yet to adopt any position on the effect of such invalidity.[308] Invalidity could mean that the reservation is null and void, but severable from the reserving state's consent to be bound.[309] Severability should only occur to the extent that the reserving state's consent to the treaty is not conditional on the effectiveness of its reservation.[310] The result of severance is that the reserving state (in this hypothetical Lebanon and Syria) is an unqualified party to the full treaty. Alternatively, the invalidity of the reservation could invalidate the reserving state's consent to be bound, in particular where that consent is conditional on the effectiveness of the reservation.[311] In such a case Lebanon and Syria would cease to be parties to the relevant TSC.[312] Both positions have been taken in

---

[305] See Pellet (2005). But see Human Rights Committee, General Comment 24, Reservations to the International Covenant on Civil and Political Rights, UN Doc. CCPR/C/21/Rev.1/Add.6 (1994), para 18. In reference to the International Covenant on Civil and Political Rights, the Human Rights Committee has reserved for itself the authority to objectively determine whether a reservation is contrary to object and purpose.

[306] See Pellet (2005); Higgins (2007). See also *Reservations to the Genocide Convention,* Advisory Opinion; *Armed Activities on the Territory of the Congo (DRC v. Rwanda)* (New Application: 2002), Jurisdiction and Admissibility.

[307] Pellet (2005), para 187.

[308] See Pellet (2009), para 14.

[309] This appears to be the position of the nineteen states that objected to Syria's reservation to the Terrorism Financing Convention, but stipulated that the objection did not preclude the entry into force of the Convention as between the objecting state and Syria. See also the Irish and Swedish objections to Pakistan's self-determination reservation to the Terrorist Bombing Convention, in which they stipulate that the objection shall not preclude the entry into force of the Convention between the reserving state and Pakistan, and that the Convention enters into force, without Pakistan benefiting from its reservation. See generally Redgwell (1993), 257. Several states have supported the severability of reservations that are incompatible with object and purpose in their comments on the ILC 'Reservations to Treaties' project: See UNGA, Sixth Committee, UN Doc. A/C.6/60/SR.14 (2005), paras 22–3 (Sweden (on behalf of the Nordic countries); UNGA, Sixth Committee, UN Doc. A/C.6/60/SR.18 (2005), para 86 (Malaysia); UNGA, Sixth Committee, UN Doc. A/C.6/60/SR.19 (2005), para 39 (Greece). But see UNGA, Sixth Committee, UN Doc. A/C.6/60/SR.14 (2005), para 3 (UK); UNGA, Sixth Committee, UN Doc. A/C.6/60/SR.14 (2005), para 40 (Australia); UNGA, Sixth Committee, UN Doc. A/C.6/60/SR.14 (2005), para 72 (France); UNGA, Sixth Committee, UN Doc. A/C.6/60/SR.16 (2005), para 20 (Italy); UNGA, Sixth Committee, UN Doc. A/C.6/60/SR.16 (2005), para 44 (Portugal); UNGA, Sixth Committee, UN Doc. A/C.6/62/SR.25 (2007), paras 28–9 (Greece); UNGA, Sixth Committee, UN Doc. A/C.6/62/SR.25 (2007), para 20 (Sweden). See also Report of the International Law Commission on the work of its fifty-ninth session, UN Doc. A/62/10 (2007), para 23.

[310] *Belilos v. Switzerland* (ECtHR, 1988).

[311] See *Reservations to the Genocide Convention,* Advisory Opinion; Bowett (1977), 88; UNGA, Sixth Committee, UN Doc. A/C.6/62/SR.19 (2007), para 21(Germany). This appears to be the position taken by states in reference to Burundi's reservation to the Internationally Protected Persons Convention. *Supra* note 294.

[312] While both states might nevertheless have an obligation to prevent acts of hostage-taking as a matter of customary international law, they would have no obligation to extradite or submit to

reference to reservations to the TSCs which were objected to by individual states as incompatible with object and purpose. It has also been suggested that the effects of a reservation that is objected to as incompatible with object and purpose could depend on a 'reservations dialogue' commenced between the reserving and object-ing state.[313] Whether states have an obligation to criminalize, extradite or submit to prosecution under the TSCs against which they have made a self-determination reservation will depend in part on the unsettled (and unlikely to be easily settled) outcome of the ILC's work on treaty reservations.

Whether injured states can rely on the TSC compromissory clauses as a basis of the ICJ's jurisdiction in reference to breaches of those obligations will also depend on the effect (if any) to be given to such reservations. If a reservation were found to be severable (on the basis of its incompatibility with object and purpose), the reserving state would be a party to the TSC without benefit of the reservation and the Court would have jurisdiction pursuant to that TSC's compromissory clause over a dispute that would otherwise have fallen within the scope of the reservation. But if the effect of the reservation were that the reserving state, having expressed contradictory intentions, would not be a party to the TSC against which it had made an incompatible reservation, the Court would not have jurisdiction over any dispute with the reserving state regarding that TSC. As will be discussed in Chapter 4, it is not unknown for the ICJ to favour (in a principled manner) the position that supports a finding of jurisdiction.

The argument that reservations which are held to be incompatible with object and purpose should be severable from the agreement to be bound by the relevant TSC might find further support from Article 103 of the UN Charter and the obligations to prevent international terrorism imposed on all states by the Security Council. Acting under Chapter VII, the Security Council decided that all states *shall* '[p]revent and suppress the financing of terrorist acts' and '[t]ake the necessary steps to prevent the commission of terrorist acts, including by provision of early warning to other States by exchange of information'.[314] The Security Council drew no distinction between terrorist acts and violence carried out in furtherance of a struggle for self-determination.[315] Obligations set out in Security Council resolu-tions adopted under Chapter VII are mandatory for all member states of the UN,[316] and obligations of member states under the UN Charter prevail over

---

prosecution, as the alternative criminal law enforcement obligations under the Geneva Conventions would not apply to the acts of hostage-taking because Israel is not a party to API and the hostage-taking was not committed during the course of an international armed conflict.

[313] See Ruda (1975), 190, arguing that Article 19(c) of the VCLT is 'a mere doctrinal assertion, which may serve as a basis for guidance to states regarding acceptance of reservations, but no more than that'. See also Gaja (1987), 314. A number of states that responded to the ILC questionnaire on the effect of an objection to a reservation as incompatible with object and purpose considered such objections to form the basis of a 'reservations dialogue' with the reserving state. See Pellet (2006), 11, para 37; UNGA, Sixth Committee, UN Doc. A/C.6/62/SR.23 (2007), paras 64–7 (France).

[314] UNSC Resolution 1373 (2001), paras 1(a) and 2(b).

[315] See the Security Council's definition of 'terrorism' in UNSC Resolution 1566 (2004).

[316] Arts. 25 and 48(1), UN Charter.

obligations under other international agreements.[317] The ICJ has accounted for general customary international law in its interpretation of treaties through the mechanism of Article 31(3)(c) of the VCLT.[318] It might also interpret declarations to treaties through the prism of Security Council legislation with a similar application of Article 31(3)(c) of the VCLT, thereby concluding that declarations which are incompatible with the object and purpose of a treaty are severable therefrom in an effort to impose symmetry between the scope of treaty and Security Council obligations.

Further support for severability, at least in reference to the regime of Terrorism Suppression Conventions, results from state practice. States that have objected to self-determination reservations as contrary to object and purpose (or as attempting to unilaterally limit the scope of the Convention) have generally stipulated that the relevant TSC nevertheless remains in force between the objecting and reserving state.[319] The one exception was in reference to Burundi's reservation to the Internationally Protected Persons Convention, which was the first TSC against which a self-determination reservation was made.[320] State practice has evolved since then, suggesting (unsurprisingly) that at least objecting states prioritize broad treaty participation over a strictly consensual approach to reservations.

3.4 Conclusion

Evaluating compliance with international terrorism prevention obligations calls for a balanced approach. As terrorism prevention obligations are imbued with more and more specificity, whether in virtue of notice of a particular threat or in virtue of the decrease in the margin of appreciation following the 9/11 terrorist attacks, the limitations imposed by a state's resource and territorial capacity (or incapacity) are infused with heightened importance—to ensure that states are not held responsible where diligence is exercised to the extent for which means allow. Barring such incapacity, however, and given the institutional support readily available to states, a failure to exercise due diligence in preventing terrorism in the post-9/11 world looks more and more like acquiescence.

This *rapprochement* will have important consequences in the sphere of state responsibility, because a state can be held responsible for a failure to prevent (effectively amounting to acquiescence in) terrorism whether or not a terrorist attack has occurred as a result of the state's inaction. Its consequences are equally far reaching in the *jus ad bellum* context. In light of the *rapprochement*, failures to prevent which border on the deliberate amount to a prohibited use of force

---

[317] Art. 103, UN Charter. See also the ICJ's treatment of conflict between a Security Council Chapter VII Resolution and the Montreal Convention. *Lockerbie Case (Libya v. US)*, Preliminary Objections.
[318] See discussion of the ICJ's decision in *Oil Platforms (Iran v. US)*, *infra* Chapter 4, note 58.
[319] *Supra* notes 295–6.
[320] *Supra* note 294.

pursuant to the UN Declaration on Friendly Relations.[321] Such failures may also account for the necessity of uses of force in the acquiescing state's territory to defend against terrorist attacks emanating therefrom.[322] The stakes are therefore very high in correctly evaluating whether a host state is acting to prevent international terrorism (but is missing the mark of diligence required in the post-9/11 world), or whether a state (given the notice and capacity development available in the post-9/11 world) is acquiescing in international terrorism and is thereby susceptible to breaches of its territorial integrity in response to terrorist attacks by non-state actors launched against foreign states from within its borders.

Analysis of the TSC *aut dedere aut judicare* obligations set out above reveals several important features that bear on an evaluation of compliance. First, the *aut dedere aut judicare* obligation in the TSCs does not require states to extradite alleged terrorist offenders held in their custody. A requested state's decision to extradite is subject to a broad discretion, and acceding to an extradition request remains within the (mostly unfettered) sovereign authority of the requested state. Custodial states that refuse to extradite an alleged offender, however, are thereby bound to submit the case to their competent authorities for prosecution. But the obligation to submit to prosecution, absolute as it is, does not necessarily guarantee that a terrorist offender will be brought to justice. While the obligation is subject to good faith, it does not require the custodial state to in fact proceed with a prosecution or to punish the alleged offender. For instance, insufficient evidence or state immunity (except in reference to immunity *ratione materiae* in cases where the alleged terrorist acted in foreign territory without the custodial state's consent, or the state of nationality is party to a relevant TSC) may result in a case proceeding no further than referral to competent authorities. In this way, the obligation in the TCSs to extradite or submit to prosecution attempts to balance the international community's interest in eliminating impunity for terrorist offences against a measure of non-interference in each state party's domestic criminal regulation. While the balance will not always be perfect (and indeed will often allow for non-prosecution that is TSC compliant), it will be most imperfect when the *aut dedere aut judicare* obligation is asked to bear the weight of state terrorism, which it was not designed to carry. The *aut dedere aut judicare* obligation in the TSCs was intended to secure the criminal responsibility of individual terrorist actors, and contemplated the custodial state's commitment to an international legal order in which there is no impunity for terrorist offences. To the extent that states are involved (directly or indirectly) in acts of terrorism and alleged offenders find refuge in their territory, states support the cause in furtherance of which the relevant terrorist act was carried out, or are otherwise in bad faith, we encounter the limits of the *aut dedere aut judicare* obligation in its respect for a sphere of sovereign discretion in criminal law matters.[323]

---

[321] See Section 2.1.2.
[322] See Section 2.2.3.
[323] The 2010 Protocol to the Hague Convention and Beijing Convention (both adopted on 10 September 2010 and not yet in force) may address some of this difficulty, in that both Conventions

There are other limitations on the *aut dedere aut judicare* obligation in the TSCs (and possibilities for the judicial settlement of disputes in regard to such obligations) that result not from a state's participation in acts of terrorism, but rather from states' sympathy with the cause of non-state actors who commit such acts. These limitations are principally a product of the self-determination debate and the negotiated rules of regime interaction between the TSCs and humanitarian law that followed from that debate. Where the regime interaction is seamless and there are no gaps in coverage, as in the Hostages Convention, all defined acts of terrorism are subject to an extradite or submit to prosecution obligation, irrespective of the cause for which they were committed. Rather, the victory of the proponents of a distinction between terrorism and acts carried out in furtherance of a struggle for self-determination is in ensuring that the Hostages Convention does not apply to acts of war, which are thereby assessed on the basis of humanitarian law. The impact of the shift in the source of the obligation to extradite or submit to prosecution from the Hostages Convention to humanitarian law is on the possibilities for resolving disputes regarding breach of that obligation. As the Geneva Conventions and API do not have compromissory clauses, a state's breach of its criminal law enforcement obligations in reference to a hostage-taking that is excluded from the scope of the Hostages Convention may not fall within the ICJ's jurisdiction.

But there are also gaps in coverage between the TSCs and the laws of war, in particular as regards the Terrorist Bombing Convention, Nuclear Terrorism Convention, 2005 Protocol to the SUA Convention, and the 2010 Protocol to the Hague Convention and Beijing Convention (adopted on 10 September 2010 and not yet in force), which bear on the substantive obligations (and not merely possibilities for judicial settlement of disputes) to which states are subject. While there has been a serious increase in the number of substantive obligations bearing on non-state actors in the context of non-international armed conflicts (including conflicts in which a people are fighting in exercise of their right of self-determination), the development of a criminal law enforcement framework applicable to breaches of those obligations has been slow and patchy, depending in part on the ratification of humanitarian law treaties by relevant states. As a result, some acts of terrorism falling within the scope of the TSCs listed above will not be subject to the *aut dedere aut judicare* obligation of the TSCs or to a prosecute or hand over obligation under the Geneva Conventions or API, despite also being in breach of the laws of war. And for those acts of terrorism meeting the elements of the TSCs that are not committed in the context of an armed conflict, there may nevertheless be a reservation to the relevant TSC that purports to exclude criminal law enforcement obligations in

require states to criminalize being an after the fact accessory to the defined offences. As discussed in Section 4.2.1, on an application of the *Bosnia Genocide Case* analysis, these provisions capture the wrongfulness of a state's harbouring alleged terrorists, and may (once in force) better serve as a basis of state responsibility than would a failure to extradite or prosecute, given the discretion built into meeting both obligations.

reference thereto, the effect of which is unsettled as a matter of international law. While any resulting exemptions from the *aut dedere aut judicare* obligation in the TSCs certainly suggest an imperfect commitment to non-impunity, they do reflect the value judgments of some states parties to the TSCs, including their support for certain causes irrespective of means used.

4

The ICJ's jurisdiction over disputes relating to state responsibility for international terrorism

A breach of the primary rules of international law related to terrorism considered in Chapters 2 and 3 gives rise to a state's responsibility for an internationally wrongful act by operation of the law.[1] As a result of such responsibility, the wrongdoing state is under a secondary obligation to cease the wrongful conduct and to make full reparation for any injury caused thereby.[2] There has yet to be a case, however, in which a state has acknowledged its responsibility for international terrorism following protest of such responsibility by the injured state. If the injured state wishes to pursue its demands for cessation and reparation, it will have to rely on the mechanisms available under international law to implement the wrongdoing state's responsibility.

One possible mechanism for implementing responsibility, envisaged in Chapter VI of the UN Charter, is the peaceful judicial settlement of disputes.[3] The presence of an authoritative mechanism to establish (with binding effect) that a primary obligation has been breached, and the legal consequences of that breach, does not, of itself, enforce the secondary obligations that flow from responsibility. Judicial settlement of disputes may impose further primary obligations on the wrongdoing state, for instance the primary obligation to abide by the decisions of the ICJ under the UN Charter,[4] but the treaty obligation to abide by decisions of the Court is no more binding on a wrongdoing state than the primary obligation it has breached (which is the subject of judicial determination) and the secondary obligations that flow from its responsibility for that breach under customary international law. That said, a binding determination of responsibility both pressures and gives rise to additional possibilities for pressuring a wrongdoing state into complying with its secondary obligations. For instance, an objective determination of wrongfulness that is binding on the wrongdoing and injured states can eliminate the risks associated with the adoption of self-help countermeasures by the injured state, as discussed in Chapter 5. Equally, a determination of responsibility by the principal

[1] Commentary to Art. 43, ILC Articles on State Responsibility, para 2.
[2] Arts. 30(a) and 31, ILC Articles on State Responsibility.
[3] Art. 33(1), UN Charter.
[4] Art. 94(1), UN Charter.

judicial organ of the UN can trigger the Security Council's power to decide upon measures to give effect to the judgment as discussed in Section 4.5 below.

In order that the judicial settlement of disputes amount to a potential mechanism for implementing a state's responsibility for international terrorism, there must be an available forum for such settlement. Despite the proliferation of international courts and tribunals,[5] the ICJ remains the only international court with a general jurisdiction that might cover disputes relating to a state's responsibility for international terrorism. The ICJ's jurisdiction, however, is not compulsory and is based on the consent of the applicant and respondent states. Consent can be expressed in an *ad hoc* fashion with reference to a particular dispute,[6] pursuant to an optional clause declaration,[7] or through compromissory clauses.[8] Given the unlikelihood that a respondent state will accept the ICJ's jurisdiction on an *ad hoc* basis in cases of its responsibility for international terrorism, this chapter examines the latter two bases of jurisdiction.

As examined in Chapter 2, the rule of international law prohibiting state terrorism is an instantiation of more general rules and principles of customary international law, in particular the prohibition of aggression, the prohibition of the use of force, and the principle of non-intervention. Equally, as examined in Chapter 3, the obligation to prevent international terrorism is both an obligation of customary international law, and a treaty obligation under the TSCs. Breach of the customary obligations can form the substantive basis of an invocation of responsibility before the ICJ in cases where the terrorist act is *not* covered by a TSC, or involved states are not party to a relevant TSC. Absent *ad hoc* consent, such breaches of customary international law will only fall within the ICJ's jurisdiction to the extent that the involved states have made applicable optional clause declarations under Article 36(2) of the ICJ Statute. Section 4.1 examines such declarations as a basis of the ICJ's jurisdiction in cases of internationally wrongful acts related to terrorism.

The TSCs each contain a compromissory clause conferring jurisdiction on the ICJ over disputes 'between two or more State Parties concerning the interpretation or application of' the relevant TSC.[9] As a result, at least in reference to a dispute

---

[5] See generally Shany (2004).

[6] Art. 36(1), Statute of the International Court of Justice, 26 June 1945, [1946–47] United Nations Yearbook 843 [hereinafter 'ICJ Statute']. *Ad hoc* consent can be expressed through a *compromis*, in which the parties jointly submit a particular dispute to the ICJ, or through the respondent's acceptance of jurisdiction following the unilateral reference of a dispute by the applicant state, as France has done in two recent cases: *Certain Criminal Proceedings in France (Congo v. France)*, Consent to the Jurisdiction of the Court (application withdrawn by the Congo, *Case removed from the Court's List at the request of the Republic of the Congo*, ICJ Press Release, 17 November 2010); *Certain Questions Concerning Mutual Assistance in Criminal Matters (Djibouti v. France)*, Consent to the Jurisdiction of the Court. See also Oda (2000), 274.

[7] Under Article 36(2) of the ICJ Statute, states may recognize the compulsory jurisdiction of the ICJ, in advance, for all legal disputes they have with any other state which has also accepted the ICJ's jurisdiction (subject to any reservations made to the optional clause declaration).

[8] Art. 36(1), ICJ Statute.

[9] Art. 12, Hague Convention; Art. 14, Montreal Convention; Art. 13, Internationally Protected Persons Convention; Art. 16, Hostages Convention; Art. 16, SUA Convention; Art. 20, Terrorist Bombing Convention; Art. 24, Terrorism Financing Convention; Art. 23, Nuclear Terrorism Convention.

over breach of the obligation to prevent acts of international terrorism, there will be more than one possible bases of jurisdiction (assuming the relevant act of terrorism falls within the scope of a TSC): an Article 36(2) declaration applicable to the customary obligation to prevent international terrorism generally; and the TSC compromissory clauses applicable to the parallel treaty obligation to prevent particular acts of terrorism covered by the TSCs.[10]

The TSC compromissory clauses will be very important in reference to disputes regarding the breach of an obligation to extradite or submit terrorist actors to prosecution. This is because the *aut dedere aut judicare* obligation is treaty-based and has not developed into customary international law.[11] The scope of exclusion clauses, discussed in reference to struggles for self-determination in Chapter 3, and in reference to state activity in Section 4.2.2 below, will be particularly important in this regard as the Geneva Conventions and Additional Protocols (the alternative treaty source of the substantive obligation to prosecute or hand over that might apply to relevant conduct) do not contain compromissory clauses conferring jurisdiction on the ICJ to settle disputes.

The TSC compromissory clauses might also be a relevant basis of jurisdiction for claims of state terrorism. In its judgment on the merits of the *Bosnia Genocide Case*, the ICJ held that a state's obligation to prevent genocide under the Genocide Convention necessarily implies a prohibition of the commission of genocide by the state itself. Like the Genocide Convention, the TSCs do not expressly prohibit state conduct, but require states to prevent and punish the terrorist offences defined therein. The *Bosnia Genocide Case* precedent suggests that an applicant state could successfully argue that the TSCs impliedly prohibit state terrorism through their obligation of prevention. Section 4.2 below examines the TSCs as a basis of the ICJ's jurisdiction in cases of state terrorism. There are, however, limits to the type of state conduct that might be covered by the TSCs, and Section 4.2.2 considers the extent to which military conduct is excluded from their scope.

The TSCs are subject to reservations and their compromissory clauses each set out pre-conditions for the seisin of the ICJ. Section 4.4 considers the impact of these conditions and reservations on the potential for judicial settlement of disputes regarding state responsibility for international terrorism. Finally, Section 4.5 explores the Security Council enforcement options available to a state that has successfully established another state's responsibility for international terrorism before the ICJ.

4.1 Optional clause declarations

As discussed in Sections 4.2 and 4.3 below, disputes relating to sponsorship of, support for, or a failure to prevent acts of international terrorism may fall within the

[10] In theory, a state might make an Article 36(2) declaration that would also cover disputes under a TSC, but reserve against the TSC's compromissory clause. In such a case, the ICJ would have jurisdiction to hear a dispute regarding the TSC pursuant to Article 36(2) of the ICJ Statute. In practice, however, states which make reservations to compromissory clauses in the TSCs have not made Article 36(2) declarations. See *infra* notes 15–19 and 229–31 and accompanying text.

[11] *Supra* Chapter 3, notes 109–11 and accompanying text.

ICJ's jurisdiction pursuant to the compromissory clauses in the Terrorism Suppression Conventions. But the compromissory clauses will only serve as a basis of the Court's jurisdiction to the extent that the act of terrorism is one that meets the elements of the offences defined therein,[12] is not excluded from the scope of the TSC, and the states involved in the dispute are parties to that TSC (including its compromissory clause). In all other cases, and assuming a refusal to grant *ad hoc* consent, compulsory jurisdiction under Article 36(2) of the ICJ Statute will be the only basis of the Court's jurisdiction for disputes relating to state responsibility for international terrorism. The merits of such disputes will be decided on the basis of customary international law.

There are two factors that militate against the ICJ's having jurisdiction over international terrorism disputes pursuant to an optional clause declaration. The first results from the limited number of relevant declarations accepting the ICJ's compulsory jurisdiction under Article 36(2) of the ICJ Statute. Only approximately one-third of UN member states have accepted the ICJ's compulsory jurisdiction,[13] and very few are states that are habitually charged with sponsorship of, support for, or failure to prevent international terrorism. With the exception of the Sudan,[14] none of the current US designated 'State Sponsors of Terrorism' have filed optional clause declarations.[15] Libya and North Korea have recently been removed from the US State Sponsors list, but were ever-present members of the list throughout the 1980s and 1990s.[16] Neither has made an optional declaration accepting the ICJ's compulsory jurisdiction. Finally, a number of states with terrorist organizations operating from their territory, including Yemen, Algeria, Lebanon and Afghanistan, have not accepted the compulsory jurisdiction of the Court under Article 36(2) of the ICJ Statute.[17] Of the remaining four states identified as terrorist safe

---

[12] Some acts which are intended to cause death or serious bodily injury for a terrorist purpose, and would therefore fit the definition of terrorist acts set out in Section 1.3, are not covered by the existing TSCs. For instance the wilful propagation of epidemics, animal disease or other calamity (see Fourth International Conference for the Unification of Penal Law, Brussels, 26–30 June 1930, Actes de Conférence (Brussels: Office de publicité, 1931)), causing the pollution, fouling or poisoning of drinking water or food (see Sixth International Conference for the Unification of Penal Law, Copenhagen, 31 August – 2 September 1935, Actes de Conférence (Paris: Éditions A. Pédone, 1938)), or wilfully destroying railways or damaging public power installations without the use of explosives (see Scharf (2001), 393) do not fall within the scope of any of the TSCs. Absent an Article 36(2) declaration, a failure to prevent such acts or submit the case to prosecution would therefore not fall under the ICJ's jurisdiction.

[13] For a list of states which have made optional clause declarations, and the text of any reservations to such declarations, see <http://treaties.un.org/pages/ViewDetails.aspx?src=TREATY&mtdsg_no=I-4&chapter=1&lang=en>.

[14] The Sudan's optional clause declaration contains a reservation regarding disputes arising out of hostilities in which it is a belligerent, which will make its Article 36(2) declaration an improbable source of the ICJ's jurisdiction in reference to acts of state terrorism.

[15] Cuba, Iran, Syria and the Sudan are designated as state sponsors of terrorism in the US Department of State Country Reports on Terrorism (2008) and none have made optional clause declarations pursuant to Article 36(2) of the ICJ Statute.

[16] Libya last appeared on the list in the US Department of State Country Reports on Terrorism (2005) and North Korea was removed from the list in 2008. See <http://www.state.gov/s/ct/rls/crt/>.

[17] See <http://treaties.un.org/pages/ViewDetails.aspx?src=TREATY&mtdsg_no=I-4&chapter=1&lang=en>.

havens by the US Department of State that have made an optional clause declaration,[18] one has done so subject to a reservation.[19]

This capacity to carve out certain disputes or disputants from acceptance of the ICJ's jurisdiction under Article 36(2) of the ICJ Statute further decreases the chances of the Court having jurisdiction over a dispute based on the breach of customary international law, including one relating to state responsibility for international terrorism.[20] Of the sixty-six states that have accepted the ICJ's compulsory jurisdiction under Article 36(2) of the ICJ Statute at the time of writing, more than one-third have reserved against the ICJ having jurisdiction over one or more of the following disputes: disputes related in some way to the use of armed force;[21] disputes with particular groupings of states;[22] disputes concerning the interpretation or application of a multilateral treaty unless all the parties to the treaty are also party to the case before the ICJ;[23] disputes in respect of which any other party to the dispute has accepted the compulsory jurisdiction of the ICJ only in relation to or for the purpose of the dispute, or where the acceptance of the ICJ's compulsory jurisdiction on behalf of any other party to the dispute was deposited less than twelve months before the filing of the application.[24]

The ICJ has given the fullest possible effect to these reservations to optional clause declarations. While the ICJ has refrained from elaborating a 'doctrine of restrictive interpretation' in so far as optional clause declarations are concerned,[25] it has repeatedly emphasized that declarations under Article 36(2) of the ICJ Statute

---

[18] Pakistan, Somalia, Colombia, and the Philippines, US Department of State Country Reports on Terrorism (2008), Ch. 5.

[19] Of relevance, Pakistan has made a multilateral treaty reservation to its optional clause declaration. <http://treaties.un.org/pages/ViewDetails.aspx?src=TREATY&mtdsg_no=I-4&chapter=1&lang=en#5>.

[20] While the majority of states which have accepted (but made some reservation against) the ICJ's Article 36(2) jurisdiction are not today associated with internationally wrongful acts related to terrorism, the changing membership of the US Department of State Country Reports on Terrorism state sponsorship and safe haven lists suggests that states' attitudes to terrorism as an instrument of foreign policy have changed at different stages of their history, and the fact that a state does not now appear on those lists says little in regard to its future activities.

[21] Twelve out of sixty-seven states have made such a reservation to the ICJ's jurisdiction.

[22] Eight states have excluded disputes with Commonwealth countries from their optional clause declarations. For an application of the Commonwealth reservation by the ICJ, see *Aerial Incident of 10 August 1999 (Pakistan v. India)*, Jurisdiction.

[23] Five states have made a multilateral treaty reservation. The US optional clause declaration (before it was withdrawn) contained a multilateral treaty reservation on the basis of which the ICJ held that it did not have jurisdiction to decide Nicaragua's claims arising under the UN Charter and the Charter of the Organization of American States in its suit against the US. *Nicaragua (Nicaragua v. US)*, Merits, 38, para 56. On multilateral treaty reservations, see generally Alexandrov (1995), 112–19.

[24] Seventeen states have made such a reservation, including the UK and Spain, on the basis of which the ICJ held that it did not have jurisdiction under Article 36(2) of the ICJ Statute in *Legality of Use of Force (Yugoslavia v. Spain)*, Provisional Measures, and *Legality of Use of Force (Serbia and Montenegro v. United Kingdom)*, Provisional Measures.

[25] See Tomuschat (2006), 610, para 33. Instead, the ICJ has characterized its approach to optional clause declarations and reservations thereto as one which 'interpret[s] the relevant words of a declaration including a reservation contained therein in a natural and reasonable way, having due regard to the intention of the state concerned at the time when it accepted the compulsory jurisdiction of the ICJ'. *Fisheries Jurisdiction Case (Spain v. Canada)*, Jurisdiction, para 48.

are different from compromissory clauses in that the ICJ must place a particular emphasis on the intention of the declaring state.[26] The result of such an approach, whether strictly a 'doctrine of restrictive interpretation' or not, is that in most cases in which the applicant state relied on Article 36(2) as the basis of the ICJ's jurisdiction, and the respondent state raised a preliminary objection based on a limitation or reservation to its own optional clause declaration, the ICJ has upheld the preliminary objection.[27] The ICJ has equally given the fullest effect to reservations to Article 36(2) declarations made by applicant states and has declined to exercise jurisdiction on the basis of reciprocity when the reservation formed the basis of a preliminary objection by the respondent state.[28] Given the limited number of optional clause declarations, the large number of reservations thereto, and the ICJ's propensity to give such reservations their fullest effect, the potential scope of the ICJ's jurisdiction under Article 36(2) is generally limited,[29] and, given the likely identity of disputants (as discussed above), particularly so in reference to disputes relating to terrorism.

4.2 The Terrorism Suppression Conventions

The state itself is the subject of the customary international law prohibition of state terrorism examined in Section 2.1. The prohibition bears on states as international actors, requiring that they refrain from certain conduct in their international relations. The TSCs, on the other hand, generally view the state as a mechanism of control through which individual terrorist conduct is addressed, imposing obligations on states to legislate, exercise jurisdiction, and extradite or submit terrorist criminals to prosecution. The ICJ's decision in the *Bosnia Genocide Case* suggests that these two types of obligations (one prohibiting the state itself, the other regarding the state as the enforcer of prohibitions imposed on non-state actors) overlap in the obligation to prevent. In its judgment on the merits, the ICJ held

---

[26] See *Aegean Sea Continental Shelf (Greece v. Turkey)*, Judgment, para 69; *Anglo-Iranian Oil Co. Case (UK v. Iran)*, Jurisdiction, 104; *Fisheries Jurisdiction Case (Spain v. Canada)*, Jurisdiction, para 48; *Aerial Incident of 10 August 1999 (Pakistan v. India)*, Jurisdiction, paras 42–4.

[27] See *Anglo-Iranian Oil Co. Case (UK v. Iran)*, Jurisdiction; *Nicaragua (Nicaragua v. US)*, Jurisdiction and Admissibility; *Fisheries Jurisdiction Case (Spain v. Canada)*, Jurisdiction; *Aerial Incident of 10 August 1999 (Pakistan v. India)*, Jurisdiction; *Legality of Use of Force (Yugoslavia v. Spain)*, Provisional Measures; and *Legality of Use of Force (Yugoslavia v. US)*, Provisional Measures. But see *Certain Phosphate Lands in Nauru (Nauru v. Australia)*, Preliminary Objections.

[28] See *Legality of Use of Force (Serbia and Montenegro v. Belgium)*, Provisional Measures; *Legality of Use of Force (Serbia and Montenegro v. Canada)*, Provisional Measures; *Legality of Use of Force (Serbia and Montenegro v. Netherlands)*, Provisional Measures; *Legality of Use of Force (Serbia and Montenegro v. Portugal)*, Provisional Measures. Despite the on-going nature of the NATO bombing campaign, the ICJ held that the dispute between Yugoslavia and the NATO countries arose when the first bomb was dropped, which was before the date on which Yugoslavia accepted the ICJ's jurisdiction. This narrow interpretation of the timeframe within which the dispute arose made the applicant state's *ratione temporis* limitation to its optional clause declaration applicable, and on the basis of reciprocity, the ICJ held that it lacked *prima facie* jurisdiction. For a critique of the ICJ's ruling on this point, see Gray (2003), 735.

[29] See generally Merrills (1993); Merrills (2002).

that a state's obligation to prevent genocide under the Genocide Convention necessarily implies a prohibition of the commission of genocide by the state itself[30] and that a dispute regarding breach of the prohibition by a state is thereby decidable by the Court pursuant to the compromissory clause of the Genocide Convention.

The ICJ's decision in the *Bosnia Genocide Case* raises an obvious question: can the TSCs, which require states to prevent certain acts of terrorism, be interpreted as impliedly prohibiting states from engaging in those same acts?[31] While states are clearly prohibited from engaging in the acts of violence defined in the TSCs as a matter of customary international law,[32] the question examined in this section is whether that obligation is duplicated in the TSCs. In its *Bosnia Genocide Case* decision, the ICJ was very careful to restrict its reasoning to the particular circumstances of the Genocide Convention, and later in the judgment expressly stated that it did not 'purport to establish a general jurisprudence applicable to all cases where a treaty instrument, or other binding legal norm, includes an obligation for states to prevent certain acts'.[33] Nevertheless, and despite some difficulties with the ICJ's reasoning discussed below, the *Bosnia Genocide Case* decision will figure heavily in any attempt to argue that the TSCs impliedly prohibit state terrorism. This interpretive question is one bearing on the scope of the substantive obligations under the TSCs. But given that state terrorism is prohibited as a matter of customary international law, the question of interpretation will generally only arise in the context of a dispute referred to the ICJ in which the disputants are both party to a relevant TSC and there are no (or not enough) applicable Article 36(2) declarations on the basis of which the customary international law issue could be settled. In reference to the invocation and implementation of state responsibility for international terrorism in any other context, including in reference to demands for cessation and reparation or the adoption of countermeasures, the source of the obligation is irrelevant.[34] Whether a TSC obligation to prevent terrorism impliedly duplicates the prohibition of state terrorism existing at customary international law is therefore of interest because it may have important jurisdictional consequences, securing the ICJ as an available forum for dispute settlement.

The ICJ's decision that there is an implied prohibition of state genocide in the Genocide Convention was based on two separate arguments. The first argument relied on the Convention's characterization of genocide as an 'international crime'. While the ICJ was clear that the state responsibility envisioned in the Genocide

---

[30] *Bosnia Genocide Case*, Judgment, para 166.

[31] In the *Lockerbie Case*, the US and the UK both argued that the Montreal Convention did not apply to disputes bearing on an act of state sponsored terrorism. While the Court decided that it had jurisdiction to consider the dispute between Libya and the US and UK (which ultimately turned on the *applicability* of the Montreal Convention to acts of state sponsored terrorism), it did not resolve the issue owing to a settlement between the state parties, and the discontinuance of the case. See discussion of *Lockerbie Case* in Section 4.3 below.

[32] See Section 2.1.

[33] *Bosnia Genocide Case*, Judgment, para 429.

[34] Art. 12, ILC Articles on State Responsibility. See also *Rainbow Warrior (France/New Zealand)* (1990), 251, para 75; *Gabčíkovo–Nagymaros Project (Hungary v. Slovakia)*, Judgment, para 47.

Convention is not criminal in nature,[35] it considered that a state's undertaking not to commit acts falling within the scope of the Convention follows *logically* from the characterization of genocide as a crime under international law.[36] Whether one considers the understanding of 'crime under international law' at the time the Genocide Convention was drafted or at the time the *Bosnia Genocide Case* was decided, the argument as to logical implication is not entirely convincing. The General Assembly first requested the Economic and Social Council ('ECOSOC') to draw up a convention on genocide in its Resolution 96(I) of 1946.[37] The text of the Convention was unanimously adopted by the General Assembly in 1948.[38] During this brief period, the concept of a crime under international law was still firmly rooted in the Nuremberg precedent of individual criminal responsibility and there was a good deal of confusion surrounding the extent or nature of state responsibility for the international crime of genocide.[39] By the time the *Bosnia Genocide Case* was decided, the long-running debate within the ILC as to the desirability of a special regime of aggravated state responsibility for international crimes had come and gone. The concept of crimes of state had been dropped from the Articles on State Responsibility under Special Rapporteur Crawford's stewardship, and the ILC addressed responsibility for such crimes under the rubric of serious breaches of obligations arising under peremptory norms and *erga omnes* invocations of responsibility.[40] There is therefore no *logical* reason why characterizing conduct as an international crime should inform the scope of a state's direct delictual responsibility with regard thereto.

---

[35] *Bosnia Genocide Case*, Judgment, para 170. Whether holding a state directly responsible for the commission of genocide under the Genocide Convention amounts to holding it *criminally* responsible (as opposed to delictually responsible for the commission of an international crime) was the source of some confusion. See e.g. *Bosnia Genocide Case*, Merits, Joint Declaration of Judges Shi and Koroma, para 4; Declaration of Judge Skotnikov, 371.

[36] *Bosnia Genocide Case*, Judgment, para 166. See also Dominicé (1999), 150–1, arguing that the consequence of this unique feature of the Convention is that it prohibits both states and individuals from committing acts of genocide.

[37] ECOSOC carried out its mandate in cooperation with the Secretary General, experts in the field of international law, an *Ad Hoc* Committee on Genocide, and the Sixth Committee of the GA. See ECOSOC Resolution 47 (IV) (1947); ECOSOC Resolution 117 (VI) (1947); UNGA, Sixth Committee, Genocide: Draft Convention and Report of the Economic and Social Council, UN Doc. A/C.6/289/Rev.1 (1948).

[38] UNGA Resolution 260A (1948).

[39] See e.g. the ILC's survey of international law in relation to its work of codification, UN Doc. A/CN.4/1/Rev.1 (1949), 57, in which it is reported that the Secretary General characterized the new issues of state responsibility which arose as a result of the Nuremberg experience as 'the question of the criminal responsibility of States as well as that of individuals acting on behalf of the State'. The *travaux préparatoires* of the Genocide Convention also clearly evidence some confusion regarding whether state responsibility for genocide should be criminal or delictual in nature, which ultimately led to the failure to include any substantive provision regarding state responsibility for the commission of genocide in the Convention. See the rejected UK proposal to extend criminal responsibility for genocide to states under the Convention (UNGA, Sixth Committee, Genocide: Draft Convention and Report of the Economic and Social Council, UN Doc. A/C.6/236 and Corr. 1 (1948); UNGA, Sixth Committee, UN Doc. A/C.6/SR.96 (1948)). See also Jorgensen (2000), 35–41; Seibert-Fohr (2009), 355–6.

[40] Arts. 40 and 48, ILC Articles on State Responsibility. See also Crawford and Olleson (2006), 464 and discussion in Section 1.2.1.

The TSCs do not characterize the crimes defined therein as 'international crimes'. As a result, this part of the ICJ's approach to implied obligations is not strictly relevant to the TSC context. That said, there was some discussion during the ILC's drafting of the Internationally Protected Persons Convention whether the offences under consideration should be characterized as 'international crimes' in the Convention's preamble. Mr Roberto Ago, who at the time was serving as the Special Rapporteur on State Responsibility, and was therefore heavily involved in discussions regarding whether there should be aggravated state responsibility for international crimes,[41] argued that the term 'international crime':

suggest[s . . .] *at the present time* the notion of an international wrongful act by a State, in other words a violation of international law at the inter-State level. But there was no wrongful act by a State if a diplomat was kidnapped on its territory without that State having failed to fulfil any of its obligations. Hence the acts dealt with in the draft belonged solely to internal criminal law, and there was nothing international about them except the concern they caused.[42]

Most delegates took Mr Ago's view,[43] and the proposed term 'international crime' was therefore not used in the Internationally Protected Persons Convention (or the TSCs negotiated thereafter), replaced instead with a characterization of the terrorist offences criminalized therein as 'a matter of grave concern to the international community'.[44] Given that the ICJ did not elaborate on its conclusion that a prohibition of state genocide logically follows from the characterization of genocide as an 'international crime', it is difficult to say whether or not the characterization of terrorist offences as 'a matter of grave concern to the international community' should equally imply a prohibition of state terrorism. As the *travaux préparatoires* are silent on the question of direct state responsibility for an offence against internationally protected persons,[45] the Court could certainly extend its *Bosnia*

---

[41] See Section 1.2.1.

[42] Emphasis added. ILC, summary record of meeting, UN Doc. A/CN.4/SR.1151 (1972), [1972] YBILC, Vol. 1, 11, para 26.

[43] See ILC, summary record of meeting, UN Doc. A/CN.4/SR.1151 (1972), [1972] YBILC, Vol. 1, 15, para 18 and 18, para 6. But see the comments of Mr Yaseen, who considered that 'an international crime seemed to mean, not a crime committed by a State, but a crime which, although committed by a private person or persons, constituted a grave danger for the international community, such as piracy or the slave trade'. ILC, summary record of meeting, UN Doc. A/CN.4/SR.1151 (1972), [1972] YBILC, Vol. 1, 12, para 39. Despite the different views taken on the perpetrator of an 'international crime', the common ground seems to be that the Internationally Protected Persons Convention was contemplated as an instrument which addressed individual criminal responsibility and a state's obligations *vis à vis* the implementation of individual criminal responsibility. The ILC did not contemplate direct state responsibility for the offences defined in the Convention, and having not done so, it cannot be said that the ILC included or excluded such responsibility.

[44] Internationally Protected Persons Convention, preamble; Hostages Convention, preamble; 1988 Protocol to the Montreal Convention, preamble; SUA Convention, preamble. Beginning with the Terrorist Bombing Convention, the preamble characterized the defined crimes as a 'matter of grave concern to the international community *as a whole*'. Emphasis added. Terrorist Bombing Convention, preamble; Terrorism Financing Convention, preamble. The Nuclear Terrorism Convention notes 'that acts of nuclear terrorism may result in the gravest consequences and may pose a threat to international peace and security'. Nuclear Terrorism Convention, preamble.

[45] Recourse to the *travaux préparatoires* for the purposes of treaty interpretation is only permissible to confirm an interpretation arrived at through reliance on certain rules of interpretation (in particular

Genocide Case reasoning to crimes that are 'a matter of grave concern to the international community'. Indeed, given that the phrase 'a matter of grave concern to the international community' is neutral as to its individual criminal or state responsibility implications in a way that 'international crimes' is not, the *Bosnia Genocide Case* argument as to logical implication would be less objectionable in the TSC context.

The ICJ's second argument in the *Bosnia Genocide Case* was that a state's obligation of prevention necessarily implies a prohibition of the commission of genocide.[46] While this argument has an intuitive appeal that the first argument perhaps does not, it does seem to be at odds with the criminal law enforcement framework of the Genocide Convention. The obligations set out in the Genocide Convention are primarily concerned with the prosecution and punishment of genocide, suggesting that the state is viewed (for the purposes of the treaty) as a mechanism of control through which individual behaviour is addressed rather than as a subject of prohibitions in its own right. In keeping with the logic of a criminal law enforcement treaty, the ICJ held that the obligation to prevent genocide 'requires the State parties, *inter alia*, to employ the means at their disposal, [. . .] to prevent persons or groups *not directly under their authority*, from committing an act of genocide or any other acts enumerated in Article III'.[47] An obligation of prevention, aimed as it is at the conduct of third parties, does not *necessarily imply* that the state is prohibited from engaging in the conduct it must prevent others from engaging in.[48]

The ICJ did note, in support of its necessary implication conclusion, that it would be paradoxical if states were under an obligation to prevent the commission of genocide, but were not forbidden from committing such acts themselves.[49] Indeed that would be paradoxical, and therein lays the intuitive appeal of this argument. But the paradox is resolved if one considers the *source* of the distinct obligations. To the extent that the prohibition of state genocide existed at customary international law at the time of the conclusion of the Genocide Convention,[50]

---

interpretation in accordance with the ordinary meaning of terms in their context and in light of the treaty's object and purpose), or where the application of such rules of interpretation leaves the meaning ambiguous or obscure. Art. 32, VCLT. In this case, the meaning of the terms themselves is not obscure—characterizing a matter as 'of grave concern to the international community' is clear enough. Rather, it is the implication of those terms that might be qualified as obscure, perhaps justifying recourse to the *travaux préparatoires*. In this case however, such recourse would be of no particular assistance.

[46] *Bosnia Genocide Case*, Judgment, para 166. In order to reach its conclusion as to necessary implication, the Court first had to reject Yugoslavia's arguments that (i) state responsibility under the Convention was limited to responsibility for a failure to prevent or punish (see *Bosnia Genocide Case*, Preliminary Objections, para 32), and (ii) the emphasis on criminal repression in the Genocide Convention suggests that the obligation of prevention is subsumed in the obligation to punish (see *Bosnia Genocide Case*, Judgment, para 162).

[47] Emphasis added. *Bosnia Genocide Case*, Judgment, para 166. See also the ICJ's discussion of the obligation to prevent at the end of the Judgment, paras 430–2.

[48] For further critique of the ICJ's argument as to necessary implication, see Gaeta (2007), 639–40.

[49] *Bosnia Genocide Case*, Judgment, para 166.

[50] See *Reservations to the Genocide Convention*, Advisory Opinion, 23.

the General Assembly may well have decided to address the obligations of prevention and individual criminal responsibility (which were not obviously customary law at the time)[51] in a treaty framework, while leaving the prohibition of state conduct to customary international law.

Despite the difficulties with the Court's reasoning identified above, the question remains whether its interpretation of the obligation to prevent in the *Bosnia Genocide Case* can form the basis of an argument that the TSCs impliedly prohibit states from engaging in the terrorist conduct defined therein. One apparent basis for distinguishing the Genocide Convention from the terrorism context is that the obligation of prevention in the Terrorism Suppression Conventions is territorially limited,[52] whereas the Court held in the *Bosnia Genocide Case* that the obligation to prevent genocide under the Genocide Convention is not territorially limited.[53] This should not, however, have any impact on the applicability of the *Bosnia Genocide Case* reasoning to the TSCs. The Court did not in any way condition its conclusion that the obligation to prevent genocide necessarily implies a prohibition of state genocide on the extra-territoriality of the obligation to prevent. The Court was right to divorce the question of the territorial scope of the obligation to prevent from its argument as to necessary implication because (assuming acceptance of the Court's logic) a prohibition on state conduct may be implied whether or not the obligation to prevent is territorial. The territorially limited obligation to prevent in the TSCs requires states to prevent preparations in their territory for the commission of acts of terrorism carried out within *or outside* their territories. Even if that territorial limitation were applied *mutatis mutandis* to an implied prohibition of state terrorism, any act of terrorism carried out by a state will, in some measure, be prepared or planned within its territory—thereby satisfying the territorial limitation.

A more significant difference between the Genocide Convention and the Terrorism Suppression Conventions is in the scope of their compromissory clauses. One feature of the Genocide Convention that supported the Court's broad interpretation of the obligation to prevent was the language in the compromissory clause of Article IX. Article IX confers jurisdiction on the Court over disputes 'relating to the responsibility of a State for genocide or for any other acts enumerated in Article III'. The Court correctly refused to read substantive obligations into

---

[51] See Schabas (2000), 3–4. See also UNGA Resolution 96(I) (1946) in which the GA *affirms* that genocide is a crime under international law, but *invites* states to enact legislation to prevent and punish the crime; and *recommends* international co-operation for the prevention and punishment of genocide. Were it clear that customary international law at the time required states to prevent and punish genocide, the GA would surely have used less tentative language.

[52] See Section 3.1.

[53] In its decision on Jurisdiction and Admissibility in the *Bosnia Genocide Case*, the ICJ noted that 'the obligation each State thus has to prevent and to punish the crime of genocide is not territorially limited by the Convention'. *Bosnia Genocide Case*, Preliminary Objections, para 31. In its decision on the merits, the Court held that '[t]he substantive obligations arising from Articles I and III are not on their face limited by territory. They apply to a State wherever it may be acting or may be able to act in ways appropriate to meeting the obligations in question'. *Bosnia Genocide Case*, Judgment, para 183. See also *ibid*, para 430, in which the Court held that a state's capacity to prevent must be assessed in light of its capacity to influence, which capacity depends on 'the geographical distance of the State concerned from the scene of the events'.

the compromissory clause,[54] but did rely on Article IX to support its interpretation of the obligation to prevent under the Genocide Convention. Unless the obligation to prevent genocide had been interpreted broadly, the reference in Article IX to state responsibility for genocide would have had no legal effect. The principle of effectiveness has long been a tool of treaty interpretation enabling courts and tribunals to read rights and obligations into treaties that are otherwise silent,[55] and the Court apparently considered that its broad interpretation of the obligation to prevent gave effect to the phrase 'the responsibility of a State for genocide or any of the other acts enumerated in Article III'. The TSCs do not *expressly* contemplate direct state responsibility for terrorism in their compromissory clauses. That said, a number of the TSCs implicitly contemplate certain acts of state terrorism (for instance acts of terrorism carried out by non-military state organs or by non-state actors on behalf of or supported by a state) by expressly excluding others.[56] Another difference between the TSCs and the Genocide Convention is that the TSCs do not *expressly* stipulate that individual criminal responsibility is to be imposed whether the perpetrator is a constitutionally responsible ruler, public official, or private individual, as does the Genocide Convention—suggesting that genocide which is attributable to a state is contemplated by the Genocide Convention.[57] The imposition of criminal responsibility on state officials was, however, contemplated by state parties to the TSCs. States considered that the reference to 'any person' in the definition of the covered terrorist offences was broad enough to cover state officials.[58] But the absence of an express reference to state responsibility for terrorism in the TSC compromissory clauses, replaced by an implicit contemplation of such responsibility, and only an implicit contemplation of individual criminal responsibility for state officials, distinguishes the TSCs from the Genocide Convention and the basis on which the Court supported its broad interpretation of the obligation to prevent. A broad interpretation of the obligation to prevent in the TSCs would therefore be somewhat less convincing than that adopted in the *Bosnia Genocide Case*, although such approaches to treaty interpretation are not beyond the Court when its jurisdiction hangs in the balance.[59] Nor perhaps should they be.

---

[54] *Bosnia Genocide Case*, Judgment, para 166.

[55] Merrills has identified the 'principle of effectiveness' as the interpretive tool for the development of positive obligations under the European Convention for the Protection of Human Rights and Fundamental Freedoms, which he describes as 'a means of giving the provisions of the treaty the fullest weight and effect consistent with the language used and with the rest of the text and in such a way that every part of it can be given meaning'. Merrills (1993), 98. Shelton similarly considers implied positive obligations to be the result of the ECtHR's 'doctrine of effectiveness'. See Shelton (2003), 137. While not expressly set out in Article 31 of the VCLT, the principle of effectiveness is embodied in the requirement that a treaty be interpreted in good faith in accordance with the ordinary meaning to be given to its terms in the context of the treaty and in the light of its object and purpose. See Report of the International Law Commission on the second part of its seventeenth session and on its eighteenth session, Draft Articles on the Law of Treaties with Commentaries, UN Doc. A/6309/Rev.1 (1966), 219, para 6.

[56] See Section 4.2.2 below.

[57] Art. IV, Genocide Convention.

[58] *Supra* Chapter 3, notes 208–10 and accompanying text.

[59] See the Court's interpretation of Article XX(1)(d) of the Treaty of Amity, Economic Relations, and Consular Rights between the United States of America and Iran, 15 August 1955, 284 UNTS 93, in its *Oil Platforms (Iran v. US)*, Judgment. See also the very strong critique of the majority decision by

Judge Simma, in his separate opinion in the *Oil Platforms* case, made a compelling argument that the Court should use every possible opportunity to address unlawful uses of force by states, to 'secure that the voice of the law of the Charter rise above the current cacophony'.[60] And although jurisdictionally expansionist treaty interpretation by the Court in individual cases may well have a long-term impact on states' willingness to accept compromissory clauses, there is something to be said for the Court making the most of its capacity to peacefully settle disputes in cases where flagrant breaches of the peace are alleged to have been committed. The Court may need to save its reputational currency for rainy days, but certainly a case of state-sponsored terrorism in which the only basis of jurisdiction was a TSC would be such a day.

A *Bosnia Genocide Case* type analysis was implicitly relied on by Djibouti in its suit against France, in reference to the Internationally Protected Persons Convention. Djibouti argued that France, by sending witness summonses to the head of state of Djibouti and to senior Djiboutian officials, had failed to prevent attacks on the person, freedom or dignity of internationally protected persons. Djibouti further argued that the obligation to prevent attacks was not only a positive obligation to take all appropriate measures to prevent attacks by third parties, but also a negative obligation on the state to refrain from committing acts that are likely to prejudice the protection of these persons, and relied on the Internationally Protected Persons Convention as a source of both the positive and negative obligations.[61] The Court dismissed Djibouti's claim, holding that the purpose of the Convention:

is to prevent serious crimes against internationally protected persons and to ensure the criminal prosecution of presumed perpetrators of such crimes. It is consequently not applicable to the specific question of immunity from jurisdiction in respect of a witness summons addressed to certain persons in connection with a criminal investigation, and the Court cannot take account of it in this case.[62]

The Court certainly emphasized the obligation to prevent and the individual criminal responsibility focus of the Internationally Protected Persons Convention in its decision. But the Court rejected Djibouti's argument on the basis that issuing a summons does not amount to the commission of a serious crime (in particular the

---

Judge Burgenthal, arguing that interpreting the clause consistently with the broader corpus of international law, in reliance on Article 31(3)(c) of the VCLT, should not have the effect of conferring jurisdiction on the ICJ over questions of customary international law that would not otherwise fall within its jurisdiction. *Oil Platforms (Iran v. US)*, Judgment, Separate Opinion of Judge Buergenthal. Judge Higgins described the majority's reasoning as having invoked the concept of treaty interpretation to displace the applicable law. *Oil Platforms (Iran v. US)*, Judgment, Separate Opinion of Judge Higgins, para 49. See also Berman (2004), 319–20; Kammerhofer (2004), 702–4.

[60] *Oil Platforms (Iran v. US)*, Judgment, Separate Opinion of Judge Simma, 328. See also Cannizzaro and Bonafé (2005), 496 (arguing that 'the enlargement of the scope of its jurisdiction and the taking into consideration of this wider set of rules applicable to the dispute, constitute the only way to set aside the incumbent danger of fragmentation of the law'); Koskenniemi (2006), paras 451–60.

[61] *Certain Questions of Mutual Assistance in Criminal Matters (Djibouti v. France)*, Judgment, *para* 157.

[62] *Ibid*, para 159.

'murder, kidnapping or other attack upon the person or liberty of an internationally protected person', which are the offences defined in the Internationally Protected Persons Convention)[63]. The Court did not reject Djibouti's argument (expressly or implicitly) on the basis of the inapplicability of the *Bosnia Genocide Case* analysis to the Convention. Given the other bases of jurisdiction in the case, there was no need for the Court to interpret expansively. If, however, a state committed a serious offence against an internationally protected person (as defined in the Convention), with the Internationally Protected Persons Convention as the only possible basis of the Court's jurisdiction,[64] there might be good reason for the Court to interpret broadly to jurisdictional effect—relying on its reasoning in the *Bosnia Genocide Case* to decide that the obligation to prevent particular acts of international terrorism impliedly prohibits states from engaging in those very terrorist activities.

4.2.1 Application of the *Bosnia Genocide Case* analysis to the TSCs

If the interpretation of the obligation to prevent in the TSCs were consistent with that in the *Bosnia Genocide Case*, the TSCs would prohibit state sponsorship of terrorism because the state would be prohibited from carrying out, through its organs or through non-state actors whose conduct is attributable to the state, the very terrorist acts it is required to prevent.[65] Given the difficulties in applying the rules of attribution relating to state organs in the terrorism context identified in Section 2.2.1 above, and unless the ICJ takes a more flexible approach to the standard of control required for attribution under Article 8 of the ILC Articles on State Responsibility,[66] states might have a forum in which to claim that a state is directly responsible for a terrorist attack, without much chance of success in establishing that responsibility.

In deciding that the obligation to prevent in the Genocide Convention impliedly prohibits states from committing genocide, the ICJ also concluded that states are prohibited (*mutatis mutandis*) from engaging in all accessory activities defined as punishable offences under Article III of the Genocide Convention.[67] This conclusion forced the Court to stretch the principles of state responsibility so as to encompass the modes of accessory criminal responsibility covered by the Genocide Convention and a similar approach could be taken to the TSCs. For instance, most of the TSCs define being an accomplice to a person who commits a relevant

---

[63] Art. 2(1), Internationally Protected Persons Convention.

[64] See Section 4.2.2 for a discussion of the circumstances in which the only conventional basis of responsibility for state violence against an internationally protected person would be the Internationally Protected Persons Convention.

[65] Some of the more recent TSCs also define 'direct[ing] others to commit [the defined] offence[s]' as an offence. See Art. 2(3)(b), Terrorist Bombing Convention; Art. 2(5)(b), Terrorism Financing Convention; Art. 2(4)(b), Nuclear Terrorism Convention. This mode of accessory liability under the TSCs adds nothing to the prohibition of state sponsorship of terrorism, because directing the commission of terrorist crimes would fulfil the standard of attribution under Article 8 of the ILC Articles on State Responsibility (see Section 2.2).

[66] See Section 2.2.

[67] See generally Milanovic (2007).

terrorist offence as falling within the scope of the Conventions.[68] Accomplice liability is not usually a matter for state responsibility, but on a slightly strained interpretation, the ICJ considered Article 16 of the ILC Articles on State Responsibility (aid or assistance to another state) to be a relevant state responsibility model for complicity in genocide committed by non-state actors.[69] The Court might well apply the same reasoning to accomplice liability under the TSCs. On the basis of such reasoning, aid or assistance provided by a state to non-state actors carrying out a TSC-covered offence, where the state 'acted knowingly, that is to say [. . .] was aware of the [. . .] intent of the principal perpetrator',[70] would give rise to state responsibility for a breach of the implied prohibition of a state's 'participating as an accomplice' in the TSC-covered offence. The SUA Convention criminalizes abetting the commission of the defined offences,[71] analysis of which could equally be modelled on Article 16 of the ILC Articles on State Responsibility.[72] Some of the TSCs also require states to criminalize 'intentionally and knowingly contributing to the commission of the [defined] offence[s]'.[73] On a *Bosnia Genocide Case* analysis, this accessory offence would cover most types of support a state knowingly provided to non-state terrorist actors with the aim of furthering the general terrorist activity of those non-state actors. As a result, the TSCs would broadly (albeit impliedly) prohibit state support of terrorism based on an application of the *Bosnia Genocide Case* analysis.

---

[68]   Art. 1(b), Hague Convention; Art. 1(2)(b), Montreal Convention; Art. 2(1)(e), Internationally Protected Persons Convention; Art. 1(2)(b), Hostages Convention; Art. 3(2)(b), SUA Convention; Art. 2(3)(a), Terrorist Bombing Convention; Art. 2(5)(a), Terrorism Financing Convention; Art. 2(4)(a), Nuclear Terrorism Convention; Art. 1(3)(c), Beijing Convention.

[69]   See *Bosnia Genocide Case*, Judgment, paras 420–1. In equating 'aid or assistance' (which might be considered the state responsibility equivalent of the criminal law concept of 'aiding and abetting') with complicity, the Court's decision skates over contradictions in the jurisprudence of the international criminal tribunals—in particular regarding whether 'aiding and abetting' and 'complicity' have the same requirements of intention. See *Akayesu* (ICTR-96-4-T), paras 545–7 (holding that complicity requires knowledge of genocidal intent, while aiding and abetting requires specific genocidal intent); *Kayishema and Ruzindana* (ICTR-95-1-T), paras 205–7 (holding exactly the opposite); *Musema* (ICTR-96-13-A), para 181 (holding that complicity requires only knowledge, without expressly addressing the distinction between complicity and aiding and abetting under the ICTR Statute). In support of the Court's conclusion that complicity and aiding and abetting require the same element of intention, at least one ICTR decision holds that 'there is no material distinction between complicity in Article 2(3)(e) of the [ICTR] Statute and the broad definition accorded to aiding and abetting in Article 6(1) [of the ICTR Statute]' and that the 'redundancy can be explained by the drafters' *verbatim* incorporation into the [ICTR] Statute of Art. III of the Genocide Convention' (*Semanza* (ICTR-97-20-T), paras 391–5). The ICTY Appeal Chamber decision in *Krstić* (ICTY-98-33-A) also seems to allow for some overlap between complicity and aiding and abetting—but to the extent that complicity is broader than aiding and abetting, requires proof of specific genocidal intent. This approach was endorsed by the ICTR Appeals Chamber in *Elizaphan Ntakirutimana* and *Gérard Ntakirutimana* (ICTR-96-10-A; ICTR-96-17-A), paras 500–1. On the general confusion regarding the requirement of intention for aiding and abetting and complicity in genocide in the ICTY and ICTR jurisprudence, see Schabas (2000), 300–3; van Sliedregt (2009), 169–71.

[70]   *Bosnia Genocide Case*, Judgment, para 421.

[71]   Art. 3(2)(b), SUA Convention.

[72]   See the ICTY's analysis in *Krstić* (ICTY-98-33-A), para 139, in which the Appeals Chamber held that aiding and abetting is an included offence in complicity.

[73]   Art. 2(3)(c), Terrorist Bombing Convention; Art. 2(5)(c), Terrorism Financing Convention; Art. 2(4)(c), Nuclear Terrorism Convention.

Finally, the three newest TSCs adopted under the auspices of the IMO and ICAO require states to criminalize being an accessory after the fact. The 2005 Protocol to the SUA Convention requires states to criminalize the unlawful and intentional transport of another person on board a ship in the knowledge that such person has committed an offence as defined in the relevant Convention *or* any of the other TSCs already in force at the time of the Convention's adoption.[74] The Beijing Convention (which is not yet in force) requires states to criminalize assisting another person to evade investigation, prosecution or punishment, knowing that the person has committed an act that constitutes an offence set out in the Convention (which includes all the offences set out in the Montreal Convention and the 1988 Protocol to the Montreal Convention) or that the person is wanted for criminal prosecution by law enforcement authorities for such an offence or has been sentenced for such an offence.[75] The 2010 Protocol to the Hague Convention (which is not yet in force) requires states to criminalize precisely the same conduct, only in reference to offences committed under the Hague Convention as amended by the 2010 Protocol.

The accessory offence defined in the 2005 Protocol to the SUA Convention is both broader and narrower than those set out in the ICAO TSCs adopted in 2010. The offence is broader because it criminalizes after the fact assistance in reference to all offences defined in existing TSCs, whereas the Beijing Convention and 2010 Protocol to the Hague Convention are limited to after the fact assistance with hijackings and acts against the safety of civil aviation. The 2005 Protocol to the SUA Convention is narrower in that after the fact assistance is only criminalized if provided through transport aboard a ship covered by the SUA Convention, whereas the ICAO TSCs adopted in 2010 are unrestricted as to the type or mode of assistance.

The accessory offences covered by these new TSCs are particularly relevant modes of state participation in acts of terrorism. Injured states often accuse wrongdoing states of assisting terrorists in escaping prosecution. That said, applying the defined offence under the 2005 Protocol to the SUA Convention to state conduct in reliance on a *Bosnia Genocide Case* analysis will be difficult because the mode of transportation covered by the Convention is effectively private. The 2005 Protocol only requires the criminalization of assisting a person to evade justice through transport aboard a ship—and the SUA Convention does not apply to warships or ships owned or operated by states in connection with naval, customs or police operations.[76] As states will not often be in control of transport aboard ships covered by the SUA Convention, the *Bosnia Genocide Case* analysis will generally be inapplicable to this mode of accessory liability.

The Beijing Convention and the 2010 Protocol to the Hague Convention, however, do not restrict the methods of assisting a person in evading justice— requiring that any such assistance, however delivered, be criminalized. States often

---

[74] Art. 4, 2005 Protocol to the SUA Convention.
[75] Art. 1(4)(d), Beijing Convention.
[76] Art. 2(1), SUA Convention.

accuse a wrongdoing state of harbouring individual terrorists, particularly in reference to hijackings. Such harbouring would certainly meet the elements of the offence of assistance in evading investigation, prosecution or punishment as defined under the new ICAO Conventions. The Beijing Convention and 2010 Protocol to the Hague Convention, when they enter into force, may therefore provide a treaty basis of state responsibility for harbouring alleged terrorists in reliance on a *Bosnia Genocide Case* analysis. But suggestions that a state is an accessory after the fact generally take the form of accusing a custodial state of a failure to comply with the obligations to extradite or submit to prosecution.[77] The question remains whether state responsibility for being an accessory after the fact might be more easily established by relying directly on the obligations to extradite or submit to prosecution (without needing to stretch the principles of state responsibility to cover accessory modes of criminal liability).

As examined in Section 3.2 above, the *aut dedere aut judicare* obligation can be complied with even though no extradition or prosecution actually takes place. Where the custodial state's *bona fide* is in question, relying on the after the fact accessory provisions of the 2010 Protocol to the Hague Convention and the Beijing Convention may better capture the essence of the custodial state's wrongful conduct. In particular, the after the fact accessory provisions of both Conventions require an intention to help an accused evade justice in knowledge that he has committed an offence within the Convention—which addresses precisely the elements of a custodial state's bad faith in refusing to extradite or genuinely submit to prosecution. As the ICJ would have to read a good faith element into the *aut dedere aut judicare* obligations in order that a state might be held responsible for assisting an accused in evading justice—the Court might also rely on the provisions requiring states to criminalize being an accessory after the fact, coupled with a *Bosnia Genocide Case* analysis, to hold states responsible for harbouring persons accused of having committed terrorist acts related to civil aviation.

4.2.2 Exclusion from the scope of the TSCs

The Court's analysis in the *Bosnia Genocide Case* may be strained, adapting as it does the international law of state responsibility to a Convention that creates a regime of individual criminal responsibility,[78] but it is otherwise uncomplicated by questions regarding the interaction of substantive regimes of international law. Even if conspiracy to commit genocide[79] or incitement to commit genocide[80] were prohibited to states as a matter of customary international law, reading the

---

[77] See e.g. discussions regarding the 2 March 1981 hijacking of a Pakistan International Airlines domestic flight to Kabul (Section 5.1.4); the measures adopted against Lebanon in response to its failure to extradite or submit the alleged hijackers of Flight TWA 847 to prosecution (Section 5.1.4); and Sudan's failure to extradite persons accused of the assassination attempt against President Mubarak in Addis Ababa (Section 6.2.5).
[78] See Section 4.2.1.
[79] Art. III(b), Genocide Convention.
[80] Art. III(c), Genocide Convention.

Genocide Convention as impliedly prohibiting states from committing these acts simply duplicates existing obligations without affecting other regimes of applicable substantive law. The same is not true in the terrorism suppression context. Acts that might be defined as terrorist within the scope of some of the TSCs would, if committed by a state's organs or agents, be covered by other applicable regimes of substantive law—in particular the *jus ad bellum*[81] and the *jus in bello*—and might not be prohibited under those regimes.

In the terrorism suppression context, the question of whether state conduct should be characterized as terrorism has long been controversial and the subject of much negotiation. There is no doubt that international humanitarian law prohibits the armed forces of a state party to a conflict from carrying out acts of terrorism.[82] The issue addressed in this section, however, is not whether state military forces *can* carry out acts of terrorism, but whether such conduct falls within the regime of treaties aimed at the prevention and suppression of terrorism generally, or whether such conduct has been left to more directly applicable bodies of international law, including the *jus ad bellum* and IHL.

In the context of negotiations on the draft comprehensive terrorism suppression convention, discussed further below, the Coordinator of the *Ad Hoc* Committee has emphasized that:

the focus [...] had been on developing a law enforcement instrument for individual criminal responsibility, strengthening international cooperation in that regard on the basis of an extradite or prosecute regime. In other words, the individual rather than the State had been at the centre of the efforts to draft a comprehensive convention. The core rationale for focusing on the individual had been that other fields of law—in particular the Charter of the United Nations, international humanitarian law and the law relating to the responsibility of States for internationally wrongful acts—adequately covered the obligations of States in situations where acts of violence were perpetrated by States or their agents. However, since States acted through the agency of individuals, there had nevertheless been an attempt to address the conduct of such agents during armed conflict and in peacetime.[83]

The Coordinator further noted that it is essential that the Convention not encroach upon any of those other applicable regimes of international law—and in particular that it was necessary to preserve the integrity of IHL.[84]

This approach to regime interaction—which views the international treaty regime applicable to terrorism suppression as supplementing existing international law, seamlessly so as to leave no gaps, but without overlap—is only partially reflected in the existing TSCs. What is not clearly reflected in the existing TSCs is the principle, emphasized by the Coordinator, that the Conventions create criminal law enforcement regimes only and do not contemplate direct state responsibility for the acts of terrorism they require states to prevent and extradite or submit to prosecution. As a result, the door has been left open for a *Bosnia Genocide*

---

[81] See Section 2.1.
[82] See Art. 51(2), API; Arts. 4(2)(d) and 13(2), APII.
[83] UNGA, Sixth Committee, UN Doc. A/C.6/63/SR.14 (2008), para 41.
[84] *Ibid*, para 44.

Case analysis to be applied to the existing regime of TSCs. However, some of the TSCs do contain exclusion clauses in reference to particular kinds of state activity (in particular military activity). This means that even if the *Bosnia Genocide Case* analysis is applied to the TSCs, there is a range of state conduct over which the Court could not exercise jurisdiction on the basis of their compromissory clauses. The following sections examine the exclusion of state conduct from the TSCs, and the principles of regime interaction that they give effect to, to determine the precise scope of the ICJ's potential jurisdiction over acts of state terrorism under the Terrorism Suppression Conventions.

(i) Express exclusion of military conduct

The Terrorist Bombing Convention, Nuclear Terrorism Convention, and Hostages Convention all contain clauses that exclude military conduct, to a greater or lesser extent, from their scope. The purpose of these exclusion clauses seems to be to ensure that the TSCs do not amount to a *lex specialis* (which would thereby displace more generally applicable regimes) and are instead principally supplementary to existing regimes. The Conventions do this by defining prohibited conduct broadly in terms that, on their face, overlap with existing rules of international law (such as the *jus ad bellum* and IHL), but then exclude their applicability to at least some of the area of overlap, giving priority to the pre-existing (and often more directly applicable) regime of law.

The Terrorist Bombing and Nuclear Terrorism Conventions

The Terrorist Bombing Convention and the Nuclear Terrorism Convention contain provisions that exclude conduct from their scope to the extent that it is (i) carried out by armed forces during an armed conflict[85] *and* governed by IHL, *or* (ii) carried out by the military forces of a state in the exercise of their official duties *and* otherwise governed by general international law.[86] These carve-out provisions were heavily negotiated and the subject of heated debate. With regard to the Terrorist Bombing Convention, the Non-Aligned Movement sought to limit the exclusion to military action that was in conformity with international law and the UN Charter.[87] What was referred to as a 'compromise' position was only achieved under heavy pressure from Western states which argued that the Convention text was carefully balanced and that the urgency of the need to address terrorist bombings required immediate action.[88]

---

[85] The terms 'armed forces' and 'armed conflict' in the Terrorist Bombing Convention and the Nuclear Terrorism Convention are as understood under IHL. Art. 19, Terrorist Bombing Convention; Art. 4, Nuclear Terrorism Convention.

[86] *Ibid.*

[87] See UNGA, Sixth Committee, Measures to eliminate international terrorism, UN Doc. A/C.6/ 52/SR.33 (1997), paras 41–59.

[88] See e.g. UNGA, Sixth Committee, UN Doc. A/C.6/52/SR.33 (1997), paras 4, 16 and 18. See also Report of the *Ad Hoc* Committee established by General Assembly Resolution 51/210 of 17 December 1996, UN Doc. A/52/37 (1997), Annex II-IV; UNGA, Sixth Committee, Report of the working group on measures to eliminate international terrorism, UN Doc. A/C.6/52/L.3 (1997),

The Nuclear Terrorism Convention negotiations provided another forum in which states could debate the legality of nuclear weapons.[89] Proposals during negotiation of the Convention either insisted that it apply equally to state and non-state actors,[90] or called for a compromise position such as that set out in Article 12 of the Hostages Convention.[91] The military carve-out, as finally adopted, is identical to that in the Terrorist Bombing Convention, except that it expressly stipulates that the exclusion clause 'shall not be interpreted as condoning or making lawful otherwise unlawful acts, or precluding prosecution under other laws'.[92] Acceptance of the carve-out, which was surprising given the protracted negotiations,[93] was undoubtedly facilitated by the Security Council's adoption of Chapter VII Resolution 1540 on the proliferation of weapons of mass destruction to non-state actors.[94]

The first basis of exclusion in both the Terrorist Bombing Convention and the Nuclear Terrorism Convention applies to the activities of armed forces (including the armed forces of a state)[95] during an armed conflict.[96] As state military activity will be covered by the second broader basis of exclusion considered below, this first basis of exclusion is principally relevant to the non-state actor context, including that in which a people is fighting in exercise of their right of self-determination.[97] This first basis of exclusion requires only that relevant conduct be 'governed by' rules of IHL (to be distinguished from a requirement that conduct be 'compliant with' such rules), and draws on both customary international law and

Annex II. Delegates suggested that only the activities of a state's armed forces carried out in accordance with international law should be excluded from the scope of the Convention (UN Doc. A/52/37 (1997), Annex IV), which proposal was not reflected in Article 19(2) of the Terrorist Bombing Convention, but has been raised again in reference to the draft comprehensive terrorism suppression convention (see *infra* note 125 and accompanying text).

[89] The legality (or rather illegality) of the use of nuclear weapons was not conclusively decided by the ICJ in its *Nuclear Weapons Advisory Opinion*.

[90] See e.g. Report of the *Ad Hoc* Committee established by General Assembly Resolution 51/210 of 17 December 1996, UN Doc. A/53/37 (1998), Annex II (Libya); UNGA, Sixth Committee, Report of the working group on measures to eliminate international terrorism, UN Doc. A/C.6/53/L.4 (1999), Annex III, para 43; UNGA, Sixth Committee, UN Doc. A/C.6/54/SR.32 (1999), para 10 (Iraq).

[91] UNGA, Sixth Committee, Report of the working group on measures to eliminate international terrorism, UN Doc. A/C.6/53/L.4 (1999), Annex III, para 38–9. See discussion of Article 12 of the Hostages Convention, Section 3.3.

[92] Art. 19, Terrorist Bombing Convention; Art. 4, Nuclear Terrorism Convention.

[93] India proposed an initial draft of the Nuclear Terrorism Convention in 1998 (see Report of the *Ad Hoc* Committee established by General Assembly Resolution 51/210 of 17 December 1996, UN Doc. A/53/37 (1998), Annex I) and the Convention was not open for signature until September 2005.

[94] UNSC Resolution 1540 (2004).

[95] On the applicability of the exclusion clause to the activities of non-state actors fighting in exercise of a people's right of self-determination, see Section 3.3.

[96] The term 'armed conflict', as understood under IHL, encompasses both international armed conflicts and non-international armed conflicts. The exclusion clause can never operate, however, to exclude activities during a purely internal armed conflict (in which there is no foreign participation and no foreign victims) because the Terrorist Bombing Convention and the Nuclear Terrorism Convention do not apply to such situations in the first place. See Art. 3, Terrorist Bombing Convention; Arts. 3 and 9(2), Nuclear Terrorism Convention.

[97] See Section 3.3.

the Geneva Conventions and Additional Protocols.[98] Ongoing negotiations regarding the draft comprehensive terrorism suppression convention suggest that 'governed by' should be understood in its broadest sense, recognizing that IHL prohibits conduct, but rarely expressly permits it. As a result, that which is not prohibited is considered permitted,[99] and any activities of armed forces during an armed conflict will at least be 'governed by' IHL.

The second basis of exclusion under the Terrorist Bombing and Nuclear Terrorism Conventions covers all state military activity that might fall within the scope of the first basis of exclusion. It requires only that the conduct of a state's armed forces be in exercise of their official duties *and* governed by other rules of international law. As all military conduct in exercise of official duties *will* be subject to other bodies of international law, the latter qualification does not restrict the scope of exclusion. If a state's armed forces are acting officially within that state's territory (with the assistance of or against foreign nationals),[100] human rights law will apply; and if acting officially outside its territory, the *jus ad bellum* or international law regulating the exercise of extra-territorial enforcement jurisdiction will apply. The only way for the conduct of a state's armed forces to be included in the scope of the Terrorist Bombing Convention and the Nuclear Terrorism Convention is therefore if the armed forces are acting in a purely private capacity (i.e. not in exercise of their official duties). But state military forces in a position to carry out acts that are required to be criminalized under the Terrorist Bombing Convention or Nuclear Terrorism Convention will generally only be able to do so in virtue of the tools (explosive or incendiary weapons and nuclear weapons) placed at their disposal as a result of their military status. In carrying out such acts, they will therefore generally be acting at least under colour of authority,[101] thereby meeting the qualification of official conduct as defined in the ILC Articles on State Responsibility.[102]

The provisions discussed above do not condition exclusion from the scope of the Terrorist Bombing Convention or the Nuclear Terrorism Convention on the conduct of the armed forces being in compliance with IHL or other applicable

---

[98] The ICRC has determined that most rules set out in API, which might be inapplicable to a particular armed conflict because of the non-API state party status of a state party to the conflict, nevertheless apply because they are customary international law. See generally Henckaerts (2005). These rules would therefore be relevant for the purposes of excluding conduct from the scope of the Terrorist Bombing and Nuclear Terrorism Conventions, even if they might be irrelevant for the purposes of exclusion under Article 12 of the Hostages Convention in virtue of that Article's conditioning exclusion on the applicability of the Geneva Conventions and Additional Protocols (rather than international humanitarian law more generally). See Section 3.3 on Article 12 of the Hostages Convention and its relationship with API state party status.

[99] See UNGA, Sixth Committee, UN Doc. A/C.6/63/SR.14 (2008), para 45.

[100] To the extent that a state's armed forces are operating within its own territory without foreign assistance and only against its own nationals, the conflict is an internal conflict to which the TSCs are inapplicable. *Supra* note 96.

[101] It is possible to conceive of a group of active military officers who create a terrorist cell whilst acting solely in their private capacity, thus not engaging Art. 7, ILC Articles on State Responsibility. There are no known cases in which this has happened, and it will obviously be exceptional.

[102] See Articles 4 and 7 of the ILC Articles on State Responsibility and the discussion of state actors acting under colour of their authority in Section 2.2.1.

bodies of international law,[103] or on those bodies of law imposing individual criminal responsibility for that conduct. Indeed, given the definition of the offence of terrorist bombing, which includes detonating an explosive in or against a state or government facility,[104] such acts would not necessarily be unlawful under IHL. To the extent that any of the prohibited targets under the Terrorist Bombing Convention are legitimate military targets under IHL, bombing such targets will not amount to a grave breach of the Geneva Conventions or Additional Protocols (subject to their proportionality) and will therefore not be subject to prosecution as a war crime.[105] The exclusion clause thereby attempts to respect the balance between military necessity and humanitarian considerations achieved by IHL without affecting future developments in respect thereof. To that effect, the penultimate preambular paragraph of both the Terrorist Bombing and Nuclear Terrorism Conventions reads:

Noting that the activities of military forces of States are governed by rules of international law outside the framework of this Convention and that the exclusion of certain actions from the coverage of this Convention does not condone or make lawful otherwise unlawful acts, or preclude prosecution under other laws.

But in failing to make exclusion conditional on the availability of alternative mechanisms for the imposition of individual criminal responsibility, and conditioning exclusion instead on the applicability of any alternative regime (including state responsibility for military acts contrary to the *jus ad bellum* and the UN Charter), the exclusion clauses could be read as supporting the application of a *Bosnia Genocide Case* analysis to the Terrorist Bombing and Nuclear Terrorism Conventions, albeit in a much more limited way. Both Conventions appear to implicitly contemplate certain acts of state terrorism (for instance those carried out by non-state actors on behalf of or supported by a state[106] or by non-military state organs) by expressly excluding others.[107] Indeed, the exclusion clauses discussed above are both prefaced by a 'without prejudice' clause that reads as follows: 'Nothing in this Convention shall affect *other* rights, obligations and *responsibilities*

---

[103] But see Egypt's reservation to the Terrorist Bombing Convention: 'The Government of the Arab Republic of Egypt declares that it shall be bound by article 19, paragraph 2, of the Convention to the extent that the armed forces of a state, in the exercise of their duties, do not violate the norms and principles of international law'. In response, the German Government declared 'that it does not consent to the Egyptian declaration [. . .] with regard to any armed forces other than those of the Arab Republic of Egypt, and in particular does not recognize any applicability of the Convention to the armed forces of the Federal Republic of Germany'. <http://treaties.un.org/pages/ViewDetails.aspx? src=TREATY&mtdsg_no=XVIII-9&chapter=18&lang=en>. On Egypt's reservation and the German declaration in regard thereto, see Pellet (2008), paras 293–6.

[104] Art. 2(1), Terrorist Bombing Convention.

[105] *Supra* Chapter 3, notes 284–5 and accompanying text.

[106] The Geneva Conventions do contemplate non-state actors forming part of a state's armed forces or belonging to a Party to the conflict so as to be treated as a state's armed forces (see Art. 4A, GCIII; Del Mar (2010)), but references to non-state actors in this book contemplate non-state actors which do not fall within the scope of Article 4A of GCIII.

[107] This principle of treaty interpretation is the converse of the maxim *expressio unius est exclusio alterius*, and has been applied by international courts and tribunals, like the WTO Appellate Body. See Van Damme (2009), 130.

of states and individuals under international law, in particular the purposes and principles of the Charter of the United Nations and international humanitarian law'.[108] Were the Court minded to apply a *Bosnia Genocide Case* analysis to the TSCs, it might consider that excluding *other* responsibilities of states under international law from the scope of the Convention (in particular those regarding the military forces of a state referenced in the next paragraph of the exclusion clause) suggests that at least *some* responsibilities of states are contemplated (for instance state responsibility for an act of terrorism carried out by non-military actors). Such an interpretation would be consistent with the approach the ICJ took to Article IX of the Genocide Convention, relying on its reference to state responsibility to bolster a broad interpretation of the obligation to prevent.

The result of applying the *Bosnia Genocide Case* analysis, coupled with the exclusion clauses, is that the Court would have jurisdiction pursuant to the compromissory clauses of the Terrorist Bombing and Nuclear Terrorism Conventions to decide disputes regarding a state's responsibility for sponsoring or supporting non-state actors to commit acts meeting the elements of the offences defined therein, as well as disputes regarding a state's responsibility for such conduct by non-military state organs. For instance, had the Terrorist Bombing Convention been in force at the time of the Rainbow Warrior incident,[109] and had France and New Zealand both been parties to the Convention, New Zealand might have invoked France's state responsibility for the act of terrorism carried out by its secret services agents before the ICJ, establishing the Court's jurisdiction under the compromissory clause of the Terrorist Bombing Convention. But had France carried out the 'Rainbow Warrior' bombing through military forces, the Court would have had no jurisdiction under the Terrorist Bombing Convention to decide the dispute in virtue of the exclusion clauses discussed above.

The Hostages Convention

The only other TSC that expressly addresses regime interaction is the Hostages Convention. Article 12 excludes an act of hostage-taking from the scope of the Convention to the extent that it is carried out in the course of an armed conflict as defined in the Geneva Conventions and the Additional Protocols, and to the extent that their prosecute or hand over obligation applies thereto. As discussed in Section 3.3 above, the carve-out was intended to ensure that acts committed in furtherance of a people's struggle for self-determination were not characterized as terrorist under the Convention.[110] The perhaps unintended effect of the provision

---

[108] Emphasis added. Art. 19(1), Terrorist Bombing Convention; Art. 4(1), Nuclear Terrorism Convention.

[109] See *supra* Chapter 2, notes 69–75 and accompanying text for details of the incident.

[110] See Report of the *Ad Hoc* Committee on the drafting of an International Convention against the Taking of Hostages, UN Doc. A/32/39 (1977), Annex, paras 28–9; Proposal by Lesotho, Tanzania, Algeria, Egypt, Libya and Nigeria to the *Ad Hoc* Committee on the drafting of an International Convention against the Taking of Hostages, UN Doc. A/AC.188/L.5 (1978), para 11; Summary record of the 27th meeting of the *Ad Hoc* Committee on the drafting of an International Convention against the Taking of Hostages, UN Doc. A/AC.188/SR.27 (1978), para 1.

is to equally exclude acts of a state from the scope of the Hostages Convention *if* committed during an armed conflict as defined under Geneva Law, *and* if otherwise subject to a prosecute or hand over obligation under the Geneva Conventions and Additional Protocols. The analysis that applied in reference to acts of hostage-taking committed in furtherance of a people's right of self-determination applies equally in reference to the armed forces of a state. The result is that, in cases where state parties to the Hostages Convention are party to the Geneva Conventions (but not to API), only the taking of civilian hostages in the context of an international armed conflict will be excluded from the scope of the Hostages Convention.[111] All other activities of a state's armed forces that otherwise meet the elements of the offence defined in the Hostages Convention (including any hostage-takings committed during a non-international armed conflict and taking active combatants or persons *hors de combat* hostage during an international armed conflict)[112] will fall within the scope of the Hostages Convention. In cases where state parties to the Hostages Convention are also party to API, any hostage-taking of civilians and persons who are *hors de combat*, and the perfidious hostage-taking of active combatants, committed during the course of an international armed conflict (including armed conflicts in which a people is fighting in exercise of their right of self-determination),[113] will be excluded from the scope of the Hostages Convention.[114]

This analysis of the way in which IHL and the terrorism suppression regime interact under Article 12 has two implications for the relevance of the *Bosnia Genocide Case* reasoning to the Hostages Convention. First, the fact that exclusion is conditioned on the applicability of an alternative criminal law enforcement regime should suggest that the Hostages Convention was viewed purely as an individual criminal responsibility enforcement regime, and that there is no room for finding an implied prohibition of state conduct to which state responsibility could attach, beyond responsibility for a failure to properly implement the criminal law enforcement regime created by the Convention. This is consistent with the way in which states negotiating the draft comprehensive terrorism suppression convention view the existing regime of TSCs.[115] The ICJ was, however, not convinced by the similar criminal law focus of the Genocide Convention in its *Bosnia Genocide Case* decision. Second (assuming the Court found a *Bosnia Genocide Case* analysis to be nevertheless relevant), the Court could only hold a state directly responsible under the Hostages Convention (with its jurisdiction established on the basis of the compromissory clause) for taking non-civilians hostage during the course of an international armed conflict (with respect to parties to the Geneva Conventions); or for taking active combatants hostage (in a non-perfidious manner) in the course of an international armed conflict, including Article 1(4) API conflicts (with respect to parties to API).

---

[111] *Supra* Chapter 3, notes 245–55 and accompanying text.
[112] *Supra* Chapter 3, note 249 and accompanying text.
[113] Art. 1(4), API.
[114] *Supra* Chapter 3, note 253–5 and accompanying text.
[115] *Supra* note 83 and accompanying text.

The Terrorism Financing Convention

The Terrorism Financing Convention does not have an exclusion clause like those examined above. Rather, any exclusion from the scope of the Convention results from the definition of terrorist acts, the financing of which is prohibited. The Terrorism Financing Convention prohibits the financing of:

    (a) An act which constitutes an offence within the scope of and as defined in one of the treaties listed in the annex; or

    (b) Any other act intended to cause death or serious bodily injury to a civilian, or to any other person not taking an active part in the hostilities in a situation of armed conflict, when the purpose of such act, by its nature or context, is to intimidate a population, or to compel a government or an international organization to do or to abstain from doing any act.[116]

In reference to the first part of the definition of acts of terrorism, the financing of any act excluded from the scope of an existing TSC pursuant to its exclusion clause will not be prohibited under Article 2(1)(a) of the Terrorism Financing Convention. The catch-all definition of terrorist acts in Article 2(1)(b), however, covers state conduct that would be excluded from the scope of the TSCs examined above. For instance, the Terrorist Bombing Convention and Nuclear Terrorism Convention exclude all activities of a state's military forces from their scope (provided such forces are not acting in a purely private capacity)—including the deliberate killing of civilians. It would therefore not be possible, in applying a *Bosnia Genocide Case* analysis, to argue that those Conventions impliedly create a regime of state responsibility for military activities meeting the elements of the defined offences. But if a state's military forces deliberately kill civilians to compel a government to do or abstain from doing something, the *financing* of such acts could be prohibited pursuant to Article 2(1)(b) of the Terrorism Financing Convention on a *Bosnia Genocide Case* analysis even though the regime of TSCs does not apply to the acts themselves when committed by a state's military.

It should, however, be exceptionally difficult to argue that the obligation to prevent the financing of terrorism implicitly prohibits a state from funding its own military (to the extent that the military commits acts that otherwise meet the definition of terrorist acts in Article 2(1)(b)). The object and purpose of the Terrorism Financing Convention is to prevent terrorism by cutting off available funding, and to cut off available funding by filling a gap in international law that had not expressly created a criminal law framework applicable to such financing.[117] There is, however, no gap in international law in relation to the activities (financing or otherwise) of states. States control both their militaries and their budgets, and are prohibited from deliberately killing civilians either as a matter of human rights law or as a matter of IHL. The foundational premise of the Terrorism Financing Convention—that the source of funds is separate from those carrying out the

---

[116] Arts. 2(1) (a) and (b), Terrorism Financing Convention.
[117] See Preamble, Terrorism Financing Convention: '*Noting* that the number and seriousness of acts of international terrorism depend on the financing that terrorists may obtain; *Noting also* that existing multilateral legal instruments do not expressly address such financing'.

acts of terrorism and needs to be addressed in addition to the regime that addresses the conduct directly—is therefore inapplicable to the case of states funding their own military activities. But where states are funding non-state activities that meet the definition of terrorism set out in Article 2(1)(b) of the Terrorism Financing Convention or are otherwise covered by the TSCs, there is nothing particular in the Convention to suggest that the *Bosnia Genocide Case* analysis should not apply—on which basis the Court could exercise jurisdiction over claims of state financing of terrorism under the Terrorism Financing Convention compromissory clause.

Draft Comprehensive Terrorism Suppression Convention

The ongoing negotiation of the draft comprehensive terrorism suppression convention is instructive in terms of the relationship between the TSCs and other bodies of international law—in particular as regards the TSCs potentially being a source of state responsibility for acts of 'state terrorism'. As discussed above,[118] the Coordinator of the *Ad Hoc* Committee has emphasized the criminal law enforcement framework of the draft convention, noting that there are other bodies of international law—which the draft convention should not affect or be affected by—that address acts of violence perpetrated by states and their agents.[119] Nevertheless, the Coordinator has noted persistent efforts to include specific obligations bearing on states, for instance obligations prohibiting states from engaging in acts of terrorism, within the draft comprehensive terrorism suppression convention.[120] Her response to these efforts has been to emphasize that the criminal responsibility focus of the draft convention 'did not, in and of itself, mean that international law was silent on the obligations of states',[121] and to call on states to respect the *acquis* of the TSC regime—as law enforcement instruments for ensuring individual criminal responsibility on the basis of an obligation to extradite or submit to prosecution.[122]

While the Coordinator's position is principled in its attempt to respect the spheres of application of different regimes of international law, it has not been fully reflected in the TSCs discussed above. Conduct that amounts to a use of force by a state (and is therefore regulated by the *jus ad bellum*), in particular when committed by non-military personnel or outside the context of an armed conflict (in the case of the Hostages Convention), still falls within the scope of the existing TSCs (at least in so far as criminal responsibility for such conduct is concerned). That said, the vast majority of state conduct that is regulated by other regimes, in particular military conduct (regulated by the *jus ad bellum* and *jus in bello*) is

---

[118] *Supra* notes 83–4 and accompanying text.

[119] UNGA, Sixth Committee, UN Doc. A/C.6/63/SR.14 (2008), para 41.

[120] See Reports of the *Ad Hoc* Committee established by General Assembly Resolution 51/210 of 17 December 1996, UN Doc. A/64/37 (2009), para 6; UN Doc. A/65/37 (2010), para 11. Other delegates, however, have insisted that the draft convention should be a purely law-enforcement instrument based on an *aut dedere aut judicare* regime and that the notion of state terrorism must be avoided. See UN Doc. A/65/37 (2010), para 14.

[121] See UNGA, Sixth Committee, UN Doc. A/C.6/63/SR.14 (2008), para 48.

[122] *Ibid*, para 49.

excluded from the scope of the TSCs. This is precisely the compromise the Coordinator is trying to achieve in respect of the draft comprehensive terrorism suppression convention, but the scope of the exclusion clause is one of the reasons for the protracted negotiations.[123]

The proposal that is most closely aligned with the inclusion of 'state terrorism' in the draft comprehensive terrorism suppression convention is that of the OIC, put forward in 2002.[124] The OIC's proposal, which continues to enjoy wide support, suggests that state military conduct should only be excluded from the scope of the draft convention to the extent that it is 'in conformity with international law'[125] (to be distinguished from the Coordinator's proposal which excludes conduct 'because [it is] governed by other rules of international law').[126] Were the Coordinator's proposal adopted, the regime interaction between the draft comprehensive terrorism suppression convention and the *jus ad bellum* and *jus in bello* would be as described in reference to the Terrorist Bombing and Nuclear Terrorism Conventions above: there would be minimal overlap between the regimes. Were the OIC proposal adopted, however, any state military conduct that is in breach of the *jus ad bellum* or *jus in bello* would—in virtue of its unlawfulness under those regimes—also amount to an act of terrorism falling within the scope of the draft comprehensive terrorism suppression convention.

In reference to the divide between her own proposal and that of the OIC, the Coordinator stated that:

[123] The other flashpoint in negotiations has been whether the general definition of terrorism should cover acts committed in exercise of a people's right of self-determination, although there is more and more consensus amongst delegates to the *Ad Hoc* Committee that any exclusions from the scope of the draft comprehensive terrorism suppression convention should be achieved through an exclusion clause like those discussed in Section 4.2.2 above, rather than in the definition of terrorist acts in the convention. See e.g. UN Doc. A/65/37 (2010), para 3; UN Doc. A/64/37 (2009), para 6.

[124] A proposal by Cuba, submitted in 2005, attempted to apply the draft comprehensive terrorism suppression convention to acts of state terrorism—but for the purposes of the individual criminal responsibility of the state officials. Cuba has proposed that the following offence be added to the definition of terrorist offences in the draft convention: 'Being in a position to control or direct effectively the actions of troops belonging to the armed forces of the state, orders, permits, or actively participates in the planning, preparation, initiation or execution of any of the offences set out in paragraphs 1, 2 or 3 of the present article, in a manner incompatible with international law, including the Charter of the United Nations'. Reports of the *Ad Hoc* Committee established by General Assembly Resolution 51/210 of 17 December 1996, UN Doc. A/65/37 (2010), para 11; UN Doc. A/60/37 (2005), Annex III.

[125] The OIC's proposal for the exclusion clause (in Article 18 of the draft comprehensive terrorism suppression convention) reads as follows: 'The activities undertaken by the military forces of a state in the exercise of their official duties, inasmuch as they are in conformity with international law, are not governed by this Convention'. Report of the *Ad Hoc* Committee established by General Assembly Resolution 51/210 of 17 December 1996, UN Doc. A/57/37 (2002), Annex IV, 17. The proposal, which was first made (but rejected) in reference to the Terrorist Bombing Convention (see UNGA, Sixth Committee, Measures to eliminate international terrorism, UN Doc. A/C.6/52/SR.33 (1997), paras 41–59) enjoys support more than seven years after the OIC first put it to the *Ad Hoc* Committee. See Report of the *Ad Hoc* Committee established by General Assembly Resolution 51/210 of 17 December 1996, UN Doc. A/65/37 (2010), para 12.

[126] The Coordinator's proposal simply adopts the language of the exclusion clauses already agreed to in the Terrorist Bombing and Nuclear Terrorism Conventions. *Supra* note 85 and accompanying text. See Report of the *Ad Hoc* Committee established by General Assembly Resolution 51/210 of 17 December 1996, UN Doc. A/62/37 (2007), para 14.

if there was any agreement at all on the approach, it was in the fact that it was essential not to encroach upon any of those regimes [i.e. IHL]. It was recalled that the necessity to preserve the integrity of international humanitarian law had been reiterated throughout the discussions by many delegations. Any attempt to rectify what some might consider gaps or deficiencies in that regime should be avoided.[127]

This certainly seems to be the case. Both the OIC proposal and the Coordinator's proposal leave the *jus ad bellum* and the *jus in bello* intact. The difference is that the Coordinator's proposal excludes conduct from the scope of the draft comprehensive convention whenever it is *regulated* by those other regimes, whatever they have to say about the lawfulness of the conduct, whereas the OIC proposal includes acts of state in the draft comprehensive convention—but bases inclusion on the unlawfulness of the conduct, as determined independently by the *jus ad bellum* and *jus in bello* regimes.

Given that language in line with the Coordinator's proposal was adopted over that of the OIC proposal in reference to the Terrorist Bombing Convention, and the preference for consistency in regard to the terrorism suppression treaty regime,[128] it is unlikely that the OIC proposal will win the day—but it certainly highlights the potential for overlap between the terrorism suppression regime and the *jus in bello* and *jus ad bellum*. Whatever the conclusion of the negotiations, the draft comprehensive terrorism suppression convention will not upset the regime interaction rules operative in respect of the existing TSCs, as the comprehensive convention is only intended to apply in the event the existing TSCs do not.[129]

(ii) Implied exclusion of state military activities?

With the exception of the Terrorist Bombing Convention, Nuclear Terrorism Convention, 2005 Protocol to the SUA Convention,[130] and to a lesser extent the

---

[127] Report of the *Ad Hoc* Committee established by General Assembly Resolution 51/210 of 17 December 1996, UN Doc. A/65/37 (2010), para 5.

[128] See e.g. IMO, Report of the *Ad Hoc* Preparatory Committee on the Suppression of Unlawful Acts against the Safety of Maritime Navigation, 2nd Session, 18–22 May 1987, IMO Doc. PCUA 2/5 (1987), para 65; ICAO Assembly, 36th Session, Legal Committee, Acts or Offences of Concern to the International Aviation Community and not Covered by Existing Air Law Instruments, ICAO Doc. A36-WP/12, LE/4 (2007).

[129] The relationship between the draft comprehensive terrorism suppression convention and the existing TSCs (where the comprehensive convention and a TSC applied to the same act as between state parties) was the subject of much debate, with some states preferring that the existing TSCs should apply as a *lex specialis*, and other states proposing to allow the sectoral TSCs and the comprehensive convention to apply in parallel. See Report of the *Ad Hoc* Committee established by General Assembly Resolution 51/210 of 17 December 1996, UN Doc. A/58/37 (2003), Annex II, paras 7–11. Art. 2*bis* drafted by the Coordinator in 2002 (which proposes the *lex specialis* status of the existing TSCs) remains, however, the only proposal considered by the *Ad Hoc* Committee. See Art. 2*bis*, Report of the *Ad Hoc* Committee established by General Assembly Resolution 51/210 of 17 December 1996, UN Doc. A/57/37 (2002), Annex II; Art. 3, Report of the Coordinator of the draft convention, attached to the letter of the Chairman of the Sixth Committee to the President of the General Assembly, UN Doc. A/59/294 (2005), Appendix II. See further Reports of the *Ad Hoc* Committee established by General Assembly Resolution 51/210 of 17 December 1996, UN Doc. A/59/37 (2004), para 7; UN Doc. A/60/37 (2005), para 7; UN Doc. A/61/37 (2006), para 6; UN Doc. A/62/37 (2007), para 6; UN Doc. A/63/37 (2008), para 6; UN Doc. A/64/37 (2009), para 6; UN Doc. A/65/37 (2010), para 6.

[130] See discussion below in reference to the IMO TSCs.

Hostages Convention and the Terrorism Financing Convention, the TSCs in force at the time of writing are silent on the 'state terrorism' issue. There is, however, some practice suggesting that the military activities of a state that meet the elements of offences defined in the remaining TSCs are not considered subject to those TSCs, and are rather considered subject to more directly applicable legal regimes— practice that might inform an interpretation of the scope of those TSCs. TSCs adopted under the auspices of the IMO in 2005 and the ICAO in 2010 confirm this implicit analysis by incorporating exclusion provisions identical to those in the Terrorist Bombing and Nuclear Terrorism Conventions, as discussed further below.

Internationally Protected Persons Convention

The Internationally Protected Persons Convention does not expressly exclude any state activities from its scope, but states do not tend to invoke the Internationally Protected Persons Convention to condemn state activities unless attempting to establish the ICJ's jurisdiction over a dispute.[131] Instead, state force against diplomatically protected persons is, to the extent possible, dealt with as a matter regulated by the Vienna Convention on Diplomatic Relations and Vienna Convention on Consular Relations, and not as a question of state responsibility under the Internationally Protected Persons Convention.

For instance, states protesting action taken by Iraqi soldiers against foreign consulates, embassies and their ambassadors or attachés in Kuwait after Iraq's invasion in 1990 did not invoke the Internationally Protected Persons Convention.[132] Similarly, in a letter to the Secretary-General regarding an attack by Ecuadorian military personnel on the Peruvian Vice-Consul, Peru invoked both the Vienna Convention in Diplomatic Relations and the Vienna Convention on Consular Relations, not the Internationally Protected Persons Convention.[133] Finally, the Sudan informed the Secretary-General of an assault on its Ambassador to Egypt by Egyptian security forces, characterizing the assaults as 'flagrant violation[s] of the Charter of the United Nations, the Vienna Convention on Diplomatic Relations of 18 April 1961 and the resolutions of the General Assembly', but not of the Internationally Protected Persons Convention.[134]

This practice suggests an application of the regime interaction principles discussed above in reference to the Terrorist Bombing and Nuclear Terrorism Conventions—treating the Internationally Protected Persons Convention as supplementary to existing bodies of international law, without overlap. In its *Tehran Hostages* decision, the Court showed an appreciation for these regime interaction principles, relying on more directly applicable rules to decide the case.

---

[131] *Supra* notes 61–4 and accompanying text, in reference to *Certain Questions of Mutual Assistance in Criminal Matters (Djibouti v. France)*, Judgment.

[132] See UNSG, Report on effective measures to enhance the protection, security and safety of diplomatic and consular missions and representatives, UN Doc. A/45/455/Add.2 (1990).

[133] See UNSG, Report on effective measures to enhance the protection, security and safety of diplomatic and consular missions and representatives, UN Doc. A/INF/50/3 (1995), 17.

[134] *Ibid*, 22.

In particular, the Court did not consider it necessary to decide the question of responsibility under the Internationally Protected Persons Convention given that the Vienna Conventions applied to the facts before the Court and both Iran and the US were state parties to the Vienna Conventions and their accompanying Optional Protocols concerning the compulsory settlement of disputes.[135] But this will not always be the case. While the Vienna Conventions on Diplomatic and Consular Relations are (marginally) more widely ratified than the Internationally Protected Persons Convention,[136] only one-third of state parties to the Vienna Conventions have ratified their accompanying Optional Protocols conferring jurisdiction on the ICJ,[137] compared with 136 state parties to the Internationally Protected Persons Convention that have accepted the compulsory jurisdiction of the ICJ under the Convention's compromissory clause.[138] As a result, the issue of the applicability of the Internationally Protected Persons Convention to state conduct (whether the Vienna Conventions are more directly applicable to the conduct or not) may well arise in the context of disputes before the ICJ. In cases where relevant states have not ratified the Optional Protocols to the Vienna Conventions, the Court could well abandon the principled approach it took in *Tehran Hostages* (in which it relied on the more directly applicable Conventions), in favour of a position that supports its jurisdiction to hear a dispute.

There is also a broad spectrum of potential state conduct that falls outside the scope of the Vienna Conventions on Diplomatic and Consular Relations, to which the Internationally Protected Persons Convention would apply. For instance, the Vienna Conventions impose obligations on states as receiving states—and therefore the obligations resulting from the inviolability of diplomatic representatives of the sending state are limited to territory within the receiving state's jurisdiction or control. In addition, the Vienna Conventions on Diplomatic and Consular Relations are more limited in scope than the Internationally Protected Persons Convention in so far as the former only apply to persons connected with the diplomatic and consular relations between a sending and receiving state. The Internationally Protected Persons Convention applies more broadly to heads of state and other internationally protected persons (including diplomatic agents), as defined under general international law.[139] As a result, there are gaps in coverage in the Vienna

---

[135] See *Tehran Hostages (US v. Iran)*, Judgment, paras 45–9 and 55.

[136] The Vienna Convention on Diplomatic Relations, 18 April 1961, 500 UNTS 95 has 187 state parties, and the Vienna Convention on Consular Relations, 24 April 1963, 596 UNTS 261 has 173 state parties. The Internationally Protected Persons Convention has 173 state parties, all of which are parties to the Vienna Conventions.

[137] Sixty-six states have ratified the Optional Protocol to the Vienna Convention on Diplomatic Relations concerning the Compulsory Settlement of Disputes, 18 April 1961, 500 UNTS 241 and forty-eight states have ratified the Optional Protocol to the Vienna Convention on Consular Relations concerning the Compulsory Settlement of Disputes, 24 April 1963, 596 UNTS 487. <http://treaties.un.org/pages/Treaties.aspx?id=3&subid=A&lang=en>.

[138] Of the 173 state parties to the Internationally Protected Persons Convention, only thirty-seven have made a reservation against the compulsory jurisdiction of the ICJ pursuant to the Convention's compromissory clause. <http://treaties.un.org/pages/ViewDetails.aspx?src=TREATY&mtdsg_no=XVIII-7&chapter=18&lang=en>.

[139] Art. 1, Internationally Protected Persons Convention.

Conventions that might be filled by the Internationally Protected Persons Convention. Employing a *Bosnia Genocide Case* analysis, the Internationally Protected Persons Convention could impose obligations on states directly to refrain from uses of force against protected persons that would not otherwise be unlawful under the Vienna Convention regime.[140] For instance, a state's conduct against internationally protected persons, when perpetrated outside of its territory or territory it controls, or against an internationally protected person who is not protected pursuant to the Vienna Conventions, has been treated as falling within the scope of the Internationally Protected Persons Convention. In a letter to the Security Council, in which South Korea accused North Korea of having sent captains of its army to Rangoon in Burma to attack the South Korean President with explosives, South Korea characterized North Korea's conduct as 'criminal acts of terrorism' that amounted to a violation of the UN Charter *and* the Internationally Protected Persons Convention.[141]

IMO TSCs

At the SUA Conference in 1988, Saudi Arabia,[142] Libya[143] and Nicaragua[144] proposed that the Convention should apply to states as well as to individuals. Kuwait, recognizing that the Convention was one that addressed individual criminal responsibility (which would not be easily applicable to states or governments), refined the idea and suggested that 'any person' in the definition of the offence be replaced by 'any person, even if acting on behalf of a Government'. Kuwait justified its proposal on the basis of the Nuremberg jurisprudence, in particular that it was well accepted that persons who carry out acts of state are personally accountable for

---

[140] While a use of force by a state in foreign territory against an internationally protected person would be unlawful as a matter of customary international law, a dispute in regard to responsibility for such a use of force would not be subject to the Court's jurisdiction absent an Article 36(2) declaration.

[141] UNSG, Report on measures to prevent international terrorism, UN Doc. A/38/355/Add.2 (1983), 3.

[142] The Saudi proposal included preambular language expressing concern 'about the world-wide escalation of acts of terrorism in all its forms, by persons or governments' and proposed that the article defining the offence read 'any ordinary person *or government* commits an offence if that person unlawfully and intentionally [. . .]'. Emphasis added. IMO, International Conference on the Suppression of Unlawful Acts Against the Safety of Maritime Navigation, Rome 1988, Working papers for the Committee of the Whole (submitted by Saudi Arabia), IMO Doc. SUA/CONF/CW/WP.14 (1988). See also IMO, International Conference on the Suppression of Unlawful Acts against the Safety of Maritime Navigation, Sixth Committee, Record of decisions, 10 March 1988, IMO Doc. SUA/CONF/RD/6 (1989), 9.

[143] Libya proposed both that the Convention not apply in cases where the relevant offence was committed during an armed conflict as defined in Article 1(4) of API, and took up the substance of the Saudi proposal in its proposal that the article defining the SUA offence should read 'any Government or persons commits an offence if [. . .]'. IMO, International Conference on the Suppression of Unlawful Acts Against the Safety of Maritime Navigation, Rome 1988, Working papers for the Committee of the Whole (submitted by Libya), IMO Doc. SUA/CONF/CW/WP.15 (1988).

[144] Nicaragua proposed that Article 3(1) read 'Any person or Government commits an offence if that person or Government unlawfully and intentionally [. . .]'. IMO, International Conference on the Suppression of Unlawful Acts Against the Safety of Maritime Navigation, Rome 1988, Working papers for the Committee of the Whole (submitted by Nicaragua), IMO Doc. SUA/CONF/CW/WP.33 (1988).

their behaviour. Kuwait further emphasized that its proposal did not affect state responsibility as it was concerned only with individual criminal responsibility.[145] Objections to the Kuwaiti proposal included that it would complicate interpretation of parallel provisions in the Montreal and Hague Conventions, which did not contain similar language, and that the added language was unnecessary in any event because the existing language was broad enough to include criminal responsibility for acts carried out on behalf of governments.[146] While Kuwait's proposal was not reflected in the final draft, the language was left open enough to allow for an interpretation that covered acts of terrorism committed by state officials. For instance Syria emphasized that it considered the words 'wherever and by whomever committed' in the preambular condemnation of all acts of terrorism as referring to 'States which practice terrorism'.[147] That said, the debate over whether the Convention should cover the acts of a state was entirely in reference to the potential individual criminal responsibility of state actors, not state responsibility for the offences defined under the Convention.

In reference to whether the *Bosnia Genocide Case* analysis should apply to the SUA Convention, the SUA Convention defines the scope of its applicability in a manner that is consistent with some of the principles of regime interaction discussed above. In particular, language in the SUA Convention signals that it was intended to supplement applicable bodies of international law, not to supplant those bodies of law through the creation of a *lex specialis*. For instance, Article 2(1) of the SUA Convention renders the Convention inapplicable to acts committed against warships and naval auxiliary ships—to which the *jus ad bellum* and *jus in bello* would be more obviously applicable. Uses of military force against such ships are therefore addressed within the framework of generally applicable international law.[148] The negotiating history of the IMO Conventions also reflects a concern

---

[145] IMO, Report of the *Ad Hoc* Preparatory Committee on the Suppression of Unlawful Acts against the Safety of Maritime Navigation, 2nd Session, 18–22 May 1987, IMO Doc. PCUA 2/5 (1987), para 65.

[146] *Ibid*, para 66.

[147] IMO, International Conference on the Suppression of Unlawful Acts against the Safety of Maritime Navigation, Sixth Committee, Record of decisions, 10 March 1988, IMO Doc. SUA/CONF/RD/6 (1989), Annex, 9.

[148] For instance, on 26 March 2010, an underwater explosion caused by a submarine-fired torpedo sunk South Korea's 'Cheonan' naval ship, resulting in the loss of forty-six lives. Seoul released a report, drafted in cooperation with teams of experts from the US, UK, Australia and Sweden, which determined that the torpedo had been fired by a submarine belonging to North Korea. BBC, 'Investigation Result on the Sinking of ROKS "Cheonan"', 20 May 2010, <http://news.bbc.co.uk/nol/shared/bsp/hi/pdfs/20_05_10jigreport.pdf>. South Korea invoked the responsibility of North Korea on several occasions, most particularly in letters to the Security Council, and consistently relied on the UN Charter, the 1953 Korean Armistice Agreement and the 1992 Agreement on Reconciliation, Non-aggression and Exchanges and Cooperation as a basis for condemning North Korea's use of military force. See Letter dated 4 June 2010 from the Permanent Representative of the Republic of Korea to the United Nations addressed to the President of the Security Council, UN Doc. S/2010/281; Letter dated 30 June 2010 from the Permanent Representative of the Republic of Korea to the United Nations addressed to the President of the Security Council, UN Doc. S/2010/349. The South Korean invocation of responsibility was rejected by North Korea, which claimed that the investigative results were a fabrication serving US interests. See Letter dated 8 June 2010 from the Permanent Representative of the Democratic People's Republic of Korea to the United Nations addressed to the

that any rules relating to terrorism suppression not displace or modify UNCLOS as the general law of the sea.[149] Article 9 of the SUA Convention in particular stipulates that nothing in the Convention shall affect in any way the rules of international law pertaining to the competence of states to exercise investigative or enforcement jurisdiction on board ships not flying their flag. The SUA Convention also has an unusual preamble which stipulates that matters not regulated by the Convention continue to be regulated by the rules and principles of general international law. These articles quite clearly indicate that acts of state which are subject to other regimes of international law were not intended to be covered by the SUA Convention, and, properly interpreted, they should suggest to the Court that the *Bosnia Genocide Case* analysis is inapplicable to the SUA Convention to the extent of any overlap with existing regimes of international law.

As a result of the availability of other regimes of international law within which to evaluate uses of force by states against merchant shipping, the IMO TSCs have not generally been invoked to condemn a state's military activities against the safety of civil maritime navigation. While the use of military force against merchant ships (without flag state consent) is very unusual, incidents involving such uses of force[150] are dealt with as a matter of general maritime law and the *jus ad bellum*. A telling example of this practice is the condemnation of Israel's use of force against a flotilla of ships destined for Gaza in May 2010. The flotilla was allegedly delivering aid to Gaza, in defiance of a blockade imposed by Israel after Hamas took power in 2007. Israeli military commandos stormed the largest vessel of the flotilla (the Turkish-flagged 'Mavi Marmara') to prevent it from breaching the blockade.[151] Israel's use of force was the subject of two letters of complaint to the Security Council from Turkey and Lebanon, in response to

President of the Security Council, UN Doc. S/2010/294; Letter dated 6 July 2010 from the Permanent Representative of the Democratic People's Republic of Korea to the United Nations addressed to the President of the Security Council, UN Doc. S/2010/358.

[149] IMO, Report of the *Ad Hoc* Preparatory Committee on the Suppression of Unlawful Acts against the Safety of Maritime Navigation, 2nd Session, 18–22 May 1987, IMO Doc. PCUA 2/5 (1987), paras 36–8; See also IMO, International Conference on the Suppression of Unlawful Acts against the Safety of Maritime Navigation, Sixth Committee, Record of decisions, 10 March 1988, IMO Doc. SUA/CONF/RD/6 (1989), Annex, 3 (Austria, emphasising that the SUA Convention filled gaps in the generally applicable regime of international law).

[150] Whether the exercise of enforcement jurisdiction on board a ship amounts to a use of force against that ship (as that term is used in Article 2(4) of the UN Charter) is a matter of some controversy (see Randelzhofer (2002a), 124; Guilfoyle (2007)). Neither military force nor the exercise of enforcement jurisdiction aboard a foreign ship are addressed in the SUA Convention. Art. 9, SUA Convention. But the 2005 Protocol to the SUA Convention—which addresses a use of force while boarding a ship with flag state consent to investigate the possible commission of offences defined under the Convention (Art. 8(2), 2005 Protocol to the SUA Convention) *and* excludes military activities from the scope of the Convention (Art. 2*bis*, 2005 Protocol to the SUA Convention)—suggests that uses of military force against a ship are to be distinguished from any use of force during the exercise of enforcement jurisdiction. A proposal to address the use of force in self-defence in the context of the provision addressing the use of force while boarding and searching a ship for criminal law enforcement purposes was rejected by the Legal Committee, further suggesting that the exercise of enforcement jurisdiction on board a ship (even if involving a use of force) is not to be confused with a use of force regulated by the *jus ad bellum*. See IMO, Report of the Legal Committee on the work of its ninetieth session, IMO Doc. LEG 90/15 (2005), para 89.

[151] Keesing's, Vol. 56, May 2010, 49865.

which the Council met on 31 May 2010.[152] Most delegates making statements before the Council restricted themselves to calling for an investigation into the event, calling on Israel to end its blockade of Gaza, and calling for a long-term (and peaceful) solution to the Arab–Israeli conflict. And although the Turkish delegate characterized Israel's conduct as 'a grave breach of international law [. . .] tantamount to banditry and piracy [. . .]',[153] it relied principally on applicable regimes of international law (including the law of the sea, the *jus in bello* and the absence of any *jus ad bellum* justification (such as self-defence)) to condemn Israel's attack on the flotilla.[154] Of the other states that condemned Israel's conduct in reference to particular rules of international law, none relied on the SUA Convention, invoking instead the Geneva Conventions, Additional Protocols and humanitarian law principles more generally,[155] Security Council Resolution 1860,[156] the law of the sea,[157] and the Charter of the United Nations.[158] The international fact-finding mission charged with investigating violations of international law resulting from the Israeli attack on the flotilla considered the law of naval warfare, international humanitarian law and human rights law to be the applicable legal framework within which to assess the lawfulness of Israeli conduct. Nowhere in the report is the SUA Convention mentioned.[159]

The interpretation of the SUA Convention suggested above, which implicitly excludes direct state responsibility for the offences defined therein to the extent that such conduct is regulated by other regimes of international law, is confirmed in the 2005 Protocol to the SUA Convention (amending the SUA Convention as between state parties to the Protocol). The 2005 Protocol contains a clause identical to the exclusion clause examined above in reference to the Terrorist Bombing and Nuclear Terrorism Conventions. But the 2005 Protocol to the SUA Convention came into force five years after its adoption (on 28 July 2010), and is only in force (at the time of writing) as between thirteen states. The SUA Convention, unamended by the 2005 Protocol, therefore remains in force between the other 140 state parties to the SUA Convention that have not yet ratified the Protocol. As a result, unless the ICJ was

---

[152] See Letter dated 31 May 2010 from the Permanent Representative of Turkey to the President of the Security Council, UN Doc. S/2010/266; Letter dated 31 May 2010 from the Permanent Representative of Lebanon to the President of the Security Council, UN Doc. S/2010/267; SC 6326th meeting (2010).

[153] SC 6326th meeting (2010), 4.

[154] *Ibid.* Turkey has invoked Israel's responsibility for the killing of Turkish citizens and has demanded an apology and compensation. BBC, 'Israel and Turkey hold talks to heal rift over flotilla', 6 December 2010, <http://www.bbc.co.uk/news/world-middle-east-11929258>.

[155] See SC 6326th meeting (2010), 7 (Mexico), 9 (Russian Federation), 12 (Lebanon).

[156] *Ibid*, 7 (Brazil). Security Council Resolution 1860 called for the unimpeded provision and distribution throughout Gaza of humanitarian assistance (including food, fuel and medical treatment). UNSC Resolution 1860 (2009), para 2.

[157] SC 6326th meeting (2010), 9 (Russian Federation), 12 (Lebanon).

[158] *Ibid*, 12 (Lebanon).

[159] See Report of the international fact-finding mission to investigate violations of international law, including international humanitarian and human rights law, resulting from the Israeli attacks on the flotilla of ships carrying humanitarian assistance, UN Doc. A/HRC/15/21 (2010). See further Shany (2010), criticising the Report's conclusions as to applicable law (particularly in its assumptions that the Fourth Geneva Convention and human right law applies on the high seas), without suggesting that the SUA Convention was applicable law.

minded to implicitly exclude state activities from the scope of the SUA Convention on the basis of the analysis above—the SUA Convention might well be relied on to ground the Court's jurisdiction in reference to an Israeli type use of force against maritime navigation on the basis of the *Bosnia Genocide Case* analysis.

ICAO TSCs

The issue of whether a state's use of military force can qualify as an act of terrorism has most often been raised in reference to the ICAO TSCs. In public statements condemning the use of force against a civil aircraft, states have consistently relied on rules of international law *other than* the ICAO TSCs as the basis for qualifying such activities as unlawful. But for the purposes of international dispute settlement, states have invoked the ICAO TSCs as a source of legal obligation (and ICJ jurisdiction) in disputes regarding state responsibility for military activities against the safety of civil aircraft. The inconsistency of this practice—indicating on the one hand a principled approach to regime interaction similar to that taken in reference to the Terrorist Bombing and Nuclear Terrorism Conventions discussed above, and on the other a more opportunistic approach when the ICJ's jurisdiction hangs in the balance—has forced the ICAO to adopt a legal position on the question of the applicability of the ICAO TSCs to state activities. In September 2010, the ICAO adopted the 2010 Protocol to the Hague Convention and the Beijing Convention (which consolidates the Montreal Convention and 1988 Protocol to the Montreal Convention, in addition to requiring states to criminalize the use and transport of explosives and BCN weapons from civil aircraft), both amending the existing ICAO TSCs to more closely accord with the position on regime interaction adopted in the Terrorist Bombing and Nuclear Terrorism Conventions and the non ICJ-related state practice discussed below.

State practice

When states condemn a use of military force against a civil aircraft or airport, they generally do so within the parameters of the Chicago Convention[160] and customary international law rather than through an invocation of the Montreal Convention. For example, in presentations to the ICAO Assembly regarding Israel's downing of a Libyan airliner on 21 February 1973 over occupied Egyptian territory, states invoked the Chicago Convention to condemn Israel's use of force, but not the Montreal Convention (to which Israel was a party).[161] Similarly, the ICAO resolution adopted in response to the USSR's downing of Korean Airlines flight 007 ('KAL 007') on 1 September 1983 characterized the military action as incompatible with the Chicago Convention, but not the Montreal Convention

---

[160] Convention on International Civil Aviation, 7 December 1944, ICAO Doc. 7300/9 [hereinafter 'Chicago Convention']. For further discussion of the Chicago Convention, see Section 5.2.3.

[161] See ICAO Assembly, 19th Session Extraordinary, Resolutions and Minutes, 2 March 1973, ICAO Doc. 9061 (1973), 11–64 (in particular, the statement by Lebanon, 35, characterizing the Israeli conduct as terrorist, but only invoking the Chicago Convention as the basis for Israeli responsibility). See also the resolution adopted by the ICAO Council on 4 June 1973, condemning the Israeli use of force as a flagrant violation of the principles and objectives of the Chicago Convention. ICAO News Release, June 1973, <http://www.icao.int/icao/en/nr/1973/pio197303_e.pdf>.

(to which the USSR was a party).[162] A proposed draft Security Council resolution condemning the Soviet downing of KAL 007 also invoked the Chicago Convention and made no mention of the Montreal Convention, but was not adopted owing to the USSR's exercise of its veto.[163] During the Security Council debate on the Soviet downing of KAL 007, many states had occasion to address the applicable law and each invoked the Chicago Convention and general international law prohibiting recourse to armed force, rather than the Montreal Convention.[164]

Similarly, in Iran's letters to the Security Council, complaining of the Iraqi air force's shooting down of an Iranian passenger plane on 20 February 1986, Iran characterized the Iraqi conduct as a 'blatant violation of the Chicago Convention regarding the guarantee for the safety of passenger airliners',[165] and as a 'gross violation of the Chicago Convention',[166] but nowhere as a violation of the Montreal Convention (to which both Iran and Iraq were parties). Libya's letter dated 17 April 1986 to the Security Council, in which it protested that the US had interfered with a Bulgarian civilian aircraft on its way from Sophia to Tripoli, invoked the Chicago Convention, but not the Hague Convention (to which the US, Libya and Bulgaria were a party).[167] Finally, in reference to the shooting down by the Cuban air force of two private US civil aircraft on 24 February 1996, both the ICAO and the Security Council 'deplored' the downing of the aircraft on the basis of general international law on the use of force and the Chicago Convention (in particular Article 3*bis* discussed below), without any reference to the ICAO TSCs.[168]

The consistent exception to this practice are expressions of condemnation by states regarding some (but not all) Israeli uses of force against civil aircraft and airports—in which cases the ICAO TSCs are sometimes invoked as a basis for characterizing Israel's conduct as terrorist. For instance, in reference to Israel's forcible diversion of a Lebanese aircraft on lease to Iraqi Airways on 10 August 1973, states invoked the Chicago Convention, Hague Convention, and Montreal Convention before the Security Council[169] and the ICAO Assembly[170] as a basis for condemning Israel's conduct. The Security Council unanimously adopted Resolution 337 (1973), which characterized Israel's conduct as a violation of the

---

[162] See ICAO Council, 24th Session Extraordinary, Resolution adopted 16 September 1983, ICAO Doc. A24-WP/49 (1983), 2.

[163] SC 2476th meeting (1983).

[164] SC 2470th meeting (1983), paras 38, 63–4 and 82; SC 2472nd meeting (1983), paras 18 and 96; SC 2473rd meeting (1983), para 139; SC 2476th meeting (1983), paras 14 and 101.

[165] Letter dated 25 February 1986 from the Permanent Representative of the Islamic Republic of Iran to the United Nations addressed to the Secretary-General, UN Doc. S/17864 (1986).

[166] Letter dated 5 March 1986 from the Chargé D'Affaires a.i. of the Permanent Mission of the Islamic Republic of Iran to the United Nations addressed to the Secretary-General, UN Doc. S/17896 (1986).

[167] See Letter dated 21 April 1986 from the Permanent Representative of the Libyan Arab Jamahiriya to the United Nations addressed to the Secretary-General, UN Doc. A/41/306 (1986).

[168] See ICAO Council, 148th Session, Resolution adopted 28 June 1996, ICAO Doc. C-DEC 148/20 (1996); UNSC Resolution 1067 (1996).

[169] SC 1737th meeting (1973), paras 46–7; SC 1738th meeting (1973), para 32.

[170] See ICAO Assembly, 20th Session Extraordinary, Resolutions and Plenary Minutes, 21 September 1973, ICAO Doc. 9087 (1973), 93, 112. Most states, however, only invoked the Chicago Convention. *Ibid*, 108–15.

1949 Armistice Agreement, the ceasefire resolutions of the Security Council of 1967, the provisions of the Charter, and 'the international conventions on civil aviation'.[171] Similarly, in presentations to the Security Council regarding Israel's forcible diversion of a Syrian aircraft on 4 February 1986, states invoked the Hague and Montreal Conventions as a basis for characterizing Israel's conduct as terrorist and condemning it.[172]

As subsequent practice in the application of a treaty is only relevant to its interpretation if it is accepted by all the state parties as reflecting their agreement,[173] the more relevant practice is the adoption of ICAO Assembly and Council Resolutions that require consensus or at least a majority of participating states to agree with the text of the resolution.[174] With one ambiguous exception, also in reference to an Israeli use of force,[175] ICAO Resolutions address military uses of force against civil aviation or airports within the parameters of the Chicago Convention and general international law.[176] Indeed, when the international community became convinced of the need to codify general international law prohibiting a state's use of military force against civilian aircraft (in response to

[171] UNSC Resolution 337 (1973), para 2. The Security Council did not expressly invoke the ICAO TSCs, but might be understood as qualifying the Israeli use of force as a breach of the Chicago Convention *and* the ICAO TSCs, given its plural reference to international conventions on civil aviation.

[172] SC 2653rd meeting (1986), 6; SC 2651st meeting (1986), 24–5; SC 2655th meeting (1986), 28, 37, in which Ghana argued that the ICAO TSCs were meant to cover acts by a state's military and to prohibit hijacking precisely because the seizure by a state's military needlessly introduces civilian aircraft into military operations. No resolution was adopted owing to a US veto. But see the ICAO Council resolution, condemning Israel's conduct only as a violation of the principles of the Chicago Convention. ICAO Council, 117th Session, Resolution adopted 28 February 1986, ICAO Doc. 9485-C/1094 (1986).

[173] Art. 31(3)(b), VCLT. See Commentary to Arts. 27 and 28, ILC Draft Articles on the Law of Treaties with Commentaries, [1966] Yearbook of the International Law Commission, Vol. II, 187, 222.

[174] Arts. 46(c) and 52, Chicago Convention.

[175] ICAO Council, 165th Session, Resolution adopted 13 March 2002, ICAO Doc. C-DEC 165/10 (2002), in its preamble, noted that Israel's destruction of Gaza International Airport facilities in December 2001 and January 2002 was 'contrary to the principles of the [Montreal Convention] and the [1988 Protocol to the Montreal Convention], which consider that unlawful acts of violence jeopardizing the safety of airports disturb the safe and orderly conduct of civil aviation for all states'. The resolution did not condemn the Israeli military operation as a violation *per se* of the Montreal Convention and 1988 Protocol to the Montreal Convention, invoking only their underlying principles. Furthermore, the operative paragraphs of the Resolution urged Israel to comply with the aims and objectives of the Chicago Convention (para 4), making no mention of the Montreal Convention or its 1988 Protocol.

[176] See e.g. ICAO Council, 24th Session Extraordinary, Resolution adopted 16 September 1983, ICAO Doc. A24-WP/49 (1983), 2; ICAO Council, 148th Session, Resolution adopted 28 June 1996, ICAO Doc. C-DEC 148/20 (1996); ICAO Council, 117th Session, Resolution adopted 28 February 1986, ICAO Doc. 9485-C/1094 (1986). Even in reference to Israel's forcible diversion of a Lebanese aircraft on lease to Iraqi Airways on 10 August 1973, in regard to which Member states made representations to the ICAO Assembly characterizing the conduct as terrorist and invoking the Hague and Montreal Conventions (*supra* note 170), Resolution A20–1 adopted following the debate only condemned Israel for violating the Chicago Convention and made no mention of the Montreal or Hague Conventions. ICAO Assembly, 20th Session Extraordinary, Resolutions and Plenary Minutes, 21 September 1973, ICAO Doc. 9087 (1973).

the USSR's downing of KAL 007 on 16 September 1983), the amendment was to the Chicago Convention,[177] not the Montreal Convention.[178]

Disputes before the International Court of Justice

Despite the reasonably consistent state practice discussed above, which addresses military activities against civil aviation in the context of general international law, the ICAO TSCs have been the jurisdictional hook on which states have attempted to hang their litigation hats when challenging such military activities before the ICJ. States have tried to rely on the more tenuously connected ICAO TSCs in cases of state military action against civil aircraft, rather than the directly relevant Article 3*bis* of the Protocol to the Chicago Convention, because Article 3*bis* only came into force on 1 October 1998. As there are a number of relevant states that are not yet party to the Protocol, including the US and the DRC (both of which appeared before the ICJ in relation to the military downing of civilian aircraft, as discussed below), the Chicago Convention has not been, to date, an available source of the ICJ's jurisdiction. In any event, the ICJ's jurisdiction under the Chicago Convention is appellate only, for the purposes of reviewing a prior decision by the ICAO Council on a 'disagreement between two or more contracting States relating to the interpretation or application of [the Chicago] Convention'.[179] As such, any invocation of the Chicago Convention as a basis for the ICJ's jurisdiction should fail unless the ICAO Council had first been seized of the dispute, under the very particular procedure provided for in Article 84 of the Chicago Convention, and rendered a decision in relation thereto.[180]

The question of the Montreal Convention's applicability to military force against civil aircraft was put directly to the ICJ in Iran's suit against the US, filed in 1989. On 3 July 1988, civilian flight IR 655 was destroyed by surface-to-air missiles launched from the 'USS Vincennes', stationed in the Persian Gulf, killing all 290 passengers and crew aboard. Iran, in its suit against the US for the downing of flight IR 655, invoked the Montreal Convention, the Chicago Convention[181] and

---

[177] Art. 3*bis*, Protocol Relating to an Amendment to the Convention on International Civil Aviation, 10 May 1984, ICAO Doc. 9436, reads as follows: 'The contracting states recognize that every state must refrain from resorting to the use of weapons against civil aircraft in flight and that, in case of interception, the lives of persons on board and the safety of aircraft must not be endangered. This provision shall not be interpreted as modifying in any way the rights and obligations of states set out in the Charter of the United Nations'.

[178] A 1973 proposal to amend the Montreal Convention, adding an obligation 'not to interfere by force or threat of force with an aircraft of another state' was defeated (ICAO Assembly, 20th Session Extraordinary, Resolutions and Plenary Minutes, 21 September 1973, ICAO Doc. 9087 (1973), 120), and was not raised again during the negotiation of Article 3*bis* of the Chicago Convention. See ICAO Assembly, 24th Session, Executive Committee Report and Minutes, 20 September – 7 October 1983, ICAO Doc. 9409 (1983), 10–15; ICAO Council, 24th Session Extraordinary, Resolution adopted 16 September 1983, ICAO Doc. A24-WP/49 (1983); ICAO Assembly, 24th Session, Plenary Meeting, 20 September – 7 October 1983, ICAO Doc. 9415 (1983); ICAO Assembly, 25th Session Extraordinary, Executive Committee, Reports and Minutes, 24 April – 10 May 1984, ICAO Doc. 9438 (1984), 3.

[179] Art. 84, Chicago Convention.

[180] See *Aerial Incident of 3 July 1998 (Iran v. US)*, Observations of the International Civil Aviation Organization, 619.

[181] The ICAO, in its submission to the ICJ, made it clear that Iran had not submitted its dispute with the US to the ICAO Council pursuant to Article 84 of the Chicago Convention. *Aerial Incident of*

its Treaty of Amity with the US as a basis for the ICJ's jurisdiction.[182] The US fiercely disputed that the Montreal Convention applied to military uses of force against civil aircraft.[183] To make military activities fit within the definition of offences set out in the Montreal Convention,[184] the Iranians were forced to concede that a military operation in self-defence targeting a civilian aircraft would not amount to a breach of the Montreal Convention.[185] On Iran's reading of the Montreal Convention, the *jus ad bellum* would need to be incorporated by reference into the Convention to determine whether the state's armed forces acted unlawfully. This might seem like an implausible extension of the scope of the Montreal Convention but for the ICJ's willingness to analyse uses of force (and their permissibility under general international law) within the four corners of treaty provisions that make no express mention of the *jus ad bellum*.[186] As the case was settled by negotiation,[187] it remains uncertain whether the ICJ would be willing to interpret treaty provisions as impliedly incorporating the *jus ad bellum* outside the context of a Treaty of Amity that bears more evidently on friendly relations between states.

The DRC equally invoked the Montreal Convention (alongside the Chicago Convention) in its suits against Uganda, Rwanda and Burundi before the ICJ as they related to the downing of a Congolese Airlines aircraft at Kindu Airport on 10 October 1998. As regards the Chicago Convention, even though Article 3*bis* was in force at the time of the DRC's Applications, the DRC was not a state party to the relevant Protocol.[188] In any case, no decision on the DRC's dispute with Uganda, Rwanda and Burundi had been rendered by the ICAO Council under Article 84 of the Chicago Convention on the basis of which the ICJ might have had appellate jurisdiction. As to the Montreal Convention violation, it was unclear whether the

---

3 July 1998 (Iran v. US), Observations of the International Civil Aviation Organization, 618. Pursuant to the terms of Article 84, the ICJ would therefore not have jurisdiction with respect to the Chicago Convention.

[182] In *Aerial Incident of 3 July 1998 (Iran v. US)*, Application, 10, Iran contended that the US conduct violated certain provisions of the Montreal Convention (in particular Articles 1, 3 and 10(1)). It should be noted that in its letter to the Security Council regarding the incident, Iran only invoked the Chicago Convention as a basis for US responsibility, and did not claim that the downing of the aircraft was in violation of US obligations under the Montreal Convention. See Letter dated 3 July 1988 from the Acting Permanent Representative of the Islamic Republic of Iran to the United Nations addressed to the Secretary-General, UN Doc. S/19979 (1988).

[183] The US argued more specifically that the Montreal Convention only addressed criminal acts by individuals against the safety of civil aircraft, and was not intended to address the responsibility of states for their own actions against civil aircraft or actions taken by their armed forces engaged in hostilities. The US argued that the American downing of IR 655 was governed by the laws of armed conflict. See *Aerial Incident of 3 July 1988 (Iran v. US)*, Preliminary Objections of the US, 149.

[184] Article 1 of the Montreal Convention defines the offence as the *unlawful* and intentional performance of an act which endangers the safety of a civil aircraft in flight.

[185] See *Aerial Incident of 3 July 1988 (Iran v. US)*, Memorial of Iran, para 4.58ff.

[186] See brief discussion of the ICJ's interpretation of the US/Iran Treaty of Amity in *Oil Platforms (Iran v. US)*, Judgment, *supra* note 59.

[187] See *Aerial Incident of 3 July 1988 (Iran v. US)*, Removal from List, Order.

[188] See <http://www.icao.int/icao/en/leb/3bis.pdf>. In its complaint to the Security Council, the DRC urged the Council to condemn the act of aggression, and only highlighted the Chicago Convention as the source of the prohibition of illicit acts of intervention against civil aircraft. See UN Doc. S/1998/945, 3.

DRC was claiming that each respondent state had itself (through its armed forces) shot the aircraft down,[189] or whether the violation of the Montreal Convention resulted from the respondents' alleged support for Congolese rebels[190] who might have downed the aircraft.[191] To the extent that the obligation to prevent in the TSCs is interpreted consistently with the ICJ's decision in the *Bosnia Genocide Case*,[192] state support for rebels would likely amount to a breach of the implied prohibition of state terrorism under the provision providing for accomplice liability.[193] Whether the DRC was alleging that the respondent states were directly responsible (through the mechanism of attribution) or indirectly responsible (through accomplice liability), the issue was never settled by the ICJ because the DRC's suits were either discontinued,[194] the Montreal Convention was not pleaded on the merits,[195] or the ICJ determined that it did not have jurisdiction based on the DRC's failure to meet the procedural requirements of Article 14(1) of the Montreal Convention.[196]

The ICAO's Position

In 2007, the ICAO Legal Committee, in the context of a working paper regarding the effectiveness of the existing ICAO TSCs (in particular the Hague and Montreal Conventions), claimed that '[i]n [the] ICAO, it has been widely understood that the aviation security instruments which criminalize certain acts [against civil aircraft] are not applicable to [. . .] military activities'.[197] To reflect this under-

---

[189] See *Armed Activities on the Territory of the Congo (DRC v. Rwanda)*, Application (1999), 19; *Armed Activities on the Territory of the Congo (DRC v. Burundi)*, Application, 19; *Armed Activities on the Territory of the Congo (DRC v. Uganda)*, Application, 19. See also *Armed Activities on the Territory of the Congo (DRC v. Rwanda)*, Requête (2002), 32.

[190] The US Congressional Research Service, in a report to Congress on 'Protecting Airliners from Terrorist Missiles', noted that Tutsi rebels had admitted to the shooting, claiming that they believed the airplane to be carrying military supplies. See Congressional Research Service, Report for Congress, 'Homeland Security: Protecting Airliners from Terrorist Missiles', November 2003, <http://fpc.state.gov/documents/organization/26580.pdf>, 9.

[191] See *Armed Activities on the Territory of the Congo (DRC v. Rwanda)*, Application (1999), 19; *Armed Activities on the Territory of the Congo (DRC v. Burundi)*, Application, 17; *Armed Activities on the Territory of the Congo (DRC v. Uganda)*, Application, 17. The DRC's new Application against Rwanda does not reiterate the facts on which the Montreal and Hague Convention claims are made, but Rwanda, in its counter-memorial, assumes that the claim is still based on its alleged support for rebels who shot down the aircraft (rather than its direct military intervention). See *Armed Activities on the Territory of the Congo (DRC v. Rwanda)* (New Application: 2002), Contre-Mémoire, para 3.59.

[192] See Section 4.2.1.

[193] *Supra* note 68 and accompanying text.

[194] See *Armed Activities on the Territory of the Congo (DRC v. Burundi)*, Removal from List, Order.

[195] See *Armed Activities on the Territory of the Congo (DRC v. Uganda)*, Judgment. Given that Article 36(2) of the ICJ Statute formed the basis of jurisdiction in the DRC's suit against Uganda, and the resulting ability to rely on customary international law and the UN Charter as a basis for Ugandan responsibility, the DRC did not need to stretch the scope of the Montreal Convention in order to found the ICJ's jurisdiction.

[196] See *Armed Activities on the Territory of the Congo (DRC v. Rwanda)* (New Application: 2002), Jurisdiction and Admissibility, para 118. See further Section 4.4.

[197] ICAO Assembly 36th Session, Legal Committee, Acts or Offences of Concern to the International Aviation Community and not Covered by Existing Air Law Instruments, ICAO Doc. A36-WP/12, LE/4 (2007), para 2.1.3.2. The exclusion being referred to here by the ICAO Legal Committee is different from that set out in Article 3(2) of the Hague Convention and Article 4(1) of the Montreal

standing and to 'achieve uniformity and clarity and to prevent any interpretative confusion', the Legal Committee recommended that a clause of military exclusion be included in any instrument amending the ICAO TSCs,[198] but noted that the ICAO would consider a military exclusion clause as declaratory in nature.[199]

A Special Sub-Committee of the ICAO Legal Committee, established to prepare draft instruments addressing new and emerging threats to civil aviation, proposed an amendment to the Montreal and Hague Conventions that incorporates the military exclusion clause of the Terrorist Bombing Convention and the Nuclear Terrorism Convention.[200] At the September 2010 International Conference on Air Law held in Beijing, ICAO Member states adopted the 2010 Protocol to the Hague Convention and the Beijing Convention (which consolidates and amends the Montreal Convention and the 1988 Protocol to the Montreal Convention). Both contain military exclusion clauses identical to that contained in the Nuclear Terrorism Convention.[201] As regards the Hague Convention, the military exclusion clause seems unnecessary given that it is highly unlikely that state military conduct could meet the elements of the Hague Convention offences. The Hague Convention defines the relevant offences as acts committed *inside* the aircraft,[202] but military uses of force against an aircraft, in the form of forcibly diverting civil aircraft with fighter planes, will always take place from *outside* the aircraft, and therefore do not meet the elements of the defined offences. That said, states do not always rely on legally relevant treaties in condemning state action and the Hague Convention has been invoked in condemnation of the forcible diversions of civilian aircraft by the Israeli military.[203] The military exclusion clause may therefore help clarify the inapplicability of the Hague Convention to military diversions. As regards the Montreal Convention, the state practice before the ICAO and Security Council is for the most part consistent with the principles of regime interaction (as discussed above) suggested by a military exclusion clause. But state practice in invoking the Montreal Convention before the ICJ is at odds with the diplomatic practice and the issue of applicability to military conduct will therefore benefit from such clarification.

Convention, both of which expressly exclude aircraft used in military, customs or police services from the scope of the ICAO TSCs. Articles 3(2) and 4(1) make it clear that the Hague and Montreal Conventions only require states to criminalize acts *against* the safety of civil aircraft (not *against* military or police aircraft), but say nothing about whether the Convention requires the criminalisation of acts against civil aircraft *by* military or police aircraft. It is this latter exclusion that the quote above addresses.

[198] ICAO Assembly 36th Session, Legal Committee, Acts or Offences of Concern to the International Aviation Community and Not Covered by Existing Air Law Instruments, ICAO Doc. A36-WP/12, LE/4 (2007), para 2.1.3.2.

[199] *Ibid.*

[200] See ICAO Legal Committee, 34th Session, Draft Report, ICAO Doc. LC/34-WP/5-3 (2009), Attachments D and E, Art. 4*bis*.

[201] See Art. 4(2), Nuclear Terrorism Convention; Art VI, 2010 Protocol to the Hague Convention; Art. 6(3) Beijing Convention.

[202] Article 1 of the Hague Convention defines the unlawful seizure of an aircraft as a crime committed by 'any person who *on board an aircraft in flight* [. . .]'. Emphasis added.

[203] *Supra* notes 169–72 and accompanying text.

The 2010 Protocol to the Hague Convention and the Beijing Convention, adopted in September 2010, each require twenty-two ratifications before entering into force. Once in force, as between state parties, these issues of 'military force as state terrorism' in the civil aviation context will become moot. Until then, based on the state practice reviewed above, and the ICAO Legal Committee's pronouncements on the matter, a state should have difficulties in successfully invoking the ICAO TSCs as the basis of another state's responsibility for the conduct of its armed forces, even where such conduct meets the elements of the offences defined therein. That said, in the absence of an express military exclusion clause, the ICJ would have to 'interpret' a military exclusion into the ICAO TSCs—which would limit both its jurisdiction and undermine the substantive basis of the claim. The Court's approach to treaty interpretation in cases where it would not otherwise have jurisdiction, however, has been expansive rather than restrictive. As such, attempts to establish a state's responsibility for the conduct of its armed forces meeting the elements of at least the Montreal Convention (as the Court should decide that state military diversions simply do not meet the elements of the offences defined in the Hague Convention) may well be successful, until the Beijing Convention is in force between relevant states, at which point the express military exclusion clause will apply. In reference to uses of force against civil aviation by non-military state officials, however, there is nothing in the state practice examined above or the exclusion clauses in the 2010 protocols and amendments to the ICAO TSCs to suggest that the *Bosnia Genocide Case* analysis is inapplicable. As a result, disputes regarding direct responsibility for acts against the safety of civil aviation committed by states through secret service agents or non-state actors should be subject to the ICJ's jurisdiction on the basis of a *Bosnia Genocide Case* analysis.

(iii)   Conclusion

The regime interaction clauses in the TSCs concluded after 1997 exclude state military conduct from the scope of those TSCs to the extent that the relevant conduct is governed by IHL or international law in general. This is consistent with the diplomatic practice related to the ICAO and IMO TSCs. The TSCs related to civil aviation and maritime navigation are not generally invoked to condemn military force because there is an alternative conventional and customary international law regime which more directly addresses such uses of force. This practice is further supported by the recent IMO and ICAO amendments and protocols to existing TSCs, all of which contain exclusion clauses like that in the Nuclear Terrorism Convention.

The TSCs with express military exclusion clauses very clearly do not apply to military operations—even when those operations meet the material elements of the terrorist offences defined therein. And there are compelling arguments, as set out above, in support of the conclusion that the TSCs without express exclusion clauses (or those for which express exclusion clauses are not yet in force) should not be read to apply to military operations when other conventional regimes apply. The question to ask, then, is precisely what type of 'state terrorism' might the TSCs impliedly prohibit pursuant to a *Bosnia Genocide Case* analysis? What is left are the different levels of involvement a state can have in terrorist acts carried out by non-military organs and *de facto* agents, as contemplated in the UN Declaration on Friendly Relations and the UN Definition of Aggression. As states are much more likely to engage in acts of terrorism through secret service agents and non-state actors,[204] the potential scope of application of the *Bosnia Genocide Case* analysis to the TSCs remains (despite the exclusion clauses) very broad indeed.

4.3 The existence of a dispute as to the interpretation or application of a TSC

The TSCs have yet to be successfully invoked as the basis of state responsibility for a failure to prevent, extradite or submit for prosecution before the ICJ. The only case before the ICJ in which the obligation of prevention under a TSC was invoked as a basis of state responsibility was the *Tehran Hostages* case.[205] Given the other bases of the Court's jurisdiction (and Iranian responsibility), in particular the Vienna Conventions on Diplomatic and Consular Relations, the ICJ did not 'find it necessary [. . .] to enter into the question whether, in the particular circumstances of the case, Article 13 of the [Internationally Protected Persons] Convention provides a basis for the exercise of the ICJ's jurisdiction with respect to those claims'.[206]

For cases in which a TSC is the only basis of the ICJ's jurisdiction, however, the Court will need to determine whether the dispute is one bearing on the interpretation or application of the relevant TSC. And there are two possible challenges to any such determination: (i) that a TSC does not apply to cases of state terrorism (as argued in the *Lockerbie Case*—which would require distinguishing the TSCs from the Genocide Convention and the Court's decision in the *Bosnia Genocide Case*) or that if it does, the relevant act falls outside the scope of the TSC on the basis of its exclusion clause; or (ii) that a TSC does not apply to the act in question because it was committed in furtherance of a struggle for self-determination on the basis either of an exclusion clause or a reservation to the TSC.[207] But based on its judgment in the *Lockerbie Case*, discussed below, the ICJ would almost certainly decide that a dispute as to the applicability of the relevant TSC is a dispute as to the application of that TSC, over which the Court has jurisdiction pursuant to the Convention's compromissory clause.

The facts of the *Lockerbie Case* are well known. On 21 December 1988, Pan Am flight 103 (en route from Heathrow International Airport to John F. Kennedy Airport in New York City) exploded over Lockerbie, Scotland. All 259 passengers and flight crew on board died immediately, and eleven people in the town of

---

[204] See Section 2.2.
[205] See *Tehran Hostages (US v. Iran)*, Application, 6; *Tehran Hostages (US v. Iran)*, Memorial of the US, 176–8.
[206] *Tehran Hostages (US v. Iran)*, Judgment, para 55. All other invocations of the TSCs as a basis of state responsibility before the ICJ have applied the Conventions to a state's military conduct, rather than a state's failure to prevent terrorist conduct which was not attributable to it. See Section 4.2.2.
[207] See Section 3.3.

Lockerbie were killed by falling debris from the aircraft.[208] Forensic investigations indicated a Libyan connection, and in November 1991, the Lord Advocate of Scotland issued arrest warrants for two Libyan secret service agents in connection with the bombing.[209] On the basis of the arrest warrants, the US and UK demanded that Libya 'surrender for trial all those charged with the crime, that it accept responsibility for the actions of its officials, and that it pay appropriate compensation'.[210] When Libya did not accommodate the request for surrender, the Security Council adopted resolutions first urging Libya to do so,[211] and then requiring Libya to do so under Chapter VII, in addition to imposing sanctions.[212] Libya filed an application before the ICJ against the US and UK after the Security Council had urged it to comply with the requests for surrender, but before the Security Council had compelled Libya to do so under Chapter VII.[213] Libya invoked the Montreal Convention as the basis for the Court's jurisdiction, and claimed that under the Convention it had a right to exercise jurisdiction over its two nationals accused of blowing up Pan Am 103. Libya further argued that in threatening sanctions (and perhaps a use of force)[214] and initiating Security Council action aimed at compelling Libya to surrender the suspects for trial, the US and UK were violating Libya's rights under the Montreal Convention and were seeking to prevent it from meeting its obligations under the Convention.

The US and the UK both argued that the Montreal Convention did not apply to the dispute—which they characterized as one bearing on an act of state terrorism, constituting a threat to international peace and security and therefore a matter for the Security Council.[215] As such, both the *ratione materiae* scope of the Montreal

---

[208] Keesing's, Vol. 35, January 1989, 36409.

[209] Foreign and Commonwealth Office, *Country Profiles; Middle East and Northern Africa; Libya*, <http://www.fco.gov.uk/en/about-the-fco/country-profiles/middle-east-north-africa/libya?profile=intRelations&pg=4>.

[210] See e.g. Letter dated 20 December 1991 from the Permanent Representative of the United States of America to the United Nations addressed to the Secretary-General, UN Doc. A/46/827 (1991).

[211] UNSC Resolution 731 (1992), para 3.

[212] UNSC Resolution 748 (1992). All of the measures against Libya were suspended when Libya delivered the two suspects to a Scottish Court sitting in the Netherlands. See Statement made on behalf of the Security Council, 9 July 1999, UN Doc. S/PRST/1999/22.

[213] Libya also filed a request for the indication of provisional measures with the ICJ, requesting an order enjoining the US and UK from 'taking any action against Libya calculated to coerce or compel Libya to surrender the accused individuals to any jurisdiction outside of Libya', before the Security Council adopted Resolution 748 (1992). On the basis of the intervening Chapter VII Security Council resolution, the Court decided that 'the rights claimed by Libya under the Montreal Convention cannot now be regarded as appropriate for protection by the indication of provisional measures'. *Lockerbie Case (Libya v. UK)*, Provisional Measures, paras 11 and 40.

[214] The UK strongly objected to Libya's persistent characterization of its conduct as amounting to a threat of a use of force. In its pleadings, the UK argued that for Libya 'to maintain the accusation without the slightest shred of proof or even probability is nothing less than shameful' and called on Libya, in all conscience, to withdraw the accusation before the Court. *Lockerbie Case (Libya v. UK)*, Preliminary Objections, Oral Proceedings, CR 1997/16, para 1.15.

[215] *Lockerbie Case (Libya v. UK)*, Preliminary Objections, paras 24–5; *Lockerbie Case (Libya v. US)*, Preliminary Objections, paras 23–4. The applicability of the Montreal Convention to Libya's alleged sponsorship of the Lockerbie bombing is not resolved by the new Beijing Convention, as the exclusion clause of the new Convention, like those in the Terrorist Bombing and Nuclear Terrorism Conventions,

Convention and a choice between applicable legal regimes was in issue. The Court did not carefully consider these issues, holding only that a dispute as to the *applicability* of the Montreal Convention amounted to a dispute as to its interpretation and *application*, falling within the terms of the compromissory clause.[216] As such, the ICJ deferred a decision on the scope of the Montreal Convention to the merits phase of the proceedings. Under sanctions pressure, and as a result of extraordinary diplomatic efforts by the UN Secretary-General and South African President Nelson Mandela, Libya agreed to surrender its two officials for trial to a Scottish Court sitting in the Hague in April 1999.[217] As the *Lockerbie Case* was thereafter discontinued with prejudice by agreement of the parties,[218] the ICJ never rendered a decision on the scope of the Montreal Convention.

More recently, the ICJ has reaffirmed (albeit by a bare majority) that a dispute as to the applicability of a Convention is a dispute as to its 'interpretation and application' falling within the scope of that Convention's compromissory clause. In reference to Georgia's Application against Russia regarding the conflicts in Abkhazia and South Ossetia (and Russian involvement in those conflicts), the Court held that it had *prima facie* jurisdiction to issue an order for provisional measures on the basis of a dispute between Georgia and Russia as to the *applicability* of the International Convention on the Elimination of all Forms of Racial Discrimination ('CERD').[219] Like in the *Lockerbie Case*, part of the dispute between Georgia and Russia was in regard to the appropriate legal regime for addressing their differences. In particular, Russia argued that the factual situation before the Court was governed by international law on the use of force, principles of non-intervention and self-determination, and humanitarian law.[220] Russia further maintained that Georgia had not invoked the CERD in connection with the conflicts in Abkhazia and South Ossetia, either in its correspondence with Russia, before the Security Council or the Organization for Security and Co-operation in Europe, or before the Committee on the Elimination of Racial Discrimination[221]—suggesting that Georgia's invocation of the CERD before the Court was purely for jurisdictional purposes (as there was no other available basis of

---

applies only to acts committed by armed forces during an armed conflict or acts of military forces of a state. The Lockerbie bombers were secret service agents, not military agents, and the exclusion clause in the Beijing Convention (once in force) would therefore be inapplicable.

[216] *Lockerbie Case (Libya v. UK)*, Preliminary Objections, para 25; *Lockerbie Case (Libya v. US)*, Preliminary Objections, para 24. But see the Court's decision in *Oil Platforms*, in which it held that '[i]n order to answer [the question as to whether or not there is a dispute "as to the interpretation or application" of the Treaty of Amity], the Court cannot limit itself to noting that one of the Parties maintains that such a dispute exists, and the other denies it. It must ascertain whether the violations of the Treaty of 1955 pleaded by Iran do or do not fall within the provisions of the Treaty'. *Oil Platforms (Iran v. US)*, Judgment, para 16.

[217] Keesing's, Vol. 45, April 1999, 42914; the guardian, 'Lockerbie trial: what happened when', 31 January 2001, <http://www.guardian.co.uk/uk/2001/jan/31/lockerbie.derekbrown>.

[218] See e.g. *Lockerbie Case (Libya v. UK)*, Removal from List, Order (2003).

[219] See *Case Concerning Application of the International Convention on the Elimination of all Forms of Racial Discrimination (Georgia v. Russian Federation)*, Provisional Measures, para 112.

[220] *Ibid*, paras 97 and 110–11.

[221] *Ibid*, para 98.

jurisdiction, in particular Russia had not made an Article 36(2) declaration that might have applied to the disputes regarding general international law). The Court gave virtually no consideration to these arguments in its preliminary decision on jurisdiction, deciding only that the facts *could* give rise to claims of discrimination even if they might also be governed by humanitarian law, and that a dispute as to applicability was indeed a dispute as to the 'interpretation and application' of CERD on the basis of which it had *prima facie* jurisdiction to issue an order for provisional measures. While the decision is a victory for the human rights community, confirming the Court's position that humanitarian law does not displace human rights law,[222] the Court's order was subject to a strong dissent by seven judges—arguing that the facts in question raised humanitarian law issues but were not matters of racial discrimination capable of falling with the scope of the CERD.[223]

Based on the *Lockerbie Case* precedent, confirmed (albeit weakly) by the Court's decision in *Georgia v. Russia*, a respondent state wishing to argue that a particular TSC does not apply to acts of state terrorism or to acts committed in furtherance of a people's struggle for self-determination could expect to have a decision on the applicability of the relevant TSC deferred to the merits phase of the proceedings. Deferring such questions to the merits phase of the proceedings has the advantage of enabling the creation of a historical record of the events in question (from the perspectives of both the applicant and respondent states) through the written and oral pleadings before the International Court of Justice.

4.4 TSC compromissory clauses: conditions of seisin and reservations

In order that the ICJ have jurisdiction under the TSCs, the applicant state must meet the conditions for the ICJ's seisin set out in the compromissory clauses. The TSC compromissory clauses all read identically as follows:

Any dispute between two or more State Parties concerning the interpretation or application of this Convention which cannot be settled by negotiation shall, at the request of one of them, be submitted to arbitration. If, within six months from the date of the request for arbitration, the parties are unable to agree on the organization of the arbitration, any one of those [P]arties may refer the dispute to the International Court of Justice, by application, in conformity with the Statute of the ICJ.[224]

---

[222] See *Palestinian Wall Advisory Opinion*, para 106.
[223] See *Case Concerning Application of the International Convention on the Elimination of all Forms of Racial Discrimination (Georgia v. Russian Federation)*, Provisional Measures, Joint Dissenting Opinion of Vice-President Al-Khasawneh and Judges Ranjeva, Shi, Koroma, Tomka, Bennouna and Skotnikov, paras 9–10.
[224] Art. 12(1), Hague Convention; Art. 14(1), Montreal Convention; Art. 13(1), Internationally Protected Persons Convention; Art. 16(1), Hostages Convention; Art. 16(1), SUA Convention; Art. 20(1), Terrorist Bombing Convention; Art. 24(1), Terrorism Financing Convention; Art. 23(1), Nuclear Terrorism Convention; Art. 20, Beijing Convention.

Based on the ICJ's jurisprudence, applicant states would do well to invoke the relevant TSC in their diplomatic discourse (although not necessarily the precise provisions in dispute), and to offer to arbitrate before seeking redress before the ICJ.[225]

A further factor in determining the likelihood that a claim of state terrorism or failures to prevent or punish acts of terrorism will fall within the ICJ's jurisdiction relates to a state's capacity to make a reservation against the TSC compromissory clauses. On average, almost 85 per cent of state parties to the TSCs have not made such a reservation (and have thus accepted the Court's jurisdiction),[226] in comparison to the much smaller proportion (approximately one-third) of states which have made optional clause declarations under Article 36(2) of the ICJ's Statute.[227] Given that each of the TSCs in force has at least 150 state parties, a significantly larger number of states have accepted the ICJ's jurisdiction over disputes relating to the TSCs than under Article 36(2) of the ICJ Statute.[228] That said, states that have been identified as state sponsors of terrorism, or from whose territory terrorists are known to operate, are among the states that have made reservations to the TSC compromissory clauses. For instance, Cuba, Syria and Algeria have made reservations against the compromissory clauses of the TSCs to which they are state

---

[225] See *Nicaragua (Nicaragua v. US)*, Jurisdiction and Admissibility, 426–7; *Nicaragua (Nicaragua v. US)*, Merits, para 274; *Tehran Hostages (US v. Iran)*, Judgment, 26–8; *Lockerbie Case (Libya v. US)*, Preliminary Objections, para 20; *Armed Activities on the Territory of the Congo (DRC v. Rwanda)* (New Application: 2002), Jurisdiction and Admissibility, paras 92 and 118; *Questions relating to the Obligation to Prosecute or Extradite (Belgium v. Senegal)*, Provisional Measures, para 52. See also Scheffer (1990). But see *Case Concerning Application of the International Convention on the Elimination of all Forms of Racial Discrimination (Georgia v. Russian Federation)*, Provisional Measures, para 115, in which the Court held that 'the fact that CERD has not been specifically mentioned in a bilateral or multilateral context is not an obstacle to the seisin of the Court on the basis' of the CERD's compromissory clause. This particular aspect of the Order was the subject of a very strong dissent by seven judges (*ibid*, Joint Dissenting Opinion of Vice-President Al-Khasawneh and Judges Ranjeva, Shi, Koroma, Tomka, Bennouna and Skotnikov, paras 12–16), who relied on some of the jurisprudence cited in this footnote to argue that the Court has always required that contact between the parties at least reference the particular convention being invoked before the Court will exercise its jurisdiction pursuant to that convention's compromissory clause. The Court, however, distinguished the CERD's compromissory clause from those which were the subject of its prior decisions on the basis that the CERD clause did not require 'that a period of time should have elapsed or that arbitration should have been attempted before initiation of any proceedings before the Court' (*ibid*, para 114). While this distinction was rejected by the dissenting judges as a relevant difference (*ibid*, Joint Dissenting Opinion of Vice-President Al-Khasawneh and Judges Ranjeva, Shi, Koroma, Tomka, Bennouna and Skotnikov, para 15), it does at least suggest that the Court will not depart from the requirement that the relevant convention be invoked in diplomatic correspondence before the Court can be seised of a dispute in reference to treaties which do require 'that a period of time should have elapsed or that arbitration should have been attempted before initiation of any proceedings before the Court', as do the TSCs.

[226] At the time of writing, reservations have been made by 25/185 states parties to the Hague Convention, and 27/188 state parties to the Montreal Convention, <http://www.icao.int/eSHOP/conventions_list.htm>; 38/173 state parties to the Internationally Protected Persons Convention, 25/168 state parties of the Hostages Convention, 27/164 state parties to the Terrorist Bombing Convention, 37/173 state parties to the Terrorism Financing Convention, <http://treaties.un.org/pages/Treaties.aspx?id=18&subid=A&lang=en>; and 20/150 state parties to the SUA Convention (status of SUA Convention on file with the author).

[227] *Supra* note 13.

[228] *Supra* notes 13–19 and accompanying text.

parties.[229] Iran has only recognized the Court's jurisdiction in reference to disputes under the Hague and Montreal Conventions and the Internationally Protected Persons Convention. It has reserved against the Court's jurisdiction for disputes relating to the Hostages Convention and is not a state party to any of the other TSCs. Other states that have been identified as having some involvement in terrorism[230] have accepted the Court's jurisdiction over disputes under some of the TSCs, while reserving against the Court's jurisdiction for others.[231] Even so, given the high number of ratifications and the number (and identity) of states that have accepted the Court's jurisdiction over the TSCs, a dispute that amounts to the 'application or interpretation' of a Terrorism Suppression Convention is significantly more likely to fall within the ICJ's jurisdiction than a dispute under general international law pursuant to an optional clause declaration.

4.5 Security Council enforcement of ICJ decisions

Under Article 94(2) of the UN Charter, 'if any party to a case fails to perform the obligations incumbent upon it under a judgment rendered by the Court, the other party may have recourse to the Security Council, which may, if it deems necessary, make recommendations or decide upon measures to be taken to give effect to the judgment'. This provision of the UN Charter has rarely been invoked in practice,[232] and the Security Council has never adopted enforcement measures against a

---

[229] Cuba and Algeria are a state party to all the TSCs and have made a reservation against each of their compromissory clauses; Syria is state party to all but the Terrorist Bombing Convention, and has made a reservation against the compromissory clauses of those other TSCs (except for the SUA Convention, over which it recognizes the Court's jurisdiction).

[230] *Supra* notes 14–19.

[231] The Sudan has made a reservation against the Terrorist Bombing Convention's compromissory clause, but otherwise accepts the Court's jurisdiction over disputes relating to the TSCs (and is a state party to all of them). North Korea has accepted the Court's jurisdiction over disputes relating to the Hague and Montreal Conventions, but has made a reservation to the Court's jurisdiction over disputes under the Internationally Protected Persons Convention, Hostages Convention and Terrorism Financing Convention, and is not a state Party to the Terrorist Bombing or SUA Conventions. Yemen has made reservations against the Court's jurisdiction under the Internationally Protected Persons and Terrorism Financing Conventions, but is otherwise a state party to the TSCs without reservation. Lebanon has accepted the Court's jurisdiction for all TSCs to which it is a state party (and is only a non-state party to the Terrorism Financing Convention). Afghanistan has accepted the Court's jurisdiction in relation to disputes under all the TSCs with the exception of the Montreal Convention. Pakistan has made reservations against the Court's having jurisdiction under the Internationally Protected Persons Convention and the Terrorism Financing Convention, but has otherwise accepted the Court's jurisdiction as a state party to the other TSCs. Somalia is not a party to any of the TSCs, although has signed the Terrorism Financing Convention. Colombia accepted the Court's jurisdiction over disputes under the Hague and Montreal Conventions, and the Internationally Protected Persons Convention, but has reserved against the Court's jurisdiction in reference to the Hostages Convention, Terrorist Bombing and Terrorism Financing Conventions and is not a state party to the SUA Convention. Finally, the Philippines accepts the Court's jurisdiction over disputes under the TSCs—to all of which it is a state party.

[232] Part of the reason for the dearth of practice may well be the reasonably high compliance rate with ICJ judgments. See Schachter (1960), 1; Schulte (2004), 403; Llamzon (2008). Article 94(2) has only been invoked expressly twice in the last thirty years: by Bosnia, *infra* note 233; and by Libya,

state in particular response to that state's failure to perform its obligations under a judgment rendered by the Court.[233] Given the dearth of practice, there are some unresolved questions regarding the nature of the Security Council's power under Article 94(2), including whether the recommendations it makes, or measures it decides upon, fall within the scope of Chapter VI or Chapter VII[234] of the UN Charter, or indeed whether Article 94(2) is an independent basis of Security Council enforcement power.[235] The distinction (if any) between powers under Article 94(2) and Chapter VII of the UN Charter is irrelevant to the extent that the

asking the Security Council to take action to give effect to the ICJ's Judgment on Preliminary Objections in the *Lockerbie Case* (see UN Doc. S/1998/192). The Security Council took no action on Libya's request, presumably having agreed with the US and UK that decisions as to jurisdiction and admissibility are not susceptible to Article 94(2) action (see SC 3864th meeting (1999); UN Doc. S/1999/239). The US requested the Council to meet in reference to Iran's failure to comply with the Court's order for provisional measures in *Tehran Hostages (US v. Iran)*, but did not expressly invoke Article 94(2). See Letter dated 22 December 1979 from the Permanent Representative of the United States of America to the United Nations addressed to the President of the Security Council, UN Doc. S/13705 (1979). The Council 'deplore[d] the continued detention of the hostages contrary to its resolution 457 (1979) and the Order of the International Court of Justice [. . .]', but did not expressly demand compliance with the Court's decision (see UNSC Resolution 461 (1979)). Nicaragua requested the Council to meet following the Court's decision in *Nicaragua (Nicaragua v. US)*. See UN Doc. S/18187 (1986); UN Doc. S/18230 (1986). Owing to a US veto, a Security Council resolution calling on the US to comply with the ICJ's judgment (as proposed by Congo, Ghana, Madagascar, Trinidad and Tobago, and United Arab Emirates, UN Doc. S/18250 (1986)) was not adopted by the Security Council. See SC 2704th meeting (1986).

[233] The closest the Security Council has come to adopting measures under Chapter VII to enforce a judgment of the Court was in reference to Bosnia's invocation of Article 94(2) of the UN Charter, in which it requested the Security Council to 'take immediate measures under Chapter VII of the Charter [. . .] to enforce the [provisional measures] order of the International Court of Justice [against Yugoslavia]'. UN Doc. S/25616 (1993). The Court had, in its provisional measures decision, required Yugoslavia to 'take all measures within its powers to prevent commission of the crime of genocide'. *Bosnia Genocide Case*, Provisional Measures, para 52A(1). The Security Council adopted Resolution 819 (UNSC Resolution 819 (1993)) under Chapter VII, taking note of the Court's provisional measures decision, and demanding, *inter alia*, that Yugoslavia cease its supply of military equipment and arms to the Bosnian Serb paramilitary forces (presumably in furtherance of the Court's order that Yugoslavia take measures within its power to prevent genocide). The Security Council's demands were otherwise directed at the Bosnian Serb paramilitary forces or all parties to the conflict. No enforcement measures were adopted in UNSC Resolution 819 (1993). In a subsequent resolution (which recalled UNSC Resolution 819 (1993)), the Security Council authorized member states to take all necessary measures to support UNPROFOR in its establishment of safe areas in Bosnia (see UNSC Resolution 836 (1993), para 10), but such measures were to enforce the Security Council's own demands (which were partially co-extensive with the Court's order for provisional measures), rather than specifically and expressly enforcing the provisional measures order of the Court in the *Bosnia Genocide Case*.

[234] Bosnia's application to the Council under Article 94(2) suggests that it considered Article 94(2) of the UN Charter to provide the basis for Chapter VII measures to be adopted in response to non-compliance with a judgment of the ICJ. See UN Doc. S/25616 (1993).

[235] Arguing that Article 94(2) is an independent basis of enforcement power, see e.g. Kelsen (1950), 541–2; Mosler and Oellers-Frahm (2002), 1177; Schulte (2004), 49; Pillepich (2005), 1996. See also Tanzi (1995), 17–20, arguing that Article 94(2) Security Council action, while independent, will generally be co-extensive with both Chapters VI and VII, depending on the circumstances (in particular whether non-compliance amounts to a threat to international peace and security). But see Kerley (1976), 277–8; Schachter (1960), 21–2, noting that the relationship between Article 94 and other provisions in the Charter had been rendered controversial by statements from the US State Department suggesting that Article 94 is limited to the powers of Chapters VI and VII, but arguing that there is good reason to consider Article 94 as an independent basis for enforcement action.

Security Council decides that non-compliance with a decision of the ICJ also amounts to a threat to the peace or breach of the peace (pursuant to Article 39 of the UN Charter). In such circumstances, the Security Council could clearly adopt enforcement measures against the non-complying state, irrespective of the interpretation of Article 94(2). Such measures would render an otherwise bilateral situation (between the injured/applicant state and the wrongdoing/respondent state)[236] *erga omnes* in that all UN member states are required to carry out the Security Council's decisions.[237] The Security Council's practice, however, has been to recall (in the preambular paragraphs) an uncomplied-with ICJ decision, but to only call upon (or demand) that a wrongdoing state undertake action in terms similar to the obligations set out in the Court's decision (rather than demanding compliance with the decision itself).[238] Even if acting under Chapter VII, the Security Council's decisions in this regard, without the adoption of enforcement measures to make its demands effective, add nothing to the binding nature of the Court's decisions. The Security Council's decisions and the Court's decisions are equally binding on relevant states under Articles 25 and 94(1) respectively of the UN Charter.

The threat posed by international terrorism has spurred the Security Council to innovate, in particular as regards its newly adopted legislative role.[239] That the Security Council has yet to adopt enforcement measures (whether in reliance on Chapter VII or directly under Article 94(2) of the UN Charter) to give effect to an ICJ determination of the secondary obligations flowing from a wrongdoing state's responsibility is not to say that it will never do so. Indeed, were the *Bosnia Genocide Case* analysis applied to the terrorism context (within the limits identified above), a determination of state responsibility for an act of international terrorism might be precisely the catalyst needed for the adoption of Security Council enforcement measures to secure compliance with a decision by the ICJ.

4.6 Conclusion

Optional clause declarations are an unlikely source of the ICJ's jurisdiction to hear disputes regarding the breach of international terrorism obligations. As a result, whether the ICJ would have jurisdiction to hear a dispute bearing on an internationally wrongful act related to terrorism depends on a number of different factors, including whether (i) both the applicant and respondent state are parties to a

---

[236] ICJ decisions are only binding *inter partes*. Art. 94(1), UN Charter.

[237] Art. 25, UN Charter.

[238] *Supra* notes 232–3, in reference to non-compliance with the Court's *Tehran Hostages (US v. Iran)* and *Bosnia Genocide Case* decisions.

[239] See e.g. UNSC Resolution 1373 (2001). The legitimacy of the Security Council's assuming the role of international legislature has been debated in the academic literature (see e.g. Szasz (2002); Happold (2003); Rosand (2005); Talmon (2005)), but in practice, states have complied with at least the reporting obligations imposed on them pursuant to relevant Security Council Chapter VII resolutions.

relevant TSC; (ii) the failure to prevent, punish or refrain from engaging in terrorism bears on conduct meeting the elements of the offences defined in the TSC; (iii) there are any reservations to the relevant TSC (and the effect of such reservations), or any reservations to the TCS's compromissory clause; and (iv) the applicant state has satisfied the conditions of seisin in the compromissory clause. These conditions are not particular to the terrorism context, and are similar to those applicable in any other dispute brought before the ICJ pursuant to a compromissory clause.

The extent of the ICJ's jurisdiction will also depend on the scope of the TSCs. While the ICJ's decision in the *Bosnia Genocide Case* is not without its logical difficulties, it has established a promising basis for the Court's jurisdiction in cases of state-sponsored or supported terrorism. As a result of the Court's expansive interpretation of the obligation to prevent, the TSCs—drafted with a view to ending impunity for international terrorism committed by natural persons— might also be the vehicle for judicial determinations of a state's responsibility for such offences. As the TSCs are very widely ratified, including by states consistently associated with sponsorship and support of international terrorism, the promise of peaceful settlement of disputes inherent in the Court's jurisdiction is more likely to be actualized under the TSCs than if the injured state were required to rely on jurisdiction pursuant to an optional clause declaration.

Unfortunately, states have not relied on the power of judicial settlement in regard to disputes regarding state responsibility for international terrorism (whether direct responsibility for acts of terrorism or indirect responsibility for a failure to prevent, extradite or submit to prosecution). The only case before the ICJ in which the obligation of prevention under a TSC was asserted as a basis of state responsibility was the *Tehran Hostages* case,[240] but the issue was not decided by the Court. Failures to prevent and punish terrorist offences have generally been treated as threats to international peace and security by the Security Council,[241] rather than being dealt with as a matter of state responsibility under the Terrorism Suppression Conventions. The *Bosnia Genocide Case* precedent, in which a criminal law enforcement treaty (the Genocide Convention) formed the basis of Serbian responsibility for failing to prevent and punish acts of genocide, may stimulate similar claims in regard to terrorism under the TSCs.

---

[240] See *Tehran Hostages (US v. Iran)*, Application, 6; *Tehran Hostages (US v. Iran)*, Memorial of the US, 176–8.
[241] See Sections 4.3 and 6.2.1 (discussing the *Lockerbie Case*); Section 6.2.5(ii) (discussing the assassination attempt on President Mubarak); and Section 6.2.5(iii) (discussing the Harriri assassination).

5

Measures adopted in response to international terrorism

There are a number of different ways in which an injured state can seek to make its invocation of a state's responsibility for internationally wrongful acts related to terrorism effective. One such option, involving pressure brought to bear in virtue of a binding ICJ determination of responsibility, or Security Council enforcement action following such a binding determination, was considered in Chapter 4 through an exploration of the bases for the ICJ's jurisdiction. Based on the *Bosnia Genocide Case* decision and its possible application to the terrorism context (with appropriate limitations based on the exclusion clauses in the TSCs), the ICJ's jurisdiction to hear a dispute regarding the breach of international terrorism obligations is broad. To date, however, the dispute settlement power inherent in the TSC compromissory clauses has not been relied on by injured states. In the absence of any such binding determination and the resulting possibility of relying on institutional remedies for breaches of international law, states must rely on other mechanisms to implement responsibility for terrorism-related wrongs. Chapter 2 examined one possible unilateral response to internationally wrongful acts related to terrorism, taken in a *jus ad bellum* context. To the extent that states cannot rely on their neighbours to prevent acts of international terrorism, injured states can legitimately respond to terrorist conduct within the framework of Articles 2(4) and 51 of the UN Charter.[1] Such a response, however, operates on the basis of a security paradigm, and does nothing to restore the primary legal relationship as between the injured and wrongdoing states. Section 5.1 of this book explores the permissibility of *non-military* responses to a breach of international terrorism obligations under general international law, in particular measures adopted with the aim of securing a wrongdoing state's compliance with its secondary obligations of cessation and reparation.

Certain sub-systems of international law articulate both primary rules and, to a greater or lesser extent, secondary rules with respect to those primary rules, which may affect the right of states to respond to internationally wrongful acts related to terrorism through the adoption of non-military measures. Section 5.2 considers three separate sub-systems of international law that regulate (in varying degrees of

---

[1] See Section 2.2.3.

self-containedness)[2] the primary rules most often implicated by such measures: obligations in the field of diplomatic relations; trade obligations; and air service arrangements. The focus of the examination is on the extent to which these sub-systems expand (or perhaps limit) the right of states to adopt non-military measures for the purposes of securing a wrongdoing state's compliance with its secondary obligations, as compared to the right of response under the general international law of state responsibility.

5.1 The adoption of measures in response to international terrorism under general international law

In the context of a decentralized international legal system, injured states occasionally have to engage in 'self-help' for the purposes of 'vindicating their rights and [...] restor[ing] the legal relationship with the responsible State which has been ruptured by the internationally wrongful act'.[3] States will, as far as possible, attempt to respond to breaches of international law without breaching their own international obligations toward the wrongdoing state. The adoption of measures that are not in breach of the measure-adopting state's international obligations, but are adopted for the purposes of securing the wrongdoing state's compliance with its secondary obligations of cessation and reparation, are referred to as retorsion and are examined in Section 5.1.1 below. It will sometimes be the case, however, that measures adopted by an injured state against a wrongdoing state are themselves in breach of the injured state's international obligations toward the wrongdoing state. International law recognizes that the commission of an internationally wrongful act by one state may excuse a responsive breach by the injured state for the limited purposes of securing the wrongdoing state's compliance with its primary and secondary obligations. Such measures are referred to as countermeasures within the framework of the ILC Articles on State Responsibility,[4] and will be examined in Section 5.1.2 below. Finally, international law recognizes that certain measures, in breach of international law, may be necessary to protect essential interests, and the wrongfulness of those measures is precluded to the extent of that necessity. Section 5.1.3 below examines necessity as a circumstance precluding wrongfulness in the terrorism context.

---

[2] Some sub-systems of international law are referred to as 'self-contained' regimes, as where the sub-system is 'intended to exclude more or less totally the application of the general legal consequences of wrongful acts, in particular the application of countermeasures normally at the disposal of an injured party'. Simma (1985), 117. See also Simma and Pulkowski (2010), 142–50. The term is not used in this book, given that the 'self-containedness' of a sub-system is a matter of degree, and will always turn on a careful analysis of the relevant treaty language. See Koskenniemi, (2006) 85, para 159. Reference will be made, however, to the degree of 'self-containedness' of a sub-system in examining the extent to which relevant sub-systems interact with general international law as regards the right of response to breaches of international terrorism obligations.
[3] Commentary to Part Three, Chapter II, ILC Articles on State Responsibility, para 1.
[4] See Art. 22, ILC Articles on State Responsibility.

5.1.1 Acts of retorsion

Retorsion is unfriendly conduct, often adopted in response to the internationally wrongful conduct of a state, which is not in breach of any primary international obligation of the retorsion-adopting state.[5] There are two ways in which responsive measures might amount to retorsion. The first is where the measures bear on a sphere of discretionary[6] or unregulated state activity.[7] Where a sphere of state activity is regulated, the second way in which responsive measures might amount to retorsion is if the relevant measure is subject to an exception within the framework of the primary rules applicable thereto. States may attempt to justify or excuse the adoption of responsive measures through the very primary rules that the measures might otherwise be in breach of. For instance, certain economic measures adopted in response to the breach of international terrorism obligations may be excused or justified within the sub-system of international law created by the Word Trade Organization Agreement, examined in Section 5.2.2 below. A significant international effort was also made within the ICAO to provide for (and justify) the breach of international air service agreements in response to a state's failure to comply with its obligations to prevent and punish terrorist offences against the safety of civil aviation. There was no final agreement on an appropriate way to respond to the breach of international terrorism obligations related to the safety of civil aviation, but the proposals were an instructive attempt to transform breaches of international air service obligations into acts of retorsion from within the framework of the primary rules applicable thereto, and are examined in Section 5.2.3.

While states adopt measures amounting to retorsion principally in response to alleged breaches of international law for the purposes of pressuring the wrongdoing state into complying with its primary and secondary obligations,[8] a state can adopt measures of retorsion in response to any situation. Retorsive measures are not limited to responses to an initial breach of international law by the target state. For instance, a state that is a victim of terrorist attacks launched by non-state actors from another state's territory might consider it necessary to respond to that other state's failure to prevent its territory from being used as a base of terrorist operations, even if the failure did not amount to an internationally wrongful act in virtue of the territorial state's exercise of due diligence.[9] Indeed, as long as the responsive measure is not itself in violation of an

---

[5] For instance, restrictions on diplomatic relations in response to internationally wrongful acts related to terrorism are acts of retorsion. The ICJ noted, in its *Tehran Hostages* Judgment, that states are under no obligation to maintain diplomatic or consular relations with other states. *Tehran Hostages (US v. Iran)*, Judgment, para 41. Similarly, restrictive economic measures, absent particular treaty obligations, are not prohibited under general international law, and therefore amount to retorsion. See *Nicaragua (Nicaragua v. US)*, Merits, para 276.

[6] See Leben (1982), 14.

[7] See Zoller (1984), 5.

[8] See Section 5.1.4 on state practice. While measures amounting to retorsion are not dealt with in the ILC Articles on State Responsibility, because they are not in need of wrongfulness-preclusion (see Commentary to Part Three, Chapter II, ILC Articles on State Responsibility, para 3), they are relevant for the purposes of this study given that they are often used in response to internationally wrongful acts related to terrorism.

[9] See Section 3.1 for a discussion of the standard of due diligence to which states are held in meeting their obligation to prevent international terrorism.

international obligation, there are no restrictions on the measures which can be adopted.[10] States do not have to be specially affected to take measures amounting to retorsion,[11] and therefore the right to respond collectively to internationally wrongful acts related to terrorism is unambiguous to the extent that the response does not itself breach the international obligations of the responding states.

5.1.2 Countermeasures

The ILC Articles on State Responsibility preclude the wrongfulness of counter-measures, otherwise in breach of international law, if those measures are (i) adopted by an injured state in response to the prior breach of an international obligation by the wrongdoing (and target) state;[12] (ii) proportionate to the injury suffered by the injured state as a result of the target state's internationally wrongful act;[13] and (iii) intended to re-establish the primary legal relationship between the injured (and measure-adopting) state and the wrongdoing (and target) state.[14] Countermeasures must therefore be terminated once the primary legal relationship has been re-established and secondary obligations have been met.[15] Finally, countermeasures:

shall not affect: (a) the obligation to refrain from the threat or use of force in international relations embodied in the UN Charter; (b) obligations for the protection of fundamental human rights; (c) obligations of a humanitarian character prohibiting reprisals; (d) other obligations under peremptory norms of general international law.[16]

---

[10] The only limits on the adoption of retorsive measures are the limits on state action under international law generally, for instance pursuant to the principle of non-intervention. This, however, is not a limit on the types of retorsive measures that can be adopted, but the very limit of retorsion itself, in that a measure that is in violation of an international obligation (like the obligation not to intervene in the domestic affairs of another state) ceases to be an act of retorsion, and becomes a countermeasure in need of wrongfulness-preclusion under the secondary rules of state responsibility. In the human rights context, the Institut de droit international has determined that the principle of non-intervention should not be considered a dividing line between acts of retorsion and countermeasures, in that the adoption of individual or collective measures (not otherwise in breach of international law) in response to violations of human rights 'cannot be considered an unlawful intervention in the internal affairs of the [human rights violating state]'. Art. 2, Institut de droit international (1990), 340. The same argument might be made in the terrorism context.

[11] See Section 5.1.2(iii) on collective responses amounting to countermeasures.

[12] Art. 49(1), ILC Articles on State Responsibility.

[13] Art. 51, ILC Articles on State Responsibility.

[14] While the ILC Articles on State Responsibility clearly consider countermeasures as strictly instrumental, in that their purpose must be to secure cessation of, and reparation for, an internationally wrongful act (Art. 49(1), ILC Articles on State Responsibility; Commentary to Part Three, Chapter II, ILC Articles on State Responsibility, para 6), the question of the purpose of countermeasures was long a matter of controversy in the literature. Some commentators considered countermeasures as purely instrumental in line with the position finally adopted by the ILC (see Zoller (1984), 46; Riphagen (1985), 11, para 1; Elagab (1988), 44–5; Arangio-Ruiz (1992), 6–7, para 3); while others considered that countermeasures could serve both a coercive and retributive function (see Bowett (1972), 3; Ago (1980), 54, para 90; Dominicé (1982), 34–5). See also Bederman (2002), 822, suggesting that the non-punitive focus of countermeasures as conceptualized in the ILC Articles on State Responsibility is not necessarily in keeping with early state practice.

[15] Art. 49, ILC Articles on State Responsibility; Commentary to Art. 49, ILC Articles on State Responsibility, para 7.

[16] Art. 50(1), ILC Articles on State Responsibility.

This Section therefore only considers peaceful countermeasures which do not affect human rights obligations or other obligations under a peremptory norm.

Countermeasures that do not meet the conditions set out in the paragraph above do not benefit from the 'shield against an otherwise well-founded claim for the breach of an international obligation'[17] provided for under Part One, Chapter V (Circumstances Precluding Wrongfulness) of the ILC Articles on State Responsibility.[18] This section considers the resulting limitations on a state's right to respond to breaches of international terrorism obligations through the adoption of countermeasures.

(i) 'At your own risk' element of countermeasures

Characterization of conduct as internationally wrongful

One of the conditions for a countermeasure to be legitimate (and its wrongfulness thereby precluded) is that it be in response to a prior breach of international law by the target state.[19] But an injured state 'which resorts to countermeasures based on its unilateral assessment of the situation does so at its own risk and may incur responsibility for an unlawful act in the event of an incorrect assessment'.[20] The 'at your own risk' element of countermeasures will be particularly evident in the terrorism context, as examined in Section 5.1.4 below, given difficulties in establishing connections between terrorist actors and state sponsors or supporters of terrorism.[21] Special Rapporteur Arangio-Ruiz, when considering the degree of certainty that a countermeasure-adopting state should have with regard to the internationally wrongful character of the target state's conduct, had this to say:

[T]his does not mean that the existence of such an act and the allegedly injured State's right to take countermeasures have to have been the subject of a prior determination by an arbitral or judicial procedure or of action by a political or fact-finding body. Nor does it mean that there has to have been prior agreement between the allegedly injured State and the alleged wrongdoing State as to the existence of an internationally wrongful act. On the other hand, it would not be sufficient for the allegedly injured State to believe in good faith that an internationally wrongful act has been committed in violation of its right.[22]

---

[17] Commentary to Part One, Chapter V, ILC Articles on State Responsibility, para 1.

[18] There was some debate in the ILC as to whether countermeasures, or indeed circumstances precluding wrongfulness, were strictly secondary rules, or whether they should be characterized as primary rules which modify the operation of other primary rules. Both circumstances precluding wrongfulness and countermeasures were included in the ILC Articles on State Responsibility, suggesting that they were (in the end) conceptualized as secondary rules, but the issue is still one addressed in the literature. See David (2010).

[19] Art. 49(1), ILC Articles on State Responsibility.

[20] Commentary to Art. 49, ILC Articles on State Responsibility, para 3. See also Crawford (1999a), 12, fn. 724.

[21] See Sections 2.2.1 and 2.2.2 for a discussion of the complicated questions of law and fact involved in attributing terrorist conduct to a state.

[22] Arangio-Ruiz (1992), 6, para 2. Arangio-Ruiz further argued, in respect of countermeasures, that 'in no other area in the "society of States" is the lack of an adequate institutional framework for present or conceivable future regulation of State conduct so keenly felt'. Arangio-Ruiz (1991), 7, para 3. But see Damrosch (1980), 795 and Dominicé (1982), 40–1, suggesting that certainty on the part of the

There is very little legal space, however, between the certainty afforded by a third party assessment of the internationally wrongful character of a state's conduct (or an admission of responsibility), and an injured state's good faith belief in the internationally wrongful character of that conduct. Either the matter has been determined in an objective manner by persons outside the structure of the injured state, or that state is left to its own (presumably good faith) assessment of the facts.[23] In the absence of compulsory dispute settlement in international law, these dangers of auto-determination can (and, as examined below, sometimes do) give rise to an escalation in tensions between the parties to a dispute—particularly in cases where the target state does not accept that its conduct is internationally wrongful.[24] In response to this concern, some commentators considered that the right to take countermeasures should be subject to the exhaustion of international procedures for the peaceful settlement of disputes. In particular, Special Rapporteur Riphagen argued that, to the extent that the target state disputes the facts or law on which the allegation of its breach is based, 'it can really not be required to do more than accept third party settlement of the claim'.[25] Special Rapporteur Arangio-Ruiz similarly argued that failing to require the initiation of peaceful settlement procedures before resorting to countermeasures amounts to a regression in the development of international law, in that it undermines the treaty regimes which contemplate a dispute settlement mechanism.[26] The Articles on State Responsibility as finally adopted by the ILC do not require a state to have prior recourse to dispute settlement before adopting countermeasures[27]—even where the wrongdoing state disputes the internationally wrongful character of the conduct in response to which countermeasures are adopted—but a state adopting countermeasures is not thereby relieved from fulfilling its obligations under any dispute settlement procedure applicable between it and the wrongdoing state.[28]

injured state as to the internationally wrongful character of an injurious act is not a prerequisite for the taking of countermeasures.

[23] See Alland (2010), 1129, stating that the adoption of countermeasures 'is not, as is often immediately said, the consequence of an internationally wrongful act committed by the [target] State, but the consequence of the belief of the reacting State that such a wrongful act has been committed'.

[24] See Provost (2002), xv, arguing that 'the right of States unilaterally to assess a breach by another State and to validate what would otherwise be an illegal act has the potential of significantly destabilising international relations'.

[25] Riphagen (1983), 19, para 103. See also Riphagen (1985), 11–12; Tomuschat (1994a), 81. But see Simma (1988), 30.

[26] Arangio-Ruiz (1994), 15, para 7. See also Arangio-Ruiz (1992), 19–20, paras 41–7; Arangio-Ruiz (1994), 7–12, paras 18–53. But see Simma (1994), 103–4.

[27] The failure to agree on prior recourse to dispute settlement as a condition for the adoption of legitimate countermeasures was largely the result of concerns regarding the undue burden such a condition would impose on the injured state. See ILC, summary record of meetings, UN Doc. A/CN.4/SR.2266 (1992), 81, para 43; UN Doc. A/CN.4/SR.2274 (1992), para 11; UN Doc. A/CN.4/SR.2277 (1992), para 9; UN Doc. A/CN.4/SR.2279 (1992), paras 4 and 21; UN Doc. A/CN.4/SR.2280 (1992), para 32; Tomuschat (1994), 77; Simma (1994), 104; Vereshchetin (1994), 58. See also Arangio-Ruiz (1994a), 28.

[28] Art. 50(2)(a), ILC Articles on State Responsibility.

The effect of ICJ and Security Council determinations of responsibility

While states do not have to submit their disputes for judicial settlement before resorting to countermeasures, they may well do so. As discussed in Section 4.5, determinations of responsibility by the International Court of Justice are binding on state parties to a dispute in virtue of the UN Charter.[29] Such a determination of responsibility would therefore eliminate completely the 'at your own risk' element of adopting countermeasures. Subject to the necessity and proportionality of adopted countermeasures (as discussed below), an injured state which relied on an ICJ determination of wrongfulness, and adopted countermeasures against the wrongdoing state in response to that state's failure to abide by its primary and secondary obligations under international law (including its obligation to comply with a decision of the ICJ), would not run the risk of being held responsible for its adoption of countermeasures.

In the absence of states making use of the dispute settlement potential of the TSCs to determine the internationally wrongful character of a state's conduct, Security Council pronouncements might also minimize the 'at your own risk' element of countermeasures, particularly when adopted within a Chapter VII resolution. The ICJ has treated Security Council pronouncements of fact as evidence of the truth of those facts,[30] suggesting that a measure-adopting state could rely on the Security Council's pronouncements regarding internationally wrongful acts related to terrorism should the legality of its countermeasures be put to the test. While the Security Council has not yet expressly attributed direct responsibility for a terrorist attack to a state[31] in the context of a Chapter VII resolution, it has done so implicitly. For instance, in the context of a resolution on the Lockerbie bombing, the Security Council decided that the 'Libyan Government must commit itself definitively to cease all forms of terrorist action and all assistance to terrorist groups and that it must promptly, by concrete actions, demonstrate its renunciation of terrorism'.[32] Similarly in the context of a Chapter VII resolution regarding the assassination attempt against President Mubarak in Ethiopia, the Security Council demanded that the Sudan (whose involvement had been suggested by both Egypt and Ethiopia):[33]

---

[29] Art. 94(1), UN Charter.

[30] See *Armed Activities on the Territory of the Congo (DRC v. Uganda)*, Judgment, paras 150–4.

[31] The Security Council, in UNSC Resolution 1267 (1999), para 1, determined that the Taliban was responsible for providing sanctuary and training for international terrorists, but did not hold the Taliban directly responsible for any terrorist attacks, and only imposed sanctions in response to the Taliban's failure to 'turn over' Usama Bin Laden to a state with jurisdiction to prosecute him for the 1998 bombings of US embassies in Africa (UNSC Resolution 1267 (1999), paras 2–3). See further UNSC Resolution 1333 (2000). While Afghanistan as a state would be responsible for the Taliban's conduct had the Taliban managed to become the government of Afghanistan (Art. 10, ILC Articles on State Responsibility), the civil war with the Taliban is ongoing, and the post-9/11 internationally supported Government of Hamid Karzai is generally recognized as the legitimate Government of Afghanistan.

[32] UNSC Resolution 748 (1992), para 2.

[33] See Section 6.2.5.

[d]esist[...] from engaging in activities of assisting, supporting and facilitating terrorist activities and from giving shelter and sanctuary to terrorist elements; and henceforth acting in its relations with its neighbours and with others in full conformity with the Charter of the United Nations and with the Charter of the OAU.[34]

The Security Council does not explicitly hold either Libya or the Sudan responsible for the relevant act of terrorism, but a determination to that effect would certainly have reduced (if not eliminated) the 'at your own risk' element of countermeasures. In the event, the injured states did not adopt countermeasures within the framework of the secondary rules on state responsibility, and instead relied on the Security Council imposed sanctions against the terrorist-supporting states to pressure them to extradite or surrender the accused for prosecution.

(ii) Necessity and proportionality

In order to benefit from the wrongfulness-preclusion of Article 22 of the ILC Articles on State Responsibility, countermeasures adopted in response to an internationally wrongful act must be both 'necessary to induce the responsible state to comply with its [primary and secondary] obligations',[35] and proportionate to the injury suffered by the measure-adopting state.[36] As long as the adoption of countermeasures is in response to an internationally wrongful act, is not a colourable attempt at punishment, and the countermeasures are not clearly disproportionate,[37] their necessity will often be presumed. The analysis of proportionality, however, is more complicated. Proportionality is not strictly a matter of balancing the relative harm suffered by the injured state as a result of the initial breach against that suffered by the wrongdoing state as a result of the countermeasure.[38] The importance of the interests being protected by the injured state in its adoption of countermeasures[39] must also be balanced against the importance of the interests affected by the countermeasures.[40]

Assessing the character and severity of an internationally wrongful act related to terrorism, for the purposes of adopting a proportionate response, may be difficult for an injured state. Absent third party dispute settlement, it is for the injured state alone to assess the breach of an international terrorism obligation, including whether the wrongdoing state is 'directly' responsible for an act of terrorism, or 'indirectly' responsible for acts of terrorism through its support for, acquiescence in,

---

[34] UNSC Resolution 1054 (1996), para 1(b).
[35] Art. 49(1), ILC Articles on State Responsibility; Commentary to Art. 49, ILC Articles on State Responsibility, para 1; Commentary to Art. 51, ILC Articles on State Responsibility, para 7.
[36] Art. 51, ILC Articles on State Responsibility.
[37] Commentary to Art. 51, ILC Articles on State Responsibility, para 7.
[38] *Air Services Arbitration (United States/France)*, para 83.
[39] *Ibid.*
[40] *Gabčíkovo–Nagymaros Project (Hungary v. Slovakia)*, Judgment, paras 85–7. See also Crawford (1994), 68, characterizing the proportionality rule as seeking to measure the *character* and *effects* of the internationally wrongful act as against the *character* and *effects* of the countermeasures taken in response thereto.

or failure to exercise the required due diligence in preventing terrorism.[41] Depending on the injured state's appreciation of the facts and law, there is a danger of over-responding with measures that are not proportionate to the actual wrong committed.[42] This is particularly the case given the difficult application of the rules of attribution, which should be applied in a context-sensitive manner but have to date been applied rigidly by the ICJ, and the *rapprochement* between the obligation to diligently prevent and the prohibition of acquiescing in terrorism, which calls for a sensitive evaluation of capacity that may be beyond the injured state's appreciation. It is important to bear in mind, however, that the interest being protected in responding to the breach of an international terrorism obligation is clearly held to be of the highest importance by the international community.[43] As balanced against the importance of the interests affected by the types of measures states usually adopt (for instance trade and air service measures, examined below), states will likely have some flexibility in deciding on responsive measures to state involvement in international terrorism.

(iii) The permissibility of collective countermeasures

In order to benefit from the wrongfulness-preclusion of Article 22 of the ILC Articles on State Responsibility, countermeasures must be adopted by the injured state, in the sense of Article 42 of the ILC Articles on State Responsibility.[44] The desirability of a further right to act in the collective interest has, however, long been on the academic agenda. In the first half of the twentieth century, a number of commentators focused their attention on whether collective responses to serious breaches of international law should be permissible.[45] Their writings, largely supportive of such a right, reflected an underlying concern with the systemic implications of unenforceable law, in particular where the violation being responded to undermined the international legal order.[46] These concerns, however, have generally been framed in terms of the *lex ferenda*, rather than the *lex lata*, and

---

[41] See Chapters 2 and 3 for a discussion of the complications involved in assessing, both factually and legally, whether a state is directly responsible for an act of terrorism; responsible for its own conduct in relation to an act of terrorism; or responsible for a failure to exercise diligence in preventing international terrorism.

[42] See Axelrod and Keohane (1985), 235; Abbott (1987), 310.

[43] See generally United Nations Global Counter-Terrorism Strategy, UNGA Resolution 60/288 (2006); UNSG Report, Uniting against terrorism; recommendations for a global counter-terrorism strategy, UN Doc. A/60/825 (2006); UNSC Resolution 1822 (2008).

[44] Art. 49(1), ILC Articles on State Responsibility.

[45] See Root (1915), 8–9; Stowell (1921), 46–7; Hall (1924), 65–6.

[46] But see Akehurst (1970), 14. Akehurst considered Root's argument that a collective right of response to serious breaches of international law is essential for the purposes of protecting the international legal order, but concluded from the dearth of state practice that the ability of non-affected states to remedy breaches of international law must not be 'so essential to the effectiveness of international law as writers like [...] Root suggest'. See also Scobbie (2009), 295, noting that state responsibility is 'confined within a bilateral straitjacket' and has made little progress towards communitarian responses to state criminality.

the situation has not changed significantly since then. As a result, the ILC Articles on State Responsibility were adopted without prejudice:

[to] the right of any State, entitled under article 48, paragraph 1, to invoke the responsibility of another State, to take *lawful* measures against that State to ensure cessation of the breach and reparation in the interest of the injured State or of the beneficiaries of the obligation breached.[47]

The Commentary notes that state practice in the area of collective responses to breaches of obligations *erga omnes* is embryonic,[48] limited to the practice of a particular group of states,[49] and that 'there appears to be no clearly recognized entitlement of States referred to in article 48 to take countermeasures in the collective interest'.[50]

Commentators in the latter half of the twentieth century have argued that the auto-determination of state responsibility, coupled with a decentralized and collective right of response, may undermine the international legal order rather than protect it. Professor Weil is most famous for articulating this position when he argued that:

any State, in the name of higher values determined by itself, could appoint itself the avenger of the international community. Thus, under the banner of law, chaos and violence would come to reign among States, and international law would turn on and rend itself with the loftiest of intentions.[51]

---

[47] Emphasis added. Art. 54, ILC Articles on State Responsibility. See Sicilianos (2010), 1144–5, discussing the deliberate ambiguity of Article 54, which can be read either as legally uninteresting in its confirmation that non-injured states can adopt retorsive measures, or as non-committal in its reference to the legitimacy of collective countermeasures (which could be described as 'lawful' if they met the conditions of necessity and proportionality, because their 'unlawfulness' would be precluded).

[48] Commentary to Art. 54, ILC Articles on State Responsibility, para 3.

[49] *Ibid*, para 6. The Commentary does not identify the limited number of states which have taken measures in response to the breach of an obligation *erga omnes*, but the practice reviewed is that of the US and European countries.

[50] Commentary to Art. 54, ILC Articles on State Responsibility, para 6. But see Special Rapporteur Crawford's third report in which he concluded that the Articles on State Responsibility 'should allow States parties to a community obligation to take collective countermeasures in response to a gross and well-attested breach of that obligation, in particular in order to secure cessation and to obtain assurances and guarantees for non-repetition on behalf of the non-State victims'. Crawford (2000b), 21. Some members of the ILC reluctantly accepted the possibility for collective countermeasures in cases where the obligation breached was established for the collective interest or there was no injured state (see Report of the International Law Commission on the work of its fifty-fifth session, UN Doc. A/55/10 (2000), 134–9; Koskenniemi (2001), 343), but these proposals proved too controversial, and were not reflected in the final draft Articles on State Responsibility adopted on second reading.

[51] Weil (1983), 433. See also Akehurst (1970), 16; Leben (1982), 76; Dupuy (1983), 546; Hutchison (1988), 204; Charney (1989), 87, 89; Koskenniemi (2001), 340 (noting that states have been reluctant to accept the legitimacy of collective countermeasures 'out of the prudent fear that once the door to collective reaction is opened, it can no longer be closed in order to prevent the hegemon from walking right through it, less as a policeman than as a bully', and concluding that such measures should not be legally codified). States have expressed similar concerns. See e.g. comments by Germany (UNGA, Sixth Committee, UN Doc. A/C.6/39/SR.36 (1984), 4) and the US (UNGA, Sixth Committee, UN Doc. A/C.6/39/SR.42 (1984), 4). But see Schachter (1982), 200–1; Simma (1988), 293.

As is the case in regard to the 'at your own risk' element of injured-state counter-measures, commentators have attempted to balance the potential for 'chaos' inherent in auto-determinative collective countermeasures against an institutional element of oversight. For instance, Charney considered whether collective decision-making, as required for the suspension of a multilateral treaty by non-injured states in the face of a material breach,[52] might be appropriate in the context of collective countermeasures.[53] He concluded, however, that the international community is not yet appropriately structured for such a requirement, particularly given the absence of compulsory dispute settlement and limitations on the Security Council's sphere of competence.[54]

As examined in Section 5.1.4 below, the condition that countermeasures can only be adopted in response to a prior breach of international law, and the uncertainties surrounding any such determination (particularly in the terrorism context), lends itself to a very obvious practice. States attempt, as far as possible, to limit their responses to breaches of international terrorism obligations to acts of retorsion. The uncertainty surrounding the legality of collective countermeasures lends itself to a similar preference, particularly given the widely perceived need—at least in the West—to respond collectively to breaches of international terrorism obligations.

5.1.3 Necessity as a circumstance precluding wrongfulness

The principle of necessity might, in very limited circumstances, preclude the wrongfulness of measures taken in response to the breach of an international terrorism obligation. Article 25 of the ILC Articles on State Responsibility frames the defence of necessity in the negative, to highlight its exceptional nature and the strict limitations to which it is subject:[55]

Necessity may not be invoked by a State as a ground for precluding the wrongfulness of an act not in conformity with an international obligation of that State *unless* the act:

(a) is the only means for the State to safeguard an essential interest against a grave and imminent peril; and

(b) does not seriously impair an essential interest of the State or States towards which the obligation exists, or the international community as a whole.[56]

Necessity, as a circumstance precluding wrongfulness, is different from counter-measures in at least one significant respect: the relevant measure (in breach of the

---

[52] Art. 60(2)(b), VCLT.

[53] See Charney (1989), 91–2. See also Frowein (1994), 423. But see Klein (2002), 1249, arguing that replacing the subjective assessment of non-injured states as to whether there has been a breach of international law necessitating responsive measures with an assessment by, for instance, the Security Council, would be 'replacing one subjectivity (of states) with another (of the Security Council)'.

[54] See Charney (1989), 91–2. But see White and Abass (2006), 511, arguing that there are alternative forums, such as the UN, for addressing collective interests and that non-injured states should restrict themselves thereto.

[55] *Gabčíkovo–Nagymaros Project (Hungary v. Slovakia)*, Judgment, para 51.

[56] Emphasis added. Art. 25, ILC Articles on State Responsibility.

measure-adopting state's international obligations) need not be in response to an internationally wrongful act, as long as it is the only way to safeguard an *essential interest*. As a result, states can invoke necessity to justify measures adopted in response to a state's failure to prevent terrorism, even where that failure is not an internationally wrongful act owing to the territorial state's exercise of due diligence (within its capacity). But the peril against which the adopted measure is safe-guarding has to be both 'objectively established and not merely apprehended as possible'[57] and imminent,[58] which will require a careful evaluation of the facts. Equally, whether the adopted measure is the *only way* to safeguard the essential interest will depend on the particular circumstances of each case. In cases of a failure to prevent, an injured state might do better to offer the wrongdoing state technical or even resource assistance, in the place of adopting measures against it which might further decrease the wrongdoing (and target) state's counter-terrorism capacity. In either event, necessity as a circumstance precluding wrongfulness is clearly relevant in the terrorism context, and will be examined in relation to the state practice set out below.

5.1.4 State practice

The state practice of adopting measures in response to internationally wrongful acts related to terrorism (outside the framework of Security Council enforcement action) is broad, but is most prolific in response to the breach of international terrorism obligations related to the safety of civil aviation. This section therefore focuses primarily on the practice relating to civil aviation in highlighting the practical and conceptual difficulties with a decentralized system of law enforcement examined in Section 5.1.2. The measures examined in this section fall within the framework of general international law set out above in the form of acts of retorsion; countermeasures; or exceptionally (but not always obviously) on the basis of their necessity.

(i) G7 measures against Afghanistan in response to the hijacking of a PIA flight (1981)

The Bonn Declaration

In response to the alarming increase in hijackings in the late 1970s, the G7 issued a joint statement on international terrorism. The heads of state of the G7 pledged to take immediate action to cease all flights to any country that refused to extradite or prosecute those responsible for international hijackings.[59] The Bonn Declaration is not expressly limited in its application to state parties to the ICAO TSCs, or to

---

[57] Commentary to Art. 25, ILC Articles on State Responsibility, para 15.

[58] See *Gabčíkovo–Nagymaros Project (Hungary v. Slovakia)*, Judgment, para 54.

[59] Joint Statement on International Terrorism, issued 17 July 1978 in Bonn, Germany, by Canada, the Federal Republic of Germany, France, Italy, Japan, the United Kingdom and the United States, reproduced in 17 International Legal Materials (1978) 1285 (the 'Bonn Declaration').

states that otherwise have extradition obligations pursuant to bilateral treaties, and there is no consensus on the customary international law status of an *aut dedere aut judicare* obligation with respect to terrorist (or other) offences.[60] Absent an obligation to extradite or submit to prosecution, a state's failure to do so would not amount to an internationally wrongful act, and could therefore not form the basis of a legitimate countermeasure.[61]

Implementation of the Bonn Declaration

On 2 March 1981, Pakistani political dissidents (including former Prime Minister Zulfikar Bhutto's eldest son) hijacked a Pakistan International Airlines (PIA) domestic flight between Karachi and Peshawar to Kabul.[62] The hijackers' demands included the release of political prisoners in Pakistan. The hijackers maintained control over the aircraft and the hostages for five days in Kabul, before proceeding to Damascus—where the hijacking ended on 12 March 1981.[63] From Syria, the hijackers reportedly returned to Kabul, and Pakistan made a formal request to the Afghan Government for the extradition of the hijackers, pursuant to the Hague Convention.[64] Afghanistan insisted that the hijackers were not in its territory, and that it was therefore not in a position to extradite them. In addition to a potential breach of *aut dedere aut judicare* obligations under the Hague Convention (depending on the actual whereabouts of the hijackers), Pakistan and the US accused Afghanistan of complicity in the hijacking, including through the provision of weapons to the hijackers.[65] To the extent that the Hague Convention prohibits states from engaging in the conduct criminalized therein (in line with the ICJ's analysis in the *Bosnia Genocide Case* examined in Section 4.2), Afghanistan's complicity in the hijacking would be in breach of Article 2 of the Hague Convention, which creates accomplice liability for hijackings. Support for the hijackers, particularly the provision of weapons, would equally amount to a breach of the customary international law prohibition of the use of force.[66]

The Bonn Declaration was applied for the first time in July 1981, in response to the PIA hijacking. The G7 declarants issued a statement following the Montebello

---

[60] See *supra* Chapter 3, notes 109–11.

[61] Art. 49(1), ILC Articles on State Responsibility. Some authors have argued that the obligations in the ICAO TSCs (in particular the *aut dedere aut judicare* obligation and the obligation to prevent) are instantiations of general obligations under the Chicago Convention—namely to ensure the safe and orderly development of international civil aviation. See Kraiem (1978), 1044; Chamberlain (1983), 631; Schwenck (1979), 314. See also India's arguments in its dispute with Pakistan, *infra* note 218 and accompanying text. But see Busuttil (1982), 479. The Chicago Convention was much more widely ratified than the ICAO TSCs when the Bonn Declaration was adopted. If a failure to extradite or prosecute hijackers could amount to a breach of the Chicago Convention, the conditions for the adoption of countermeasures under the international law of state responsibility would have been more likely to be met. Such an argument, however, is untested, and in their only implementation of the Bonn Declaration, the G7 were very careful to specifically invoke the target state's breach of the Hague Convention.

[62] Keesing's, Vol. 27, January 1981, 31071.

[63] *Ibid.*

[64] Akhtar, 'Hijackers' Return Sought', *The Times* (London), 19 May 1981, 9.

[65] *NY Times*, 16 March 1981, A8; *Washington Post*, 17 March 1981, A1.

[66] See Section 2.1.2 regarding military and technical support for terrorist conduct.

Economic Summit, stating that the Afghan Government's conduct during and following the hijacking (including its failure to apprehend and extradite or submit those responsible to prosecution) was in 'flagrant breach of its international obligations under the Hague Convention [...] and constitute[s] a threat to air safety'.[67] The G7 therefore 'propose[d] to suspend all flights to and from Afghanistan in implementation of the Bonn Declaration unless Afghanistan immediately [took] steps to comply with its obligations'.[68] The G7 further called upon all states 'which share[d] their concern for air safety to take appropriate steps to persuade Afghanistan to honour its obligations'.[69]

The US favoured an immediate application of the Bonn declaration.[70] The three G7 states with regular flights to and from Afghanistan, however, preferred to suspend their air service agreements with Afghanistan in accordance with the terms of those agreements.[71] France's air services agreement was the only one to have a termination clause subject to a one-year notice requirement, and the G7's measures against Afghanistan took effect two days after the year anniversary of France's notice of termination to Afghanistan.[72] Given that the air services agreements between the Bonn Declaration participants and Afghanistan were suspended in accordance with the terms of those air service agreements, the suspension was not in breach of international law, and therefore did not amount to a countermeasure, but rather to an act of retorsion.

The Afghan Government's response to the suspension of air traffic, which it delivered to the US Mission to the UN, was to offer an assurance that it would honour its international obligations with regard to the hijackers, including through their arrest and prosecution, and to request that the suspension of air services be lifted.[73] Had the measure adopted pursuant to the Bonn Declaration been a veritable countermeasure (rather than an act of retorsion), a state's offering assurances and promising to abide by its primary obligations might have a bearing on the continuing legality of the countermeasure.[74] With respect to retorsive measures adopted in response to an internationally wrongful act, however, there is no requirement that the measures be lifted when the primary legal relationship is re-established.

---

[67] Statement on Terrorism, issued in Ottawa, Canada, by Prime Minister Trudeau on behalf of the participants in the Montebello Economic Summit, reproduced in 20 International Legal Materials (1981) 956.

[68] *Ibid.*

[69] *Ibid.* States indirectly supported the G7 initiative by refusing to establish alternative air service arrangements with Afghanistan, despite Ariana Afghan Airline's efforts. See Chamberlain (1983), 628. In addition, the US claimed that non-G7 states had made unilateral commitments to abide by the terms of the Bonn Declaration, but did not signal which states had done so—or indeed how many. (1981) Digest of United States Practice in International Law, 494.

[70] Murphy et al. (1991), 40.

[71] See Chamberlain (1983), 628; Guillaume (1989), 501; Frowein (1994), 418.

[72] Guillaume (1989), 501.

[73] Department of State Cable No. USUN 3081 (28 October 1982), quoted in Levitt (1990), 111.

[74] *Supra* note 14. The sanctions remained in effect until 1986, when they were quietly terminated. Murphy et al. (1991), 41.

The way in which the G7 states implemented the Bonn Declaration, in particular through the termination of air services agreements in accordance with their terms, suggests that they were not confident that their treaty obligations could be disregarded in the form of legitimate countermeasures.[75] The first difficulty with the adoption of countermeasures against Afghanistan bears on the extent to which Afghanistan was in breach of its primary obligations. Pakistan and the US alleged that the hijackers were in Afghan territory, on the basis of which they considered Afghanistan to be in breach of its *aut dedere aut judicare* obligation under the Hague Convention, and alleged that Afghanistan had supported the hijackers through the provision of weapons. Afghanistan of course maintained exactly the opposite.[76] In the face of contested facts, which form the basis of an invocation of responsibility in response to which countermeasures are adopted, it was indeed safer to opt for an act of retorsion.[77] The second difficulty with adopting countermeasures (instead of responding to an alleged breach of international terrorism obligations through measures of retorsion) bears on the uncertainty regarding the legitimacy of collective countermeasures. The hijacked aircraft was registered to Pakistan and it is highly unlikely that there were citizens from all G7 countries on the internal flight between Karachi and Peshawar. To the extent that the G7 states were not injured states within the meaning of Article 42 of the ILC Articles on State Responsibility, the legality of a collective response in the form of countermeasures (rather than acts of retorsion) to Afghanistan's alleged breach of an international terrorism obligation would have been at best uncertain.

(ii) US measures against Lebanon in response to the hijacking of a TWA flight (1985)

Flight TWA 847, en route from Athens to Rome, was hijacked on 14 June 1985 by Lebanese Shiites. The hostage crisis that ensued lasted for two weeks, during which time the plane was flown back and forth between the Algiers and Beirut airports.[78] A US navy diver was killed in Beirut by the hijackers, and 104 out of the 145 passengers were US citizens.[79] In response to the hijacking, the US halted all flights to and from Beirut International Airport (in breach of its limited air services arrangement with Lebanon, which required a one-year notice period before the suspension of air services could take effect).[80] The initial justification for this

---

[75] See Frowein (1994), 418.

[76] The difficulties in determining, for certain, the exact location of terrorist criminals is very common. See for instance Section 6.2.5, in reference to the Sudan's failure to extradite the men who had attempted to assassinate President Mubarak, claiming that they were not in Sudanese territory.

[77] See Hutchison (1988), 162, arguing that it may be very difficult to convince well-wishing states to join in solidarity measures against a wrongdoing state absent a clear and incontestable establishment of the breach.

[78] Keesing's, Vol. 31, September 1985, 33850.

[79] United States, 'Public Report of the Vice President's Task Force on Combating Terrorism' (1986), <http://www.population-security.org/bush_report_on_terrorism/bush_report_on_terrorism.htm>, i.

[80] The Exchange of notes constituting an agreement concerning a limited air service between Beirut and New York, 22 December 1982, 1751 UNTS 19, amended the Air Transport Services Agreement

measure was that, from a security perspective, Beirut International Airport (and the safe haven it provided to hijackers) increased the terrorist threat to all civil aviation in Europe and the Middle East and, as a result, should be subject to quarantine.[81] This justification seems to evoke necessity as a circumstance precluding wrongful-ness, in characterizing the suspension of air services as a means of safeguarding an essential interest against a grave and imminent peril. Whether the suspension of air services with Lebanon (in violation of air service agreement obligations) was the *only* means to safeguard US security interests is another matter, and the US subsequently claimed that the measures were justified on the basis of the Lebanese failure to apprehend, extradite or submit the hijackers to prosecution.[82] As both the US and Lebanon were state parties to the Hague Convention,[83] Lebanon's failure to extradite or submit the hijackers to prosecution amounted to an internationally wrongful act in violation of its *aut dedere aut judicare* obligations under Article 7 thereof, and, as an injured state,[84] the US was entitled under the law of state responsibility to take countermeasures against Lebanon in response to that breach.

In a letter to the Secretary-General, Lebanon protested against the US measures to isolate Beirut International Airport and to prevent Lebanese aircraft from flying to American airports. Lebanon emphasized that the TWA hijacking had political roots and was not merely a criminal or terrorist act, and claimed that isolating Lebanon and preventing its two national airlines from operating normally were measures out of proportion to the harm suffered as a result of the hijacking.[85] In particular, the Lebanese Government considered an appropriate response to be one aimed at punishing the hijackers, rather than a government that had condemned the hijacking (which is how Lebanon characterized itself), or companies and people that were not involved in the hijacking.[86] Lebanon's evaluation of the proportion-ality of the US countermeasures is limited to balancing the relative harm suffered by the US as a result of the hijacking, and that suffered by the Lebanese aviation industry as a result of the US countermeasures. As noted above,[87] however, there are other considerations that bear on an assessment of proportionality, including the importance of the interests being protected by the countermeasures.

---

between the Government of the United States of America and the Government of Lebanon, 1 September 1972, TIAS 7546. Article 15 of the latter (which was left unamended) required a one-year period between notice of termination and such termination taking effect.

[81] See Murphy et al. (1991), 44.

[82] *Keesing's*, Vol. 31, September 1985, 33850.

[83] <http://www.icao.int/icao/en/leb/Hague.pdf>.

[84] TWA is an airline registered to the US. Pursuant to Article 4(1)(a) of the Hague Convention, the US is required to establish its jurisdiction to prosecute unlawful seizures of TWA flights, and would therefore be entitled under Article 7 of the Hague Convention to demand extradition of the alleged hijackers. In addition, as most of the victims of the hijacking were American, the US would be entitled to exercise jurisdiction over the hijackers on the basis of the passive personality principle, giving it a further basis for an extradition request under the Hague Convention.

[85] Letter dated 5 July 1985 from the Permanent Representative of Lebanon to the United Nations addressed to the Secretary-General, UN Doc. A/40/462 (1985), Annex.

[86] *Ibid.*

[87] See Section 5.1.2 (ii).

Responding to Lebanon's letter, the US maintained that the aim of the measures was not to punish Lebanon, but that Beirut International Airport had become a haven for international hijackers, and that while Lebanon was beginning to take actions to meet security deficiencies, further action was required. The US did not consider Lebanon to have demonstrated that it had *the will or the means* to counter the threat to civil aviation effectively, and highlighted that, although a party to international conventions setting standards of behaviour toward hijackers, Lebanon had not demonstrated that it could abide by its commitments. The US administration characterized the measures as 'a first step in the corrective process'.[88] The US response to Lebanon's complaint on proportionality is of interest in that it invokes Lebanon's failure to prevent international hijackings as a basis for countermeasures (as distinct from its second justification based on Lebanon's failure to apprehend and extradite or submit the hijackers to prosecution). The obligation of prevention set out in the Hague Convention is subject to a due diligence standard of conduct.[89] The US acknowledged, however, that Lebanon may not have had the means to comply with its obligations. Depending on the facts, limited means could militate against Lebanon's international responsibility for a failure to prevent.[90] But in the absence of Lebanese responsibility with respect to the hijacking, there is no basis under international law for the US countermeasures. The countermeasures would therefore best be justified as a measure in response to Lebanon's failure to extradite or submit the hijackers to prosecution—which is not subject to a due diligence standard of conduct.[91] The American characterization of the suspension of air services between the US and Lebanon as 'a first step in the corrective process' suggests that the purpose of the measures is to pressure Lebanon into complying with its primary obligations, which accounts for the necessity of the measures under the general international law of state responsibility related to countermeasures.[92]

(iii) *US and EU measures against Libya in response to the terrorist attacks against the Vienna and Rome Airports (1985)*

On 27 December 1985, seven gunmen killed over twenty people in virtually simultaneous attacks at the international airports in Vienna and Rome. Responsibility for the attacks was widely attributed to the Palestinian terrorist group Abu Nidal.[93] US intelligence services reviewed evidence related to the airport attacks and concluded that Libya had provided both support for the attacks and sanctuary to the terrorists.[94] In response to the attacks, the President issued an executive

---

[88] Letter dated 24 July 1985 from the Permanent Representative of the United States of America to the United Nations addressed to the Secretary-General, UN Doc. A/40/504 (1985).
[89] See Section 3.1.
[90] See Section 3.1.2.
[91] See Section 3.2.
[92] See Section 5.1.2.
[93] Keesing's, Vol. 32, March 1986, 34260.
[94] See President Reagan's Press Conference, 7 January 1986, reproduced in 25 International Legal Materials (1986) 175. The evidence, at the time of the President's news conference, was admitted to be

order, which declared that a 'national emergency' existed,[95] and adopted a series of economic measures against Libya. Libya's alleged support for the terrorist attacks was in violation of customary international law obligations.[96] The 1988 Protocol to the Montreal Convention, which requires states to prevent attacks against international airports (and, pursuant to a *Bosnia Genocide Case* analysis, thereby prohibits Libyan support or sponsorship of such attacks),[97] was adopted in response to the Rome and Vienna Airport attacks, and Libya's conduct was therefore not in breach of treaty-based international terrorism obligations.

As there were a number of US victims of the attacks,[98] the US constituted an 'injured state' in the sense of Article 42 of the ILC Articles on State Responsibility. The US measures included a prohibition of trade and certain business transactions with Libya by US persons, and a freeze on the Libyan Government's assets.[99] The prohibition of business transactions was far reaching in that it prohibited any US person from performing 'any contract in support of an industrial or other commercial or governmental project in Libya'.[100] The prohibition was effective immediately and made no exception for existing contracts.[101] Given that the prohibition precluded US persons from performing contracts even where they had been performed in relevant part by their Libyan contractual counterparts, it could (depending on the precise facts) amount to an expropriation of property rights without compensation, in breach of international law.[102] The asset freeze was equally far reaching, in that it prohibited all transfers, payments, exports, withdrawals, and other dealings in 'property or interests in property of the Government of Libya [. . .] that are in the United States, that hereafter come within the United States or that are or hereafter come within the possession or control of US persons',[103] and could (again depending on the precise facts) have amounted to a breach of Libya's sovereign immunity. The US measures against Libya could

---

circumstantial—but the US administration later claimed to be in possession of evidence that directly linked Libya to the airport attacks. See Press Conference of the Deputy Secretary of State, the Honourable John C. Whitehead, 27 January 1986, reproduced in 25 International Legal Materials (1986) 209, 221.

[95] The President characterized Libya's provision of material support to terrorist groups which attack US citizens as an act of 'armed aggression [. . .] just as if [Libya] had used its own armed forces'. President Reagan's Press Conference, 7 January 1986, reproduced in 25 International Legal Materials (1986) 175.

[96] See Section 2.1.2.

[97] See Section 4.2.

[98] United States, 'Public Report of the Vice President's Task Force on Combating Terrorism' (1986), <http://www.population-security.org/bush_report_on_terrorism/bush_report_on_terrorism.htm>, ii.

[99] Executive Order No. 12543, 7 January 1986, reproduced in 25 International Legal Materials (1986) 173; Executive Order No. 12544, 8 January 1986, reproduced in 25 International Legal Materials (1986) 181.

[100] Executive Order No. 12543, 7 January 1986, reproduced in 25 International Legal Materials (1986) 173.

[101] See Bialos and Juster (1986), 813.

[102] See generally *German Interests in Polish Upper Silesia (Germany v. Poland)*, Merits.

[103] Executive Order No. 12544, 8 January 1986, reproduced in 25 International Legal Materials (1986) 181.

therefore amount to countermeasures adopted by an injured state against a wrong-doing state in response to the breach of international terrorism obligations.[104]

The US economic measures were significantly more far reaching than those imposed by Europe. Given the location of the attacks, Austria and Italy were injured states within the meaning of Article 42 of the ILC Articles on State Responsibility, but the measures taken against Libya in response to the airport attacks were taken collectively by the European Community ('EC'). The measures, had they amounted to countermeasures, could have put in issue the lawfulness of a collective response to the breach of international terrorism obligations. On the assumption that there were no relevant arms sale treaties between the EC member states and Libya at the time, the European Community's decision not to export arms or other military equipment to countries that 'were clearly implicated in supporting terrorism' (including Libya)[105] amounted to an act of retorsion.

The G7 also took measures against Libya, largely in response to its alleged participation in the Rome and Vienna Airport attacks. In a second statement on international terrorism issued after the Tokyo Economic Summit, the G7 specified a list of measures it intended to take against terrorism-supporting states, and invited the participation of 'any government concerned to deny to international terrorists the opportunity and the means to carry out their aims, and to identify and deter those who perpetrate such terrorism'.[106] The measures included an arms embargo, limitations of diplomatic relations, and stricter visa and immigration requirements, and the G7 expressed their joint intention to apply these measures 'in respect of any state which is clearly involved in sponsoring or supporting international terrorism, and in particular of Libya, until such time as the state concerned abandons its complicity in, or support for, such terrorism'.[107] As these measures amount to acts of retorsion, implementation of the Tokyo Declaration avoided any issues regarding the legality of collective countermeasures.

(iv) Various measures in response to Syrian support for terrorism (1986–present)

On 29 March 1986, the German–Arab Friendship Society in West Berlin was bombed, injuring nine people.[108] A German court convicted Ahmed Hasi of the

---

[104] The US subsequently characterized the measures as a concerted multilateral effort against terrorism, which served as an important deterrent to states considering support of terrorist acts or groups. Such a deterrent effect could be characterized as a means of pressuring Libya into complying with its primary obligation to refrain from supporting international terrorism. See UNSG, Reports on measures to prevent international terrorism, UN Doc. A/48/267/Add.1 (1993), 3; UN Doc. A/49/257 (1994), 23.

[105] Statement of Ministers of Foreign Affairs of the Twelve Meeting in Brussels on Combating International Terrorism, 27 January 1986, reproduced in 25 International Legal Materials (1986) 208, 209.

[106] Joint Statement on International Terrorism, issued on 5 May 1986 in Tokyo, Japan, by Canada, the Federal Republic of Germany, France, Italy, Japan, the United Kingdom and the United states, reproduced in 25 International Legal Materials (1986) 1005.

[107] *Ibid.*

[108] Keesing's, Vol. 32, December 1986, 34835.

bombing and ruled that he had obtained the explosives from the Syrian Embassy in East Berlin.[109] In response to Syria's involvement in the terrorist attack, the German Government expelled five Syrian diplomats, halted development aid, as well as $73 million in low-interest loans to Damascus, and announced that it would not replace its ambassador to Syria. The German Government also stopped honouring certain Syrian passports that it suspected were used by terrorists.[110] Most of the measures fall clearly within the category of retorsion. Only the cessation of low-interest loans to Damascus could amount to a countermeasure, depending on the terms of the loan agreement. Based on evidence of the Syrian Embassy's involvement in the plot—for which Syria would be responsible—Germany, as an injured state within the meaning of Article 42 of the ILC Articles on State Responsibility, would have been entitled to adopt countermeasures against Syria.

On 17 April 1986, Nezar Hindawi (Ahmed Hasi's brother) attempted to smuggle a bag containing explosives and a timing and detonation device concealed in a calculator onto an El Al flight between Heathrow International Airport and Tel Aviv Airport. Mr Hindawi persuaded his pregnant Irish girlfriend unwittingly to carry the explosives on board with the promise that he would meet her in Israel the following day.[111] The explosives were discovered by an El Al security official who searched the girlfriend's bag.[112] Following the discovery of the explosives, Mr Hindawi, a Jordanian national carrying a Syrian diplomatic passport, was apprehended while leaving a Syrian safehouse.[113] In October 1986, he was convicted of attempting to place on an aircraft an explosive device likely to destroy or damage the aircraft.[114] In response to the conviction, which included conclusive evidence of Syrian involvement in the plot, the UK broke off diplomatic relations with Syria and expelled the Syrian ambassador,[115] both of which amounted to acts of retorsion.

In relation to both attacks discussed above, the injured states had a high degree of certainty regarding the internationally wrongful nature of Syria's conduct, based on a determination of Syrian involvement by national courts. Given that the 'at your own risk' element of countermeasures had been minimized, it is striking that both Germany and the UK nevertheless resorted exclusively (or primarily) to retorsive measures.

In response to Syria's involvement in the attacks, Canada, Austria and Belgium withdrew their ambassadors from Syria,[116] and the EC banned arms sales to Syria

---

[109] Hull et al., 'West Germany Verdict Against Damascus', Time, 8 December 1986, <http://www.time.com/time/magazine/article/0,9171,963053,00.html>.

[110] *Ibid.*

[111] See *R. v. Nezar Nawat Mansour Hazi Hindawi*, England (Court of Appeal, 7 March 1988), 10 Criminal Appeal Reports (S.) 104.

[112] BBC, 'On this Day: 1986: UK cuts links with Syria over bomb plot', <http://news.bbc.co.uk/onthisday/hi/dates/stories/october/24/newsid_2478000/2478505.stm>.

[113] *Ibid.*

[114] Mr Hindawi was refused leave to appeal the conviction. *R. v. Nezar Nawat Mansour Hazi Hindawi*, England (Court of Appeal, 1988).

[115] *Supra* note 112. The UK restored diplomatic relations with Syria in November 1990, after having received assurances from the Syrian Government that it rejected acts of international terrorism and would take action against convicted terrorists. Keesing's, Vol. 36, November 1990, 37873.

[116] See Lerner (1989), 264.

and reviewed the number of Syrian diplomats in the EC.[117] Finally, the US imposed further trade controls and restrictions against Syria.[118] All these measures amounted to retorsion, and thereby avoided the legal uncertainty regarding the right of non-injured states to adopt countermeasures in response to an internationally wrongful act related to terrorism.

The US adopted further retorsive measures against Syria in 2003, in response to Syria's support for Hezbollah, Hamas, Palestinian Islamic Jihad and the Popular Front for the Liberation of Palestine (General Command)—all of which the US qualifies as terrorist organizations.[119] The measures included trade restrictions and restrictions on exports to Syria[120]—neither of which are in breach of US obligations owed to Syria (as Syria is not a member of the WTO and the US and Syria have no other trade treaty relations), and therefore amounted to acts of retorsion. The measures also include restrictions on rights of over-flight to Syrian registered aircraft, which are not in breach of the Chicago Convention because such rights are subject to permission (for scheduled flights)[121] and the US/Syrian bilateral Air Transport Agreement (providing for a right of over-flight) was terminated pursuant to the one-year notice provision of the agreement.[122] As a non-injured state, the US did well to limit itself to acts of retorsion in response to Syria's alleged support of international terrorism, thereby avoiding the legal uncertainty regarding the lawfulness of collective countermeasures.

(v) US response to destruction of a KAL flight (1987)

The US placed North Korea on its 'State Sponsors of Terrorism' list in January 1988, following the destruction of KAL flight 858 on 29 November 1987, allegedly by North Korean agents posing as Japanese tourists.[123] The designation as a state sponsor of terrorism entails a number of economic consequences for the designated state, including restrictions on US foreign assistance; a ban on defence exports and sales; controls over exports of dual use items; and other financial restrictions.[124] In the absence of trade obligations with North Korea, the US measures amounted to acts of retorsion, which it was entitled to adopt. The

---

[117] EC Bulletin No. 11, 1986, 11. See also Keesing's, Vol. 33, January 1987, 34883.

[118] White House Statement, 'US Measures against Syria', 14 November 1986, printed in Dept. St. Bull., January 1987, 79. See also Abbott (1987), 324; Congressional Research Service, Report for Congress (January 2003), 'North Korea: Economic Sanctions', <http://www.au.af.mil/au/awc/awcgate/crs/rl31696.pdf>, 9, 14.

[119] See Syria Accountability and Lebanese Sovereignty Restoration Act of 2003, Public Law 108–75, 12 December 2003, 117 Stat. 2482.

[120] *Ibid.*

[121] See Art. 6, Chicago Convention. For a discussion of the Chicago Convention, which sets out the constitutional framework of the ICAO, see Section 5.2.3.

[122] See Art. 8, Air Transport Agreement between the United States and Syria, 28 April 1947, 262 UNTS 126, as amended (14 and 16 March 1977, 1067 UNTS 302); <http://www.state.gov/e/eeb/rls/othr/ata/index.htm>.

[123] See Section 6.3.3 for details of the terrorist attack.

[124] See <http://www.state.gov/s/ct/c14151.htm>. See also Congressional Research Service, Report for Congress (January 2003), 'North Korea: Economic Sanctions', *supra* note 118.

adoption of countermeasures would have been more problematic, assuming there were no American victims in the downing of KAL flight 858 and given that the aircraft was registered to South Korea. The US would therefore not have been an injured state within the meaning of Article 42 of the ILC Articles on State Responsibility and could not have legitimately adopted countermeasures in response to North Korea's breach of its international terrorism obligations.

(vi) Conclusion

The state practice examined in this section evidences a clear preference for resorting to retorsive measures in responding to breaches of international terrorism obligations. For the most part, the practice seems to be driven by the combination of uncertainty regarding the basis for adopting countermeasures (in particular, the 'at your own risk' element of evaluating whether the target state is responsible for an internationally wrongful act) and uncertainty regarding the lawfulness of collective countermeasures. Only in the clearest cases of responsibility for an internationally wrongful act related to terrorism have injured states (within the meaning of Article 42 of the ILC Articles on State Responsibility) resorted to the adoption of countermeasures, and even then there is some uncertainty as to the proportionality of the measures or the source of the international wrong that occasioned the response. These uncertainties are all features of a decentralized legal system. In the absence of compulsory dispute settlement, or at least an objective determination of a breach of international law giving rise to a right of response, states have generally opted for responses that reduce the 'at your own risk' element of countermeasures while permitting collective action to counter the threat posed by international terrorism.

5.2 The adoption of measures in response to international terrorism under sub-systems of international law

Whether a sub-system of international law affects the right to respond to breaches of international terrorism obligations will depend on (i) the extent to which the sub-system excludes the application of the secondary rules of state responsibility; and (ii) the extent to which rules within the sub-system are more liberal or more restrictive than the secondary rules of state responsibility under general international law bearing on the permissibility of responsive measures. Both will be evaluated below in reference to diplomatic law, the WTO the ICAO.

5.2.1 Diplomatic law

The ICJ's decision in *Tehran Hostages* described the Vienna Conventions on Diplomatic and Consular Relations as:

a self-contained regime which, on the one hand, lays down the receiving State's obligations regarding the facilities, privileges and immunities to be accorded to diplomatic missions and, on the other, foresees their possible abuse by members of the mission and specifies the means at the disposal of the receiving States to counter any such abuse.[125]

The ICJ was reacting to the implication in Iran's correspondence with the Court that the seizure of the US Embassy and resulting breach of the Vienna Conventions on Diplomatic and Consular Relations was justified (if not legally, then perhaps morally) by US abuse of its diplomatic privileges.[126] In response, the ICJ suggested that the only permissible responses to a breach by the sending state of its obligations under the Vienna Conventions on Diplomatic and Consular Relations are (i) to declare the relevant diplomat *persona non grata*,[127] or (ii) the 'power which every receiving State has, at its own discretion, to break off diplomatic relations with a sending State and to call for the immediate closure of the offending mission'.[128] The Court characterized these responses as 'by their nature, entirely efficacious', suggesting that, as a practical matter, no other response is necessary. But in characterizing diplomatic law as a self-contained regime, the judgment equally suggests that, as a matter of law, the responses set out in the Vienna Conventions are exclusive, making any other response wrongful.[129]

It is unclear whether the ICJ intended, in its characterization of diplomatic law as a self-contained regime, to exclude the applicability of the general international law on countermeasures to breaches by the sending state of its obligations under the Vienna Conventions on Diplomatic and Consular Relations.[130] Even assuming that the ICJ did so intend, the Vienna Conventions, and the ICJ's decision in *Tehran Hostages*, have nothing to say about the availability of countermeasures for a breach of non-diplomatic law by a sending state that is occasioned by a breach of its

---

[125] *Tehran Hostages (US v. Iran)*, Judgment, para 86. On the self-contained nature of the Vienna Conventions, see Riphagen (1982), 86, para 59; Riphagen (1983), paras 50–3.

[126] See *Tehran Hostages (US v. Iran)*, Judgment, paras 81–3. Some statements emanating from Iranian authorities alleged espionage and interference in Iran by the US through its Embassy in Tehran. The ICJ considered that such abuse of diplomatic privileges could amount to a breach of Article 44 of the Vienna Convention on Diplomatic Relations and Article 55 of the Vienna Convention on Consular Relations, both of which require sending states to respect the laws and regulations of the receiving state; not to interfere in the internal affairs of the receiving state; and not to use the premises of the mission in any manner incompatible with the functions of the missions. *Ibid*, paras 84–5.

[127] Art. 9, Vienna Convention on Diplomatic Relations; Art. 23, Vienna Convention on Consular Relations. See *Tehran Hostages (US v. Iran)*, Judgment, para 85.

[128] *Ibid.*

[129] Special Rapporteur Arangio-Ruiz interpreted the ICJ's characterization of diplomatic law as a self-contained regime, in combination with its further statement that '[t]he Iranian Government did not, therefore, employ the remedies placed at its disposal by diplomatic law specifically for dealing with activities of the kind of which it now complains' (*Tehran Hostages (US v. Iran)*, Judgment, para 87), as implying that 'a state injured by a violation of another state's duty in the field of diplomatic relations *could only* [employ the remedies set out in the Vienna Conventions]'. Arangio-Ruiz (1992), 39, para 109.

[130] Part of the difficulty with interpreting the ICJ's position is that it was driven by the nature of Iran's response to alleged violations by the US of its obligations under the Vienna Conventions. In particular, Iran's response was in breach of the inviolability of diplomatic agents and premises. The Court's insistence on recourse to responses set out in the Vienna Conventions may have less to do with the exclusivity of those responses (in the sense of excluding the applicability of the general international law on countermeasures), and more to do with the absolute nature of the inviolability of diplomatic agents (which is equally a limitation on countermeasures under the general international law of state responsibility (Art. 50(2)(b), ILC Articles on State Responsibility)).

obligations under the Vienna Conventions. The abuse of a diplomatic mission and privileges (and the attendant breach of the Vienna Conventions on Diplomatic and Consular Relations) is often the vehicle for breaching other primary rules of international law. For example, Syrian diplomatic staff was involved in the planning and execution of the German–Arab Friendship Society bombing in 1986. A German Court ruled that the bombers had obtained the explosives from the Syrian embassy in East Berlin.[131] For diplomatic staff to be involved in a terrorist offence, using the immunities and privileges at their disposal in virtue of their position in the receiving state, certainly amounts to an abuse of those diplomatic immunities and privileges and a breach of the Vienna Conventions. Depending on the view one takes of the ICJ's characterization of diplomatic law as a self-contained regime, the only lawful response to such abuse of privilege may be declaring the relevant diplomat *persona non grata* or breaking off diplomatic relations with the sending state.[132] The sending state's conduct, however, also amounts to a breach of its international terrorism obligations,[133] and available responses to the internationally wrongful act related to terrorism fall outside the sub-system of diplomatic law.[134]

The Vienna Conventions on Diplomatic and Consular Relations are equally silent on the right to adopt measures in response to a *receiving state's* breach of its obligations of protection,[135] and the ICJ did not directly opine on the permissibility of countermeasures under general international law in response to such breaches in its *Tehran Hostages* decision.[136] The self-contained nature of the Vienna Conventions (to the extent that the sub-system of international law is indeed self-contained as regards responses to the breach of obligations by the sending state) is therefore only partial. If acts of terrorism are carried out against the diplomatic or consular agents or premises of a sending state, with the complicity or acquiescence of the receiving state (in violation of its obligation of protection under the Vienna

---

[131] *Supra* note 109.

[132] See Simma and Pulkowski (2010), 150–1, arguing that even if *persona non grata* is the only lawful response to an abuse of diplomatic privileges, the general international law on state responsibility would nevertheless apply in respect of any economic damage inflicted on the receiving state as a result of the sending state's abuse of privileges.

[133] Material support for the commission of a terrorist act, provided by state organs, could amount to a breach of the prohibition of the use of force, and (depending on the purpose of the terrorist attack) a breach of the principle of non-intervention. See Sections 2.1.2 and 2.1.3.

[134] See Simma (1985), 120–1, arguing that acts of terrorism committed by diplomatic agents on behalf of a state justify countermeasures in the form of suspension of non-diplomatic obligations towards the wrongdoing state.

[135] In particular, diplomatic agents and premises are inviolable, and receiving states are under a special duty to protect diplomatic premises and prevent attacks on the person, freedom or dignity of diplomatic agents. Arts. 22 and 29, Vienna Convention on Diplomatic Relations.

[136] In its *Tehran Hostages* Judgment, the ICJ acknowledged that the US had taken economic measures against Iran (including an asset freeze in November 1979, and an export ban in April 1980) in response to Iran's breach of the Vienna Conventions, but did not single these measures out for censure. See *Tehran Hostages (US v. Iran)*, Judgment, paras 31 and 53. The Court did, however, note the rescue operation the US had planned, involving an incursion into Iranian territory, and characterized that operation as 'calculated to undermine respect for the judicial process in international relations'. *Ibid*, paras 31 and 93. The ICJ's acquiescence in the economic measures (to be distinguished from its censure of the planned rescue operation), should not however be interpreted as an implicit endorsement of their lawfulness, given that the issue was not before the Court.

Conventions), there are no limitations within the Vienna Conventions on the sending state's ability to adopt countermeasures under the general law of state responsibility in response thereto.

Despite its description as 'self-contained' by the ICJ, the sub-system of international diplomatic law does not, therefore, affect a state's ability to respond to breaches of international terrorism obligations by a sending or receiving state. For very good reason, nor does diplomatic law provide more wrongfulness-preclusion for the adoption of such measures than would be available under general international law.

5.2.2 World Trade Organization

The Agreement Establishing the World Trade Organization is the constitutive document of the World Trade Organization ('WTO'), which provides the 'common institutional framework for the conduct of trade relations among its Members in matters related to'[137] the WTO-covered agreements.[138] The WTO-covered agreements set out a broad range of trade-related rights and obligations between WTO members, including, of particular interest, obligations under the GATT 1994. As evidenced by the state practice examined in Section 5.1.4 above, measures adopted in response to terrorism often involve trade restrictions, and between WTO members these restrictions may either amount to a breach of Article XI of the GATT 1994, which prohibits restrictions on imports and exports through the imposition of quotas or other quantitative measures, or Article XIII of the GATT 1994, which prohibits trade restrictions applied in a discriminatory manner.

The Dispute Settlement Understanding, in the Annex to the WTO Agreement, provides for a compulsory dispute settlement system, which has exclusive jurisdiction over any dispute arising under the WTO-covered agreements.[139] One feature of the WTO's compulsory dispute settlement system is a special set of rules governing the invocation and implementation of responsibility for breaches of the primary obligations set out in the WTO-covered agreements. Articles 22 and 23 of the DSU prohibit states from taking any 'self-help' measures in response to the breach of a WTO-covered agreement obligation until the existence of the breach has been determined through recourse to the WTO dispute settlement system (either by a panel or the Appellate Body ('AB'), as adopted by the Dispute Settlement Body ('DSB')) in accordance with the rules and procedures of the DSU.

---

[137] Art. II(1), Marrakesh Agreement Establishing the World Trade Organization, 15 April 1994, 1867 UNTS 154 [hereinafter the 'WTO Agreement'].

[138] The term 'WTO-covered agreements' refers to the agreements, including the General Agreement on Tariffs and Trade, Annex to the WTO Agreement, 15 April 1994, 1867 UNTS 187 [hereinafter the 'GATT 1994'], annexed to the WTO Agreement. The WTO-covered agreements set out the substantive rights and obligations of WTO member states.

[139] Article 23.1 of the Understanding on Rules and Procedures Governing the Settlement of Disputes, Annex to the WTO Agreement, 15 April 1994, 1869 UNTS 401 [hereinafter 'DSU'] provides for the compulsory jurisdiction of the WTO dispute settlement system, and has been interpreted as establishing exclusive jurisdiction. See *US–Section 301 Trade Act*, WTO Doc. WT/DS152/R (2000), para 7.43.

Once a breach has been judicially determined, a state can only take the responsive measures provided for under the DSU, with permission of the DSB, *if* the wrongdoing state has failed to abide by the recommendations thereof within a reasonable time. These rules arguably amount to a *lex specialis* on the permissibility of countermeasures within the WTO regime,[140] although the issue remains whether countermeasures provided for under general international law should be available to an injured state, as a fall-back, if measures provided for under the DSU are not successful in securing the wrongdoing state's compliance with its primary WTO obligations.[141] In any event, this *lex specialis* only limits available responses to breaches of primary obligations arising under the WTO-covered agreements.

The DSU and other WTO-covered agreements do not expressly prohibit a state from taking WTO-inconsistent measures in response to breaches of primary obligations outside the WTO system—for instance international terrorism obligations. Some commentators have argued that, in the absence of any treaty specification to the contrary, the rules of general international law continue to apply within the WTO regime.[142] On the basis of this argument, the wrongfulness of trade measures in breach of the WTO-covered agreements, taken as legitimate countermeasures under the international law of state responsibility, should be precluded—and a WTO panel or the AB should not seek 'to secure the withdrawal of the measures concerned [...]'.[143] On another view, WTO members have prioritized trade liberalization in a way that limits the availability of WTO-inconsistent measures in response to the breach of non-WTO obligations, unless those measures can be justified on the basis of exceptions within the WTO system itself. The result of this view is that a state which would otherwise be justified in breaching WTO obligations under general international law in the form of countermeasures may nevertheless be held responsible within the WTO system for that breach. The choice between these two views depends on the answer to two separate questions examined below: what is the applicable law under the WTO dispute settlement system; and what are the limits of the WTO dispute settlement system's jurisdiction.

(i) Applicable law within the WTO dispute settlement system

The question of applicable law within the WTO dispute settlement system is unsettled. The DSU does not contain a provision comparable to Article 38 of the

---

[140] Art. 55, ILC Articles on State Responsibility. See Commentary to Part Three, Chapter II (Countermeasures), ILC Articles on State Responsibility, para 9.

[141] See generally Simma (1985); Arangio-Ruiz (1992), 40, paras 112–15. On the applicability of the regime of countermeasures under the law of state responsibility to breaches of WTO obligations, see generally Pons (1999), 64–74. See also Pauwelyn (2003), 234–6; Simma and Pulkowski (2006), 523; Eeckhout (2009); Simma and Pulkowski (2010), 157.

[142] See e.g. Pauwelyn (2003), 232. See generally McNair (1961), 466; *Namibia Advisory Opinion*, 47, para 96; *Gabčíkovo–Nagymaros Project (Hungary v. Slovakia)*, Judgment, para 100. But see Pons (1999), 102.

[143] Art. 3(7), DSU. See also Art. 19(1), DSU, providing that '[w]here a panel or the Appellate Body concludes that a measure is inconsistent with a covered agreement, it shall recommend that the Member concerned bring the measure into conformity with that agreement'.

ICJ Statute and does not expressly set out applicable or inapplicable law, except in Article 3, paragraph 2 of the DSU, with respect to the applicability of the customary international law rules of treaty interpretation. To fill in the gap, commentators have taken a broad range of views on the applicable law within the WTO dispute settlement system. Some commentators have argued that panels and the AB can apply any law applicable between the parties to the dispute,[144] while others argue that the WTO is a closed system in that the only applicable law is that set out in the WTO-covered agreements.[145]

Within the WTO dispute settlement system, panels and the AB have relied on general international law for the purposes of *interpreting* the WTO-covered agreements,[146] but have only *directly applied* general international law relating to treaties[147] and procedural issues[148] to WTO disputes. WTO adjudicative bodies have yet to rule expressly on the applicability of circumstances precluding wrongfulness under the general law of state responsibility to the breach of a WTO-covered agreement obligation.[149] There may be good reason, however, for a WTO panel or the AB to distinguish circumstances precluding wrongfulness under the general international law of state responsibility from treaty law or general principles of procedural law, which they have deemed applicable to WTO disputes. Applying the law of treaties to the WTO-covered agreements, or relying on general principles of international law to resolve procedural issues relating to dispute settlement, does not vary the rights and obligations of WTO members. Rather, these bodies of international law set a broad framework within which the rights and obligations under WTO-covered agreements can be given effect. Applying circumstances precluding wrongfulness under the general international law of state responsibility to breaches of WTO obligations may, however, vary the rights and obligations of WTO members under the WTO-covered agreements. If circumstances precluding

---

[144] See Pauwelyn (2003), 460; see also Palmeter and Mavroidis (1998), 409; Bartels (2001); Koskenniemi (2006), para 169. See also *Korea—Measures Affecting Government Procurement,* WTO Doc. WT/DS163/R (2000), para 7.96.

[145] See Charney (1998), 219; Canal-Forgues (2001), 11–13.

[146] See generally Van Damme (2009).

[147] See e.g. *Canada–Terms of Patent Protection,* WTO Doc. WT/DS170/AB/R (2000), paras 71–4 (on the non-retroactivity of treaties); *Japan–Measures Affecting Consumer Photographic Film and Paper,* WTO Doc. WT/DS44/R (1998), para 10.65 (on successive treaties); *Turkey–Restrictions on Imports of Textile and Clothing Products,* WTO Doc. WTO/DS34/R (1999), para 9.181 (on the modification of treaties); *Korea–Measures Affecting Government Procurement,* WTO Doc. WT/DS163/R (2000), paras 7.123–7.126 (on error); and *Brazil–Export Financing Programme of Aircraft,* WTO Doc. WT/DS46/ AB/R (2000), para 3.10 (on termination of treaties).

[148] See e.g. *United States–Anti Dumping Act of 1916,* WTO Doc. WT/DS136/AB/R (2000), para 54, fn. 30 (on compétence de la compétence); *United States–Measures Affecting Imports of Woven Wool Shirts and Blouses,* WTO Doc. WT/DS33/AB/R (1997), 14 (on the burden of proof); *European Communities–Regime for the Importation, Sale and Distribution of Bananas,* WTO Doc. WT/DS27/R (1997), para 133 (on the rules of standing); *India–Patent Protection for Pharmaceutical and Agricultural Chemical Products,* WTO Doc. WT/DS50/AB/R (1998), para 65 (on municipal law as evidence of compliance or non-compliance with international obligations).

[149] But see Young (2007), 911–13, discussing the WTO Panel decision in *European Communities—Measures Affecting the Approval and Marketing of Biotech Products,* noting that the decision might be interpreted either as accepting or rejecting the possibility of directly applying non-WTO law to justify a breach of WTO law.

wrongfulness under general international law were applicable to breaches of WTO obligations, a state might effectively be justified in breaching its WTO obligations (and consequently would not be required to withdraw its trade measures) in circumstances beyond those set out in the WTO-covered agreements. But Article 3, paragraph 2 of the DSU stipulates that '[r]ecommendations and rulings of the DSB cannot add to or diminish the rights and obligations provided in the covered agreements'.[150] As the specific issue of the applicability of circumstances precluding wrongfulness under general international law has yet to be decided by a WTO adjudicative body, these arguments remain speculative. Whether reliance on the general international law of state responsibility (and in particular the wrongfulness-preclusion of countermeasures) is permissible in WTO dispute settlement, however, is arguably settled by a recent decision on the scope of the DSB's jurisdiction discussed below.

(ii) Jurisdiction of the WTO dispute settlement system

While there is some suggestion in the literature that the jurisdiction of the WTO dispute settlement system should be limited to disputes that are *precipitated* by breaches of the WTO-covered agreements,[151] and should not be exercised in circumstances where trade-restrictive measures in breach of WTO-covered agreements are adopted *in response* to the prior breach of a non-WTO obligation, the AB has ruled to the contrary. In particular, the AB has ruled that WTO adjudicative bodies cannot refuse to exercise jurisdiction under the DSU with regard to the breach of an obligation under the WTO-covered agreements merely because the breach is part of a broader dispute (including where it is in response to the prior breach of a non-WTO international obligation).[152] The AB further ruled that it does not have jurisdiction to adjudicate non-WTO disputes, or to determine whether there has been a breach of non-WTO obligations.[153] In its *Mexico–Tax Measures on Soft Drinks* decision, the AB was not addressing whether it could directly apply the international law of state responsibility relating to countermeasures to justify a

---

[150] See also Art. 19(2), DSU.

[151] See e.g. Pons (1999), 94–104. See also Germany's arguments regarding its trade measures (potentially in breach of the General Agreement on Tariffs and Trade, 30 October 1947, 55 UNTS 194 [hereinafter the 'GATT 1947']) against Iceland, in response to Iceland's allegedly illegal arrest of a German fishing trawler (which Germany characterized as a violation of the prohibition of the use of force under general international law and a disregard for the judgment of the ICJ on its fishery dispute with Iceland), GATT Council, Minutes of Meeting on 3 and 7 February 1975, GATT Doc. C/M/103 (1975), 14; Comments by EC, Australian and Canadian delegates regarding trade restrictions against Argentina in response to its invasion of the Falklands, GATT Council, Minutes of Meeting on 7 May 1982, GATT Doc. C/M/157(1982), 2–13; and US arguments regarding the limitations of the WTO, in reference to the effects of the Helms Burton Act (which the EU characterized as a restrictive trade measure in violation of GATT 1994), WTO DSB, Minutes of Meeting on 16 October 1996, WTO Doc. WT/DSB/M/24 (1996). But see Bartels (2004), 871 (in reference to WTO jurisdiction over trade measures adopted in response to security concerns); Schloemann and Ohlhoff (1999).

[152] *Mexico–Tax Measures on Soft Drinks*, WTO Doc. WT/DS/308/AB/R (2006), para 53. See also Marceau (2008).

[153] *Mexico–Tax Measures on Soft Drinks*, WTO Doc. WT/DS/308/AB/R (2006), paras 56 and 78.

breach of GATT 1994 obligations. Instead, the issue before the AB was whether Article XX(d) of the GATT 1994 (which provides that 'nothing in this Agreement shall be construed to prevent the adoption or enforcement by any contracting party of measures [...] necessary to secure compliance with laws or regulations which are not inconsistent with the provisions of this Agreement [...]') excuses WTO-inconsistent measures necessary to secure compliance with non-WTO international agreements, or whether the scope of the exception is limited to securing compliance with *domestic* laws or regulations. In holding that Article XX(d) must be limited to domestic laws and regulations, the AB relied in part on the fact that:

WTO panels and the Appellate Body would have to assume that there is a violation of the relevant international agreement (such as NAFTA) by the complaining party, or they would have to assess whether the relevant international agreement has been violated. WTO panels and the Appellate Body would thus become adjudicators of non-WTO disputes [and...] this is not the function of panels and the Appellate Body as intended by the DSU.[154]

It is the latter determination that may be fatal to an attempt to preclude the wrongfulness of a breach of WTO obligations, within the WTO dispute settlement system, in reliance on the general international law of state responsibility relating to countermeasures. Without a prior determination that there is an initial breach of an international obligation, there is no basis on which to hold responsive measures in breach of WTO obligations to be legitimate countermeasures. As a result, the wrongfulness of WTO-inconsistent measures could not be precluded in reliance on the general international law of state responsibility within the WTO dispute settlement system.

(iii) Justifications for the breach of WTO-covered agreements

The combination of the WTO's exclusive jurisdiction over trade-related disputes[155] and the limitations of that exclusive jurisdiction[156] creates the danger that a state that might otherwise be justified in breaching WTO obligations under general international law in the form of countermeasures may nevertheless be held responsible within the WTO system for that breach. If states are to avoid responsibility within the WTO system for breaching WTO obligations in their responses to internationally wrongful acts related to terrorism, wrongfulness-preclusion must come from within the WTO regime. It remains to consider the justifications or excuses for breach of a primary obligation under the WTO-covered agreements,[157]

---

[154] *Ibid*, para 78.
[155] *Supra* note 139.
[156] See Section 5.2.2(ii).
[157] This section only considers countermeasures in response to breaches of international terrorism obligations. As a result, the justifications or excuses examined are those that might be particularly applicable in justifying measures taken in response to an internationally wrongful act related to terrorism. Regarding the relationship between countermeasures generally and the WTO, see further Trapp (2010).

and whether those justifications or excuses are co-extensive (or even broader) than those provided for under general international law.

Article XXI of the GATT 1994 (the 'security exception') provides a potential excuse for GATT 1994-inconsistent trade measures taken in response to the breach of international terrorism obligations.[158] In particular, paragraph (b)(iii) reads that nothing in the GATT 1994 is to be construed as 'prevent[ing] any contracting party from taking any action which it considers necessary for the protection of its essential security interests [. . .] taken in time of war or other emergency in international relations'.[159] Article XXI is not quite the equivalent of a circumstance precluding wrongfulness under general international law, in that the security exception need not be applied as a *post facto* justification for the breach of a GATT obligation (as do circumstances precluding wrongfulness) because a WTO panel or the AB could determine the applicability of the security exception whether they have determined the trade measure under consideration to be in breach of the GATT 1994 or not. Indeed, there is a fundamental conceptual difference between the security exception and circumstances precluding wrongfulness under general international law. The former is in the form of a primary rule, and if trade measures fall within the scope of the exception, they are not in breach of the primary obligation at all. Circumstances precluding wrongfulness, on the other hand, are distinctly secondary in their application to a prior breach of international law.

Nevertheless, the practice of WTO adjudicative bodies in evaluating the applicability of exceptions under the GATT 1994 is to treat them as a defence to the applicant's claim of a breach of GATT obligations.[160] The Commentaries to the ILC Articles on State Responsibility describe a circumstance precluding wrongfulness as providing 'a shield against *an otherwise well-founded claim for the breach* of an international obligation'.[161] In requesting the establishment of a panel, WTO members must 'identify the specific measures at issue and provide a brief summary of the legal basis of the complaint sufficient to present the problem clearly'[162]—which amounts to a 'well-founded claim for the breach' of a WTO-covered agreement obligation (including obligations under the GATT 1994). As invocation of the security exception provides 'a shield' or defence against such well-founded claims, the security exception establishes, *in effect*, a circumstance precluding wrongfulness under the GATT 1994.

It goes without saying that states consider their security interests to be implicated by state sponsorship or support of terrorism, and the state practice reviewed above

---

[158] Article XIV *bis* of the General Agreement on Trade in Services, Annex to the WTO Agreement, 15 April 1994, 1869 UNTS 183 [hereinafter the 'GATS'] and Article 73 of the Agreement on Trade-Related Aspects of Intellectual Property Rights, Annex 1C to the WTO Agreement, 15 April 1994, 1869 UNTS 299 [hereinafter the 'TRIPS Agreement'] contain similar exceptions to that in Article XXI of the GATT 1994. This section will consider the security exception under the GATT 1994, but the discussion applies equally to the security under the GATS and the TRIPS Agreement.

[159] Art. XXI(b)(iii), GATT 1994.

[160] See e.g. *United States–Wool Shirts and Blouses*, WTO Doc. WT/DS33/AB/R (1997), para 522; *Mexico–Tax Measures on Soft Drinks*, WTO Doc. WT/DS/308/AB/R (2006).

[161] Emphasis added. Commentary to Part One, Chapter V, ILC Articles on State Responsibility, para 1.

[162] Art. 6(2), DSU.

suggests that states often consider trade measures a necessary element of protecting those interests.[163] But the precise scope of the security exception under the GATT 1994, and the degree of deference owed to states in defining their security interests and the measures necessary for their protection, remains unsettled. There is a debate in the literature regarding the justiciability of security exception invocations. While there is nothing in the language of Article XXI of the GATT 1994 to suggest that the legitimacy of its invocation is not subject to judicial review, some commentators have argued that the question of a state's national security is entirely self-judging.[164] There are no GATT 1947 panel reports[165] or decisions by a WTO adjudicative body[166] confirming this interpretation. And while the limited practice under the GATT 1947 and within the WTO suggests that states consider their invocations of the security exception to be unreviewable,[167] the weight of academic authority is to the contrary. Most commentators consider that, at the very least, a state's good faith in invoking the security exception is subject to judicial determination, or that the more objective elements of the exception (in particular the existence of 'war or other emergency in international relations', or whether the trade measure is 'necessary' or the state 'considers it necessary') could be reviewed by a WTO panel or the AB.[168] Indeed, a GATT panel, considering whether it

---

[163] See Section 5.1.4.

[164] See Whitt (1987), 616. See also Schloemann and Ohlhoff (1999), 426.

[165] There is some GATT 1947 state practice of invoking the security exception which did not result in any panel reports. EC, Australian and Canadian trade restrictions adopted against Argentina in response to its invasion of the Falklands were justified by the measure-adopting states under the 'inherent rights of which Article XXI of the General Agreement was a reflection'. Communication by the Commission of the European Communities, *Trade Restrictions Affecting Argentina Applied for Non-Economic Reasons*, GATT Doc. L/5319/Rev.1 (1982). See further Comments by EC, Australian and Canadian delegates regarding trade restrictions against Argentina in response to its invasion of the Falklands, GATT Council, Minutes of Meeting on 7 May 1982, GATT Doc. C/M/157 (1982), 10. See also Tams (2005a), 216, suggesting that the measure-adopting states were not invoking a treaty-specific justification under the GATT 1947, but rather general international law as codified in Article XXI of the GATT 1947. In reference to the EC's invocation of Article XXI of the GATT 1947 to justify the trade measures it adopted against Yugoslavia in 1991, see Communication from the European Communities, *Trade Measures Taken by the European Community against the Socialist Federal Republic of Yugoslavia*, GATT Doc. L/6948 (1991); GATT Council, *EEC–Trade Measures Taken for Non-Economic Reasons—Recourse to Article XXIII:2 by Yugoslavia*, GATT Doc. DS27/2, 18 February 1992; GATT Council, Minutes of Meeting on 30 April 1992, GATT Doc. C/M/256 (1992), 32; GATT Council, Minutes of Meeting on 19 June 1992, GATT Doc. C/M/257 (1992), 3; GATT Council, Minutes of Meeting on 17 June 1993, GATT Doc. C/M/264 (1993), 3. See also GATT, Report of the Panel (unadopted), *United States–Trade Measures Affecting Nicaragua*, GATT Doc. L/6053 (1986), in reference to the US embargo against Nicaragua in 1985.

[166] See <http://www.wto.org/english/res_e/booksp_e/analytic_index_e/gatt1994_08_e.htm#article21B>.

[167] *Supra* note 165. Within the WTO, the US threatened to invoke Article XXI of the GATT 1994 to justify penalties against international companies trading with Cuba, authorized under the US Helms Burton Act, which the EU characterized as a restrictive trade measure in violation of the GATT 1994. The US argued that its invocation of Article XXI would not be reviewable by a WTO Panel. See Jackson and Lowenfeld (1997). Nicaragua made similar arguments regarding its restrictions on imports from Honduras and Colombia. See *Nicaragua—Measures Affecting Imports from Honduras and Colombia—Statements by Nicaragua*, WTO Doc. WT/DSB/COM/5/Rev.1 (2000).

[168] See Hahn (1991), 558–67; Swaak-Goldman (1996); Akande and Williams (2003); Bartels (2004), 871; Simma and Pulkowski (2006), 523, fn. 204; Boisson de Chazournes and Boutruche (2009).

could review an invocation of the security exception if its terms of reference had allowed for it, suggested that review would be permissible.[169] It is widely agreed, however, that a state's determination of its own essential security interests would not be subject to review.[170]

Essential security interests

Subject to the requirements of 'war or other emergency in international relations' and 'necessity' discussed below, the broad discretion states might have in determining their own essential security interests results in a greater freedom to adopt trade-related responses to international terrorist attacks under the GATT 1994 than under the general international law related to countermeasures. This is because a state's discretion to determine its own security interests (and whether those interests are in need of protection) under the security exception is not limited to situations in which there is an initial breach of international law by the target state. Under general international law, a state that considered its security interests to be endangered by the conduct of another state could not legitimately adopt countermeasures unless the target state had breached its international obligations toward the countermeasure-adopting state.[171]

Consider, for instance, a state's failure to prevent part of its territory from being used as a base of terrorist operations, where such failure is not due to a want of diligence on the part of the territorial state (but is rather due to an absence of capacity).[172] The territorial state would not be responsible under general international law for an internationally wrongful act, and countermeasures could not legitimately be adopted against it. It is certainly conceivable, however, that a state victim of terrorist attacks launched from the territorial state would consider it necessary to impose import restrictions on goods originating from the territory from which the terrorist organization operates (to limit the resources available to the terrorist organization).[173] Such import restrictions between WTO members, even though targeted, would amount to a violation of Articles XI and XIII of the GATT 1994. While the wrongfulness of these measures would not be precluded

---

[169] The panel decision under the GATT 1947, in reference to the US trade embargo against Nicaragua in 1985, took care to suggest that it considered invocations of the security exception reviewable: '[i]f it were accepted that the interpretation of Article XXI was reserved entirely to the contracting party invoking it, how could the Contracting Parties ensure that this general exception to all obligations under the General Agreement is not invoked excessively or for purposes other than those set out in this provision?' GATT, Report of the Panel (unadopted), *United States–Trade Measures Affecting Nicaragua*, GATT Doc. L/6053 (1986), para 5.17. The Panels' terms of reference precluded it from examining the US invocation of Article XXI to justify its embargo against Nicaragua. *Ibid*, para 5.3.

[170] See e.g. Hahn (1991), 580, 597; Swaak-Goldman (1996), 367, 369; Schloemann and Ohlhoff (1999); Akande and Williams (2003), 396–9.

[171] Art. 49, ILC Articles on State Responsibility. See also *Gabčíkovo–Nagymaros Project (Hungary v. Slovakia)*, Judgment, 55, para 83: Countermeasures only preclude wrongfulness when they are 'taken in response to a previous international wrongful act of another State and [. . .] directed against that State'.

[172] See Section 3.1.2.

[173] Consider, for instance, the targeted sanctions imposed by the Security Council, including in relation to the trade of arms and military assistance, to Taliban-controlled territory (rather than to the whole of Afghan territory). See e.g. UNSC Resolution 1333 (2000), para 5.

under the general international law of countermeasures because of the absence of an internationally wrongful act on the part of the target state,[174] the WTO-inconsistent measures could be excused under the security exception of the GATT 1994 because there is no requirement that conduct posing a security risk *also* amount to a breach of international law.

Furthermore, the broad discretion states enjoy in defining their own essential security interests affects the permissibility of collective measures in response to internationally wrongful acts related to terrorism. Under the security exception, third party states may well have more freedom to adopt trade measures (in breach of GATT obligations) against a terrorist-sponsoring or supporting state than they would under the general international law relating to countermeasures. This is because there is no limitation under Article XXI of the GATT 1994 to the effect that the essential security interests of only injured states can form the basis of an invocation of the security exception. Indeed, the security exception is invocable in response to an 'emergency in international relations', which provides a broad basis of justification. At least Western states consider Article XXI to be invocable generally, and not merely by the injured state (if there is one), in response to breaches of the peace.[175] The lawfulness of collective countermeasures taken in response to violations of international terrorism obligations is, however, unsettled. While Article 48 of the ILC Articles on State Responsibility allows for an invocation of responsibility by any state in the case of the breach of an obligation *erga omnes*, there is no international consensus on whether non-injured states have a right to implement such responsibility through the adoption of countermeasures.[176]

War or other emergency in international relations
One element of the security exception that a WTO adjudicative body might be called on to review is whether a 'war or other emergency in international relations' exists.[177]

---

[174] The wrongfulness of the measures might, however, be precluded under Article 25 of the ILC Articles on State Responsibility (Necessity). See Section 5.1.3.

[175] In reference to the Balkan war and EC trade measures adopted under Article XXI of the GATT 1947 against Yugoslavia, see Communication from the European Communities, *Trade Measures Taken by the European Community against the Socialist Federal Republic of Yugoslavia*, GATT Doc. L/6948 (1991). In reference to trade measures adopted against Argentina by the EC, Australia and Canada, in response to Argentina's invasion of the Falklands, see Communication by the Commission of the European Communities, *Trade Restrictions Affecting Argentina Applied for Non-Economic Reasons*, GATT Doc. L/5319/Rev.1 (1982). Some GATT 1947 contracting parties questioned whether EC member states (other than the UK), Australia and Canada could legitimately invoke Article XXI of the GATT 1947 as justification for trade measures against Argentina, but the matter was not settled by a GATT panel. See Comments by EC, Australian and Canadian delegates regarding trade restrictions against Argentina in response to its invasion of the Falklands, GATT Council, Minutes of Meeting on 7 May 1982, GATT Doc. C/M/157(1982), 5 (Brazil), 6 (Spain).

[176] See Commentary to Art. 54, ILC Articles on State Responsibility. See also Section 5.1.2(iii).

[177] Art. XXI, GATT 1994 reads that nothing in the GATT 1994 is to be construed as 'prevent[ing] any contracting party from taking any action which it considers necessary for the protection of its essential security interests [. . .] taken in time of war or other emergency in international relations'. See Bartels (2004), 871, arguing that the existence of a state of war or other emergency in international relations is subject to objective determination. See also Akande and Williams (2003), 399–402; Emmerson (2008), 146.

Some authors have argued that 'other emergency in international relations' should be interpreted as the situation in international relations created by the breach of an international obligation giving rise to the right to take countermeasures.[178] As a result, the right to take countermeasures under the general international law of state responsibility, and the right to take measures in breach of GATT obligations in reliance on the security exception, would be co-extensive. This would be a very tidy answer to the possibility of a fragmented approach to circumstances precluding wrongfulness under the general international law of state responsibility and the GATT 1994, but it would unduly restrict the scope of Article XXI(b)(iii) of the GATT 1994. The right to invoke the security exception under the GATT 1994 is not conditioned on a prior breach of international law, as is the right to take countermeasures under the law of state responsibility. Any effort to force symmetry of application between circumstances precluding wrongfulness under general international law and the GATT 1994 security exception therefore has the potential to restrict the scope of application of Article XXI(b)(iii).

In any case, such a reading of the security exception is not necessary in the terrorism context, because it is self-evident that state sponsorship or support for acts of international terrorism amounts to an 'emergency in international relations' in response to which trade-restrictive measures could, subject to the requirement of necessity discussed below, be justified under the security exception. As a result, in so far as the condition of 'war or other emergency in international relations' is concerned, the permissibility of trade measures in breach of GATT obligations in response to internationally wrongful acts related to terrorism is at least co-extensive with that under the general international law of state responsibility. In fact, the permissibility of GATT-inconsistent measures under the security exception is likely broader in so far as an emergency in international relations could equally cover circumstances in which a state has failed to prevent its territory from being used as a base of international terrorist operations, but that failure does not amount to an internationally wrongful act for the purposes of adopting countermeasures under the law of state responsibility.[179]

Necessity

Article XXI(b)(iii) of the GATT 1994 entitles states to adopt potentially WTO-inconsistent measures 'which it considers necessary for the protection of its essential security interests'. A WTO adjudicative body might review the necessity of a particular trade measure to protect essential security interests. As with the security exception in general, commentators are divided on whether the necessity of measures should be reviewable by a WTO panel or the AB. Some argue that a WTO adjudicative body should make its own assessment of the extent to which the relevant trade measure is necessary to protect essential security interests (as defined

---

[178] See Kuilwijk (1997), 54. See also Hahn (1991), 589–602. But see Pons (1999), 98–9, arguing that there is no need to broaden the scope of Art. XXI(b)(iii), GATT 1994 beyond security-related incidents, because the use of trade measures in response to breaches of general international law fall outside the scope of the GATT and the WTO system.

[179] *Supra* notes 171–3 and accompanying text.

by the respondent state).[180] Other commentators consider that the language of Article XXI(b)(iii), in particular that a state may adopt measures 'which *it considers necessary* for the protection of its essential security interests',[181] suggests that a WTO adjudicative body should only consider whether the state in fact believed that the measures were necessary (leaving assessment of the actual necessity of the measure to the judgment of the measure-adopting state).[182] Again there is no WTO jurisprudence on the question, but the ICJ's decision in *Nicaragua* supports the latter position. In *Nicaragua*, the ICJ distinguished the security exception in the US–Nicaragua FCN from that contained in Article XXI(b)(iii) of the GATT 1947 on the basis that the former requires that measures *be* necessary for the protection of security interests, while the latter requires only that the state party *considers* the measures to be necessary. Given this distinction, the ICJ suggested that the question of necessity under Article XXI(b)(iii) of the GATT 1947 is 'purely a question for the subjective judgment of the party'.[183]

Assuming *arguendo* that a WTO adjudicative body would interpret its competence to review the necessity of measures taken in protection of essential security interests rather more broadly than suggested by the ICJ, it might rely on the approach it has taken to necessity in reference to the general exception under Article XX(b) of the GATT 1994. Article XX(b) provides, in relevant part, that 'nothing in [the GATT 1994] shall be construed to prevent the adoption or enforcement by any contracting party of measures [...] necessary to protect human, animal or plant life or health'. WTO panels and the AB have held measures to be necessary 'if an alternative measure which [a member] could reasonably be expected to employ and which is not inconsistent with other GATT provisions is [not] available to it'.[184] The AB has attenuated the strict effect of the WTO-consistent alternative measures test through the elaboration of two further considerations which (i) account for 'whether [the] alternative measure [...] would achieve the same end' as the measure in fact adopted;[185] and (ii) balance the strictness of the test against the importance of the values being protected.[186] The AB has further clarified that a measure will be considered necessary to the extent of the contribution it makes to the achievement of its objective and that a 'contribution exists when there is a genuine relationship of ends and means between the objective pursued and the measure at issue'.[187]

---

[180] See e.g. Schloemann and Ohlhoff (1999), 443; Emmerson (2008), 146; Boisson de Chazournes and Boutruche (2009), 700.

[181] Emphasis added. Art. XXI(b)(iii), GATT 1994.

[182] See Akande and Williams (2003), 389. See also Bartels (2004), 871; Simma and Pulkowski (2006), 524, fn. 204.

[183] *Nicaragua (Nicaragua v. US)*, Merits, 141, para 282.

[184] *EC–Asbestos*, WTO Doc. WT/DS135/AB/R (2001). See also *Thailand–Cigarettes*, GATT Doc. DS10/R - 37S/200 (1990), paras 73 and 75.

[185] *EC–Asbestos*, WTO Doc. WT/DS135/AB/R (2001), para 172. See also *Brazil–Retreaded Tyres*, WTO Doc. WT/DS332/AB/R (2007), para 178.

[186] *EC–Asbestos*, WTO Doc. WT/DS135/AB/R (2001). paras 170–2, quoting *Korea–Beef*, WTO Doc. WT/DS161/AB/R (2001), paras 163–6. See also *Brazil–Retreaded Tyres*, WTO Doc. WT/DS332/AB/R (2007), para 178.

[187] See *Brazil–Retreaded Tyres*, WTO Doc. WT/DS332/AB/R (2007), para 210. See also Marceau and Trachtman (2009), 217.

If a WTO adjudicative body adopts the 'WTO-consistent alternative measure' test to necessity set out above, the justification for GATT-inconsistent trade measures provided for under the security exception may well be narrower than circumstances precluding wrongfulness under the general international law of state responsibility. Under general international law, as long as the purpose of the countermeasure is to bring pressure to bear on the wrongdoing state, and the countermeasure is not clearly disproportionate to the initial harm suffered (taking into account the importance of the rule breached by the target state and the seriousness of that breach),[188] a countermeasure is likely to be considered legitimate.[189] The 'WTO-consistent alternative measures' test set out above, however, is not dissimilar from the circumstance precluding wrongfulness of 'necessity' examined in Section 5.1.3, which was drafted to be very restrictive.[190] The possibility of accounting for the importance of the interests being protected through the WTO-inconsistent measures may afford some flexibility, but it is far from clear how a WTO adjudicative body would balance terrorism-related interests against those of trade liberalization in assessing necessity under the security exception. In addition, the requirement of a 'genuine relationship' between the objective pursued and the measure adopted[191] is more restrictive than what is required of a legitimate countermeasure. As noted above, the test for what amounts to a legitimate countermeasure is purposive. The AB's 'genuine relationship' test, however, suggests that unless a measure bore some relationship to terrorism-related obligations, it would not be considered 'necessary' under the WTO general exceptions. If the WTO were to apply the 'genuine relationship' test to the security exception, measures that would be legitimate countermeasures under general international law would be wrongful as a matter of WTO law.

(iv) Relationship between wrongfulness preclusion under the GATT 1994 and under the general international law of state responsibility

Under the security exception, states can adopt measures that are inconsistent with GATT obligations in response to international terrorism—whether or not the relevant terrorist incident results from the breach of an international obligation by the target state, and whether or not the measure-adopting states are 'injured states' within the meaning of Article 42 of the ILC Articles on State Responsibility. The 'at your own risk' element of countermeasures, which requires an accurate assessment of a wrongdoing state's responsibility, and the uncertainty regarding the legitimacy of collective countermeasures, is therefore absent in the WTO context. As a result, the justificatory power of the security exception is potentially broader than the general international law of state responsibility on countermeasures, subject to the WTO's approach to necessity. A narrow approach to the necessity

---

[188] See Commentary to Art. 51, ILC Articles on State Responsibility, para 6.
[189] *Ibid*, para 7. See also Section 5.1.2(ii).
[190] See Commentary to Art. 25, ILC Articles on State Responsibility.
[191] *Supra* note 187.

of GATT-inconsistent measures under the security exception would restrict the scope of its wrongfulness-preclusion, more so than under the general international law related to countermeasures. The possibility therefore remains that a state that would be justified in breaching WTO obligations in the form of countermeasures under general international law would nevertheless be held responsible within the WTO system for that breach. WTO members may have (deliberately or unwittingly) prioritized trade in a way that limits available responses to breaches of international terrorism obligations.

To the extent that a WTO-inconsistent measure, adopted in response to an internationally wrongful act related to terrorism, can be justified or excused in reliance on the security exception under the GATT 1994, the measure is not in breach of an international obligation. As a result, the measure is not itself an internationally wrongful act and amounts to an act of retorsion whose wrongfulness need not be precluded in reliance on the secondary rules of state responsibility.

5.2.3 International Civil Aviation Organization

The International Civil Aviation Organization ('ICAO'), a specialized UN agency, is the global forum for civil aviation. Its primary purpose is to coordinate international efforts to achieve the safe, secure and sustainable development of civil aviation.[192] The Chicago Convention sets out the constitutional framework of the ICAO, the general regime of air navigation between state parties (including rights of over-flight, measures to facilitate air navigation and best practices), and provides for a dispute settlement mechanism. Disputes under the Chicago Convention between state parties may be submitted to the ICAO Council (on application of one of the parties), with a right of appeal to the ICJ.[193] In the case of a state's non-compliance with a decision of the ICAO Council, the defaulting state's voting rights in the ICAO Assembly and ICAO Council 'shall' be suspended.[194]

The jurisdiction of the ICAO Council over civil aviation disputes falling within the terms of the Chicago Convention (for instance, disputes arising out of the suspension of air services in breach of the Chicago Convention taken in response to a prior violation of international terrorism obligations) is, unlike the jurisdiction of the WTO adjudicative bodies, non-exclusive. In addition, there are no limitations on the law applicable by the ICAO Council in its consideration of a dispute.[195] As such, the self-containedness of the ICAO regime is limited, and there is no real danger that a state responding to the breach of an international terrorism obligation through the suspension of air service obligations under the Chicago Convention (in

---

[192]   See <http://www.icao.int/icao/en/strategic_objectives.htm>.
[193]   Art. 84, Chicago Convention.
[194]   Art. 88, Chicago Convention.
[195]   In reference to a dispute between India and Pakistan (discussed in Section 5.2.3), the ICAO Council considered India's argument that its obligations under the Chicago Convention and the International Air Services Transit Agreement (1944) had been suspended *vis à vis* Pakistan in virtue of Pakistan's breach of obligations outside the Chicago Convention regime (in particular the Tokyo and Hague Conventions).

the form of a legitimate countermeasure) could be held responsible for that breach within the ICAO system when it would not be held responsible under the general international law of state responsibility.

There was a movement in the 1970s, however, to increase the self-containedness of the ICAO regime, particularly as regards the ICAO Terrorism Suppression Conventions.[196] With the rising number of hijackings and offences against the safety of civil aviation, there was an increasing perception within the ICAO membership that the Hague and Montreal Conventions were inadequate to their purpose. The principal concern expressed by states was the failure of the ICAO TSCs to provide for enforcement mechanisms in the event of breach.[197] While both the Montreal and Hague Convention have compromissory clauses conferring jurisdiction on the ICJ in the event of a dispute as to their interpretation or application, judicial settlement of disputes was apparently not considered a sufficient 'enforcement mechanism'. This position fails to appreciate the potential role of determinations by the ICJ in giving effect to state responsibility for international terrorism (as explored in Chapter 4). Nevertheless, the ICAO Legal Committee was asked to consider either an international convention (or an amendment to existing conventions) to provide a basis for ICAO member states to take collective measures in the case of a state's failure to respond appropriately to an unlawful seizure of a civil aircraft, and to propose an amendment to bilateral air transport agreements conferring authority to participate in such measures against any state breaching its international terrorism obligations with respect to civil aviation.[198] A number of proposals were put before the Legal Committee for consideration. While ultimately not adopted, the proposed amendments address the broader issues with the law on countermeasures examined in Section 5.1.2 (in particular the 'at your own risk' element of countermeasures and the uncertainty regarding the legitimacy of collective countermeasures), and provide an illustration of the potential of sub-systems of international law to resolve difficulties in the application of—while remaining flexible in their interaction with—general international law.

(i) Proposals for the collective enforcement of the ICAO Terrorism Suppression Conventions

The first proposal providing for the collective enforcement of the ICAO TSCs was a draft convention put forward by the US and Canada.[199] The draft convention provided, in the first instance, for an impartial determination of the facts. The proposal empowered an interested state (which was not limited to an injured state)

---

[196] The Hague and Montreal Conventions, which were adopted under the auspices of the ICAO, are independent treaties that do not form part of the Chicago Convention regime and are not subject to the dispute settlement mechanism therein.

[197] See ICAO Council, Resolution of 1 October 1970, ICAO Doc. 8923-C/998 (1970).

[198] *Ibid.*

[199] The draft was supported by Australia, Italy, the Netherlands, New Zealand, Nicaragua, and the UK. See ICAO Legal Committee, 20th Session (Special), 9–30 January 1973, Documents, ICAO Doc. 9050-LC/169–2 (1973), 265.

to convene a fact-finding commission if it believed that another state was harbouring hijackers or other persons who had committed offences against the safety of civil aviation.[200] In the event the fact-finding commission determined that the investigated state was indeed harbouring such persons, interested states could then decide on the appropriate collective action. Under the proposal, states in respect of whose conduct a fact-finding commission could be convened were not limited to state parties to the ICAO TSCs. As a result, states that were not under any primary obligation to extradite or submit to prosecution pursuant to the ICAO TSCs might—under the terms of the US and Canadian proposal—still be the subject of an investigation.

A second proposal for the collective enforcement of the ICAO TSCs was an amendment to the Chicago Convention, for the purposes of enforcing ICAO TSCs, put forward jointly by the UK and Switzerland.[201] The crux of the proposal was (i) to insert the basic obligations of the Hague and Montreal Conventions (in particular the obligation of prevention and the *aut dedere aut judicare* obligation) into the Chicago Convention and (ii) to amend the dispute settlement and enforcement mechanisms of the Chicago Convention such that the ICAO Council could require all ICAO member states to refuse the operation of any airline registered to a state that the Council had determined was in violation of its Hague or Montreal Convention obligations. Article 87 of the Chicago Convention requires contracting states to suspend an *airline's* right to fly over its territory in the event the ICAO Council determines that the *airline* is not conforming to a final decision of the Council. The UK and Switzerland proposed that an equivalent sanction be provided for in the Chicago Convention to be applied against a *state* that is held not to be conforming to a final decision of the Council (in particular as regards the breach of Hague or Montreal Convention obligations). The result of the proposal would be to provide for sanctions in response to breaches of the Hague or Montreal Conventions that would not themselves breach bilateral air services agreements between the sanction-adopting and wrongdoing states, given the provision for this type of measure within the Chicago Convention framework.[202] France subsequently joined the UK and Switzerland in their proposal, and their revised joint submission contained a fact-finding element, in that a commission would be created to investigate violations of the obligations set out in the Hague and Montreal Conventions.[203]

Finally, a third proposal was put forward by the Nordic states in the form of a draft convention[204] which empowered the ICAO Council to make binding deter-

---

[200] See ICAO Legal Committee, 18th Session, Report, ICAO Doc. 8910-LC/163 (1970), Part III, Annex 2.

[201] See ICAO Legal Committee, 20th Session, Summary report of the work of the Legal Committee, ICAO Doc. 9049-LC/168 (1973), Part II, Annex 3, 53–5.

[202] *Ibid*, Part II, Annex 6, 65.

[203] ICAO Assembly, 20th Session Extraordinary, Sub-amendment to the Amendment of the Chicago Convention, proposed by the Delegations of France, Switzerland and the United Kingdom, ICAO Doc. A20-WP/5 (1973).

[204] ICAO Legal Committee, 20th Session, Summary report of the work of the Legal Committee, ICAO Doc. 9049-LC/168 (1973), Part II, Annex 4, 57.

minations of fact with regard to breaches of the Hague or Montreal Conventions, but did not provide for sanctions if the Council determined that the accused state was in default of its ICAO TSC obligations. The proposal did allow for the convening of a conference to make recommendations regarding further measures if the ICAO Council determination of a breach (and the international embarrassment associated therewith) was not sufficient to bring the wrongdoing state into compliance with its ICAO TSC obligations.

(ii) *Broader concerns regarding the general international law on countermeasures addressed in the ICAO TSC enforcement proposals*

The proposals put before the Legal Committee on the enforcement of ICAO TSCs addressed a number of broader concerns regarding the right under general international law to adopt countermeasures against a wrongdoing state. The first and most obvious concern addressed by the proposals bears on a state's authority to determine for itself that there has been a breach of an international terrorism obligation. Each of the proposals sought to establish an independent fact-finding capacity within the ICAO—whether through a commission of experts, or by using the ICAO Council—to determine 'objectively' whether or not a state was in violation of its international terrorism obligations under the Hague and Montreal Conventions. While two Special Rapporteurs on State Responsibility argued that attempts to judicially settle a dispute should be a condition for the adoption of countermeasures,[205] the ILC Articles on State Responsibility ultimately left any evaluation of the internationally wrongful character of an act to the appreciation of the injured state. The ILC Articles on State Responsibility make it clear that an injured state adopts countermeasures at its own risk (if it is mistaken in considering the target state's conduct to be internationally wrongful),[206] and the proposals before the ICAO Legal Committee effectively sought to minimize that risk.

The second concern reflected in the proposals touches on the legitimacy of collective responses to internationally wrongful conduct. All three proposals attempted to legitimize the adoption of collective measures in response to the breach of ICAO terrorism obligations, albeit in slightly different ways. The US/Canadian and Nordic proposals sought legitimacy in a collective or institutionalized decision-making process. Both proposals avoided the 'at your own risk' element of countermeasures through a mechanism for third party determination of a breach of the ICAO TSCs, and sought to minimize the dangers of chaos and vigilantism resulting from the availability of collective countermeasures[207] by formalizing the decision-making process in regard to a collective response. The Nordic proposal attempted to institutionalize decision-making in a conference setting, whereas the US/Canadian proposal appeared to suggest a more *ad hoc* form of collective decision-making, but both required a response to the breach of ICAO TSC obligations to be

---

[205] *Supra* notes 25–6.
[206] *Supra* note 20 and accompanying text.
[207] *Supra* note 51.

genuinely collective. The often-raised danger in reference to collective counter-measures as a matter of general international law is that they might be used by individual states as a cover for aggressive conduct under the guise of law enforce-ment in the collective interest. Institutional or collective decision-making has certainly been proposed as a means of limiting that danger,[208] and the proposals for ICAO enforcement mechanisms tap into the potential of truly collective enforcement, as distinct from unilateral enforcement in the subjectively-deter-mined interests of the collective. The UK and Switzerland equally sought to institutionalize collective responses, but their proposal went beyond those of the US, Canada and Nordic countries. Effectively, the UK/Swiss proposal provided for an institutionalized mechanism that transformed legitimate countermeasures in the field of air services arrangements into acts of retorsion.[209] Through a collective decision-making process (using the ICAO Council), measures adopted against a state found to be in breach of its ICAO TSC obligations would have been truly collective in that they would have been decided on by a representative body, and would have been obligatory for all member states of the ICAO. The provision for an institutionalized decision-making process and a mandatory collective response within the ICAO framework (such that the suspension of air services obligations in response to a breach of ICAO TSC obligations would not in itself be an interna-tionally wrongful act because it would be sanctioned within the ICAO regime) responds to the difficult issues raised by the availability of collective counter-measures under general international law identified in Section 5.1.2(iii) above.

These rather elegant solutions to the potential for abuse inherent in a decen-tralized system of law enforcement were not adopted, principally because there was no consensus on whether states should give prior consent to the possibility of sanctions being imposed against them. A number of states insisted that any draft convention or amendment to the Chicago Convention providing for third party fact determination or the imposition of sanctions should only apply *inter partes*— that is to say that a fact-finding commission should not be instituted or measures adopted against a wrongdoing state unless it too was a party to the new convention or Chicago Convention amendment.[210] As some of the proposals would have had the effect of allowing for the investigation of, or adoption of measures against, states that were either not bound by the relevant Terrorism Suppression Convention or had not signed on to the new enforcement mechanisms, consensus within the ICAO proved impossible. Despite the ultimate failure of the effort to create a sub-system of international law that both elaborated primary obligations and provided

[208] *Supra* note 52.

[209] The Canadian delegation had proposed language that could be added in amendment to bilateral services agreements, which would justify the breach of those agreements as against states providing sanctuary to aerial terrorists, and would have achieved the same objective as that pursued in the UK/Swiss proposal. ICAO Legal Committee, 18th Session, Report, ICAO Doc. 8910-LC/163 (1970), Part III, Annex 5.

[210] ICAO Legal Committee, 20th Session, Summary report of the work of the Legal Committee, ICAO Doc. 9049-LC/168 (1973), Part II, Annex 2, 42; ICAO Legal Committee, 20th Session (Special), 9–30 January 1973, Minutes, ICAO Doc. 9050-LC/169–1 (1973), 50.

for collective measures to be adopted against wrongdoing states in the event of their breach (thereby precluding the wrongfulness of those measures within the sub-system and transforming them into acts of retorsion from the perspective of general international law), it remains an excellent illustration of the potential for sub-systems of international law to address the difficulties inherent in the application of the general international law of countermeasures identified in Section 5.1.2 above. The following section examines a particular example of a dispute regarding the suspension of air service obligations in response to the breach of international terrorism obligations related to civil aviation, bearing in mind the potential of the proposals set out above to have contributed to the peaceful resolution of the dispute.

(iii) Dispute between India and Pakistan (1971)

On 30 January 1971, an Indian Airlines aircraft was hijacked on an internal flight between Srinagar and Jammu by Kashmiri militants.[211] The flight was diverted to Lahore, Pakistan by the militants, where the crew and passengers were released unharmed. The hijackers remained on board the aircraft for several days and then destroyed the aircraft with explosives India alleged had been provided to them by Pakistani officials.[212] After a period of hospitalization in Lahore, the hijackers were released without charge.[213] India invoked Pakistan's responsibility for the destruction of the aircraft, the failure to apprehend and punish the hijackers,[214] and its alleged support for the hijackers, and claimed damages in respect of the destroyed aircraft.[215] India initially characterized Pakistan's conduct as a breach of its obligations under the Tokyo and Hague Conventions.[216] As Pakistan was not a party to either the Tokyo or Hague Conventions at the time of the hijacking,[217] India subsequently characterized the conduct as in breach of the Chicago Convention and International Air Services Transit Agreement (1944).[218]

---

[211] Keesing's, Vol. 17, April 1971, 24561.

[212] *Ibid.*

[213] *Ibid.*

[214] Pakistan refused India's request that the hijackers be surrendered for trial in India. See Letter from the High Commission of India in Pakistan, Islamabad, to the Ministry of Foreign Affairs, Government of Pakistan, dated 5 February 1971, reprinted in *Appeal Relating to the Jurisdiction of the ICAO Council (India v. Pakistan)*, Indian Memorial, Attachment C, 79.

[215] Letter from the High Commission of India in Pakistan, Islamabad, to the Ministry of Foreign Affairs, Government of Pakistan, dated 3 February 1971, reprinted in *Appeal Relating to the Jurisdiction of the ICAO Council (India v. Pakistan)*, Indian Memorial, Attachment C, 77.

[216] Letter from the Ministry of External Affairs, New Delhi to the High Commission of Pakistan in India, dated 9 February 1971, reprinted in *Appeal Relating to the Jurisdiction of the ICAO Council (India v. Pakistan)*, Indian Memorial, Attachment C, 82, 83.

[217] See <http://www.icao.int/icao/en/leb/Hague.pdf>; <http://www.icao.int/icao/en/leb/Tokyo.pdf>.

[218] India did not specify which obligations under the Chicago Convention or the International Air Services Transit Agreement, 7 December 1944, ICAO Doc. 7500, were violated by Pakistan's alleged support for the hijacking and the aircraft's subsequent destruction, and instead used vague language to claim that Pakistan's alleged support 'was most reprehensible and amounted to the very negation of all the aims and objectives, the scheme and provisions, of the Chicago Convention and of the International Air Services Transit Agreement'. Preliminary Objections to the Jurisdiction of the ICAO Council by the Government of India under Article 5 of the Rules for the Settlement of Differences Approved by the Council of the International Civil Aviation Organization on 9 April 1957, dated

India and Pakistan were both parties to the Chicago Convention and the International Air Services Transit Agreement (1944). In the absence of an immediate response by Pakistan to its demand for damages, India informed Pakistan that it had 'decided to suspend, with immediate effect, the over-flight of all Pakistani aircraft, civil or military, over the territory of India' and explained that the decision was 'taken in the hope that the Government of Pakistan will settle [the] matter amicably and peacefully without delay'.[219]

Pakistan disputed both the facts alleged by India, and the measures adopted by India in response thereto. Pakistan emphasized in particular the efforts it had made to negotiate with the hijackers to release the crew and passengers, and their consequent safe return to India under Pakistani escort.[220] In reference to the destruction of the aircraft, Pakistan claimed that it was 'in no way responsible for the [...] blowing up of the plane by desperate Kashmiri young men' and considered India's charge of its complicity to be completely baseless.[221] Pakistan did not generally address India's claim that it had failed to apprehend and punish the hijackers. As Pakistan denied any responsibility for the hijacking and the subsequent destruction of the Indian Airlines aircraft, it considered India's suspension of over-flights to be in breach of several international agreements to which both India and Pakistan were a party:[222] the Chicago Convention, a bilateral air agreement between India and Pakistan, and the International Air Services Transit Agreement (1944). The Chicago Convention permits operation of international scheduled air services over the territory of a contracting state;[223] the bilateral Air Agreement between India and Pakistan (1948) permitted Pakistan's scheduled air services to over-fly India and Indian planes to over-fly Pakistan;[224] and under the

---

28 May 1971, ICAO Doc. SG 602/71, LE 6/1 (1971), 99, para 6; *Appeal Relating to the Jurisdiction of the ICAO Council (India v. Pakistan)*, Indian Memorial, 33.

[219] Letter from the High Commission of India in Pakistan, Islamabad, to the Ministry of Foreign Affairs, Government of Pakistan, dated 4 February 1971, reprinted in *Appeal Relating to the Jurisdiction of the ICAO Council (India v. Pakistan)*, Indian Memorial, Attachment C, 78. India warned that the ban on Pakistan's flights over India's territory would not be lifted unless Pakistan accepted India's demand for compensation for the destruction of its aircraft. See Attachment B to the Memorial of the Government of Pakistan under Article 2 of the Rules of Procedure Approved by the Council on 9 April 1957, reprinted in *Appeal Relating to the Jurisdiction of the ICAO Council (India v. Pakistan)*, Indian Memorial, 72, para 5.

[220] *Ibid*, 72, paras 8–9.

[221] *Ibid*, 73, para 11. See also Letter from the Ministry of Foreign Affairs, Government of Pakistan, to the High Commission of India in Pakistan, Islamabad, dated 5 February 1971, reprinted in *Appeal Relating to the Jurisdiction of the ICAO Council (India v. Pakistan)*, Indian Memorial, Attachment C, 80, para 2; Letter from the Ministry of Foreign Affairs, Islamabad to the High Commission of India in Pakistan, Islamabad, dated 13 February 1971, reprinted in *Appeal Relating to the Jurisdiction of the ICAO Council (India v. Pakistan)*, Indian Memorial, Attachment C, 85, para 3.

[222] Letter from the Ministry of Foreign Affairs, Islamabad to the High Commission of India in Pakistan, Islamabad, dated 13 February 1971, reprinted in *Appeal Relating to the Jurisdiction of the ICAO Council (India v. Pakistan)*, Indian Memorial, Attachment C, 80, para 4. India claimed that all three agreements had been suspended or terminated as between the Parties. *Infra* note 230.

[223] Art. 5, Chicago Convention

[224] Art. I, Agreement between the Government of India and the Government of Pakistan Relating to Air Services (with Annex and Exchange of Notes), New Delhi, 23 June 1948, reprinted in *Appeal Relating to the Jurisdiction of the ICAO Council (India v. Pakistan)*, Indian Memorial, 110.

International Air Services Transit Agreement (1944), each state party grants other state parties 'two freedoms' of air in respect of scheduled international service: (i) to fly across its territory without landing (the right of over-flight); and (ii) to land for non-traffic purposes.[225] Had India suspended flights without justification, it would have done so in breach of all three international agreements. As a result, the Government of Pakistan 'request[ed] the Government of India to rescind its decision to ban the over-flights of Pakistan aircraft and invite[d] it to have recourse to established diplomatic procedures so as to allow the situation to return to normal',[226] which request was ignored.

Pakistan initiated proceedings against India for its breach of international air services obligations before the ICAO Council, in accordance with the dispute settlement procedure under the Chicago Convention,[227] and reserved the right to claim compensation for damage it incurred as a result of the breach.[228] A key element of Pakistan's claim was that the measures adopted by India (in violation of the Chicago Convention and international air services agreements) bore no relation to (and could therefore not be justified on the basis of) a hijacking from Indian-occupied territory to Pakistan.[229] India's response to the complaint was to object to the ICAO's jurisdiction to settle the matter, on the basis that the Chicago Convention and International Air Services Transit Agreement (1944) had been terminated or at least suspended as between India and Pakistan and could not form the basis of the Council's jurisdiction.[230] The Council rejected India's arguments and

---

[225] Art. I, International Air Services Transit Agreement (1944).

[226] Letter from the Ministry of Foreign Affairs, Islamabad to the High Commission of India in Pakistan, Islamabad, dated 13 February 1971, reprinted in *Appeal Relating to the Jurisdiction of the ICAO Council (India v. Pakistan)*, Indian Memorial, Attachment C, 81, para 7.

[227] Pakistan requested the Council to determine that India's suspension of over-flights was in violation of its international obligations under the Chicago Convention and the air services agreements; to declare that it had a right of over-flight; and to (should it wish) order India to pay compensation. Pakistan's Complaint to ICAO Council dated 3 March 1971, ICAO Doc. SG 588/71, LE 4/1.1 (1971), 97.

[228] Letter from the Ministry of Foreign Affairs, Islamabad to the High Commission of India in Pakistan, Islamabad, dated 13 February 1971, reprinted in *Appeal Relating to the Jurisdiction of the ICAO Council (India v. Pakistan)*, Indian Memorial, Attachment C, 86, para 5.

[229] Complaint of the Government of Pakistan to the ICAO Council filed under Articles 2 and 21 of the Rules for the Settlement of Differences Approved by the Council of the International Civil Aviation Organization on 9 April 1957, dated 3 March 1971, ICAO Doc. SG 588/71, LE 4/1.11 (1971), 95, para 5. See also Letter from the Ministry of Foreign Affairs, Islamabad to the High Commission of India in Pakistan, Islamabad, dated 13 February 1971, reprinted in *Appeal Relating to the Jurisdiction of the ICAO Council (India v. Pakistan)*, Indian Memorial, Attachment C, 86, para 5, making the same argument.

[230] See Preliminary Objections to the Jurisdiction of the ICAO Council by the Government of India under Article 5 of the Rules for the Settlement of Differences Approved by the Council of the International Civil Aviation Organization on 9 April 1957, dated 28 May 1971, ICAO Doc. SG 602/71, LE 6/1 (1971), 106, paras 29–39; ICAO Council, 74th Session, Minutes of the second meeting, 27 July 1971, ICAO Doc. 8956-c/1001, C-Min. LXXIV/2 (1971), reprinted in *Appeal Relating to the Jurisdiction of the ICAO Council (India v. Pakistan)*, Indian Memorial, Annex E, 138, 154–9, paras 41–91. See also ICAO Council, 74th Session, Minutes of the third meeting, 27 July 1971, ICAO Doc. 8956-c/1001, C-Min. LXXIV/3 (1971), reprinted in *Appeal Relating to the Jurisdiction of the ICAO Council (India v. Pakistan)*, Indian Memorial Annex E, 172, 177, para 31. By arguing that the relevant conventions were suspended, India was justifying its measures both as a countermeasure, in response to Pakistan's breach of its obligations to apprehend and punish (whether under the ICAO TSCs or the

determined that it had jurisdiction to consider Pakistan's complaint.[231] India appealed the Council's decision to the ICJ, pursuant to Article 84 of the Chicago Convention. The ICJ confirmed the ICAO's jurisdiction to consider the legality of Indian measures against Pakistan.[232] Following the ICJ's decision, however, the matter was settled extra-judicially between India and Pakistan and was removed from the ICAO Council's agenda. As a result, a final decision on the legality of India's measures (and any illegality of Pakistan's conduct in relation to the hijacking—in respect of which the measures were adopted) was never taken.[233]

The dispute between India and Pakistan clearly illustrates one of the difficulties inherent in the application of the law of state responsibility as regards acts of international terrorism. In particular, a state adopts countermeasures, in reliance on its own assessment of the internationally wrongful character of the target state's conduct, at its own risk. Pakistan maintained throughout the dispute that it had not breached its international obligations in regard to terrorism against civil aviation. As the basis for the adoption of countermeasures was in dispute, India's responsibility for breach of its own international obligations (occasioned by its adoption of countermeasures) was put before the ICAO Council. Given Pakistan's consistent denial of responsibility, it characterized India's measures as attempts to:

pressurize Pakistan to submit to her unilateral and unreasonable demands for compensation [. . .] drafted with a view to put the blame of the hijacking and destruction of the plane on Pakistan. Apart from India's charges against Pakistan being baseless; no self-respecting sovereign country could be expected to submit to illegal demands under duress.[234]

(iv) The legitimizing potential of the ICAO proposals

Had there been a mechanism in place for a third party determination of Pakistan's compliance with its international obligations to prevent and punish acts against the safety of civil aviation (as provided for in the US/Canada, UK/Swiss and Nordic proposals examined in Section 5.2.3(i) above), the dispute as to the underlying

---

Chicago Convention by implication), *and* in virtue of the law of treaties, based on a material breach by Pakistan. This section is focusing on the legitimacy of the countermeasures, and therefore does not assess the merits of the argument under the law of treaties.

[231] See ICAO Council, 74th Session, Action of the Council, 8 July 1971, ICAO Doc. 8987-C/1004 (1971), 42–6. See also ICAO Council, 74th Session, Minutes of the fifth meeting, 28 July 1971, ICAO Doc. 8956-c/1001, C-Min. LXXIV/5 (1971), reprinted in *Appeal Relating to the Jurisdiction of the ICAO Council (India v. Pakistan)*, Indian Memorial, Annex E, 234, 257–60, paras 97–114; ICAO Council, 74th Session, Minutes of the sixth meeting, 28 July 1971, ICAO Doc. 8956-c/1001, C-Min. LXXIV/6 (1971), reprinted in *Appeal Relating to the Jurisdiction of the ICAO Council (India v. Pakistan)*, Indian Memorial, Annex E, 266, 268–9, paras 2–7.

[232] See *Appeal Relating to the Jurisdiction of the ICAO Council (India v. Pakistan)*, Judgment.

[233] See ICAO Council, 88th Session, Action of the Council, 7–30 June 1976, ICAO Doc. 9171-C/1033 (1976), 22. See also ICAO Council, Annual Report, 1973, ICAO Doc. 9085 (1973), 97; ICAO Council, 88th Session, Minutes of meetings between 7–30 June 1976, ICAO Doc. 9170-C/1032, C-Min. 88/1–8 (1976), 57, para 21.

[234] See Attachment B to the Memorial of the Government of Pakistan under Article 2 of the Rules of Procedure Approved by the Council on 9 April 1957, reprinted in *Appeal Relating to the Jurisdiction of the ICAO Council (India v. Pakistan)*, Indian Memorial, 73, para 12.

breach of international terrorism obligations—which formed the basis of India's countermeasures—would have been resolved before the adoption of countermeasures. A determination that Pakistan was in breach of its Chicago Convention obligations by an independent committee of experts, or indeed the ICAO Council, would certainly have undermined the deniability of Pakistan's responsibility, and could have formed the basis, under the UK/Swiss proposal, for collective measures against Pakistan. Effectively, as to the suspension of air services obligations, the ICAO enforcement proposals examined above would (if the findings of fact supported India's claims) have both facilitated and legitimized the adoption of countermeasures, avoiding the 'at your own risk' element of countermeasures and the uncertain legitimacy of collective countermeasures under the general international law of state responsibility.

The ICAO TSC enforcement proposals could equally have legitimized the G7's suspension of air services with Afghanistan in response to the hijacking of a PIA flight examined in Section 5.1.4(i) above. The need for the G7 to wait out the one-year notice requirement in France's air services agreement with Afghanistan, to render the measure an act of retorsion (and avoid any questions as to the legitimacy of a collective countermeasure), could have been avoided by an ICAO Council decision that all ICAO member states suspend services with Afghanistan until it resumed compliance with its obligations to prevent and punish acts of international terrorism related to the safety of civil aviation.

The enforcement proposals examined above did not grant exclusive jurisdiction over breaches of the Hague and Montreal Conventions to ICAO organs, and there would have remained a freedom to adopt measures outside the framework of the Chicago Convention in response to internationally wrongful acts related to terrorism against civil aviation. While the suspension of air services with a state that is failing to prevent and punish terrorist offences against the safety of civil aviation is an effective response to the danger of an increase in such offences (given the terrorists' reliance on a safe haven), it is not the only response that states have adopted. States have equally considered trade measures to be an effective response to internationally wrongful acts related to terrorism against civil aviation. The legitimacy of such measures would fall outside the scope of Chicago Convention framework and, as between WTO members, would have to be assessed under the GATT 1994 and other WTO-covered agreements, as examined in Section 5.2.2 above.

5.3 Conclusion

As international law increasingly regulates the rights and obligations of states, the scope of unregulated activities that can form the basis of retorsive measures is correspondingly diminished. For that same reason, responses by states to internationally wrongful acts related to terrorism will increasingly have to be justified as countermeasures, or rely on sub-systems of international law to excuse what would otherwise be a breach of the primary rules affected by the responsive measure. Measures adopted pursuant to, and justified by, a sub-system of international law can draw on the legitimacy of the international institution in the context of which they are adopted. Proposals such as those put forward by ICAO member states to secure the enforcement of international terrorism obligations related to civil aviation would have ensured that a proper balance is achieved between the interests being protected and those being infringed through the adoption of responsive measures. This balance would have been achieved as a matter of principle, in that the scope of potential measures would be circumscribed within the framework of the system, and not left to the *ad hoc* determination of injured states, whose assessment of their own injury might be far from objective.

Given the shrinking scope for retorsive measures, and the absence of sub-systems like that proposed by the ICAO, countermeasures remain one of the principal available responses (in the context of the law of state responsibility) to unremedied breaches of international terrorism obligations. Despite the dangers of a decentralized system of law enforcement highlighted above, in particular as regards the potential for an escalation in tensions when a target state contests the characterization of its conduct as internationally wrongful, it bears emphasizing that the adoption of countermeasures remains a peaceful means of implementing state responsibility.[235] Measures in breach of international law adopted in reliance on the wrongfulness-preclusion of countermeasures under the law of state responsibility cannot impair the prohibition of the use of force as embodied in the UN Charter[236]—the adoption of pacific countermeasures in response to the breach of international terrorism obligations thereby pressures wrongdoing states into respecting obligations that themselves bear on the maintenance of international peace and security without in any way detracting from that peace and security.

Such measures may, however, be precluded by sub-systems of international law, most particularly the WTO. If the 'necessity' element of the Article XXI GATT security exception is interpreted narrowly, it creates a gap between wrongfulness-preclusion under general international law and wrongfulness-preclusion within the WTO system, and states may well be surprised to learn that they have prioritized trade liberalization in a way that fundamentally alters the availability of trade countermeasures under general international law in response to terrorism-related wrongs. The security exception has yet to be the subject of a WTO decision. It may be hoped that when the issue arises, the WTO will determine the scope of the security exception in a way that is sensitive to the competing priorities of security (in particular in relation to international terrorism) *and* trade liberalization. Indeed, an inward-looking approach, which seriously limited states' freedom to respond to terrorism-related wrongs under international law in the name of trade, would not serve member states interests and might well invite states to take a position not dissimilar to that taken by the US in reference to its Helms Burton Act dispute with the EU—in particular, to threaten to boycott any convened WTO panel because the dispute was one bearing on issues of essential national security and not a trade dispute. This would undermine the effectiveness of the WTO system both in terms

---

[235] See Simma (1994), 103.
[236] Art. 50(1)(a), ILC Articles on State Responsibility.

of its substantive obligations and its dispute settlement capacity, and thus potentially also the effectiveness of trade sanctions (which might thereby be viewed as illegitimate)—an unwelcome prospect, whether viewed from the WTO or terrorism-suppression perspective.

The broader the approach taken by the WTO to the security exception under the GATT, the more widely the wrongfulness of trade sanctions adopted in response to international terrorism-related wrongs would be precluded, rendering the sanctions retorsive. Article XXI of the GATT might then be relied on to protect security-related interests (whether or not such interests are engaged by an internationally wrongful act) by both injured states and those acting in solidarity with injured states. The GATT might therefore provide states with an important mechanism for implementing state responsibility for international terrorism that avoids the 'at your own risk' element of countermeasures, allows for collective responses, and, through the possibility of WTO dispute settlement, could prevent the escalation of the conflict into one of spiralling countermeasures.

6

The relationship between individual criminal responsibility and state responsibility in the terrorism context

When considering the enforcement of international law, the Nuremberg Tribunal famously suggested that state criminality should and could only be addressed through the mechanic of individual criminal responsibility: '[c]rimes against international law are committed by men, not by abstract entities, and *only* by punishing individuals who commit such crimes can the provisions of international law be enforced'.[1] State responsibility for the crimes against peace committed during World War II, however, was not displaced or absorbed by the individual criminal responsibility of German officials. In addition to the war crimes trials against high-ranking German officials (eight of whom were convicted of crimes against peace),[2] Germany was liable for heavy war damages. The result was the first case of true concurrent responsibility—with individual state actors held criminally responsible and the state held delictually responsible *for the same conduct*.[3] In keeping with this precedent, the ILC and the international community have consistently emphasized the concurrence of responsibility under international law for the commission of

---

[1] Emphasis added. *Nuremberg Judgment.* See also H. Lauterpacht (1950), 40; Allott (1988), 14; *Bosnia Genocide Case,* Preliminary Objections, Joint declaration of Judge Shi and Judge Vereshchetin, 631. The Nuremberg Tribunal's statement (suggesting exclusive individual criminal responsibility) is almost exactly the opposite of the principle of exclusive state responsibility espoused nearly 100 years prior to Nuremberg in reference to the McLeod prosecution (discussed in Section 3.2.2). The Nuremberg trials, and the development of international criminal law subsequent thereto, make it clear that the principle of exclusive state responsibility has not survived into the modern era, at least in reference to international crimes. Indeed, state comments on draft Article 19 of the ILC Articles on State Responsibility expressed the concern that international responsibility for crimes of state would embolden individual criminals to shift responsibility from themselves to the state on whose behalf they acted. See ILC, Comments and Observations received from Governments on State Responsibility, UN Doc. A/CN.4/488 (1998), 63 (US), 135 (Germany).

[2] *Nuremberg Judgment*: Goering, von Ribbentrop, Hess, Rosenberg, Keitel, Raeder, Jodl and von Neurath.

[3] There was an attempt to impose some measure of concurrent responsibility following World War I. Articles 231–2 of the Treaty of Versailles affirmed Germany's responsibility for aggression and required it to pay war damages, while Article 227 of the Treaty of Versailles provided that '[t]he Allied and Associated Powers publicly arraign William II of Hohenzollern, formerly German Emperor, for a supreme offence against international morality and the sanctity of treaties'. Article 227 was never implemented because the Netherlands refused to deliver the Kaiser to the Allied powers. See H. Lauterpacht (1944), 94.

international crimes. Individual criminal responsibility for crimes under international law has not replaced state responsibility, where the criminal conduct is attributable to the state and amounts to the breach of an international obligation.[4] Both the Rome Statute[5] and the ILC Articles on State Responsibility[6] are without prejudice to the sphere of application of the other. And in relation to terrorist offences, which have consistently been on the edge of developments in international criminal law (without ever making it to the core, as discussed in Section 6.4 below), the same applies. It is clear from the analysis in Section 3.2.2 that state officials are not necessarily shielded from individual criminal responsibility for terrorist offences committed abroad and on behalf of a state by immunity *ratione materiae*. The state's responsibility for acts of international terrorism is not exclusive. Nor is individual criminal responsibility for terrorist offences exclusive, as is evident from the Lockerbie bombing precedent discussed below.

Conceptually, individual criminal responsibility and state responsibility for criminal conduct can co-exist, each established independently from the other.[7] In practice, however, the relationship between the two forms of responsibility is much more dynamic. For instance, determinations of individual criminal responsibility can catalyse a victim state into formally invoking a wrongdoing state's responsibility and taking measures against the state to enforce that responsibility. This relationship is examined in Section 6.1 below. Determinations of individual criminal responsibility also seem to pressure wrongdoing states into accepting the secondary obligations that flow from their responsibility. The relationship between guilty verdicts and determinations of state agency by domestic courts on the one hand and wrongdoing state's acceptance of the secondary obligations flowing from their responsibility on the other is examined in Section 6.2 below. Given this relationship, injured states tend to pursue the criminal model of responsibility for terrorism before invoking state responsibility. As examined in Section 6.2.5 below, the criminal law enforcement process is often pursued through to its completion before any invocation of state responsibility is made.

A further facet of the relationship between individual criminal responsibility and state responsibility may be more formal in nature. Article 37 of the ILC Articles on State Responsibility (in particular the commentary thereto) suggests that a state's responsibility for criminal conduct could be discharged through prosecution of the criminal actors, in that punishing the responsible criminals may amount to reparation in the form of satisfaction. Section 6.3 below examines this possible intersection between individual criminal and state responsibility in the terrorism context.

---

[4] See *Bosnia Genocide Case*, Judgment, para 171. See also ILC, Comments and Observations received from Governments on State Responsibility, UN Doc. A/CN.4/488 (1998), 53 (Denmark on behalf of the Nordic countries).

[5] Art. 25(4), Rome Statute. See also the ILC Commentary to Art. 5, Draft Code on Offences against the Peace and Security of Mankind adopted on first reading, UN Doc. A/46/10 (1991), 99.

[6] Art. 55, ILC Articles on State Responsibility. See also Report of the International Law Commission on the work of its twenty-eighth session, UN Doc. A/31/10 (1976), 104, para 21.

[7] See *Bosnia Genocide Case*, Judgment, paras 180–2; *Selmouni v. France* (ECtHR, 1999), para 87. See also Nollkaemper (2008), 353–4.

Finally, determinations of individual criminal responsibility (or the absence thereof) can play a decisive role in judicial determinations of state responsibility. For instance, in the *Bosnia Genocide Case*, the ICJ relied on the fact that the ICTY *had not* found any person guilty of genocide in Srebrenica, and that the prosecutor had failed to charge relevant persons with genocide, in concluding that there *was no genocidal intent* on the part of the Serbian state for the purposes of state responsibility.[8] *À contrario*, where there is a relevant determination of individual criminal responsibility (and such responsibility depends on the state leadership role or organ status of the accused), it could certainly influence the Court in any determination of state responsibility. Equally, the ICJ relied heavily on determinations of fact by the ICTY in its assessment of the facts bearing on Serbian responsibility for genocide in its *Bosnia Genocide Case* decision. This reliance signals a willingness to engage with determinations by international criminal tribunals in assessing state responsibility for the criminal conduct in question.[9] Section 6.5 examines the potential role of the International Criminal Court ('ICC') and criminal responsibility for acts of terrorism under the Rome Statute in giving effect to a state's responsibility for acts of international terrorism.

6.1 Determinations of individual criminal responsibility as a catalyst

Even though state responsibility is deemed to arise by operation of the law on commission of an internationally wrongful act, in practice responsibility has to

---

[8] *Bosnia Genocide Case*, Judgment, paras 374–5. But see *Bosnia Genocide Case*, Judgment, Dissenting Opinion of Vice-President Al-Khasawneh, para 42, criticizing the Court's use of ICTY and prosecutorial decisions for the purposes of determining genocidal intent in a case of state responsibility.

[9] It bears repeating that state responsibility for criminal conduct will nevertheless be delictual, and not criminal. With respect to genocide, the elements of the offence for which there will be individual criminal responsibility, and the elements of the international delict for which there will be state responsibility, are exactly the same. Indeed, the ICJ held that state responsibility for genocide hung on the attributability of individual acts of genocide, as judged by the definition of the criminal offence in the Genocide Convention. See *Bosnia Genocide Case*, Judgment, paras 179–80. This precise overlap of elements defining the wrongful conduct will not necessarily be present in the terrorism context. Some of the TSCs (which define the conduct for which individuals will be criminally responsible), in addition to defining the physical elements of an offence, require a 'terrorist' purpose or intent (see e.g. Art. 1, Hostages Convention; Art. 2(1)(b), Terrorism Financing Convention). But acts of terrorism for which states can be held responsible under general international law will not generally be limited by the purpose of the conduct, relying purely on physical elements (amounting to a different international wrong than that for which the individual is held responsible—like a prohibited use of force or aggression). This will not, however, affect the extent to which determinations of individual criminal responsibility can form the basis of determinations of state responsibility, because the physical elements of the conduct are at least co-extensive, even if individual criminal responsibility will require further evidence of purpose. And if the TSCs are relied on as a basis of state responsibility pursuant to a *Bosnia Genocide Case* analysis, as examined in Chapter 4, then the elements of the offence for the purposes of individual criminal responsibility (to the extent the definition of the criminal offence has been correctly incorporated into a state's domestic criminal law), and the elements of the delict for the purposes of state responsibility, will be precisely the same.

be invoked.[10] Any such invocation will be based on an appreciation of the facts and law by the injured state, with the facts and attributability particularly difficult to determine.[11] In certain cases, domestic criminal proceedings can confirm a foreign state's involvement in terrorist conduct, and serve as a catalyst for the invocation of that state's responsibility by the injured (and prosecuting) state.

For instance, on 29 March 1986, the German–Arab Friendship Society in West Berlin was bombed.[12] A German Court convicted a Jordanian national, Ahmed Hasi, for the attack, and ruled that he had obtained the explosives from the Syrian Embassy in East Berlin.[13] In response to the conviction, Germany invoked Syrian responsibility, expelled Syrian diplomats, and halted development and other aid.[14] Shortly after the German–Arab Friendship Society attack, an attack against an El Al flight between Heathrow and Tel Aviv airports was attempted by Ahmed Hasi's brother, Nezar Hindawi.[15] In October 1986, Hindawi was convicted by an English court of attempting to place on an aircraft an explosive device likely to destroy or damage the aircraft.[16] In reaching its decision, the Court held that there was conclusive evidence of Syrian involvement in the plot. In response thereto, the UK broke off diplomatic relations with Syria and expelled the Syrian Ambassador.[17] In both cases, the breaking off of diplomatic relations (acts of retorsion in response to Syrian responsibility) followed immediately from the domestic criminal convictions, which confirmed Syrian involvement.

6.2 Determinations of individual criminal responsibility as pressure

As examined in Chapter 2, states participating in acts of terrorism through non-state actors or secret service agents maintain a high degree of deniability regarding their participation in a particular terrorist attack.[18] Such deniability makes the invocation of state responsibility by an injured state less likely to be successful, if

---

[10] See Crawford and Olleson (2006), 473.

[11] See Sections 2.2.1, 2.2.2 and 5.1.2(i).

[12] Keesing's, Vol. 32, December 1986, 34835. See also Section 5.1.4(iv).

[13] Hull et al., 'West Germany Verdict against Damascus', *Time*, 8 December 1986, <http://www.time.com/time/magazine/article/0,9171,963053,00.html>.

[14] *Ibid.*

[15] See further Section 5.1.4(iv) for details of the plot.

[16] Mr Hindawi was refused leave to appeal the conviction. *R. v. Nezar Nawat Mansour Hazi Hindawi*, England (Court of Appeal, 1988).

[17] BBC, 'On this Day: 1986: UK cuts links with Syria over bomb plot', <http://news.bbc.co.uk/onthisday/hi/dates/stories/october/24/newsid_2478000/2478505.stm>.

[18] See also United States, 'Public Report of the Vice President's Task Force on Combating Terrorism' (1986), <http://www.population-security.org/bush_report_on_terrorism/bush_report_on_terrorism.htm>, 2, noting that a state's *de facto* terrorist agents are 'agents whose association the State can easily deny'.

success is defined in terms of a wrongdoing state's acceptance of and compliance with the secondary obligations flowing from such responsibility.[19]

Hans Kelsen characterized the difficulty as follows:

[A]n obligation to make reparation exists only if an international delict has been committed, and there is, under general international law, no objective authority, especially no court, competent to ascertain the existence of a delict. This function is left by general international law to the states concerned. Consequently a state may consider itself to be under an obligation to make reparation only if it admits that it has committed a delict, that is to say, if there is an agreement of the states concerned in this respect. However such agreement might not be reached.[20]

In the absence of an international judicial determination of the internationally wrongful character of a course of conduct, the victim state's own assessment of state responsibility for international terrorism amounts to little more than the word of one state against that of another, and is unlikely to entice a wrongdoing state out from behind the veil of deniability.[21] The determination of a state's conduct as internationally wrongful by an international adjudicative body is, however, not the only way of pressuring a wrongdoing state into accepting its secondary obligation to make reparation. As examined in Chapter 5, the imposition of countermeasures by the injured state, even though not without its difficulties, can serve such a function.[22] Equally, as examined in the state practice below, domestic judicial determinations of individual criminal responsibility, where there is credible evidence that the guilty person(s) acted on behalf of a state, seem to pressure wrongdoing states into accepting their obligations to compensate for damage caused, or at least embolden injured states in their invocations of responsibility which renders negotiations more likely.

As a matter of law, individual criminal responsibility does not replace state responsibility, and indeed there are a number of strong arguments bearing on the reparatory function of state responsibility why it should not.[23] As a matter of practice, however, pursuing a criminal justice model of responsibility for acts of terrorism often *precedes* the invocation of state responsibility. There are a number of possible reasons

---

[19] The secondary obligations flowing from state responsibility include the obligation to cease the wrongful conduct and make reparation therefor. The obligation to make reparation might take the form of (i) restitution, which is often materially impossible in the case of terrorist attacks which lead to deaths or the permanent destruction of property (see Commentary to Art. 37, ILC Articles on State Responsibility, para 8); (ii) compensation for financially assessable damage (see Art. 36, ILC Articles on State Responsibility; *Gabčíkovo–Nagymaros Project (Hungary v. Slovakia)*, Judgment, 81, para 152); or (iii) satisfaction (see Section 6.3).

[20] Kelsen (1966), 18. See also Riphagen (1983), 9, para 39.

[21] See Riphagen (1983), 8, para 37, arguing that 'in most cases, a State will deny, on the grounds of the facts or of the interpretation of the applicable primary rules, that there has been on its side a non-conformity with a legal rule, an internationally wrongful act for which it bears responsibility'.

[22] Note, however, that in the absence of a judicial determination of state responsibility, the adoption of countermeasures is 'at the risk' of the measure-adopting state in virtue of the same difficulties in establishing state involvement in terrorism discussed in this section. See Section 5.1.2.

[23] *Infra* notes 166–7 and accompanying text. See also Allott (2002), 66–9, arguing that international criminal law serves to maintain the status quo by distracting attention from the need to reform states as institutions to prevent the abuses of power that give rise to international crimes.

for this, not least that the process for pursuing individual criminal responsibility in domestic systems is clearly established, whereas successful invocations of state responsibility rely on probably strained relations between the injured state and wrongdoing state.

6.2.1 Lockerbie bombing

Following the Lockerbie bombing,[24] the US and UK demanded that Libya surrender for trial all those charged with the offence, that it accept responsibility for the actions of its officials, and that it pay appropriate compensation.[25] Libya attempted to circumvent the requests for surrender by filing an application before the ICJ asserting rights under the Montreal Convention to prosecute its own nationals. On the claim of state responsibility, Libya consistently denied that it had any 'link' (beyond the obvious link of nationality) to the individuals whose surrender was sought by the US and UK.[26] Following years of Security Council imposed sanctions and negotiations, Libya surrendered the two accused to a Scottish Court seated in The Hague. In 2001, Ali Mohmed Al Megrahi, held to be a Libyan secret service agent,[27] was found guilty of murder, while Lamen Khalifa Fhimah was acquitted of all charges against him. Following Megrahi's conviction, the US and UK renewed their claims for compensation.[28] Libya subsequently accepted 'civil responsibility for the actions of its officials in the Lockerbie affair, in conformity with international civil law',[29] and agreed to pay compensation to the victims of the Lockerbie bombing.[30] It is of course impossible to establish a causal

---

[24] For details of the Lockerbie bombing, see Section 4.3.

[25] See e.g. Letter dated 20 December 1991 from the Permanent Representative of the United States of America to the United Nations addressed to the Secretary-General, UN Doc. A/46/827 (1991).

[26] See Letter dated 11 November 1991 from the Permanent Representative of the Libyan Arab Jamahiriya to the United Nations addressed to the Secretary-General, UN Doc. S/23417 (1991). When Libya refused to surrender its nationals, the Security Council first urged it to do so (UNSC Resolution 731 (1992), para 3), and then required Libya to surrender its nationals, as requested by the US and UK, under Chapter VII (UNSC Resolution 748 (1992)). UNSCR 748 (1992) also imposed sanctions against Libya, pending its compliance with the demand for surrender of the accused. Following the resolutions imposing sanctions, Libya continued to deny that it was connected in any way to acts of international terrorism. See Letter dated 9 December 1992 from the Permanent Representative of the Libyan Arab Jamahiriya to the United Nations addressed to the Secretary-General, UN Doc. S/24961 (1992); SC 3312th meeting (1993), 18–19.

[27] While the court held that Megrahi was a member of the Jamahiriya Security Organization 'of fairly high rank', it did not implicate those higher up in the Libyan Government. *Her Majesty's Advocate v. Al-Megrahi*, Scotland (High Court of Justiciary at Camp Zeist, 31 January 2001), 2001 G.W.D. 5–177, para 88.

[28] Watt, 'Allies tell Libya to accept UN demands and end isolation', the guardian, 15 March 2002, <http://www.guardian.co.uk/uk/2002/mar/15/lockerbie.unitednations>.

[29] Letter dated 15 August 2003 from the Chargé D'Affaires a.i. of the Permanent Mission of the Libyan Arab Jamahiriya to the United Nations addressed to the President of the Security Council, UN Doc. S/2003/818, in which Libya accepted responsibility 'for the actions of its officials'. See also the guardian, 'Libya agrees Lockerbie compensation payout', 29 April 2003, <http://www.guardian.co.uk/uk/2003/apr/29/lockerbie.world>.

[30] Letter dated 15 August 2003 from the Chargé D'Affaires a.i. of the Permanent Mission of the Libyan Arab Jamahiriya to the United Nations addressed to the President of the Security Council, UN Doc. S/2003/818: '[. . .] Libya as a sovereign state: Has arranged for the payment of appropriate compensation'.

link between the guilty verdict against Megrahi (and associated determination of his Libyan secret service agent status) and Libya's ultimate acceptance of 'civil responsibility' under international law—most particularly given the prolonged Security Council sanctions regime to which Libya was subject following the Lockerbie bombing—fatigue from which almost certainly played a role.[31] In addition, Libya's acceptance of responsibility is not without ambiguity. In accepting responsibility for the actions of its officials, Libya did not necessarily concede that its officials had in fact carried out the Lockerbie bombing or that it had directed them to do so.[32] Nevertheless, a credible judicial determination of the guilt of a Libyan secret service agent removed the element of deniability, and is likely to have encouraged acceptance of the obligation to make reparation on that basis.[33]

6.2.2 'La Belle' disco bombing

On 5 April 1986, a bomb exploded in West Berlin's 'La Belle' disco, killing two US servicemen and a Turkish woman and injuring another 230 people. The US, based on intercepted messages between Tripoli and Libyan agents in Europe, claimed that Libyan leader Colonel Gaddafi had ordered the attack.[34] The US launched air strikes in and around Tripoli in response to the attacks.[35] Fifteen years later, a Berlin court found a Libyan secret service agent and two staff members of Libya's diplomatic representation in East Berlin guilty of attempted murder, and the German wife of one of the staff members guilty of murder, it having been proven

---

[31] In an interview with the BBC, Colonel Gaddafi's son suggested that the Libyan Government had only accepted responsibility for the Lockerbie bombing in order to have international sanctions lifted. He confessed that '[y]es, we wrote a letter to the Security Council saying we are responsible for the acts of our employees [. . .], but it doesn't mean that we did it in fact [. . . .]. I admit that we played with words – we had to [. . .]. What can you do? Without writing that letter we would not be able to get rid of sanctions'. BBC, 'Lockerbie Evidence not Disclosed', 28 August 2008, <http://news.bbc.co.uk/1/hi/scotland/south_of_scotland/7573244.stm>.

[32] *Ibid.*

[33] The Scottish Criminal Cases Review Commission referred Megrahi's case to the High Court of Justiciary, based on new evidence that the applicant may have suffered a miscarriage of justice (in particular in regards to the line-up evidence on the basis of which Megrahi was convicted). As a result of that decision, Megrahi was entitled to a further appeal against his conviction for the murder of the 270 people who died on board Pam Am flight 103. News Release, Scottish Criminal Cases Review Commission, <http://www.sccrc.org.uk>. Before the review occurred, the Scottish Government controversially decided to release Megrahi to Libya on compassionate grounds, and dropping the appeal was one of the conditions of release. See BBC, 'Lockerbie bomber freed from jail', 20 August 2009, <http://news.bbc.co.uk/1/hi/scotland/south_of_scotland/8197370.stm>. In any event, Libya had already paid US$2.7 billion in compensation to the families of Pan Am 103 victims. And even after the Scottish Criminal Cases Review Commission decided to permit Megrahi a further appeal, Libya had agreed to further compensate the victims of the Lockerbie bombing (through funds not directly linked to the Libyan Government), in final settlement of all outstanding claims against Libya related to the bombing. See BBC, 'US-Libya compensation deal sealed', 14 August 2008, <http://news.bbc.co.uk/2/hi/americas/7561271.stm>; NY Times, 'Libya: Settlement Ends Terrorism Suits', 14 August 2008, <http://www.nytimes.com/2008/08/15/world/africa/15briefs-SETTLEMENTEN_BRF.html?ex=1219464000&en=aab8de05e638bc49&ei=5070&emc=eta1>.

[34] Malinarich, 'Flashback: The Berlin disco bombing', 13 November 2001, <http://news.bbc.co.uk/2/hi/europe/1653848.stm>.

[35] See Gray (2008), 196.

that she planted the bomb in the nightclub. In a statement issued at the close of the trial, Judge Peter Marhofer said that the Court was convinced that the Libyan state was at least to a large extent responsible for the bomb attack as it had been planned and carried out by members of the Libyan secret service in the Libyan Embassy in East Berlin.[36] Judge Marhofer also noted that prosecutors had failed to prove that the attack was planned on the personal orders of Libyan leader Colonel Gaddafi, partly because of the lack of co-operation from Western secret services, and he criticized the limited willingness of the German and US secret services to provide evidence, describing it as one of the 'disappointments' of the trial. Given the judge's determination of Libyan involvement, it is notable that immunity *ratione materiae* was not considered by the Court. This is in keeping with the general exception to immunity discussed in Section 3.2.2 above, which provides that states are not bound to give effect to the immunity of foreign states in reference to official acts of sovereign authority carried out in the forum state's territory without its consent.

Germany did not make demands for compensation from Libya in 1986, and it was only following the conviction of the Libyan secret service agent and embassy workers that the German and Libyan governments entered into nego-tiations. In August 2004, Libya agreed to pay US$35 million in compensation for non-US victims of the 'La Belle' bombing (refusing to pay compensation for the US victims of the bombing unless the US government compensated it for the deaths and property damage that resulted from air strikes which the US launched in response to the 'La Belle' bombing),[37] but maintained that the agreement did not mean that Libya had acknowledged guilt for the bombing.[38] The commen-tary to Article 36 of the ILC Articles on State Responsibility, on compensation, recognizes that in 'many cases, these payments have been made on an *ex gratia* or a without prejudice basis, without any admission of responsibility', but still treats the payments under the rubric of the obligation to make reparation.[39] In this case, the guilty verdicts prompted Germany to invoke Libyan responsibility and very likely influenced Libya's agreement to pay compensation. Whether the payment of compensation amounted to an admission of responsibility or not, it certainly played its part in re-establishing the primary legal relationship between the injured and wrongdoing states—which is indeed the very purpose of state responsibility.

---

[36] See BBC, 'Four jailed for Berlin disco bombing', 13 November 2001, <http://news.bbc.co.uk/1/hi/world/europe/1653575.stm>; Keesing's, Vol. 47, November 2001, 44482.

[37] See BBC, 'Libya inks $35m Berlin bomb deal', 3 September 2004, <http://news.bbc.co.uk/2/hi/europe/3625756.stm>. In August 2008, the US and Libya signed a comprehensive compensation deal, according to which the US would compensate Libyans for damage caused by its 1986 Tripoli bombing campaign, and Libya would compensate US citizens for damage caused by the 'La Belle' disco bombing. BBC, 'US-Libya compensation deal sealed', 14 August 2008, <http://news.bbc.co.uk/2/hi/americas/7561271.stm>.

[38] Keesing's, Vol. 50, August 2004, 46181.

[39] Commentary to Art. 36, ILC Articles on State Responsibility, para 12.

6.2.3 UTA 722

An explosion aboard UTA flight 722, leaving from Chad to Paris on 19 September 1989, caused the plane to break up over the Sahara in Niger. All 156 passengers and fourteen crew members died. Following the investigation, French Magistrate Jean-Louis Brugiére made a request to the general prosecutor in Paris that six Libyans (including Colonel Gaddafi's brother-in-law and several secret service agents) be charged in connection with the destruction of UTA flight 722.[40] UTA (which stands for 'Union des Transports Aériens') is a French registered airline, and France therefore had jurisdiction to prosecute the accused under the terms of the Montreal Convention.[41] Libya consistently denied its responsibility for the UTA bombing, and maintained that the men charged were innocent—refusing to extradite them to France.[42] All six Libyan officials were tried *in absentia* by the Cour d'assises de Paris in 1999, and convicted of murder and destruction of property.[43] As would be the case in reference to acts carried out by foreign officials in a state's territory without that state's consent, the French courts did not raise (or consider) the immunity *ratione materiae* of the Libyan agents for official acts carried out on a French registered airline.[44] In addition, both France and Libya were parties to the Montreal Convention at the time of the UTA bombing,[45] and Libya can be considered to have waived its immunity for its officials pursuant to a *Pinochet* analysis as applied to the TSCs.[46] In light of the convictions, the Cour d'assises de Paris also ordered the payment of compensation by the Libyan Government for the destruction of UTA 722.[47] The compensation finally paid to the families of the 170 victims was not paid by the Libyan Government, but by a charitable foundation headed by one of Colonel Gaddafi's sons.[48] Given that the compensation was not paid directly by the Libyan Government, it is a less obvious example of the dynamic between determinations of individual criminal responsibility and state responsibility. That said, the timing of the negotiations on compensation, and the very close connection between the Libyan Government and the fund that ultimately paid compensation, suggest that the guilty verdicts played a role in settling the UTA 722 dispute.

---

[40] Keesing's, Vol. 44, February 1998, 42102.

[41] Art. 5(1)(b), Montreal Convention.

[42] BBC, 'Libya agrees bombing deal', 1 September 2003, <http://news.bbc.co.uk/2/hi/europe/3197095.stm>.

[43] Keesing's, Vol. 45, March 1999, 42869.

[44] See Section 3.2.2 for a discussion of the general exception to immunity in reference to acts of foreign sovereign authority carried out in the forum state's territory without its consent.

[45] See <http://www.icao.int/icao/en/leb/Mtl71.pdf>.

[46] See Section 3.2.2 for a discussion of the implied waiver of immunity *ratione materiae* of state parties to the TSCs.

[47] Keesing's, Vol. 45, July 1999, 43082.

[48] *Supra* note 42.

6.2.4 Rainbow Warrior

France initially denied any link (beyond nationality) with the French couple in New Zealand's custody for the 'Rainbow Warrior' bombing, and offered its full co-operation into the 'criminal outrage committed on [New Zealand] territory'.[49] New Zealand maintained throughout that Mafart and Prieur were French secret service agents. As the trial date approached, at which both pleaded guilty to charges of manslaughter and wilful damage to a ship by means of an explosive, France incrementally abandoned its claim of non-responsibility.[50] Media reports on the case in France made it increasingly difficult for the French Defence Minister and the Head of the DGSE to deny that it had knowledge of the operation.[51] Prime Minister Laurent Fabius finally admitted that the French secret service had ordered the attack on the 'Rainbow Warrior' and accepted responsibility[52] two weeks before the 4 November 1985 trial date of its secret service agents. Given France's initial denial (despite the fact that its agents had been arrested), it is very unlikely that French responsibility would have been established absent a criminal process. Had Mafart and Prieur successfully fled New Zealand, as did their two accomplices, New Zealand would have had no basis on which to claim French responsibility, and France would have had no reason to abandon its claims of non-responsibility.

6.2.5 Ongoing criminal law enforcement processes

The state practice examined above were cases in which determinations of individual criminal responsibility preceded invocations of state responsibility. In the state practice examined below, states (and the Security Council) have also responded to terrorist attacks in which there are allegations of state involvement by focusing on criminal law enforcement. In these cases, however, the criminal law enforcement process has not yet been completed, and states, as a result, have yet to formally invoke the responsibility of other states at the international level for the prosecuted acts of terrorism.

(i) Argentine Community Centre

On 18 July 1994, a van packed with explosives was driven into a seven-storey Jewish–Argentine community centre in Buenos Aires. The explosion reduced the

---

[49] See Letter from the President of France to the Prime Minister of New Zealand, 8 August 1985, 74 International Law Reports 262. See also Section 2.2.1 for a full account of the Rainbow Warrior incident.

[50] *Supra* Chapter 2, notes 71–2 and accompanying text.

[51] See Bernstein, 'France Blames 2 Aides in Ship Raiding', *NY Times*, 26 September 1985, A12. More recent reports have confirmed that the orders to commit the act of terrorism against the 'Rainbow Warrior' went all the way up to French President Mitterand. See Gattegno, 'Greenpeace, vingt ans après: le rapport secret de l'amiral Lacoste', *Le Monde*, 10 July 2005.

[52] Communiqué from the French Prime Minister dated 22 September 1985, 74 International Law Reports 261.

building to rubble and killed 96 people, injuring another 300.[53] Initial investigations into the bombing were seriously mismanaged and marred by charges of corruption.[54] It was only in November 2005 that a joint effort by Argentinean intelligence and the FBI resulted in the identification of the suicide bomber responsible for blowing up the community centre. He was identified as Ibrahim Hussein Berro, a member of Hezbollah.[55] Even though Hezbollah issued a statement denying allegations that it had been involved in the Jewish community centre attack,[56] the Argentinean Government asked Iran to clarify its relationship with Hezbollah, which also prompted sharp denials by Iran that its Latin American embassies were involved in the terrorist attacks.[57]

One year later, the Argentinean public prosecutor charged former Iranian President Ali Akbar Hashemi Rafsanjani (1989–97) and eight of his officials with ordering guerrillas from Hezbollah to carry out the attack against the Jewish Community Centre,[58] followed shortly by the issuance of arrest warrants.[59] In response to the arrest warrants issued by Argentina, Iran has drawn up charges against the Argentinean investigative magistrate and others involved in the investigation for 'actions against the security of the Islamic Republic [of Iran]', and has threatened to take action against Argentina before the ICJ 'for damaging [the] prestige of [the] Iranian government' with its baseless accusations.[60] Nevertheless, the INTERPOL General Assembly upheld the unanimous decision made by the organization's Executive Committee to publish six out of nine Red Notices[61] requested by Argentina in connection with its issuance of arrest warrants.[62] At

---

[53] Keesing's, Vol. 40, July 1994, 40110–21.
[54] See Kiernan, 'Why Argentina's Jewish Center Bombing Remains Unsolved', *International Herald Tribune*, 28 August 1996, <http://www.iht.com/articles/1996/08/28/edserg.t.php>.
[55] BBC, 'Buenos Aires bomber "identified"', 10 November 2005, <http://news.bbc.co.uk/2/hi/americas/4423612.stm>.
[56] Keesing's, Vol. 51, November 2005, 46927.
[57] Keesing's, Vol. 40, July 1994, 40122.
[58] Keesing's, Vol. 52, November 2006, 47571.
[59] *Ibid.*
[60] Keesing's, Vol. 53, August 2007, 48075. It remains an open question whether the relevant state officials would be immune from prosecution in Argentina. The Terrorist Bombing Convention was not yet concluded at the time of the bombing, and there is therefore no basis for arguing an implied waiver of immunity under the TSCs. Equally, a general exception to immunity regarding the acts of saboteurs or unauthorized incursions by an organ of one state in the territory of the forum state would not necessarily apply, as the Iranian organs charged with ordering the bombing were not in fact present in Argentina at the time it was carried out. For a discussion of immunity *ratione materiae* from prosecution for acts of terrorism carried out by state officials, see Section 3.2.2.
[61] A Red Notice is not an international arrest warrant. It is based on warrants issued by national jurisdictions and is one of the ways in which INTERPOL informs its member countries that an arrest warrant has been issued for an individual by a domestic judicial authority, to assist the national police forces in locating those persons with a view to their arrest and extradition. See <http://www.interpol.int/Public/Wanted/Default.asp>.
[62] INTERPOL Media Release, 7 November 2007, 'INTERPOL General Assembly upholds Executive Committee decision on AMIA Red Notice dispute', <http://www.interpol.int/public/ICPO/PressReleases/PR2007/PR200754.asp>. Notices were not issued for former President of Iran, Ali Rafsanjani, former Minister of Foreign Affairs of Iran, Ali Akbar Velayati and former Ambassador of Iran in Buenos Aires, Hadi Soleimanpour. INTERPOL Media Release, 15 March 2007, 'INTERPOL Executive Committee takes decision on AMIA Red Notice dispute', <http://www.interpol.int/Public/ICPO/PressReleases/PR2007/PR200705.asp>.

the time of writing, no arrests had been made. INTERPOL hosted a meeting between Iranian and Argentinean officials on 10 March 2010 to discuss the impasse, but no apparent progress was made during the meeting.[63]

Despite the charges laid against the former President of Iran and high-ranking Iranian officials, Argentina has not formally invoked Iran's responsibility or made any public claims for reparation. Its strategy has been focused entirely on the criminal liability of those responsible for the bombing. State responsibility for an internationally wrongful act, however, has a shelf life. An injured state can lose the right to invoke a wrongdoing state's responsibility where it has, 'by reason of its conduct, validly acquiesced in the lapse of the claim',[64] including as a result of unreasonable delay in invoking responsibility.[65] Courts and tribunals have taken a flexible approach to evaluating whether too much time has elapsed between the internationally wrongful act and bringing the claim in respect thereof.[66] In this particular case, the complexity of the criminal investigation, and Argentina's announcement (through its seeking international arrest warrants) that it considered the highest authorities in Iran to be responsible as soon as practicable thereafter, might be considerations in assessing whether it had 'acquiesced in the lapse of the claim' regarding Iran's responsibility. That said, Iran has continued to protest the Red Notices published against former officials, most particularly in reference to the Red Notice published against Mr Vahidi, appointed as minister of defence in August 2009. In reference to statements made by the Argentinean prosecutor regarding the responsibility of Iranian officials, sparked by the appointment of Mr Vardi as defence minister, President Ahmadinejad's press adviser asked 'How come they didn't bring it up in the past?'[67]

(ii) Assassination attempt on President Mubarak

Egyptian President Mubarak was the target of an assassination attempt on 26 June 1995, while visiting the Ethiopian capital of Addis Ababa.[68] Rumours of Sudanese involvement immediately followed the assassination attempt. President Mubarak himself ruled out direct Sudanese Government participation, but suggested that the Sudanese National Islamic Front, which strongly influenced the Sudan's ruling Revolutionary Command Council, was responsible.[69] Ethiopia, on the other hand, alleged that the terrorists enjoyed the active support of the Sudan, claiming that its 'investigation into the terrorist crime had shown conclusively that Sudanese

---

[63] INTERPOL Media Release, 'INTERPOL hosts Argentina-Iran meeting for continued dialogue over 15-year-old AMIA terrorist incident', 12 March 2010, <http://www.interpol.int/Public/ICPO/PressReleases/PR2010/PR018.asp>.

[64] Art. 45(b), ILC Articles on State Responsibility.

[65] Commentary to Art. 45, ILC Articles on State Responsibility, para 6. See further Tams (2010), 1042–5, on a state's acquiescence as leading to the loss of a right or claim of state responsibility.

[66] Commentary to Art. 45, ILC Articles on State Responsibility, paras 6–10.

[67] BBC, 'Iran "minister" on Interpol list', 21 August 2009, <http://news.bbc.co.uk/1/hi/world/middle_east/8215293.stm>.

[68] Keesing's, Vol. 41, June 1995, 40622.

[69] *Ibid*; Keesing's, Vol. 41, June 1995, 40587.

security organs and the leadership in the Sudan were involved in assisting, facilitating and supporting the assassination attempt on the life of the Egyptian President'.[70]

Following the assassination attempt, three key suspects allegedly fled to the Sudan and Ethiopia requested their extradition. The Sudan failed to comply with the request, maintaining that the suspects were not in Sudanese territory.[71] Ethiopia first brought the matter to the Organization of African Unity ('OAU'),[72] which issued a statement calling upon the Government of the Sudan to comply with the Ethiopian extradition request, and to 'desist from engaging in activities of assisting, supporting and facilitating terrorist activities and from giving shelter and sanctuaries to terrorist elements'.[73] The OAU demand that the Sudan comply with its international obligations to refrain from supporting terrorist conduct does not amount to an invocation of state responsibility by an injured state.[74] The OAU statement—underlying which is a determination of fact as to Sudanese involvement in the assassination plot—might nevertheless have formed the basis of Ethiopia or Egypt's adoption of countermeasures in response to Sudanese responsibility.[75]

Despite allegations of Sudanese involvement (for which its international responsibility could have been invoked by either Egypt or Ethiopia), the focus has been on criminal law enforcement. Neither injured state pursued the state responsibility option. Instead, Ethiopia brought the Sudan's failure to extradite to the Security Council, maintaining its focus on the criminal justice model of responsibility. The Security Council qualified the Sudan's failure to comply with the extradition request as 'a threat to international peace and security' and, acting under Chapter VII, (a) demanded that the Sudanese government extradite the three suspects wanted in connection with the assassination attempt to Ethiopia for prosecution, (b) demanded that the Sudanese government desist from engaging in activities of assisting, supporting and facilitating terrorist activities and from giving shelter and sanctuary to terrorist elements, and (c) imposed sanctions on the Sudan pending its compliance.[76] For its part, the Sudan maintained it did not support terrorism, and that the three suspected terrorists were not in Sudanese territory.[77]

---

[70] Letter dated 9 January 1996 from the Permanent Representative of Ethiopia to the United Nations addressed to the President of the Security Council, UN Doc. S/1996/10, Annex III, 5, para 4.

[71] Letter dated 24 June 1996 from the Permanent Representative of the Sudan to the United Nations addressed to the President of the Security Council, UN Doc. S/1996/464, Annex, 2; Letter dated 2 July 1996 from the Permanent Representative of the Sudan to the United Nations addressed to the President of the Security Council, UN Doc. S/1996/513.

[72] The OAU disbanded in 2002 and was replaced by the African Union. See <http://www.africa-union.org>.

[73] Statement Issued on 11 September 1995 by the Third Extraordinary Session of the OAU Mechanism for Conflict Prevention, Management and Resolution at the Ministerial Level on the assassination attempt on H.E. Hosni Mubarak, President of Egypt, UN Doc. S/1995/10, Annex I, 2–3, paras 6–8. The Security Council reiterated the OAU demands in Resolution 1044 (1996), para 4(b).

[74] Art. 30, ILC Articles on State Responsibility.

[75] In regard to statements made by the Security Council in the human rights context, and the potential impact of those statements in reference to the 'at your own risk' element of countermeasures, see Section 5.1.2.

[76] UNSC Resolution 1054 (1996), para 1; UNSC Resolution 1070 (1996).

[77] See Letter dated 31 May 1996 from the Permanent Representative of the Sudan to the United Nations addressed to the President of the Security Council, UN Doc. S/1996/402 (1996); Letter dated

The sanctions against the Sudan were lifted on 28 September 2001,[78] and Mustafa Hamza, the primary suspect in the assassination attempt, is reported to have been surrendered to Egypt by an unnamed country (reportedly Iran) in 2005 to face trial.[79] Neither Ethiopia nor Egypt has made any demands for reparation and both have (for the time being) remained focused on pursuing the criminal justice model of responsibility. Ethiopia's public statements to the effect that its investigations revealed the Sudan's involvement in assisting, facilitating and supporting the assassination attempt[80] may well have preserved its right to invoke Sudanese responsibility in the event the trial of Mustafa Hamza reveals relevant information about his connection to the security forces of the Sudan.

(iii) Assassination of former Lebanese Prime Minister Hariri

There is evidence suggesting that Syrian intelligence forces were involved in the assassination of former Lebanese Prime Minister Hariri on 14 February 2005. The Security Council, in Resolution 1595 (2005), established an international independent investigation commission ('UNIIIC') to assist the Lebanese authorities in their investigation of the assassination. UNIIIC's initial report noted the improbability that a third party could have undertaken the necessary surveillance of Mr Hariri and maintained the resources, logistics and capacity needed to initiate, plan and carry out the assassination without the knowledge of the Lebanese security services and their Syrian counterparts.[81] As a result, UNIIIC concluded that:

> there is probable cause to believe that the decision to assassinate former Prime Minister Rafik Hariri could not have been taken without the approval of top ranked Syrian security officials and could not have been further organized without the collusion of their counterparts in the Lebanese security services.[82]

UNIIIC's follow-up investigations confirmed the evidence pointing to the involvement of high-ranking Syrian officers.[83]

---

24 June 1996 from the Permanent Representative of the Sudan to the United Nations addressed to the President of the Security Council, UN Doc. S/1996/464, Annex, 2–4; Letter dated 2 July 1996 from the Permanent Representative of the Sudan to the United Nations addressed to the President of the Security Council, UN Doc. S/1996/513.

[78] UNSC Resolution 1372 (2001).

[79] Al Jazeera, 'Egypt trial for alleged plotter', 8 January 2005, <http://english.aljazeera.net/English/Archive/Archive?ArchiveID=8763>.

[80] *Supra* note 70.

[81] UN Doc. S/2005/662, 31, paras 123–4.

[82] *Ibid*, 33, para 133.

[83] See Report of the International Independent Investigation Commission established pursuant to Security Council Resolutions 1595 (2005) and 1636 (2005), UN Doc. S/2005/775, 9, para 34. UNIIIC's subsequent reports do not reach any new conclusions as to potential Syrian responsibility for the assassination, although the Commission highlights the increased co-operation received from the Syrian authorities. See UN Doc. S/2006/161; UN Doc. S/2006/375; UN Doc. S/2006/760; UN Doc. S/2006/962; UN Doc. S/2007/150; UN Doc. S/2007/424; UN Doc. S/2007/684; UN Doc. S/2008/210; UN Doc. S/2008/752. The investigation has since been transferred to the Special Tribunal for Lebanon (discussed *infra* notes 88–93), and the nature (or extent) of Syrian responsibility remains contested. In July 2010, the prosecutor of the Special Tribunal for Lebanon asked Lebanon's

The Security Council, in Resolution 1636 (2005), acting under Chapter VII, took note 'with extreme concern of the Commission's conclusion that there is converging evidence pointing at the involvement of both Lebanese and Syrian officials in this terrorist act, and that it is difficult to envisage a scenario whereby such complex assassination could have been carried out without their knowledge';[84] determined that 'the involvement of any state in the assassination would constitute a serious violation by that state of its obligations to prevent and refrain from supporting terrorism and that it would amount to a serious violation of its obligation to respect the sovereignty and political independence of Lebanon';[85] and decided that 'Syria must detain those Syrian officials or individuals whom the Commission considers as suspected of involvement in the planning, sponsoring, organizing or perpetrating of this terrorist act, and make them fully available to the Commission'.[86] The Security Council also imposed sanctions directly against the individuals designated by the Commission or the Government of Lebanon as suspected of involvement in the planning, sponsoring, organization or perpetration of the assassination.[87]

The Secretary-General, in a report to the Security Council, recommended the establishment of a tribunal through an agreement concluded between Lebanon and the United Nations.[88] A special tribunal to prosecute persons responsible for the attack of 14 February 2005 was established by agreement between the United Nations and the Lebanese Republic.[89] The Statute of the Special Tribunal for Lebanon[90] sets out the Tribunal's jurisdiction, which covers the assassination of 14 February 2005 and is extendable to terrorist attacks determined to be related to the assassination, and the applicable law, which is limited to provisions of the Lebanese Criminal Code.[91] Criminal responsibility is to extend to any person who committed, participated as an accomplice, organized or directed others to commit the crimes within the Tribunal's jurisdiction.[92] While the Tribunal's jurisdiction is concurrent with that of national Lebanese courts, it has primacy over Lebanese courts in relation to crimes within the Tribunal's jurisdiction.[93]

---

authorities to hand over all information allegedly held by Hezbollah leader Hassan Nasrallah pertaining to the assassination. Hezbollah's involvement certainly raises questions of Iranian involvement (given Iran's alleged support for Hezbollah), although Mr Nasrallah held a press conference on 9 August 2010 during which he implicated Israel in the attack. UN News Centre, 'UN-backed probe into Hariri killings seeks information held by Hezbollah leader', 11 August 2010, <http://www.un.org/apps/news/>.

[84] UNSC Resolution 1636 (2005), para 2.

[85] *Ibid*, para 4.

[86] *Ibid*, para 11(a).

[87] In particular, states were required to prevent the relevant individuals from entering or transiting through their territory, and to freeze all funds and financial assets in their territories that are owned or controlled (directly or indirectly) by the named individuals. UNSC Resolution 1636 (2005), para 3(a).

[88] See UNSG, Report pursuant to paragraph 6 of Security Council Resolution 1644 (2005), UN Doc. S/2006/176.

[89] UNSC Resolution 1757 (2007), Annex. See the first annual report of the Special Tribunal for Lebanon, submitted by the Tribunal's President (Antonio Cassese) to the Security Council, UN Doc. S/2010/159.

[90] UNSC Resolution 1757 (2007), Attachment to Annex.

[91] Arts. 1 and 2, UNSC Resolution 1757 (2007), Attachment to Annex.

[92] Art. 3, UNSC Resolution 1757 (2007), Attachment to Annex.

[93] Art. 4, UNSC Resolution 1757 (2007), Attachment to Annex.

Despite the initial evidence of Syrian involvement in the assassination, and the Security Council's taking note of that evidence, focus has been on individual criminal responsibility, without any mention of Syria's obligation to make reparation. The political difficulties in invoking Syrian responsibility, given Syrian influence over certain segments of the Lebanese political infrastructure, confirms Cassese's observation that the 'international community currently tends to give pride of place to [individual criminal responsibility] and plays down or neglects [state responsibility], largely motivated by political factors'.[94]

(iv) Conclusion

In each of the cases examined above, the focus of both the injured state and the international community through the Security Council has (to date) been on the individual criminal responsibility of the terrorist actors, despite allegations of state involvement in the terrorist attacks. While the practice suggests that pursuing the criminal justice model of responsibility is considered, in the first instance, a more worthwhile endeavour than pursuing a state's responsibility, it certainly does not suggest anything about the formal legal relationship between the two forms of responsibility. It remains true that individual criminal responsibility does not replace state responsibility for criminal acts attributable to a state that amount to internationally wrongful conduct. It remains equally true, however, that absent a third party determination of state involvement in an act of terrorism, an invocation of state responsibility is most often met by the wrongdoing state's denial of its involvement in a terrorist attack. Individual criminal responsibility is therefore often at least the initial focus of the injured states' attempts to pursue some measure of justice. As criminal convictions can serve to pressure wrongdoing states out from behind their veil of deniability, pursuing the individual criminal responsibility model of justice to its completion may, as a matter of process, facilitate giving effect to state responsibility. The question remains, however, whether criminal prosecutions can in some way also satisfy a state's responsibility for an internationally wrongful act related to terrorism.

6.3 Determinations of individual criminal responsibility as satisfaction

A state that is responsible for an internationally wrongful act has a secondary obligation under the law of state responsibility to make full reparation for any injury caused.[95] Satisfaction, which is the least common form of reparation,[96]

---

[94] Cassese (2006), 722. See also M.D. Evans (1998) and Pellet (2001) discussing the increasing focus on individual criminal responsibility to the detriment of state responsibility.

[95] Art. 31, ILC Articles on State Responsibility.

[96] Commentary to Art. 37, ILC Articles on State Responsibility, para 1, notes that satisfaction is not a standard form of reparation, in the sense that the injury caused will often be fully repaired by restitution and/or compensation.

presents a potential 'point of convergence between State responsibility and individual criminal responsibility under international law'.[97] The Commentary to Article 37 of the ILC Articles on State Responsibility suggests that 'disciplinary or penal action against the individuals whose conduct caused the internationally wrongful act' may amount to a form of satisfaction under the law of state responsibility.[98] In other words, it proposes that a state which is responsible for an act of terrorism might discharge the secondary obligations that flow from its responsibility by holding the individual terrorist actors criminally responsible for their crimes. Such satisfaction might be offered whether the state's responsibility is direct, through the mechanism of attribution, or indirect, in virtue of its support or failure to prevent the terrorist attack.

The literature and ILC codification efforts evidence a measure of analytical confusion, however, regarding the relationship between individual criminal responsibility and remedies for the internationally wrongful act of a state. Typically, either the necessary elements of state responsibility are disregarded or primary and secondary obligations are conflated. This section sets out the conditions under which prosecution of an alleged criminal might amount to satisfaction for an internationally wrongful act related to the commission of a crime, and considers the particularities of the terrorism context that make satisfaction an unlikely point of convergence between state and individual responsibility.

6.3.1 The state must be responsible for an internationally wrongful act

It should go without saying, but prosecution can only amount to satisfaction for a state's responsibility if the prosecuting state has committed an internationally wrongful act giving rise to a secondary obligation to make reparation. Where there is no basis of international responsibility, the prosecution of international criminals (whether terrorist or otherwise) cannot amount to reparation for an internationally wrongful act. Gray notes that, in the extensive diplomatic practice on satisfaction, 'the emphasis is on the affront to the State, however caused, rather than any breach of international law'.[99] Indeed, many of the demands made by injured states for the prosecution of wrongdoers cited in the literature and ILC codification efforts were made in respect of individual conduct for which the state was not responsible (either directly by way of attribution, or indirectly through a

---

[97] ILC, Comments and Observations received from Governments on State Responsibility, UN Doc. A/CN.4/488 (1998), 138 (Czech Republic). See also Rosenne (1997), 164; Nollkaemper (2003), 637; Maison (2004), 472–3. But see Dominicé (1984).

[98] Commentary to Art. 37, ILC Articles on State Responsibility, para 5. See also Art. 45(2)(d), draft Articles on State Responsibility adopted by the ILC on first reading in 1996, which provided that, where the internationally wrongful act arose from the serious misconduct of officials or from criminal conduct, satisfaction to the injured state may consist in disciplinary action against or punishment of those responsible. Report of the International Law Commission on the work of its forty-eighth session, UN Doc. A/51/10 (1996), 63.

[99] Gray (1990), 42.

failure of due diligence), and there is therefore considerable doubt whether this practice amounted to reparation for breaches of international law.[100] For instance, in 1975, two US officers were killed in Tehran, and their murderers were executed by the Iranian Government.[101] The executions are consistently cited as practice of punishment amounting to a form of satisfaction.[102] The murders were, however, carried out by the Iranian People's Fighters' Organization (the 'IPF') in retaliation for the death of nine of its members while in Iranian custody.[103] The IPF was not acting on behalf of the Iranian Government, but against it. Furthermore, there is nothing in the factual record which indicates that the Iranian Government failed to exercise due diligence in protecting the US officers, who were air force colonels attached to the Military Assistance Advisory Group at the Iranian armed forces headquarters.[104] As a result, Iran could not be held responsible (directly or indirectly) for the murders, and the punishment (in the form of execution) of those who carried out the murders could not amount to satisfaction for an internationally wrongful act. Punishment may well have been in fulfilment of a primary obligation to punish those responsible for injury to aliens, or in furtherance of maintaining friendly relations with the US, but could not be in satisfaction of Iran's non-existent responsibility.

6.3.2 The wrongdoing state must be the prosecuting state

Prosecution only amounts to reparation for an internationally wrongful act if it is the wrongdoing state (rather than the injured state) that seeks to impose (or facilitate the imposition of) individual criminal responsibility.[105] A case that is often cited as an example of punishment in satisfaction of international responsibility is the Rainbow Warrior case.[106] The two French agents, however, were prosecuted by New Zealand (the injured state) over the protests of the French Government (the wrongdoing state).[107] As reparation is an obligation that must be discharged by the wrongdoing state,[108] punishment of the French secret service agents did not amount to a measure of satisfaction given by the responsible French State to the injured state.

---

[100] *Ibid.*

[101] Keesing's, Vol. 21, October 1975, 27374.

[102] Arangio-Ruiz (1989), 40, para 132; Report of the International Law Commission on the work of its forty-fifth session, UN Doc. A/48/10 (1993), 80, para 14; Commentary to Art. 37, ILC Articles on State Responsibility, para 5. See also Nollkaemper (2003), 637.

[103] Keesing's, Vol. 21, October 1975, 27374.

[104] Keesing's, Vol. 21, October 1975, 27374. See also Rousseau (1976), 257.

[105] Graefrath defines satisfaction as 'all measures *taken by the author state of an internationally wrongful act* to affirm the existence of the affected obligation and to prevent continuation or repetition of the wrongful act'. Emphasis added. Graefrath (1984), 86.

[106] See Sections 2.2.1 and 3.2.2 for a full discussion of the Rainbow Warrior incident. See also Report of the International Law Commission on the work of its forty-fifth session, UN Doc. A/48/10 (1993), 80, 14; Arangio-Ruiz (1989), 40, para 132; Nollkaemper (2003), 637.

[107] See *UNSG Rainbow Warrior Ruling* (1986).

[108] Art. 37, ILC Articles on State Responsibility.

6.3.3 No independent obligation to punish

In order that prosecution amount to satisfaction for an internationally wrongful act, the prosecution must have been carried out in fulfilment of the secondary obligation to make reparation that flows from state responsibility. If the obligation to prosecute (or at least to submit to prosecution) is a primary obligation, it cannot at the same time be a consequence of international responsibility.[109] That this is the case is clearly evidenced by the ILC's concern to limit the availability of punishment as a form of satisfaction, fearing that it would otherwise 'result [in] too much interference in the internal affairs of States'.[110] Requiring the performance of an obligation that the wrongdoing state has itself accepted cannot amount to interference in its internal affairs. The concern regarding interference in the internal affairs of the wrongdoing state only materializes to the extent that punishment of responsible persons is not a primary obligation that the wrongdoing state has already assumed. The logical implication of this concern is that the ILC conceived of 'punishment as satisfaction' as a new (and not previously assumed) obligation imposed on the wrongdoing state flowing from its responsibility.[111] The confusion between reparation for the breach of one international obligation and performance of another related but independent international obligation is nevertheless persistent throughout the ILC codification effort.[112] In the terrorism context, states are under two separate but related sets of primary obligations. States are under an obligation to refrain from sponsoring or supporting terrorism and to prevent the commission of terrorist acts.[113] States are equally under a primary obligation to extradite or submit individuals responsible for terrorism to prosecution.[114] Until 11

---

[109] See Dominicé (1984), 106.

[110] Report of the International Law Commission on the work of its forty-sixth session, UN Doc. A/47/10 (1992), 35, para 247.

[111] It bears noting that the obligation is not conceived in terms of an obligation to punish, but rather as an obligation to duly submit a case to relevant authorities for the purposes of investigation and prosecution. See Crawford (2000a), 41, para 192.

[112] See e.g. ILC, Comments and Observations received from Governments on State Responsibility, UN Doc. A/CN.4/488 (1998), 111 (Austria). The most widely cited example of a request for prosecution as satisfaction for international responsibility involves the murder of Count Bernadotte in Israeli-controlled territory. See e.g. Arangio-Ruiz (1989), 39–40, para 132; Report of the International Law Commission on the work of its forty-fifth session, UN Doc. A/48/10 (1993), 80, para 14; Commentary to Art. 37, ILC Articles on State Responsibility, para 5. In that case, however, the prosecution of responsible individuals was in fulfilment of a primary obligation existing under international law and Security Council Resolution 59 (19 October 1948) (which determined that the Israeli Government had the duty to make every effort to apprehend and punish persons responsible for the assassination of the UN Mediator (para 5(f)), and not as reparation for Israel's failure to exercise due diligence in preventing the assassination of Count Bernadotte or its liability for acts of irregular forces committed in territory under its control. See UNSG, Report on Reparation for Injuries Incurred in the Service of the United Nations, UN Doc. A/1347 (1950), 2. See further Crawford (2000a), 41, para 192 (in which he acknowledges that 'it may not always be clear whether prosecution of criminal conduct was sought by way of satisfaction or as an aspect of performance of some primary obligation'); Ago (1972), 107.

[113] See Sections 2.1 and 3.1.

[114] See Section 3.2.

September 2001, the obligation to submit to prosecution was treaty-based, applied only to acts of terrorism covered by the series of TSCs, and was applicable *inter partes*.[115] With the adoption of Security Council Resolution 1373 (2001), all states, whether party to the TSCs or not (and apparently whether party to the UN Charter or not), are under an obligation to (i) refrain from providing any form of support, active or passive, to entities or persons involved in terrorist acts, (ii) take the necessary steps to prevent the commission of terrorist acts, (iii) deny safe haven to those who finance, plan, support, or commit terrorist acts, and (iv) ensure that any person who participates in the financing, planning, preparation or perpetration of terrorist acts or in supporting terrorist acts is brought to justice.[116] The obligations to refrain from sponsoring and supporting terrorism, and to prevent terrorism, existed in customary international law before 11 September 2001.[117] The real impact of Security Council Resolution 1373 is to impose an obligation on all states to bring terrorists to justice. As a result, any state that might be directly or indirectly responsible for an act of terrorism is equally under a primary obligation to submit the alleged terrorist actors to prosecution. If, for example, a state is internationally responsible for failing to diligently prevent a particular course of terrorist conduct, prosecution of the alleged criminals will not amount to reparation (in the form of satisfaction) because such prosecution amounts to the performance of a separate primary obligation under a relevant TSC or the UN Charter.[118] States that are directly responsible for terrorism (in that the terrorist acts are attributable to the state) are equally under a primary obligation to submit the individual terrorist actors to prosecution, although this obligation is likely to be ineffective.[119] Nevertheless, given the existence of the primary obligation, prosecution would not amount to satisfaction.

In state practice, it is often difficult to determine whether the injured state is demanding prosecution as satisfaction for the state's responsibility, or because the wrongdoing state is under a primary obligation to submit to prosecution. Part of the reason for that difficulty is that demands for prosecution are often made in conjunction with demands for reparation. It may be the case that the injured state considers itself to be demanding satisfaction, when prosecution is not available as satisfaction because the wrongdoing state is under a primary obligation to submit to prosecution. In such cases, the correct legal characterization of the injured state's demands would be a demand for performance of the primary obligation.

---

[115] There has been a consistent debate in the literature on whether the *aut dedere aut judicare* obligation set out in the TSCs establishes universal jurisdiction for terrorist crimes (as a matter of customary international law), or whether the exceptional basis of jurisdiction provided for in the TSCs is conventional and *inter partes* only. See Kolb (2004), 272–8 for a summary of the debate.

[116] UNSC Resolution 1373 (2001), para 2(a), (b), (c) and (e).

[117] See Chapters 2 and 3.

[118] All TSCs impose an *aut dedere aut judicare* obligation on state parties (see Section 3.2), and the obligation to comply with Security Council resolutions adopted under Chapter VII, in this case UNSC Resolution 1373, is set out in Article 25 of the UN Charter.

[119] See *supra* Chapter 3, note 133 and accompanying text, regarding the obligation to fulfil *aut dedere aut judicare* obligations in good faith, discussed in reference to the *Lockerbie Case*.

Consider the destruction of KAL flight 858. A Korean Airlines (KAL) aircraft exploded off the coast of Burma on 29 November 1987, allegedly as a result of a time bomb planted on the plane by two North Korean secret service agents before they disembarked in Bahrain.[120] The two agents (a man and a woman) were stopped for questioning at the airport in Bahrain owing to irregularities with their passports, whereupon they ingested poison, resulting in the man's death. The woman survived and was extradited to South Korea, where she confessed that she had planted the bomb in her capacity as a North Korean secret service agent.[121] In spite of the confession, North Korea alleged that it was South Korea itself that had carried out the bombing.[122] South Korea brought the matter to the attention of the Security Council. Most states condemned the attack in their statements to the Security Council, without taking any position on whether it was carried out on behalf of the North Korean regime.[123] Only Japan and the US openly condemned the act as one organized and carried out on behalf of North Korea.[124] As a result of the inability to agree on responsibility, the Security Council took no action.[125] Nevertheless, the Government of South Korea 'strongly demanded that North Korea apologize for the bombing, punish those who were directly responsible, and guarantee that there would be no repetition of such a terrorist attack'.[126] An apology is a form of satisfaction,[127] and assurances of non-repetition are an obligation flowing from responsibility if circumstances so require.[128] The question is then whether prosecution of the responsible individuals can amount to a form of satisfaction, whatever South Korea intended for it to be. North Korea became a party to the Montreal Convention—which covers acts that endanger the safety of civil aircraft—before the bombing of KAL flight 858.[129] As a result, at the time of the incident, North Korea was under a primary obligation to submit those

---

[120] See Letter dated 10 February 1988 from the Permanent Observer of the Republic of Korea to the United Nations addressed to the President of the Security Council, UN Doc. S/19488 (1988), Annex, 9, para 10.

[121] *Ibid*, 9, para 10 and 14–15, paras 26–7.

[122] See SC 2791st meeting (1988), 32–56.

[123] *Ibid*, 61–3 (Federal Republic of Germany); SC 2792nd meeting (1988), 10–11 (France), 22–3 (Argentina), 18 (Yugoslavia), 54–5 (Zambia), 25 (Italy). See also communications condemning the attack, Letter dated 26 January 1988 from the Permanent Representative of the Federal Republic of Germany (on behalf of the 12 EC Member States) to the United Nations addressed to the Secretary-General, UN Doc. S/19458 (1988); Letter dated 16 February 1988 from the Chargé D'Affaires a.i. of the Permanent Mission of Bolivia to the United Nations addressed to the Secretary-General, UN Doc. S/19507 (1988); Letter dated 9 February 1988 from the Permanent Representative of Paraguay to the United Nations addressed to the Secretary-General, UN Doc. S/19493 (1988).

[124] SC 2791st meeting (1988), 23–5 (Japan); SC 2792nd meeting (1988), 64–5 (US).

[125] *Ibid*, 91.

[126] SC 2791st meeting (1988), 17 (Republic of Korea).

[127] Art. 37(2), ILC Articles on State Responsibility.

[128] Art. 30, ILC Articles on State Responsibility. Assurances of non-repetition are sometimes sought by way of satisfaction, but the ILC considered that they are better viewed as an aspect of the restoration of the legal relationship between the injured and wrongdoing state (forward looking) rather than reparation (backward looking). Commentary to Art. 30, ILC Articles on State Responsibility, para 11.

[129] North Korea ratified the Montreal Convention on 13 August 1980. <http://www.icao.int/icao/en/leb/Mtl71.pdf>.

responsible to prosecution, and any prosecution (or extradition to a jurisdiction that would prosecute) could not also amount to fulfilment of a secondary obligation resulting from North Korea's direct responsibility for the bombing. The difficulty with the obligation to submit to prosecution for acts carried out on behalf of the prosecuting state is of course that the good faith of the prosecuting state can rarely (absent regime change) be assumed, as discussed further below.

Satisfaction might provide a formal link between individual criminal responsibility and state responsibility—but not in the terrorism context. This is primarily because states are under a primary obligation to submit acts of terrorism to prosecution, and such prosecutions would be in fulfilment of that primary obligation, rather than in fulfilment of secondary obligations flowing from responsibility. It also happens to be the case that prosecutions for acts of international terrorism (which a state is alleged to be responsible for) tend to be carried out by the victim state, and not the wrongdoing state (which should be the state to discharge the secondary obligations flowing from its responsibility). As discussed below, victim states are likely to have more faith in their own criminal process than in the criminal process of the state that sponsored or supported the very crime being prosecuted. As a result, a criminal prosecution for terrorist offences by the state alleged to have sponsored or supported the act of terrorism will rarely, if ever, 'satisfy' the victim state.

6.4 An international criminal jurisdiction for terrorist offences

The difficulty with terrorism prosecutions in cases of concurrent responsibility is that the individual terrorist actors will often be within the jurisdiction of the very state alleged to have deployed or supported them. As discussed in Section 3.2 above, there is no obligation under the TSCs to extradite. But the impartiality of a state's courts or administrative bodies, when judging persons who acted as *de facto* agents of that state or with its support, should not be presumed.[130] The *Lockerbie Case* highlights the issue in that both the US and the UK argued that a state which sponsored an act of terrorism should not be the state to prosecute the actors who had physically committed the offence.[131] As there was no international criminal jurisdiction available to prosecute the Libyan agents, a compromise was reached whereby the two accused were tried by a Scottish court sitting in The Hague.[132] Similar concerns have underpinned the creation of international tribunals,[133] and part of the basis for proposals to internationalize criminal prosecutions seems to be

---

[130] See, for instance, Hersch Lauterpacht's discussion of the German trials for war crimes following WWI. H. Lauterpacht (1944), 84. In reference to terrorism prosecutions by the terrorism-sponsoring state, see Morris (2004), 65.

[131] See *Lockerbie Case (Libya v. UK)*, Counter-Memorial of the UK, paras 3.106–3.109. See also Tomuschat (1992), 42–3.

[132] Keesing's, Vol. 45, April 1999, 42914; the guardian, 'Lockerbie trial: what happened when', 31 January 2001, <http://www.guardian.co.uk/uk/2001/jan/31/lockerbie.derekbrown>.

[133] See Mégret (2008), 508–10.

that it alleviates both the victim state and wrongdoing state's concerns regarding the impartiality of criminal proceedings.[134] This section explores the international community's efforts to establish an international basis for the prosecution of terrorist offences.

Even though prosecuting individual terrorist perpetrators cannot itself fulfil the secondary obligations resulting from international responsibility for terrorism,[135] determinations of individual criminal responsibility do serve to pressure wrong-doing states into accepting (and fulfilling) those secondary obligations.[136] In addition, the ICJ has signalled a willingness to rely on determinations by international criminal tribunals in its own determinations of state responsibility.[137] A relevant determination of individual criminal responsibility, particularly where such respon-sibility depends on the state leadership role of the individual accused,[138] could therefore go a long way in settling disputes bearing on a state's responsibility for the crimes of which the accused was convicted. As examined below, despite several efforts, there is no international forum available for terrorism prosecutions *per se*, but the ICC may be available, in limited circumstances, to prosecute terrorism as a crime of aggression or a crime against humanity.

6.4.1 The League of Nations Terrorism Convention

The adoption of the first international convention for the prevention and punish-ment of terrorism was triggered by the assassination of King Alexander of Yugosla-via and Mr Louis Barthou, Foreign Minister of the French Republic, in Marseilles on 9 October 1934, by Yugoslav *émigrés* operating from Hungary. Yugoslavia brought the incident to the attention of the Council of the League of Nations, and accused Hungary of complicity in the terrorist activities of the Yugoslav *émigrés*.[139] In particular, Yugoslavia accused Hungary of tolerating terrorist training camps in its territory, from which terrorist attacks against Yugoslavia were launched, and of providing Yugoslav *émigrés* terrorists with Hungarian passports to facilitate their free movement.[140] The Council unanimously adopted a resolu-tion which held that 'certain Hungarian authorities may have assumed, at any rate through negligence, certain responsibilities relative to acts having a connection with the preparation of the crime of Marseilles'.[141]

---

[134] In reference to the expression of concern regarding US prosecutions of those responsible for the 9/11 terrorist attacks, see Morris (2004), 66. See also *Lockerbie Case (Libya v. US)*, Provisional Measures, Separate Opinion of Judge Shahabuddeen, 141, and Separate Opinion of Judge *ad hoc* El-Kosheri, 216, both suggesting that the Lockerbie bombers might not get a fair trial in the US.

[135] See Section 6.3.

[136] See Section 6.2.

[137] *Supra* note 8.

[138] On the connection between determinations of individual criminal responsibility (where an element of the offence is that it was committed by an official of the state) and state responsibility, see Jørgensen (2000), 151–7.

[139] League of Nations, Official Journal 1934 (July–December) 1712, 1713–4. See also Liais (1935).

[140] League of Nations, Official Journal 1934 (July–December) 1712, 1713–6.

[141] League of Nations, Official Journal 1934 (July–December) 1758, 1760.

In response to the assassinations, the League of Nations drafted a convention for the prevention and punishment of terrorism.[142] Given the allegations of state-supported (if not sponsored) terrorism, one might have expected the League of Nations Terrorism Convention to focus on leadership terrorist offences. But despite the Convention's reaffirmation of 'the principle of international law in virtue of which it is the duty of every State to refrain from any act designed to encourage terrorist activities directed at another State',[143] it addressed itself to terrorist offences generally. The definition of terrorism under the League of Nations Terrorism Convention was not limited to acts carried out by or at the instigation of state agents, nor did the provisions regarding the prosecution of terrorist offences suggest any such limitation. Indeed the state of nationality, if it was precluded from extraditing by its national law, was to prosecute the terrorist offences defined under the Convention—suggesting that the acts of terrorism envisaged were not those carried out by or on behalf of the state of nationality.[144] Conspiracy, incitement, wilful participation and knowing assistance were equally to be criminalized under the terms of the League of Nations Terrorism Convention,[145] each of which could amount to a relevant form of state participation in terrorism, but state organ status was not an element of these ancillary offences. The League of Nations also negotiated a Convention for the Creation of an International Criminal Court, which was only to have jurisdiction over the offences of terrorism set out in the League of Nations Terrorism Convention.[146] The creation of an international criminal jurisdiction was intended to assist states in untenable political situations based on the presence of an alleged terrorist offender in their territory and asylum or political offence exception bars to extradition.[147] The international criminal court's jurisdiction was not to be exclusive, and was to be exercised at the option of the state in whose territory the alleged offender was found. As such, even had the League of Nations Terrorism Convention limited itself to leadership terrorist offences, criminal law enforcement in cases of state-sponsored or supported terrorism would have been unlikely in the event of the terrorist actor's return to his state of nationality (i.e. the terrorism-sponsoring or supporting state). In part due to the political situation in Europe in the late 1930s,[148] neither the League of Nations Terrorism Convention nor the League of Nations ICC Convention ever entered into force.[149]

---

[142] The League of Nations Terrorism Convention was opened for signature in 1937.

[143] There was some disagreement over the purpose of Article 1, with some states arguing that the article was superfluous because the matter was one already covered by customary international law. See Saul (2006), 84.

[144] Art. 9, League of Nations Terrorism Convention.

[145] Art. 3, League of Nations Terrorism Convention.

[146] Art. 2, League of Nations Convention for the Creation of an International Criminal Court, League of Nations Doc. C.94.M.47.1938.V, [hereinafter 'League of Nations ICC Convention'].

[147] League of Nations, Records of the Seventeenth Ordinary Session of the Assembly, Plenary Meetings (1936), reprinted in Friedlander (1979), Vol. 1, 135. See also Hudson (1938), 553–4.

[148] See Lambert (1990), 29.

[149] Friedlander (1979), Vol. 1, 253.

6.4.2 Draft Code of Offences against the Peace and Security of Mankind

The question of international criminal responsibility for acts of terrorism re-emerged following the World War II German war crimes trials—this time in the form of a Draft Code of Offences against the Peace and Security of Mankind ('Draft Code'). Unlike its League of Nations predecessor, the Draft Code did condition individual criminal responsibility for terrorism on state responsibility. In fact the first Special Rapporteur concluded, from the mandate conferred on the ILC by the General Assembly, that the '"code of offences against the peace and security of mankind" is intended to refer to acts which, if committed or tolerated by a State, would constitute violations of international law and involve international responsibility'.[150] The Draft Code effectively pierced the statehood veil in that the basis of individual criminal responsibility for many of the offences set out therein was a prohibition bearing on states (for instance the prohibition on the use of force under Article 2(4) of the UN Charter or the prohibition of aggression),[151] and the offences could therefore only be committed by the authorities of a state.[152] Article 2(6) of the Draft Code adopted in 1954 defined the offence of terrorism as '[t]he undertaking or encouragement *by the authorities of a State* of terrorist activities in another State, or the toleration *by the authorities of a State* of organized activities calculated to carry out terrorist acts in another State'.[153] Interestingly, the ILC considered the source of the prohibition of state terrorism to be Article 1 of the League of Nations Terrorism Convention, which had not limited itself to leadership crimes, despite reaffirmation of a state's duty to refrain from any act designed to encourage terrorist activities directed at another state.[154]

Work on the Draft Code was suspended in 1954, pending progress on a definition of aggression. When the Draft Code was taken up again in 1981,[155] Special Rapporteur Doudou Thiam reaffirmed the role of state responsibility in defining the offences that were to fall within the scope of the Code. He considered the general prohibitions under international law supporting the preservation of peace and security to be the basis for criminalizing the state organ or authority's conduct.[156] Thiam characterized terrorism as an offence against sovereignty and territorial integrity,[157] deriving 'from the general principles of law and from

---

[150] Spiropoulos (1950), 259, para 35.
[151] See, in regard to aggression, Report of the International Law Commission on the work of its forty-eighth session, UN Doc. A/51/10 (1996), 43, para 4.
[152] Report of the International Law Commission covering the work of its third session, UN Doc. A/1858 (1951), 135. In conditioning individual criminal responsibility on state responsibility, the Draft Code further supports the argument, set out in Section 3.2.2 above, that the McLeod principle no longer applies in reference to terrorist crimes. See Spiropoulos (1950), 262.
[153] Emphasis added. Report of the International Law Commission covering the work of its sixth session, UN Doc. A/2693 (1954), 151.
[154] *Supra* note 143 and accompanying text.
[155] UNGA Resolution 36/106 (1981).
[156] Thiam (1985), 65, para 12.
[157] Thiam (1983), 91, para 16.

Article 2, paragraph 4, of the Charter of the United Nations'.[158] The definition of terrorist offences, as adopted by the International Law Commission on First Reading, read as follows:

An individual who *as an agent or representative of a State* commits or orders the commission of any of the following acts:

  undertaking, organizing, assisting, financing, encouraging or tolerating acts against another State directed at persons or property and of such a nature as to create a state of terror in the minds of public figures, groups of persons or the general public [to . . .].[159]

State comments on Article 24 revealed how controversial the link between individual and state responsibility was in the terrorism context (as distinct from, for instance, the crime of aggression, where the link is a necessary element of the crime). States either (i) argued that the connection to state conduct was the element that justified the inclusion of terrorism in the Draft Code;[160] (ii) rejected that the offence of terrorism should be limited to acts carried out by or on behalf of a state (without, however, rejecting that such offences could be committed on behalf of a state);[161] or (iii) objected to terrorism as an offence within the Draft Code generally based on the absence of an accepted definition.[162] In response to state comments, Special Rapporteur Thiam proposed that the definition of terrorism as an offence within the scope of the Draft Code extend to private individuals acting as members of a group, movement or association.[163] The ILC report on the Draft Code in 1995, in response to the Special Rapporteur's proposal, noted the different views on whether the offence of international terrorism should be included in the Code.[164] Ultimately, terrorism was excluded from the Draft Code as adopted on second reading in 1996 based on the absence of a definition of terrorism and disagreement regarding the state or private capacity of terrorist actors to be criminalized.[165]

   Even if terrorism had been incorporated in the Draft Code, prosecution of an individual for an offence against the peace and security of mankind was not intended to relieve a state of any responsibility under international law for an act or omission attributable to it.[166] Governments commenting on the draft insisted that the criminal responsibility of state organs should not replace the state's

---

[158] *Ibid*, 91, para 17.
[159] Emphasis added. Art. 24, Draft Code of Offences against the Peace and Security of Mankind, Report of the International Law Commission on the work of its forty-third session, UN Doc. A/46/10 (1991), 97.
[160] See ILC, Comments and observations received from governments on the draft code of crimes against the peace and security of mankind (Part II), including the draft statute for an international criminal court, UN Doc. A/CN.4/448 and Add.1 (1993), 73, para 14 (Brazil).
[161] See *ibid*, 70, para 22 (Belarus); 102, para 29 (UK); 105, para 19 (US).
[162] See *ibid*, 88, para 72 (the Netherlands); 104, para 17 (US).
[163] Thiam (1995), 36, para 16.
[164] Report of the International Law Commission on the work of its forty-fifth session, UN Doc. A/48/10 (1993), 28, para 105.
[165] The ILC reduced the scope of the Code with a view to reaching consensus and to obtaining the support of governments. See Report of the International Law Commission on the work of its forty-eighth session, UN Doc. A/51/10 (1996), 16, para 46.
[166] Art. 5, Draft Code of Offences against the Peace and Security of Mankind, Report of the International Law Commission on the work of its forty-third session, UN Doc. A/46/10 (1991), 94.

responsibility, given the latter's role in reparation and compensation for victims.[167] That said, had the leadership element of the offence of terrorism been maintained, prosecutions pursuant to the Draft Code of Offences against the Peace and Security of Mankind could have laid the groundwork for the implementation of state responsibility, whether through pressure brought to bear on the wrongdoing state as a result of the criminal conviction, or as a result of a judicial determination of the wrongdoing state's responsibility for an act of terrorism (in reliance on the criminal conviction). The Draft Code project was soon overtaken by the ICC project, as discussed below.

6.4.3 International Criminal Court

In 1989, Trinidad and Tobago put forward a proposal to the UN regarding the creation of an international criminal court.[168] The General Assembly, partly in response to this proposal, requested the ILC to begin drafting a statute for an international criminal court.[169] Article 20(e) of the 1994 ILC Draft Statute stipulated that the international criminal court would have jurisdiction over terrorism in cases that 'constitute exceptionally serious crimes of international concern',[170] and included offences defined in certain Terrorism Suppression Conventions within the jurisdiction of the court.[171] The time pressure of the Rome Conference, however, did not allow for agreement to be reached on terrorism as a crime within the ICC's jurisdiction. As a concession to states pushing for the inclusion of terrorism in the Rome Statute, a resolution was included in the Final Act of the Rome Conference recommending that the Review Conference[172] consider defining terrorism and including it within the ICC's jurisdiction.[173] At the 8th Session of the Assembly of State Parties, a year before the 2010 Review Conference, the Netherlands proposed that terrorism be included as a crime within the ICC's jurisdiction under Article 5 of the Rome Statute, with a deferral of the exercise of jurisdiction by the Court until the definition and the modalities for the exercise of such jurisdiction had been agreed to.[174] There was disagreement

---

[167] See Thiam (1994), paras 41–8 and 101–2.

[168] As with the League of Nations ICC Convention, the proposed international criminal court was to have jurisdiction over drug trafficking and terrorist crimes. See Report of the Sixth Committee on the international criminal responsibility of individuals and entities engaged in illicit trafficking in narcotic drugs across national frontiers and other transnational criminal activities, UN Doc. A/44/770 (1989).

[169] See Crawford (2001), 24–6.

[170] Report of the International Law Commission on the work of its forty-sixth session, UN Doc. A/49/10 (1994).

[171] *Ibid*, Art. 20(e) and Appendix II.

[172] Under Article 123 of the Rome Statute, the Review Conference is to occur seven years after the entry into force of the Rome Statute.

[173] Final Act of the United Nations Diplomatic Conference of Plenipotentiaries on the Establishment of an International Criminal Court, done at Rome on 17 July 1998, UN Doc. A/CONF.183/10 (1998), Resolution E.

[174] ICC, Assembly of States Parties, 8th Session in the Hague, 18–26 November 2009, Official Records, Vol. I, ICC-ASP/8/20, Annex, 41.

whether there was a sufficiently clear definition of terrorism for the purposes of including it within the ICC's jurisdiction,[175] and given that the 2010 Review Conference was focused on the crime of aggression, terrorism was not discussed at any length. As a result, terrorism—as an international crime in its own right—has not yet (at the time of writing) been included within the ICC's jurisdiction. There is nothing in the ICC *Ad Hoc* Committee or Preparatory Committee materials, however, to suggest that an act of terrorism should not be prosecuted as the crime of aggression or a crime against humanity, to the extent that it meets the necessary elements of those crimes.

(i) Terrorism as the crime of aggression under the Rome Statute

The crime of aggression falls within the ICC's jurisdiction,[176] and elements of the crime, including the conditions for the exercise of the ICC's jurisdiction, were finally agreed upon at the 2010 Review Conference held in Kampala.[177] Under the Rome Statute:

'crime of aggression' means the planning, preparation, initiation or execution, by a person in a position effectively to exercise control over or to direct the political or military action of a State, of an *act of aggression* which, by its character, gravity and scale, constitutes a manifest violation of the Charter of the United Nations.[178]

---

[175] *Ibid*, paras 43–50.

[176] Art. 5(1)(d), Rome Statute. See generally von Hebel and Robinson (1999), 85.

[177] Following the adoption of the Rome Statute in 1998, defining the crime of aggression was left to a Preparatory Commission (whose work ended in 2002), followed by a Special Working Group on the Crime of Aggression ('SWGCA')—a subsidiary body of the ICC Assembly of States Parties. See Final Act of the United Nations Diplomatic Conference of Plenipotentiaries on the Establishment of an International Criminal Court, done at Rome on 17 July 1998, UN Doc. A/CONF.183/10 (1998), 9; ICC, Assembly of States Parties, Continuity of Work in Respect of the Crime of Aggression, ICC-ASP/1/Res.1 (2002), para 2. Finally, the definition was taken up by the Assembly of States Parties at the 2010 Review Conference in Kampala. Definitive progress on the elements of the crime of aggression was made prior to the Review Conference by separating the question of jurisdiction from the elements of the crime. See Seibert-Fohr (2008). But agreement on the conditions for the exercise of the ICC's jurisdiction at the Review Conference was an extraordinary achievement. Until Kampala, there was very little agreement on the conditions for the exercise of the ICC's jurisdiction, debate over which centred on whether a determination by the Security Council that a state has committed an act of aggression should be a condition for the exercise of jurisdiction by the ICC. See ICC, Assembly of States Parties, Informal Inter-sessional Meeting of the Special Working Group on the Crime of Aggression, held at the Liechtenstein Institute on Self-Determination, Woodrow Wilson School, Princeton University, 11–14 June 2007, ICC-ASP/6/SWGCA/INF.1 (2007). The final resolution of the issue at Kampala does not require a Security Council determination of an act of aggression. See ICC, Review Conference of the Rome Statute, 13th Plenary Meeting, ICC-RC/Res. 6 (advance version) (16 June 2010), Annex, Art. 8*bis*.

[178] Emphasis added. ICC, Review Conference of the Rome Statute, 13th Plenary Meeting, ICC-RC/Res. 6 (11 June 2010), Annex, Art. 8*bis*. The definition is identical to that proposed by the SWGCA in 2008 (see ICC, Assembly of States Parties, Discussion Paper on the Crime of Aggression Proposed by the Chairman (revision June 2008), ICC-ASP/6/SWGCA/2 (2008), Annex, 3; ICC, Assembly of States Parties, Report of the Special Working Group on the Crime of Aggression, ICC-ASP/6/20/Add.1 (2008), Annex II, paras 18–36), and is significantly simplified from the definition proposed in 2007. The 2007 proposed definition included several further modes of participation in the act of aggression: 'being in a position effectively to exercise control over or to direct the political or military action of a State, that person (leads) (directs) (organizes and/or directs) (engages in) (orders or

While initially a point of debate, the 2010 Review Conference accepted the SWGCA's proposal that the 'act of aggression' element of the crime of aggression be defined in reliance on the UN Definition of Aggression.[179] 'Act of aggression' is therefore to be defined as 'the use of armed force by a State against the sovereignty, territorial integrity or political independence of another State, or in any other manner inconsistent with the Charter of the United Nations', and includes a non-exclusive[180] list of acts (mirroring those enumerated in Article 3 of the UN Definition of Aggression) that 'shall [. . .] qualify as an act of aggression'.[181] Article 3(g) of the UN Definition of Aggression, of particular import if terrorism is to be tried before the ICC as the crime of aggression,[182] is also included in the list of acts that constitute the 'act of aggression' element of the crime of aggression: 'sending by or on behalf of a State of armed bands, groups, irregulars or mercenaries, which carry out acts of armed force against another State of such gravity as to amount to [invasion, attack, bombardment, or blockade], or its substantial involvement therein' is an act of aggression for which a state leader could bear individual criminal responsibility under the Rome Statute.

Article 3(g) of the UN Definition of Aggression and ICC jurisdiction

Determinations of individual criminal responsibility for the enumerated acts of aggression under Article 3 of the UN Definition of Aggression will be automatically translatable into state responsibility for those acts of aggression, because the ICC must determine that an 'act of aggression' (as defined under Article 3 of the UN Definition of Aggression) has occurred as one of the elements of determining that a crime of aggression has been committed. With the exception of Article 3(g), all the listed acts of aggression are carried out by the military of a state,[183] for which the state would be internationally responsible on the basis of the organ status of the military.[184] While any guilty verdicts handed down by the ICC for the crime of

---

participates actively in) the planning, preparation, initiation or execution of an act of aggression/armed attack'. ICC, Assembly of States Parties, Discussion paper proposed by the Chairman, ICC-ASP/5/SWGCA/2 (2007), Annex, combination of Variant (a) and Variant (b), 3.

[179] See ICC, Review Conference of the Rome Statute, 13th Plenary Meeting, ICC-RC/Res. 6 (11 June 2010), Annex, Art. 8*bis*; ICC, Assembly of States Parties, Discussion paper proposed by the Chairman, ICC-ASP/5/SWGCA/2 (2007), Annex, Annex, 3; ICC, Assembly of States Parties, Report of the Special Working Group on the Crime of Aggression, ICC-ASP/6/SWGCA/1 (2007), 2, para 13. Early proposals (since rejected) were to define the state act element of the crime of aggression as an 'armed attack' within the meaning of Article 51 of the UN Charter. See Preparatory Commission for the International Criminal Court, Working Group on the Crime of Aggression, Definition of the crime of aggression and conditions for the exercise of jurisdiction, Discussion paper proposed by the Coordinator, PCNICC/2002/WGCA/RT.1/Rev.2 (2002), 1.

[180] See ICC, Assembly of States Parties, Report of the Special Working Group on the Crime of Aggression, ICC-ASP/6/20/Add.1 (2008), Annex II, paras 34–6.

[181] ICC, Assembly of States Parties, Discussion Paper on the Crime of Aggression Proposed by the Chairman (revision June 2008), ICC-ASP/6/SWGCA/2 (2008), Annex, 3.

[182] Acts of state-sponsored terrorism, of sufficient gravity, can amount to an act of aggression pursuant to Article 3(g) of the UN Definition of Aggression. See Section 2.1.1.

[183] Arts. 3(a)–(e), UN Definition of Aggression, UNGA Resolution 3314 (1974), Annex.

[184] The UN Definition of Aggression, UNGA Resolution 3314 (1974), Annex, does not define the act of state aggression in terms of leadership participation in the planning of such aggression, it being

aggression related to Articles 3(a)–(e) of the UN Definition of Aggression could certainly form the basis of a determination of state responsibility should the matter be put to the ICJ,[185] such determinations would be largely irrelevant in the terrorism context given the exclusion of military activities from the scope of most of the TSCs.[186] In the case of Article 3(g) of the UN Definition of Aggression, however, the act amounting to aggression is not carried out by the military of the state whose leaders may be held criminally responsible therefor, but by armed bands sent by or on behalf of the state. But in the same way that military conduct is attributable to a state (in virtue of the organ status of the military), the acts of aggression carried out by the armed bands will be attributable to the state (on the basis of the *lex specialis* standard of attribution set out in Article 3(g) of the UN Definition of Aggression).[187] Any ICC determination of individual criminal responsibility for an act of aggression under Article 3(g) of the UN Definition of Aggression will necessarily incorporate a determination that the elements of Article 3(g) have themselves been satisfied, and will therefore satisfy the elements of state responsibility for that act of aggression. As it is clear that acts of terrorism of sufficient gravity can amount to an act of aggression pursuant to Article 3(g) of the UN Definition of Aggression,[188] a criminal conviction by the ICC could assist in giving effect to a state's responsibility for an act of terrorism amounting to aggression, as discussed further below.

(ii) Terrorism as a crime against humanity

Under the Rome Statute, a crime against humanity ('CAH') is defined as any of a list of enumerated acts (including murder, extermination, torture, rape, persecution, and enforced disappearance of persons)[189] 'when committed as part of a widespread or systematic attack directed against any civilian population,[190] with knowledge of the attack'.[191] It is relatively uncontroversial that certain acts of terrorism, if committed on a significant enough scale, would constitute a CAH.[192] What is of

understood that large-scale conduct by the military forces of a state, such that amount to an act of aggression, is planned at the highest levels.

[185] See the ICJ's approach to findings of fact by other international criminal tribunals, most significantly the ICTY, in its *Bosnia Genocide Case* Judgment.

[186] See Section 4.2.2.

[187] See Section 2.1.1.

[188] See Section 2.1.1.

[189] Art. 7(1), Rome Statute.

[190] 'Attack against any civilian population' means a course of conduct involving the multiple commission of acts referred to in Article 7(1) (such as murder, rape etc.) against any civilian population pursuant to or in furtherance of a state or organizational policy to commit such attack. Art. 7(2), Rome Statute. See also Art. 7, ICC, Elements of Crimes, Official Journal, ICC-ASP/1/3.

[191] Art. 7(1), Rome Statute.

[192] The ICTY has explicitly recognized that crimes against humanity can be carried out by terrorist groups or organizations. *Tadić* (ICTY-94-1-T), paras 654–5. See also Report of the International Law Commission on the work of its forty-sixth session, UN Doc. A/49/10 (1994), para 21 (noting that a systematic campaign of terror committed by some group against the civilian population would fall within the category of crimes against humanity under general international law); Report of the policy

interest for the purposes of examining the relationship between individual criminal and state responsibility are the modalities of participation in a CAH set out in Article 25(3) of the Rome Statute. Individuals can be held criminally responsible for (i) ordering, soliciting or inducing the commission of a CAH (which in fact occurs or is attempted); (ii) aiding, abetting or otherwise assisting in the commission of a CAH, including providing the means for its commission; or (iii) in any other way contributing to the commission or attempted commission of a CAH by a group of persons acting with a common purpose, where such contribution is intentional and is either made with the aim of furthering the criminal activity or criminal purpose of the group or is made in the knowledge of the intention of the group to commit the CAH.[193]

The jurisprudence of the international criminal tribunals has considered that ordering the commission of an offence 'entails a person in a position of authority using that position to convince another to commit an offence'.[194] The jurisprudence has been split, however, on whether or not a superior/subordinate relationship is a necessary element of 'ordering the commission of an offence'.[195] If a superior/subordinate relationship were a necessary element of a CAH under the Rome Statute, state officials who ordered non-state actors to commit an act of terrorism (which met the elements of a CAH) would likely escape criminal responsibility, because non-state terrorist groups exist outside the formal framework of the state and tend not to be in a subordinate relationship to relevant state officials. The Rome Statute, however, avoids the difficulty by equally criminalizing solicitation and inducement,[196] neither of which requires a superior/subordinate relationship, and which therefore should not require that the person soliciting or inducing be in a position of authority over the person in fact committing the CAH.

The international criminal tribunal jurisprudence defines 'aiding and abetting' as 'knowingly participat[ing] in the commission of an offence [... where such] participation directly and substantially affected the commission of that offence through supporting the actual commission before, during, or after the incident'.[197] Again, the Rome Statute appears to have opted for a lower threshold in that a person who has not aided or abetted, but has otherwise assisted in the commission of a CAH (including by providing the means for its commission)[198] may be found criminally responsible. Finally, the Rome Statute criminalizes any other intentional and knowing contribution to the commission or attempted commission of a CAH by a group of persons acting with a common purpose.[199]

---

working group on the United Nations and terrorism, UN Doc. A/57/273 (2002), Annex, para 26; Arnold (2004), 994–5; Cassese (2004), 222–3.

[193] Art. 25(3)(a)-(d), Rome Statute.
[194] *Krstić* (ICTY-98-33-T), para 601; *Akayesu* (ICTR-96-4-T), para 483.
[195] See Schabas (2006), 301–2.
[196] Art. 25(3)(b), Rome Statute.
[197] *Tadić* (ICTY-94-1-T), para 692. See also *Delalić et al.* (ICTY-96-21-T), para 326; *Krstić* (ICTY-98-33-T), para 601.
[198] Art. 25(3)(c), Rome Statute.
[199] Art. 25(3)(d), Rome Statute.

Applied to terrorism as CAH prosecutions, these modalities of criminal participation effectively criminalize state support for terrorism.[200] The definition of a CAH is not limited to leadership crimes, but neither does it exclude responsibility of state agents who have ordered or assisted in the perpetration of a CAH. In this regard, the modalities of participation in a CAH under the Rome Statute mirror the provisions on terrorism in the Draft Code adopted on first reading—which criminalized the undertaking, organizing, *assisting, financing, encouraging* or *tolerating* of terrorist acts, by an agent or representative of a state, against another state.[201]

(iii) ICC prosecutions and state responsibility for international terrorism

Acts of terrorism carried out by non-state actors amounting to an act of aggression, which are attributable to the state in virtue of those non-state actors having been sent by the state, will one day be prosecutable before the ICC.[202] Equally, state agents who have either directly participated in or supported acts of terrorism that are of sufficient gravity and otherwise meet the elements of crimes against humanity can be prosecuted for CAH before the ICC.[203] In both cases, the conviction of a high-ranking official would, based on state practice with domestic trials, likely catalyse the invocation of state responsibility by the victim state and would certainly pressure the wrongdoing state whose official had been convicted to accept the secondary obligations flowing from such responsibility. In addition, a determination of individual criminal responsibility by the ICC could form the basis of a victim state's application to the ICJ, and the Court's decision with respect thereto.[204] The ICC's determinations of fact would effectively amount to determinations of fact as to the elements of state responsibility for international terrorism, and the ICJ has signalled a willingness to rely on such determinations by an international criminal jurisdiction. Finally, any determination of individual criminal responsibility by the ICC in respect of terrorism as aggression or terrorism as a CAH (where the accused is a state organ or agent) can form the basis of countermeasures adopted by the injured state—eliminating the risk generally associated with an injured state's own subjective assessment of the wrongdoing state's

---

[200] Non-state actors can equally be held responsible for these crimes, given that there is no leadership element to the modes of participation, as there is for the crime of aggression.

[201] See Art. 24, Draft Code of Offences against the Peace and Security of Mankind, Report of the International Law Commission on the work of its forty-third session, UN Doc. A/46/10 (1991), 97.

[202] The ICC's jurisdiction over the crime of aggression will only become operational in 2017, at the earliest. See ICC, Review Conference of the Rome Statute, 13th Plenary Meeting, ICC-RC/Res. 6 (11 June 2010), Annex, Art. 15*bis*(3); Akande (2010).

[203] While CAH prosecutions will not be limited to state agents, it is the prosecution of state agents that will be most relevant for the purposes of state responsibility.

[204] The ICJ's jurisdiction over state responsibility for acts of terrorism amounting to the crime of aggression (related to the act of aggression as defined in Article 3(g) of the UN Definition of Aggression) and CAH can be established under the TSCs in reliance on the *Bosnian Genocide Case* analysis. See Section 4.2. As neither the Article 3(g) related crime of aggression nor CAH involve military activities, such conduct will not fall within the scope of exclusion clauses in the TSCs (see Section 4.2.2), and the ICJ could therefore exercise jurisdiction over state responsibility for such crimes (to the extent they met the elements of a TSC) on the basis of the compromissory clauses in the TSCs.

conduct.[205] As a result, determinations of individual criminal responsibility by the ICC can play an important role in giving effect to a state's responsibility for terrorism.

The promise of ICC prosecutions for terrorist offences in successfully giving effect to state responsibility is, however, not unlimited. This is because the ICC's jurisdiction—like that of the ICJ—is based on state consent. The Court's jurisdiction is limited to crimes committed in the territory or by the nationals of state parties.[206] There are of course a number of states associated with international terrorism that are not party to the Rome Statute.[207] And for those states that are party (or become party) to the Rome Statute, the territoriality and nationality restrictions on the ICC's jurisdiction will often raise difficult questions regarding whether the terrorism-sponsoring or supporting state is willing or able to prosecute the alleged terrorists.[208] As such, even with a permanent international criminal jurisdiction, the tension between a consensual legal system based on state sovereignty, and the imposition of individual criminal responsibility, has not been fully resolved.[209] The Security Council has on several occasions involving allegations of state involvement in terrorism used its Chapter VII powers to facilitate the prosecution of individual terrorist actors.[210] Under the Rome Statute, the Security Council is empowered to use its Chapter VII powers to refer a matter to the ICC Prosecutor.[211] The Security Council may therefore be in a position to ensure that acts of terrorism amounting to the crime of aggression or a CAH, that would not otherwise fall within the ICC's jurisdiction (because states that sponsor or support terrorism are not parties to the Rome Statute), are prosecuted.[212] In addition to

---

[205] See Section 5.1.2 for a discussion of the 'at your own risk' element of the adoption of counter-measures.

[206] Art. 12(2), Rome Statute.

[207] Cuba, Iran, Syria and the Sudan are designated as state sponsors of terrorism in the US Department of State Country Reports on Terrorism (2008), and none are parties to the Rome Statute. See <http://www.icc-cpi.int/Menus/ASP/states+parties/>. Libya was removed from the US State Sponsors of Terrorism List in 2005, and North Korea was removed from the List in 2008. <http://www.state.gov/s/ct/rls/crt/>. Their absolute renunciation of terrorist tactics, however, is far from certain, and neither is a party to the Rome Statute. *Ibid.*

[208] Art. 17, Rome Statute.

[209] On the question of state responsibility for underlying criminal conduct, Austria noted that 'inter-State relations lack the kind of central authority necessary to decide on subjective aspects of wrongful State behaviour. In this context the instruments provided by the Charter of the United Nations, in particular Chapter VII regarding such violations of international law which threaten international peace and security, should also be taken into account'. ILC, Comments and Observations received from Governments on State Responsibility, UN Doc. A/CN.4/488 (1998), 51 (Austria).

[210] See Sections 6.2.1 and 6.2.5.

[211] Art. 13(b), Rome Statute.

[212] It should be noted, however, that the power of the Security Council to refer matters to the ICC under Chapter VII is a feature of the Rome Statute, which, as an international treaty, is applicable *inter partes*. It is unclear whether a non-state party to the Rome Statute would be bound by the co-operation provisions of the Rome Statute in virtue of such a referral. It is likely that the Security Council would impose an obligation to co-operate on a non-party state, but this is different from the full applicability of the Rome Statute co-operation obligations. The issue of Security Council referrals and the *inter partes* nature of certain Rome Statute obligations (including the waiver of state immunity in the Rome Statute) has been raised in reference to the Security Council's referral of the situation in Sudan to the ICC, and the ICC's indictment of President Al-Bashir. See Akande (2009a).

ensuring that there is no impunity for terrorist offences committed by state actors or with the active support of a state, Security Council referrals to the ICC, and successful prosecutions, could pressure wrongdoing states into accepting the secondary obligations flowing from responsibility, or form the basis of a finding of responsibility by the ICJ.

6.5 Conclusion

The international law of state responsibility is not retributive or punitive in nature.[213] It seeks to re-establish the primary legal relationship between states as a necessary element of their peaceful co-existence. The possibility of punitive measures imposed on a wrongdoing state does not sit comfortably within an international legal paradigm built on the sovereign equality of states, and was rejected by the ILC in its consideration of a regime of criminal responsibility for states.[214] In the context of state involvement in international terrorism, however, the pursuit of justice as between the injured and wrongdoing state is increasingly focused on individual criminal responsibility. Such focus maintains the illusion of sovereign equality while satisfying the victims' desire for justice. The relative merit of holding those acting on behalf of the state criminally responsible in addition to pursuing a state's responsibility for underlying criminal conduct is being worked out in state practice. Recent cases, however, suggest a preference (at least in the first instance) for pursuing the criminal justice model, as Libya and France remain the only examples of sponsors of terrorism accepting international responsibility, where the criminal responsibility of state agents was also pursued. But the ICJ's decision in the *Bosnia Genocide Case*, in which it expressed openness to treating relevant criminal convictions as evidence in a dispute regarding state responsibility, may well shift the current balance. While injured states will undoubtedly continue to pursue criminal justice in relation to terrorist offences, the promise of state responsibility in restoring legal relations as between injured and wrongdoing state should not be ignored, particularly given the potential role of criminal convictions in implementing that responsibility.

---

[213] See Section 1.2.
[214] See Crawford (2002), 19. See further *supra* Chapter 1, notes 58–64 and accompanying text.

7

Conclusions

The threat posed by international terrorism is not a new one. While the 9/11 terrorist attacks have imbued the threat with a renewed sense of urgency, terrorism has long been a phenomenon that has both united and divided the international community: united in that particularly egregious acts of international terrorism have catalysed efforts at international co-operation in their suppression; divided in that states nevertheless have used and do use force against each other that falls within the parameters of violence they have defined as 'terrorist'. A single state may even wear both hats in regard to terrorism, sponsoring or supporting violence in certain contexts (even when it accepts the characterization of such violence as 'terrorist') and co-operating in the suppression of such violence in others. The international community's response to the threat of terrorism has vacillated accordingly between a preoccupation with the acts of states and a preoccupation with the acts of individuals—conceptualizing the state alternatively as a terrorist actor and as the mechanism of control through which non-state terrorist conduct is addressed.

The framework of state responsibility as it applies to international terrorism is neutral in its conception of the state. Questions of state responsibility may arise whether states participate in acts of terrorism or fail to prevent or punish acts of terrorism, and the rules of state responsibility do not prioritize either the security or individual criminal responsibility paradigm as the appropriate framework for addressing the threat posed by international terrorism. By responding to a range of primary obligations, including breaches of *jus ad bellum* and terrorism suppression obligations, state responsibility encompasses both paradigms and can play an important role in maintaining respect for these fundamental rules of international law. Indeed, the process of state responsibility, starting with the invocation of responsibility through to successful negotiations on the form and extent of reparations, can be cathartic—mending the strained (if not broken) legal and diplomatic relationship between the wrongdoing and injured states. The focus of this book has therefore been on the mechanisms available under international law for implementing state responsibility for internationally wrongful acts related to terrorism.

Despite the potential of state responsibility as a vehicle for restoring the legal and diplomatic relationship between injured and wrongdoing states, which will undoubtedly be seriously damaged by acts of international terrorism, successful invocations of state responsibility are relatively rare. This book has sought to identify why that might be through an analysis of the problems and prospects for giving effect to state responsibility in the terrorism context. In particular, it has considered whether challenges in implementing state responsibility are the result of difficulties inherent in the primary or secondary rules themselves; difficulties resulting from a misunderstanding or misapplication of those rules; or indeed whether such problems are the implication of the particular nature of terrorism or the general consequence of a consensual system of international law based on sovereign equality.

The primary rules of international law that address the state as a terrorist actor, examined in Chapter 2, derive from the *jus ad bellum*. State terrorism is but a particular instantiation of a prohibited use of force or an unlawful intervention and the law is relatively clear in this regard. Its application, however, is complicated. In particular, the relevant standards of attribution may be difficult to satisfy. The reasons for this include both conceptual difficulties in situating terrorism within a legitimate sphere of state activity, as well as evidentiary difficulties that result from the clandestine nature of international terrorism. Neither is a difficulty that can be addressed through changes to the law and both suggest why injured states might rely on the Security Council (which is not limited by questions of legal responsibility for terrorist conduct) instead of the framework of state responsibility to address state participation in terrorism.

A third factor that makes the rules of attribution difficult to satisfy in the terrorism context stems from the ICJ's strict reading of Article 8 of the ILC Articles on State Responsibility. The Court's 'effective control' standard responds to particular concerns in the context of military and paramilitary operations, but fails to account for circumstances in which the breach of international law is inherent in the use of force—as in the terrorism context. As a result, states that are the authors of terrorist attacks as a matter of fact may not be held directly responsible for such attacks as a matter of law. Instead, such states may only be held indirectly responsible for their support of terrorism. The disconnect between what states are in fact doing, and what states can be held responsible for doing, would certainly discourage reliance on the framework of state responsibility to address state participation in terrorism. Chapter 2 therefore advocated reliance on a lower threshold of control in attributing terrorist conduct to a state (in particular the 'overall control' standard articulated in the *Tadić* decision), so as to better capture the particular nature of a state's responsibility for terrorism. If the rules of international law reflect the true significance of state sponsorship and support for terrorism, injured states will be more willing and able to rely on the framework of state responsibility to restore their legal relationships with wrongdoing states.

Other primary rules of international law conceptualize states as a mechanism of control through which non-state terrorist conduct is addressed. States are thus under an obligation, both as a matter of customary and treaty law, to prevent acts of international terrorism. As argued in Chapter 3, the evaluation of responsibility for prevention failures calls for a balanced approach, with a sensitive appreciation of the resources at the disposal of individual states. This is most particularly the case in the post-9/11 world, with its intense counter-terrorism capacity-building initiatives, because a failure to prevent terrorism in the absence of resource scarcity may equate in legal terms to acquiescence in international terrorism. In addition to amounting to a breach of the prohibition of the use of force, for which a state could be held internationally responsible, such acquiescence may also justify forceful incursions into the territory of that state in response to terrorist attacks by non-state actors on the basis of Article 51 of the UN Charter. The stakes are therefore very high in correctly evaluating whether a state is responsible for a failure to diligently prevent international terrorism—but such evaluation may be beyond the capacity of injured states, which will not necessarily have sufficient information regarding resource availability and prioritization in other states.

Finally, the international community has approached international terrorism as a criminal phenomenon, resulting in the elaboration of a framework of Terrorism Suppression Conventions that require states to extradite alleged offenders or submit the case to prosecution. While the TSCs prioritize individual criminal responsibility as a response to international terrorism, international law is not yet at a stage where such responsibility can be imposed without the active participation of states. As a result, the framework of state responsibility might have an important role to play in holding states to their criminal law enforcement obligations. These obligations are, however, tempered by respect for a sphere of state discretion in domestic criminal law matters. The TSCs do not require states to extradite, nor do they require states to punish in default of extradition. They merely require that, assuming the good faith of the custodial state, criminal law enforcement machinery be available and brought to bear against alleged terrorists. It is not that holding a state responsible for a breach of the primary rule is complicated in some way by the secondary rules of attribution, or evidentiary difficulties resulting from the clandestine nature of terrorism. Rather, the non-prosecution of an alleged terrorist offender may not amount to a breach of the primary rules at all because of the margin of appreciation built into the *aut dedere aut judicare* obligation, and the realities of international criminal co-operation (or lack thereof).

The difficulties in assessing compliance with the primary rules relating to terrorism identified above equally give rise to difficulties in implementing state responsibility for international terrorism, including through the adoption of countermeasures. While the clandestine nature of terrorism will generally give rise to evidentiary difficulties, in some circumstances these can be overcome or their impact at least minimized (as discussed further below). Equally, the difficult application of the rules of attribution for the purposes of determining the author-ship of an act of terrorism can be addressed, to a point, through a context-sensitive application of the ILC Articles on State Responsibility. But any remaining uncertainty regarding the nature or scope of a wrongdoing state's breach (for instance whether the wrongdoing state is directly responsible for an act of terrorism or 'merely' responsible for support of terrorism) affects the foundations of the injured state's implementation of responsibility through the adoption of countermeasures. As examined in Chapter 5, the countermeasure adopting state does so at its own risk, and the proportionality of its measures is assessed in relation to the internationally wrongful act in fact committed. Any misassessment might therefore leave the injured state in the role of wrongdoing state.

Some of these uncertainties—both in determining the existence of a breach and an appropriate response for the purposes of securing the wrongdoing state's compliance with its obligations of cessation and reparation—might be addressed through domestic criminal proceedings, as examined in Chapter 6. Domestic criminal convictions can play an important role in the invocation and implementation of state responsibility for international terrorism. The clearest case of this particular phenomenon is in reference to the Rainbow Warrior case. Given France's initial denial of responsibility (despite the fact that its agents had been arrested), it is very unlikely that French responsibility would have been established absent a criminal process. While domestic criminal law proceedings clearly have no direct impact on state responsibility, in that wrongdoing states are not bound in any way by the determinations of foreign domestic courts, such determinations often touch on the capacity in which the relevant individual acted and undermine to a certain extent the deniability of state participation in terrorism. At the very least, such determinations embolden injured states to invoke state responsibility where they might otherwise have given in to the uncertainties of assessment identified above. There is equally a potential role for international criminal law to play, not only in ending impunity for offences of grave concern to the international community, but in implementing state responsibility where a particular terrorist act gives rise to concurrent responsibility. Terrorism is not subject to the ICC's jurisdiction *per se*, but might be prosecuted as an act of aggression or a crime against humanity. Any such determination of individual criminal responsibility by the ICC could address uncertainties regarding the extent and scope of a state's participation in terrorism, and may well serve as the basis for a determination of state responsibility by the ICJ. Chapter 4 examined the potential bases for the ICJ's jurisdiction in cases of state terrorism and concluded that the TSCs—drafted with a view to ending impunity for international terrorism committed by natural persons—might also be the vehicle for the ICJ's determination of a state's responsibility for such offences.

This book has mapped the mechanisms available under international law for implementing a state's responsibility, with a view to laying the groundwork for successful invocations of state responsibility for international terrorism. The assessment identifies some of the limitations on available mechanisms for giving effect to a state's responsibility, but also reveals a number of under-exploited potentialities. For instance, Chapter 5 explored the potential role of sub-systems of international law in balancing the interests affected by the breach of international terrorism obligations and the interests affected by responsive measures. Some of the ICAO proposals examined in Chapter 5 required that an assessment of the breach of an international terrorism obligation related to the safety of civil aviation, and the determination of measures to implement responsibility for such breach, both occur within the institutional framework of the ICAO. Because the nature and extent of responsive measures would have been decided by the organization charged with protecting the interests affected by the initial breach *and* those affected by the responsive measures, the balance between competing interests would be achieved as a matter of principle on the basis of particular expertise, and would not be left to the *ad hoc* determination of injured states whose assessment of their own injury might be far from objective. Unfortunately these proposals were not adopted, but they do suggest the role that sub-systems of international law might play in implementing state responsibility for international terrorism.

The WTO may also have an important role to play in facilitating responses to terrorism related wrongs. Depending on the approach the WTO dispute settlement bodies take to the security exception of the GATT 1994, trade measures in response to the breach of international terrorism obligations may be legitimated within the sub-system of international law designed to protect trade interests— thereby rendering them a powerful mechanism for implementing state responsibility. As there is no requirement that conduct leading to invocation of the GATT security exception *also* amount to a breach of international law, or any express limitation on invocation of the security exception by non-injured states, trade measures adopted in response to international terrorism related wrongs pursuant to the security exception would not be subject to the uncertainties surrounding the adoption of countermeasures under the international law of state responsibility.

Other potentialities for implementing state responsibility have been highlighted by the ICJ's decision in the *Bosnia Genocide Case*. In particular, the Court's expansive interpretation of the obligation to prevent genocide under the Genocide Convention makes it more likely that a state's direct responsibility for acts of terrorism can be determined in an impartial judicial setting. The determination of Serbian responsibility for a failure to prevent and punish genocide under the criminal law enforcement framework of the Genocide Convention equally empha- sizes the potential of the TSCs as a basis for the judicial settlement of disputes relating to state responsibility for the breaches of the obligation to suppress international terrorism. Finally, the ICJ's reliance on criminal convictions in its assessment of Serbian responsibility for genocide in the *Bosnia Genocide Case* highlights the potential in such convictions to give effect to a state's responsibility for criminal conduct, including acts of terrorism. States have been exploiting some of these mechanisms, for instance the role of criminal convictions. But other mechanisms, such as the judicial settlement of disputes, have been underutilized.

Successful invocations of state responsibility for internationally wrongful acts related to terrorism should serve to maintain respect for fundamental rules of international law and to restore the (undoubtedly seriously damaged) relationship between an injured and wrongdoing state. The mere potentiality of such an invocation may also serve to dissuade states from supporting or acquiescing in the activities of terrorist groups, or using terrorist methods. It might be hoped that, informed by the analysis of both problems and prospects in this book, the ICJ's decision in the *Bosnia Genocide Case* will lead to a greater reliance on the framework of state responsibility in the terrorism context, and light the path to the successful implementation, and thus perhaps even to a reduction, of state responsibility for international terrorism.

Bibliography

Abbott, K., 'Economic Sanctions and International Terrorism', 20 Vanderbilt Journal of Transnational Law (1987) 289.

Ago, R., 'Report by Mr. Roberto Ago, Chairman of the Sub-Committee on State Responsibility', UN Doc. A/CN.4/152, [1963] Yearbook of the International Law Commission Vol. II, 227.

——, 'Second report on State responsibility', UN Doc. A/CN.4/233 (1970), [1970] Yearbook of the International Law Commission Vol. II, 177.

——, 'Third report on State responsibility: The internationally wrongful act of the State, source of international responsibility', UN Doc. A/CN.4/246 and Add.1–3, [1971] Yearbook of the International Law Commission Vol. II(1), 199.

——, 'Fourth report on State responsibility: The internationally wrongful act of the State, source of international responsibility', UN Doc. A/CN.4/264 and Add.1, [1972] Yearbook of the International Law Commission Vol. II, 71.

——, 'Fifth report on State responsibility: The internationally wrongful act of the State, source of international responsibility', UN Doc. A/CN.4/291 and Add.1 and 2 and Corr. 1, [1976] Yearbook of the International Law Commission Vol. II, 3.

——, 'Sixth report on State responsibility: The internationally wrongful act of the State, source of international responsibility', UN Doc. A/CN.4/302 and Add. 1–3, [1977] Yearbook of the International Law Commission Vol. II(1), 3.

——, 'Seventh report on State responsibility: The internationally wrongful act of the State, source of international responsibility', UN Doc. A/CN.4/307, [1978] Yearbook of the International Law Commission Vol. II(1), 31.

——, 'Addendum to the eighth report on State responsibility', UN Doc. A/CN.4/318/ Add.5–7, [1980] Yearbook of the International Law Commission Vol. II(1), 13.

Akande, D., 'International Law Immunities and the International Criminal Court', 98 American Journal of International Law (2004) 407.

——, 'The Conviction by an Italian Court of CIA Agents for Abduction—Some Issues Concerning Immunity', EJIL: Talk!, 7 November 2009, <http://www.ejiltalk.org/the -conviction-by-an-italian-court-of-cia-agents-for-abduction-some-issues-concerning -immunity>.

——, 'The Legal Nature of Security Council Referrals to the ICC and its Impact on Al Bashir's Immunities', 7 Journal of International Criminal Justice (2009a) 333.

——, 'What Exactly was Agreed in Kampala on the Crime of Aggression?' EJIL: Talk!, 21 June 2010, <http://www.ejiltalk.org/what-exactly-was-agreed-in-kampala-on-the -crime-of-aggression>.

—— and Williams S., 'International Adjudication on National Security Issues: What Role for the WTO?', 43 Virginia Journal of International Law (2003) 365.

Akehurst, M., 'Reprisals by Third States', 44 British Yearbook of International Law (1970) 1.

Alexandrov, S.A., *Reservations in Unilateral Declarations Accepting the Compulsory Jurisdiction of the International Court of Justice* (Dordrecht: Martinus Nijhoff Publishers, 1995).

Alland, D., 'The Definition of Countermeasures', in Crawford, Pellet et al. eds, *The Law of International Responsibility* (Oxford: Oxford University Press, 2010) 1127.

Allott, P., 'State Responsibility and the Unmaking of International Law', 29 Harvard Journal of International Law (1988) 1.

——, *The Health of Nations; Society and Law Beyond the State* (Cambridge: Cambridge University Press, 2002).

Alvarez, J.E., 'The Security Council's War on Terrorism: Problems and Policy Options', in de Wet and Nollkaemper eds, *Review of the Security Council by Member States* (Antwerp: Intersentia, 2003) 119.

American Institute of International Law, 'Project of the American Institute of International Law submitted to the International Commission of Jurists at Rio de Janeiro', April 1927, in *Research in International Law; Drafts of Conventions Prepared in Anticipation of the Codification Conference of International Law* (Cambridge, MA: Harvard Law School, 1929) 232.

Apollis, G., 'Le réglement de l'affaire du Rainbow Warrior', 91 Revue Générale de Droit International Public (1987) 9.

Arangio-Ruiz, G., 'Second report on State responsibility', UN Doc. A/CN.4/425 and Corr.1 and Add.1 and Corr.1, [1989] Yearbook of the International Law Commission Vol. II(1), 1.

——, 'Third report on State responsibility', UN Doc. A/CN.4/440 and Add.l, [1991] Yearbook of the International Law Commission Vol. II(1), 1.

——, 'Fourth report on State responsibility', UN Doc. A/CN.4/444 and Add.1–3, [1992] Yearbook of the International Law Commission Vol. II(1), 1.

——, 'Sixth report on State responsibility', UN Doc. A/CN.4/461 and Add.1–3, [1994] Yearbook of the International Law Commission Vol. II(1), 3.

——, 'Counter-measures and Amicable Dispute Settlement Means in the Implementation of State Responsibility: A Crucial Issue before the International Law Commission', 5 European Journal of International Law (1994a) 20.

Arnold, R., 'The Prosecution of Terrorism as a Crime Against Humanity', 64 Zeitschrift für ausländisches öffentliches Recht und Völkerrecht (2004) 979.

——, 'Terrorism as a Crime against Humanity under the ICC Statute', in Nesi ed., *International Cooperation in Counter-terrorism: The United Nations and Regional Organizations in the Fight Against Terrorism* (Aldershot: Ashgate, 2006) 121.

Aston, C.C., 'The United Nations Convention against the Taking of Hostages: Realistic or Rhetoric?', 5 Terrorism Journal (1982) 139.

Aust, A., *Modern Treaty Law and Practice* (Cambridge: Cambridge University Press, 2006).

Axelrod, R. and Keohane, R.O., 'Achieving Cooperation under Anarchy: Strategies and Institutions', 38 World Politics (1985) 226.

Bantekas, I., 'The International Law of Terrorist Financing', 97 American Journal of International Law (2003) 315.

Barbier, S., 'Assurances and Guarantees of Non-Repetition', in Crawford, Pellet et al. eds, *The Law of International Responsibility* (Oxford: Oxford University Press, 2010) 551.

Barnidge, R.P., 'States' Due Diligence Obligations with Regard to International Non-State Terrorist Organizations Post-11 September 2001: The Heavy Burden that States Must Bear', 16 Irish Studies in International Affairs (2005) 103.

Bartels, L., 'Applicable Law in WTO Dispute Settlement Proceedings', 35 Journal of World Trade (2001) 499.

——, 'The Separation of Powers in the WTO: How to Avoid Judicial Activism', 53 International and Comparative Law Quarterly (2004) 861.

Bassiouni, M.C., 'An International Control Scheme for the Prosecution of International Terrorism: An Introduction', in Evans and Murphy eds, *Legal Aspects of International Terrorism* (Lexington, MA: Lexington Books, 1978) 485.

Bassiouni, M.C., *International Extradition: United States Law and Practice* (London: Oceana Publications, 1981).

—— and Wise, E.M., *Aut Dedere Aut Judicare: The Duty to Extradite or Prosecute in International Law* (Dordrecht: Martinus Nijhoff Publishers, 1995).

Beard, J., 'America's New War on Terror: The Case for Self-Defence under International Law', 25 Harvard Journal of Law & Public Policy (2002) 559.

Becker, T., *Terrorism and the State; Rethinking the Rules of State Responsibility* (Oxford: Hart Publishing, 2006).

Bederman, D., 'Counterintuiting Countermeasures', 96 American Journal of International Law (2002) 817.

Bedjaoui, M., 'Responsibility of States: Fault and Strict Liability', 4 Encyclopedia of Public International Law (2000) 358.

Ben Naftali, O., 'The Obligations to Prevent and to Punish Genocide', in Gaeta ed., *The UN Genocide Convention; A Commentary* (Oxford: Oxford University Press, 2009) 27.

Beres, R.L., 'The Meaning of Terrorism: Jurisprudential and Definitional Clarifications', 28 Vanderbilt Journal of Transnational Law (1995) 239.

Berman, F., 'Treaty "Interpretation" in a Judicial Context', 29 Yale Journal of International Law (2004) 315.

Bialos, J. and Juster, K., 'The Libyan Sanctions: A Rational Response to State-Sponsored Terrorism?', 26 Virginia Journal of International Law (1986) 799.

Bianchi, A., 'Immunity versus Human Rights: The Pinochet Case', 10 European Journal of International Law (1999) 237.

——, 'The Security Council's Anti-Terror Resolutions and their Implementation by Member States: An Overview', 4 Journal of International Criminal Justice (2006) 1044.

——, 'Assessing the Effectiveness of the UN Security Council's Anti-Terrorism Measures: The Quest for Legitimacy and Cohesion', 17 European Journal of International Law (2006a) 881.

——, 'State Responsibility and Criminal Liability of Individuals', in Cassese ed., *The Oxford Companion to International Criminal Justice* (Oxford: Oxford University Press, 2009) 16.

Boisson de Chazournes, L. and Boutruche, T., 'International Trade Law and Economic Sanctions', in Van Damme et al. eds, *The Oxford Handbook of International Trade Law* (Oxford: Oxford University Press, 2009) 695.

Borchard, E.M., *The Diplomatic Protection of Citizens Abroad or the Law of International Claims* (New York: Banks Law Publishing, 1915).

Boulden, J., 'The Security Council and Terrorism', in Lowe ed., *The United Nations Security Council and War: The Evolution of Thought and Practice Since 1945* (Oxford: Oxford University Press, 2008) 608.

Bowett, D., *Self-Defence in International Law* (Manchester: Manchester University Press, 1958).

——, 'Reprisals Involving Recourse to Armed Force', 66 American Journal of International Law (1972) 1.

——, 'Reservations to Non-Restricted Multilateral Treaties', 48 British Yearbook of International Law (1977) 67.

——, 'Crimes of State and the 1996 Report of the International Law Commission on State Responsibility', 9 European Journal of International Law (1998) 163.

Brierly, J.L., 'The Theory of Implied State Complicity in International Claims', 9 British Yearbook of International Law (1928) 42.

——, *The Law of Nations: An Introduction to the International Law of Peace* (6th edn, Oxford: Clarendon Press, 1963).

Brown, D., 'Use of Force against Terrorism after September 11th: State Responsibility, Self-Defence and Other Responses', 11 Cardozo Journal of International and Comparative Law (2003) 1.

Brownlie, I., *International Law and the Use of Force by States* (Oxford: Clarendon Press, 1963).

——, *System of the Law of Nations, State Responsibility (Part I)* (Oxford: Clarendon Press, 1983).

——, *Principles of Public International Law* (7th edn, Oxford: Oxford University Press, 2008).

Brunnée, J. and Toope, S.J., 'The Use of Force: International Law after Iraq', 53 International and Comparative Law Quarterly (2004) 785.

Busuttil, J.J., 'The Bonn Declaration on International Terrorism: A Non-Binding International Agreement on Hijacking', 31 International and Comparative Law Quarterly (1982) 474.

Byers, M., 'Terrorism, the Use of Force, and International Law after 11 September', 51 International and Comparative Law Quarterly (2002) 401.

Byman, D., *Deadly Connections: States that Sponsor Terrorism* (Cambridge: Cambridge University Press, 2005).

Canal-Forgues, E., 'Sur l'interprétation dans le droit de l'OMC', 105 Revue Générale de Droit International Public (2001) 5.

Cannizzaro, E. and Bonafé, B., 'Fragmenting International Law Through Compromissory Clauses? Some Remarks on the Decision of the ICJ in the Oil Platforms Case', 16 European Journal of International Law (2005) 481.

Canor, I., 'When *Jus ad Bellum* Meets *Jus in Bello*: The Occupier's Right of Self-Defence against Terrorism Stemming from Occupied Territories', 19 Leiden Journal of International Law (2006) 129.

Caplan, L.M., 'State Immunity, Human Rights, and *Jus Cogens*: A Critique of the Normative Hierarchy Theory', 97 American Journal of International Law (2003) 741.

Cassese, A., 'The International Community's "Legal" Response to Terrorism', 38 International and Comparative Law Quarterly (1989) 589.

——, 'Terrorism is Also Disrupting Some Crucial Legal Categories of International Law', 12 European Journal of International Law (2001) 993.

——, 'When May Senior State Officials be Tried for International Crimes? Some Comments on the *Congo* v. *Belgium* Case', 13 European Journal of International Law (2002) 862.

——, *International Criminal Law* (Oxford: Oxford University Press, 2003).

——, 'Terrorism as an International Crime', in Bianchi ed., *Enforcing International Law Norms Against Terrorism* (Oxford: Hart Publishing, 2004) 213.

——, 'International Criminal Law', in Evans ed., *International Law* (2nd edn, Oxford: Oxford University Press, 2006) 719.

Chamberlain, K., 'Collective Suspension of Air Services with States which Harbour Hijackers', 32 International and Comparative Law Quarterly (1983) 616.

Chadwick, E., *Self-Determination, Terrorism and the International Humanitarian Law of Armed Conflict* (The Hague: Martinus Nijhoff Publishers, 1996).

Charney, J., 'Third State Remedies in International Law', 10 Michigan Journal of International Law (1989) 57.

——, 'Is International Law Threatened by Multiple International Tribunals?', 271 Recueil des Cours de l'Académie de Droit International de la Haye (1998) 105.

Chase, A.E., 'Legal Mechanisms of the International Community and the United States Concerning State Sponsorship of Terrorism', 45 Virginia Journal of International Law (2004) 41.

Cheng, B., *General Principles of Law as Applied by International Courts and Tribunals* (London: Stevens & Sons Limited, 1953).

——, 'Aviation, Criminal Jurisdiction and Terrorism: The Hague Extradition/Prosecution Formula and Attacks at Airports', in Cheng and Brown eds, *Contemporary Problems in International Law: Essays in Honour of Georg Schwarzenberger* (London: Stevens & Sons, 1988).

Christenson, G.A., 'The Doctrine of Attribution in State Responsibility', in Lillich ed., *International Law of State Responsibility for Injuries to Aliens* (Charlottesville, VA: University Press of Virginia, 1983) 321.

Combacau, J., 'Obligations de résultat et obligations de comportement: quelques questions et pas de réponse', in Bardonnet ed., *Mélanges Offerts à Paul Reuter. Le Droit International: Unite et Diversité* (Paris: Éditions A. Pédone, 1981) 181.

——, 'The Exception of Self-Defence in UN Practice', in Cassese ed., *The Current Legal Regulation of the Use of Force* (Dordrecht: Martinus Nijhoff Publishers, 1986) 9.

Condorelli, L., 'L'imputation à l'état d'un fait internationalement illicit: solutions classiques et nouvelles tendances', 189 Recueil des Cours de l'Académie de Droit International de la Haye (1984-VI) 9.

——, 'The Imputability to States of Acts of International Terrorism', 19 Israel Yearbook on Human Rights (1989) 233.

——, 'Les attentats du 11 septembre et leur suites: où va le droit international?', 105 Revue Générale de Droit International Public (2001) 829.

Conforti, B., 'The Principle of Non-Intervention', in Bedjaoui ed., *International Law: Achievements and Prospects* (Dordrecht: Martinus Nijhoff Publishers, 1991) 466.

Corten, O., 'Opération "liberté immutable": Une éxtension abusive du concept de légitime défence', 106 Revue Générale de Droit International Public (2002) 51.

——, 'The Obligation of Cessation', in Crawford, Pellet et al. eds, *The Law of International Responsibility* (Oxford: Oxford University Press, 2010) 545.

Cottereau, G., 'Resort to International Courts in Matters of Responsibility', in Crawford, Pellet et al. eds, *The Law of International Responsibility* (Oxford: Oxford University Press, 2010) 1115.

Crawford, J.R., 'Counter-Measures as Interim Measures', 5 European Journal of International Law (1994) 65.

——, 'First Report on State Responsibility, Addendum 1', UN Doc. A/CN.4/490.Add.1 (1998).

——, 'First Report on State Responsibility, Addendum 5', UN Doc. A/CN.4/490.Add.5 (1998a).

——, 'Second Report on State Responsibility', UN Doc. A/CN.4/498 (1999).

——, 'Second Report on State Responsibility, Addendum 4', UN Doc. A/CN.4/498/Add.4 (1999a).

——, 'Third Report on State Responsibility', UN Doc. A/CN.4/507 (2000).

——, 'Third Report on State Responsibility, Addendum 1', UN Doc. A/CN.4/507/Add.1 (2000a).

——, 'Third Report on State Responsibility, Addendum 4', UN Doc. A/CN.4/507/Add.4 (2000b).

——, 'The Work of the International Law Commission', in Cassese et al. eds, *The Rome Statute of the International Criminal Court: A Commentary* (Oxford: Oxford University Press, 2001) Vol. 1, 23.

——, 'Introduction', in *The International Law Commission's Articles on State Responsibility; Introduction, Text and Commentaries* (Cambridge: Cambridge University Press, 2002).

Crawford, J.R., 'The System of International Responsibility', in Crawford, Pellet et al. eds, *The Law of International Responsibility* (Oxford: Oxford University Press, 2010) 17.

——, 'International Crimes of State', in Crawford, Pellet et al. eds, *The Law of International Responsibility* (Oxford: Oxford University Press, 2010a) 405.

——, 'Overview of Part Three of the Articles on State Responsibility', in Crawford, Pellet et al. eds, *The Law of International Responsibility* (Oxford: Oxford University Press, 2010b) 932.

—— and Olleson, S., 'The Nature and Forms of International Responsibility', in Evans ed., *International Law* (2nd edn, Oxford: Oxford University Press, 2006).

D'Amato, A., 'National Prosecution for International Crimes', in Bassiouni ed., *International Criminal Law* (3rd edn, Leiden: Martinus Nijhoff, 2008) Vol. III, 285.

Damrosch, L., 'Retaliation or Arbitration or Both? The 1978 United States-France Aviation Dispute', 74 American Journal of International Law (1980) 785.

Darcy, S. and Reynolds, J., '"Otherwise Occupied": The Status of the Gaza Strip from the Perspective of International Humanitarian Law', 15 Journal of Conflict and Security Law (2010) 211.

Daudet, Y., 'International Action Against State Terrorism', in Flory and Higgins eds, *Terrorism and International Law* (London: Routledge, 1997) 201.

David, E., 'Primary and Secondary Rules', in Crawford, Pellet et al. eds, *The Law of International Responsibility* (Oxford: Oxford University Press, 2010) 27.

de Frouville, O., 'Attribution of Conduct to the State', in Crawford, Pellet et al. eds, *The Law of International Responsibility* (Oxford: Oxford University Press, 2010) 257.

Degan, V.-D., 'Responsibility of States and Individuals for International Crimes', in Sienho Yee ed., *International Law in the Post-Cold War World: Essays in Memory of Li Haopei* (London: Routledge, 2002) 202.

de Hoogh, A.J.J., 'Articles 4 and 8 of the 2001 ILC Articles on State Responsibility, the *Tadić* Case and Attribution of Acts of Bosnian Serb Authorities to the Federal Republic of Yugoslavia', 72 British Yearbook of International Law (2001) 255.

De Visscher, C., *Théories et réalités en droit international public* (4th edn, Paris: Éditions A. Pédone, 1970).

Del Mar, K., 'The Requirement of "Belonging" under International Humanitarian Law', 21 European Journal of International Law (2010) 105.

Dinstein, Y., 'The International Legal Response to Terrorism', in Zanardi et al. eds, *International Law at the Time of its Codification, Essays in Honour of Roberto Ago* (Milan: Giuffrè, 1987) 146.

——, *War, Aggression and Self-Defence* (4th edn, Cambridge: Cambridge University Press, 2005).

Dominicé, C., 'Observations sur les droits de l'Etat victime d'un fait internationalement illicite', 2 Droit International (1982) 1.

——, 'La satisfaction en droit des gens', in Dutoit and Grisel eds, *Mélanges Georges Perrin* (Lausanne: Diffusion Payot, 1984) 91.

——, 'Legal Questions Relating to the Consequences of International Crimes', in Weiler et al. eds, *International Crimes of State: A Critical Analysis of the ILC's Draft Article 19 on State Responsibility* (Berlin: de Gruyter, 1989) 260.

——, 'La question de la double responsabilité de l'Etat et de son agent', in Yakpo and Boumdera eds, *Liber Amicorum—Mohammed Bedjaoui* (The Hague: Kluwer Law International, 1999) 143.

——, 'Quelques observations sur l'immunité de juridiction pénale de l'ancien chef d'Etat', 103 Revue Générale de Droit International Public (1999a) 297.

Donnelly, E., 'Raising Global Counter-Terrorism Capacity: The Work of the Security Council's Counter-Terrorism Committee', in Eden and O'Donnell eds, *11 September 2001: A Turning Point in International and Domestic Law* (Ardsley, NY: Transnational Publishers, 2005) 757.

Duffy, H., *The War on Terror and the Framework of International Law* (Cambridge: Cambridge University Press, 2005).

Dupuy, P.-M., 'Observations sur la pratique récente des "sanctions" de l'illicite', 87 Revue Générale de Droit International Public (1983) 505.

——, 'Implications of the Institutionalisation of International Crimes of States', in Weiler et al. eds, *International Crimes of State: A Critical Analysis of the ILC's Draft Article 19 on State Responsibility* (Berlin: de Gruyter, 1989) 170.

——, 'International Criminal Responsibility of the Individual and International Responsibility of the State', in Cassese et al. eds, *The Rome Statute of the International Criminal Court: A Commentary* (Oxford: Oxford University Press, 2002) Vol. II, 1085.

——, 'State Sponsors of Terrorism: Issues of International Responsibility', in Bianchi ed., *Enforcing International Law Norms Against Terrorism* (Oxford: Hart Publishing, 2004).

Eagleton, E., *The Responsibility of States in International Law* (New York: New York University Press, 1928).

Eeckhout, P., 'Remedies and Compliance', in Van Damme et al. eds, *The Oxford Handbook of International Trade Law* (Oxford: Oxford University Press, 2009) 437.

Elagab, O.Y., *The Legality of Non-forcible Counter-Measures in International Law* (Oxford: Clarendon Press, 1988).

Elias, T.O., 'Introduction to the Debate', in Weiler et al. eds, *International Crimes of State: A Critical Analysis of the ILC's Draft Article 19 on State Responsibility* (Berlin: de Gruyter, 1989) 189.

Emmerson, A., 'Conceptualizing Security Exceptions: Legal Doctrine or Political Excuse?', 11 Journal of International Economic Law (2008) 135.

Evans, A.E., 'The Apprehension and Prosecution of Offenders: Some Current Problems', in Evans and Murphy eds, *Legal Aspects of International Terrorism* (Lexington, MA: Lexington Books, 1978) 493.

Evans, M.D., 'International Wrongs and National Jurisdiction', in Evans ed., *Remedies in International Law: The Institutional Dilemma* (Oxford: Hart Publishing, 1998) 173.

Fassbender, B., 'The UN Security Council and International Terrorism', in Bianchi ed., *Enforcing International Law Norms Against Terrorism* (Oxford: Hart Publishing, 2004) 83.

Ferencz, B.B., 'A Proposed Definition of Aggression: By Compromise and Consensus', 22 International and Comparative Law Quarterly (1973) 407.

Focarelli, C., 'Denying Foreign State Immunity for Commission of International Crimes: The *Ferrini* Decision', 54 International and Comparative Law Quarterly (2005) 951.

Fox, H., 'The International Court of Justice's Treatment of Acts of the State and in Particular the Attribution of Acts of Individuals to the State', in Ando et al. eds, *Liber Amicorum Judge Shigeru Oda* (The Hague: Kluwer Law International, 2002) Vol. I, 147.

——, *The Law of State Immunity* (2nd edn, Oxford: Oxford University Press, 2008).

Franck, T., 'Terrorism and the Right of Self-Defence', 95 American Journal of International Law (2000) 839.

——, *Recourse to Force; State Action Against Threats and Armed Attacks* (Cambridge: Cambridge University Press, 2002).

—— and Niedermeyer, T., 'Accommodating Terrorism: An Offence against the Law of Nations', 19 Israel Yearbook on Human Rights (1989) 75.

Friedlander, R.A., *Terrorism; Documents of International and Local Control* (New York: Oceana Publications, 1979) Vol. I.

Frowein, J.A., 'Reactions by not Directly Affected States to Breaches of Public International Law', 248 Recueil des Cours de l'Académie de Droit International de la Haye (1994-IV) 349.

Gaeta, P., 'On What Conditions Can a State Be Held Responsible for Genocide?', 18 European Journal of International Law (2007) 631.

Gaja, G., 'Unruly Treaty Reservations', in Zanardi et al. eds, *International Law at the Time of its Codification, Essays in Honour of Roberto Ago* (Milan: Giuffrè, 1987) Vol. I, 307.

Galicki, Z., 'Preliminary report on the obligation to extradite or prosecute (*aut dedere aut judicare*)', UN Doc. A/CN.4/571 (2006).

——, 'Second report on the obligation to extradite or prosecute (*aut dedere aut judicare*)', UN Doc. A/CN.4/585 (2007).

——, 'Third report on the obligation to extradite or prosecute (*aut dedere aut judicare*)', UN Doc. A/CN.4/603 (2008).

Garcia-Amador, F.V., 'Report on International Responsibility', UN Doc. A/CN.4/96, [1956] Yearbook of the International Law Commission Vol. II, 173.

——, 'Second Report on International Responsibility', UN Doc. A/CN.4/106, [1957] Yearbook of the International Law Commission Vol. II, 104.

——, 'Third Report on International Responsibility', UN Doc. A/CN.4/111, [1958] Yearbook of the International Law Commission Vol. II, 47.

——, 'Sixth Report on International Responsibility', UN Doc. A/CN.4/134 and Add.1, [1961] Yearbook of the International Law Commission Vol. II, 1.

Garcia-Mora, M., *International Responsibility for Hostile Acts of Private Persons Against States* (Dordrecht: Martinus Nijhoff Publishers, 1962).

Gardam, J., *Necessity, Proportionality and the Use of Force by States* (Cambridge: Cambridge University Press, 2004).

Gasser, H.-P., 'Internationalized Non-International Armed Conflicts: Case Study of Afghanistan, Kampuchea and Lebanon', 33 American University Law Review (1983) 145.

Gattini, A., 'La notion de faute à la lumiere du projet de convention de la Commission du Droit International sur la responsabilité internationale', 3 European Journal of International Law (1992) 253.

Gehr, W., 'The Counter-Terrorism Committee and Security Council Resolution 1373 (2001)', in Benedek et al. eds, *Anti-Terrorist Measures and Human Rights* (Leiden: Martinus Nijhoff Publishers, 2004) 41.

Goodwin-Gill, G.S., 'State Responsibility and the "Good Faith" Obligation in International Law', in Fitzmaurice and Sarooshi eds, *Issues of State Responsibility Before International Judicial Institutions* (Oxford: Hart Publishing, 2004) 75.

Gowlland-Debbas, V., 'Responsibility and the United Nations Charter', in Crawford, Pellet et al. eds, *The Law of International Responsibility* (Oxford: Oxford University Press, 2010) 115.

Graefrath, R., 'Responsibility and Damages Caused', 185 Recueil des Cours de l'Académie de Droit International de la Haye (1984) 73.

——, 'International Crimes—A Specific Regime of International Responsibility of States and its Legal Consequences', in Weiler et al. eds, *International Crimes of State: A Critical Analysis of the ILC's Draft Article 19 on State Responsibility* (Berlin: de Gruyter, 1989) 161.

Graditzky, T., 'Individual criminal responsibility for violations of international humanitarian law committed in non-international armed conflicts', 322 International Review of the Red Cross (1998) 29.

Gray, C., *Judicial Remedies in International Law* (Oxford: Clarendon Press, 1990).

Gray, C., 'The Use and Abuse of the International Court of Justice: Cases Concerning the Use of Force after Nicaragua', 14 European Journal of International Law (2003) 867.

——, *International Law and the Use of Armed Force* (3rd edn, Oxford: Oxford University Press, 2008).

Green, J.A., *The International Court of Justice and Self-Defence in International Law* (Oxford: Hart Publishing, 2009).

Greenwood, C., 'Terrorism and Humanitarian Law—The Debate over Additional Protocol I', 19 Israel Yearbook on Human Rights (1989) 187.

——, 'War, Terrorism and International Law', 56 Current Legal Problems (2003) 505.

——, 'A Critique of the Additional Protocols to the Geneva Conventions of 1949', in C. Greenwood, *Essays on War in International Law* (London: Cameron May, 2007) 201 (first published in Durham and McCormack eds, *The Changing Face of Conflict and the Efficacy of International Law* (Dordrecht: Kluwer Law International, 1999) 3.

——, 'Scope of Application of Humanitarian Law', in Fleck ed., *The Handbook of International Humanitarian Law* (2nd edn, Oxford: Oxford University Press, 2008) 45.

Griebel, J. and Plücken, M., 'New Developments Regarding the Rules of Attribution? The International Court of Justice's Decision in *Bosnia v. Serbia*', 21 Leiden Journal of International Law (2008) 601.

Gross, L., 'International Terrorism and International Criminal Jurisdiction', 67 American Journal of International Law (1973) 508.

Guilfoyle, D., 'Maritime Interdiction of Weapons of Mass Destruction', 56 International and Comparative Law Quarterly (2007) 69.

Guillaume, G., 'Le terrorism aérien et les sommets des septs pays industrialises: Les declarations de Bonn (1978) et de Venise (1987)', 43 Revue Française de Droit Aérien et Spatial (1989) 495.

——, 'Terrorisme et le droit international', 215 Recueil des Cours de l'Académie de Droit International de la Haye (1989a) 287.

——, 'Terrorism and International Law', 53 International and Comparative Law Quarterly (2004) 537.

Henckaerts, J.-M., 'Study on customary international humanitarian law: A contribution to the understanding and respect for the rule of law in armed conflict', 87 International Review of the Red Cross (2005) 175.

Hahn, M.J., 'Vital Interests and the Law of GATT: An Analysis of GATT's Security Exception', 12 Michigan Journal of International Law (1991) 558.

Hall, W.E., with Pearce Higgins ed., *A Treatise on International Law* (8th edn, Oxford: Clarendon Press, 1924).

Happold, M., 'Security Council Resolution 1373 and the Constitution of the United Nations', 16 Leiden Journal of International Law (2003) 593.

——, 'Security Council Resolution 1373 and the Constitution of the United Nations', in Eden & O'Donnell eds, *September 11, 2001: A Turning Point in International and Domestic Law?* (Ardsley, NY: Transnational Publishers, 2005) 617.

Harrington, J., 'The Obligation to "Extradite or Prosecute" is not an Obligation to "Prosecute or Extradite"', EJIL: Talk!, 23 February 2009, <http://www.ejiltalk.org/the-obligation-to-extradite-or-prosecute-is-not-an-obligation-to-prosecute-or-extradite/>.

Harvard Law School, *Research in International Law: Drafts of Conventions Prepared in Anticipation of the Codification Conference of International Law* (Cambridge, MA: Harvard Law School, 1929).

Higgins, R., 'The General International Law of Terrorism', in Higgins and Flory eds, *Terrorism and International Law* (London: Routledge, 1997) 13.

Higgins, R., 'Human Rights in the International Court of Justice', 20 Leiden Journal of International Law (2007) 745.

Hmoud, M., 'Negotiating the Draft Comprehensive Convention on International Terrorism: Major Bones of Contention', 4 Journal of International Criminal Justice (2006) 1031.

Hoffman, B., *Inside Terrorism* (New York: Columbia University Press, 2006).

Hudson, M.O., 'The Proposed International Criminal Court', 32 American Journal of International Law (1938) 549.

Hutchinson, D.N., 'Solidarity and Breaches of Multilateral Treaties', 59 British Yearbook of International Law (1988) 151.

Institut de droit international, 'Régime des représailles en temps de paix', Session de Paris, 1934, <http://www.idi-iil.org/idiF/resolutionsF/1934_paris_03_fr.pdf>.

——, 'La protection des droits de l'homme et le principe de non-intervention dans les affaires intérieures des États', 63 Annuaire de l'Institute de Droit International (1990) 438.

Institute of International Law, 'International Responsibility of States for Injuries on their Territory to the Person or Property of Foreigners', Lausanne, 1927, in *Research in International Law; Drafts of Conventions Prepared in Anticipation of the Codification Conference of International Law* (Cambridge, MA: Harvard Law School, 1929) 228.

International Committee of the Red Cross, *Commentary to Geneva Convention Relative to the Treatment of Prisoners of War* (Geneva: International Committee of the Red Cross, 1960).

——, 'How is the Term "Armed Conflict" Defined in International Humanitarian Law?', Opinion Paper, March 2008, <http://www.icrc.org/eng/assets/files/other/opinion-paper -armed-conflict.pdf>.

——, Henckaerts, J.-M. and Doswald-Beck, L., *Customary International Humanitarian Law* (Cambridge: Cambridge University Press, 2005).

——, with Sandoz and Zimmerman eds, *Commentary on the Additional Protocols of 8 June 1977 to the Geneva Conventions of 12 August 1949* (Dordrecht: Martinus Nijhoff Publishers, 1987).

International Law Association, *Report of the Sixty-First Conference*, Paris, 1984.

——, 'Committee on International Terrorism: Fourth Interim Report', 7 Terrorism: An International Journal (1984a) 123.

Jackson, J.H. and Lowenfeld, A.F., 'Helms-Burton, the US, and the WTO', ASIL Insight, March 1997, <http://www.asil.org/insight7.htm>.

Janse, D., 'International Terrorism and Self-Defence', 36 Israel Yearbook on Human Rights (2006) 149.

Jennings, R.Y., 'The Caroline and McLeod Cases', 32 American Journal of International Law (1938) 82.

Jiménez de Aréchaga, E., 'Crimes of State, *Ius Standi*, and Third States', in Weiler et al. eds, *International Crimes of State: A Critical Analysis of the ILC's Draft Article 19 on State Responsibility* (Berlin: de Gruyter, 1989) 255.

Jinks, D., 'Remarks', 97 American Society of International Law Proceedings (2003) 144.

——, 'State Responsibility for the Acts of Private Armed Groups', 4 Chicago Journal of International Law (2003a) 83.

——, 'The Applicability of the Geneva Conventions to the "Global War on Terrorism"', 46 Virginia Journal of International Law (2005) 165.

Jørgensen, N.H.B., *The Responsibility of States for International Crimes* (Oxford: Oxford University Press, 2000).

Joyner, C., 'International Extradition and Global Terrorism: Bringing International Criminals to Justice', 25 Loyola International and Comparative Law Review (2003) 493.

Joyner, C. and Friedlander, R.A., 'International Civil Aviation', in Bassiouni ed., *International Criminal Law* (3rd edn, Leiden: Martinus Nijhoff, 2008) Vol. I, 831.

—— and Rothbaum, W.P., 'Libya and the Aerial Incident at Lockerbie: What Lessons for International Extradition Law', 14 Michigan Journal of International Law (1992) 222.

Kammerhofer, J., 'Oil's Well that Ends Well? Critical Comments on the Merits Judgement in the Oil Platforms Case', 17 Leiden Journal of International Law (2004) 695.

Kamto, M., 'Une troublante "Immunité totale" du Ministre des affaires étrangères', 35 Revue belge de droit international (2002) 519.

Kantor, M., 'Effective Enforcement of International Obligations to Suppress the Financing of Terror', The American Society of International Law Task Force on Terrorism (2002), <http://www.asil.org/taskforce/kantor.pdf>.

Kellman, B., 'An International Criminal Law Approach to Bioterrorism', 25 Harvard Journal of Law & Public Policy (2001) 721.

Kelsen, H., *The Law of the United Nations* (New York: F.A. Praeger, 1950).

——, 'Théorie du droit international public', 84 Recueil des Cours de l'Académie de Droit International de la Haye (1953-III) 1.

——, *Principles of International Law* (2nd edn, New York: Holt, Rinehart and Winston, 1966).

Kerley, E.L., 'Ensuring Compliance with Judgments of the International Court of Justice', in Gross ed., *The Future of the International Court of Justice* (Dobbs Ferry, NY: Oceana Publications, 1976) 276.

Kiss, A.C., *L'abus de droit en droit international* (Paris: Librarie Génerale de Droit et de Jurisprudence, 1953).

Kirgis, F.L., 'Some Proportionality Issues Raised by Israel's Use of Armed Force in Lebanon', ASIL Insight, 17 August 2006, <http://www.asil.org/insights/2006/08/insights060817.html>.

Klein, P., 'Responsibility for Serious Breaches of Obligations Deriving from Peremptory Norms of International Law and United Nations Law', 13 European Journal of International Law (2002) 1241.

——, 'Le Conseil de sécurité et la lutte contre le terrorisme: dans l'exercice de pouvoirs toujours plus grands?', 19 Revue Québécoise de Droit International (2007) 133.

Klabbers, J., 'Rebel without a Cause? Terrorists and Humanitarian Law', 14 European Journal of International Law (2003) 299.

Kolb, R., 'The Exercise of Criminal Jurisdiction over International Terrorists', in Bianchi ed., *Enforcing International Law Norms Against Terrorism* (Oxford: Hart Publishing, 2004) 227.

——, 'Principles as Sources of International Law (with Special Reference to Good Faith)', 53 Netherlands International Law Review (2006) 1.

Kolodkin, R.A., 'Preliminary report on immunity of State officials from foreign criminal jurisdiction, by Roman Anatolevich Kolodkin, Special Rapporteur', UN Doc. A/CN.4/601 (2008).

Koskenniemi, M., 'Solidarity measures: State Responsibility as a New International Order?', 72 British Yearbook of International Law (2001) 337.

——, 'Fragmentation of International Law: Difficulties Arising from the Diversification and Expansion of International Law', Report of the Study Group of the International Law Commission, UN Doc. A/CN.4/L.682 (2006).

Kraiem, R., 'Recent Developments: International Terrorism; Hijacking', 19 Harvard Journal of International Law (1978) 1037.

Kress, C., 'L'organe de facto en droit international public', 105 Revue Générale de Droit International Public (2001) 93.

Kress, C., 'The Crime of Aggression before the First Review of the ICC Statute', 20 Leiden Journal of International Law (2007) 851.

——, 'Some Reflections on the International Legal Framework Governing Transnational Armed Conflicts', 15 Journal of Conflict and Security Law (2010) 245.

Kuilwijk, K.J., 'Castro's Cuba and the U.S. Helms-Burton Act: An Interpretation of the GATT Security Exemption', 31 Journal of World Trade (1997) 49.

Lambert, J.L., *Terrorism and Hostages in International Law: A Commentary on the Hostages Convention 1979* (Cambridge: Grotius Publications, 1990).

Lauterpacht, E., ed., *British Practice in International Law* (London: British Institute of International and Comparative Law, 1963).

——, ed., *British Practice in International Law* (London: British Institute of International and Comparative Law, 1964).

Lauterpacht, H., *Revolutionary Activities by Private Persons Against Foreign States* (1927), in E. Lauterpacht ed., *The Collected Papers of Hersch Lauterpacht* (Cambridge: Cambridge University Press, 1970) Vol. 3, 251.

——, 'The Law of Nations and Punishment of War Crimes', 21 British Yearbook of International Law (1944) 58.

——, *International Law and Human Rights* (London: Stevens, 1950).

Leben, C., 'Les contre-mesures inter-étatiques et les reactions a l'illicite dans la societé internationale', XXVIII Annuaire Français de Droit International (1982) 9.

Levitt, G.M., 'Is "Terrorism" Worth Defining?', 13 Ohio Northern University Law Review (1986) 97.

——, 'Collective Sanctions and Unilateral Action', in Alexander and Sochor eds, *Aerial Piracy and Aviation Security* (Dordrecht: Martinus Nijhoff Publishers, 1990) 95.

Liais, M., 'L'affaire Hungaro-Yugoslave devant le Conseil de la Société des Nations', 42 Revue Générale de Droit International Public (1935) 125.

Lillich, R.B. and Paxman, J.M., 'State Responsibility for Injuries Occasioned by Terrorist Activities', 26 American University Law Review (1977) 217.

Llamzon, A.P., 'Jurisdiction and Compliance in Recent Decisions of the International Court of Justice', 18 European Journal of International Law (2008) 815.

Lobel, J., 'The Use of Force to Respond to Terrorist Bombings: The Bombing of Sudan and Afghanistan', 24 Yale Journal of International Law (1999) 527.

Lubell, N., *Extraterritorial Use of Force Against Non-State Actors* (Oxford: Oxford University Press, 2010).

Maison, R., *La responsabilité individuelle pour crime d'état en droit international public* (Bruxelles: Bruylant, 2004).

Malzahn, S.M., 'State Sponsorship and Support of International Terrorism: Customary Norms of State Responsibility', 26 Hastings International & Comparative Law Review (2002) 83.

Mankiewicz, H., 'The 1970 Hague Convention', 37 Journal of Air Law and Commerce (1971) 195.

Marceau, G., 'Fragmentation in International law: The Relationship Between WTO Law and General International Law – A Few Comments', 17 Finnish Yearbook of International Law (2008) 8.

—— and Trachtman, J.P., 'Responding to National Concerns', in Van Damme et al. eds, *The Oxford Handbook of International Trade Law* (Oxford: Oxford University Press, 2009) 209.

Martin, J.-C., *Les règles internationales relative à la lutte contre le terrorisme* (Bruxelles: Bruylant, 2006).

McNair, A.D., *The Law of Treaties* (Oxford: Clarendon Press, 1961).

Mégret, F., 'A Special Tribunal for Lebanon: The UN Security Council and the Emancipation of International Criminal Justice', 21 Leiden Journal of International Law (2008) 485.

Meron, T., 'The Continuing Role of Custom in the Formation of International Humanitarian Law', 90 American Journal of International Law (1996) 238.

Merrills, J.G., 'The Optional Clause Revisited', 64 British Yearbook of International Law (1993) 197.

——, 'The Optional Clause at Eighty', in Ando et al. eds, *Liber Amicorum Judge Shigeru Oda* (The Hague: Kluwer Law International, 2002) 435.

——, *International Dispute Settlement* (4th edn, Cambridge: Cambridge University Press, 2005).

Milanovic, M., 'State Responsibility for Genocide: A Follow-Up', 18 European Journal of International Law (2007) 669.

——, 'State Responsibility for Acts of Non-State Actors: A Comment on Griebel and Plücken', 22 Leiden Journal of International Law (2009) 307.

——, 'What Exactly Internationalizes an Internal Armed Conflict?', EJIL: Talk!, 7 May 2010, <http://www.ejiltalk.org/what-exactly-internationalizes-an-internal-armed-conflict/>.

Mills, A., *The Confluence of Public and Private International Law; Justice, Pluralism and Subsidiarity in the International Constitutional Ordering of Private Law* (Cambridge: Cambridge University Press, 2009).

Mohr, M., 'The ILC's Distinction between "International Crimes" and "International Delicts" and its Implications', in Simma and Spinedi eds, *United Nations Codification of State Responsibility* (New York: Oceana Publications, 1987) 115.

Moir, L., *The Law of Internal Armed Conflict* (Cambridge: Cambridge University Press, 2002).

——, 'Grave Breaches and Internal Armed Conflicts', 7 Journal of International Criminal Justice (2009) 763.

——, *Reappraising the Resort to Force: International Law, the* Jus ad Bellum *and the War on Terror* (Oxford: Hart Publishing, 2010).

Morris, M., 'Arresting Terrorism: Criminal Jurisdiction and International Relations', in Bianchi ed., *Enforcing International Law Norms Against Terrorism* (Oxford: Hart Publishing, 2004) 63.

Mosler, H. and Oellers-Frahm, K., 'Article 94', in Simma ed., *The Charter of the United Nations: A Commentary* (2nd edn, Oxford: Oxford University Press, 2002) 1174.

Murphy, J., *Legal Aspects of International Terrorism: Summary Report of an International Conference, American Society of International Law* (St. Paul, MN: West Pub. Co., 1980).

——, *Punishing International Terrorists: The Legal Framework for Policy Initiatives* (Totowa, NJ: Rowman & Allanheld, 1985).

——, *State Support of International Terrorism* (Boulder, CO: Westview Press, 1989).

—— et al., 'Report of the Special Working Committee on Responses to State Sponsored Terrorism', 22 Studies in Transnational Legal Policy (1991) 9.

Murphy, S.D., ed., 'Contemporary Practice of the United States', 94 American Journal of International Law (2000) 348.

——, 'Terrorism and the Concept of "Armed Attack" in Article 51 of the UN Charter', 43 Harvard Journal of International Law (2002) 41.

——, 'Self-Defense and the Israeli Wall Advisory Opinion: An *Ipse Dixit* from the ICJ?', 99 American Journal of International Law (2005) 62.

National Commission on Terrorist Attacks Upon the United States, *Final Report of the National Commission on Terrorist Attacks Upon the United States* (New York: WW Norton & Co, 2004, Authorised Edition).

Nesi, G., 'Reflections on the Security Council's Counter-Terrorism Resolutions', in Lee ed., *Swords into Plowshares: Building Peace through the United Nations* (Leiden: Martinus Nijhoff Publishing, 2006) 85.

Nollkaemper, A., 'Concurrence between Individual Responsibility and State Responsibility in International Law', 52 International and Comparative Law Quarterly (2003) 615.

——, 'Multi-Level Accountability: A Case Study of Accountability in the Aftermath of the Srebrenica Massacre', in Broude and Shany eds, *The Shifting Allocation of Authority in International Law* (Oxford: Hart Publishing, 2008) 345.

O'Connell, D.P., *International Law* (2nd edn, London: Stevens & Sons, 1970) Vol. 2.

O'Connell, M.E., 'Evidence of Terror', 7 Journal of Conflict and Security Law (2002) 19.

O'Keefe, R., 'Universal Jurisdiction: Clarifying the Basic Concept', 2 Journal of International Criminal Justice (2004) 735.

Oda, S., 'The Compulsory Jurisdiction of the International Court of Justice: A Myth?', 49 International and Comparative Law Quarterly (2000) 251.

Orakhelashvili, A., *The Interpretation of Acts and Rules in Public International Law* (Oxford: Oxford University Press, 2008).

Palmeter, D. and Mavroidis, P.C., 'The WTO Legal System: Sources of Law', 92 American Journal of International Law (1998) 398.

Pan, E., 'Lebanon's Weak Government', Council on Foreign Relations, 20 July 2006, <http://www.cfr.org/publication/11135/>.

Paust, J., 'Use of Force against Terrorists in Afghanistan, Iraq and Beyond', 35 Cornell International Law Journal (2002) 533.

Pauwelyn, J., *Conflict of Norms in Public International Law: How WTO Law Relates to Other Rules of International Law* (Cambridge: Cambridge University Press, 2003).

Pellet, A., 'Vive le crime! Remarques sur les degrés de l'illicite en droit international', in *International Law on the Eve of the Twenty-First Century: Views from the International Law Commission* (New York: United Nations, 1997) 287.

——, 'Can a State Commit a Crime? Definitely, Yes!', 10 European Journal of International Law (1999) 425.

——, 'La responsabilité pénale individuelle, alternative aux sanctions collectives?', in Gowland-Debbas ed., *United Nations Sanctions and International Law* (The Hague: Kluwer Law International, 2001) 105.

——, 'The Responsibility of Government Leaders for International Crimes of the State from the Perspective of International Law', in Doucet ed., *Terrorism, Victims and International Criminal Responsibility* (Paris: SOS Attentats, 2003) 289.

——, 'Tenth report on reservations to treaties by Mr. Alain Pellet, Special Rapporteur, Addendum 2', UN Doc. A/CN.4/558/Add.2 (2005).

——, 'Eleventh report on reservations to treaties by Mr. Alain Pellet, Special Rapporteur', UN Doc. A/CN.4/574 (2006).

——, 'Thirteenth report on reservations to treaties by Mr. Alain Pellet, Special Rapporteur', UN Doc. A/CN.4/600 (2008).

——, 'Fourteenth report on reservations to treaties by Mr. Alain Pellet, Special Rapporteur', UN Doc. A/CN.4/614 (2009).

——, 'The Definition of Responsibility in International Law', in Crawford, Pellet et al. eds, *The Law of International Responsibility* (Oxford: Oxford University Press, 2010) 3.

Perera, A.R., 'Reviewing the UN Conventions on Terrorism: Towards a Comprehensive Convention', in Fihnaut et al. eds, *Legal Instruments in the Fight Against Terrorism; A Transatlantic Dialogue* (Leiden: Martinus Nijhoff Publishers, 2004) 567.

Pictet, J., *Commentary on the Geneva Conventions of 12 August 1949*, Vol. I (Geneva: ICRC, 1952).

——, *Commentary on the Geneva Conventions of 12 August 1949*, Vol. III (Geneva: ICRC, 1958).

Pillepich, A., 'Article 94', in Cot et al. eds, *La Charte des Nations Unies: Commentaire Article par Article* (3rd edn, Paris: Economica, 2005) 1987.

Pisillo-Mazzeschi, R., 'Due Diligence and the International Responsility of States', 35 German Yearbook of International Law (1992) 9.

Plachta, M., 'The Lockerbie Case: The Role of the Security Council in Enforcing the Principle *Aut Dedere Aut Judicare*', 12 European Journal of International Law (2001) 125.

Politis, N., 'Le problème des limitations de la soveraineté et la théorie de l'abus de droits dans les rapports internationaux', 6 Recueil des Cours de l'Académie de Droit Internation aux de la Haye (1925-I) 1.

Pons, J.F., 'Self-Help and the World Trade Organization', in Mengozzi ed., *International Trade Law on the 50th Anniversary of the Multilateral Trading System* (Milan: Giuffrè, 1999) 55.

Proulx, V.-J., 'Rethinking the Jurisdiction of the International Criminal Court in the Post-September 11th Era: Should Acts of Terrorism Qualify as Crimes Against Humanity?', 19 The American University International Law Review (2004) 1009.

——, 'Babysitting Terrorists: Should States be Strictly Liable for Failing to Prevent Transborder Attacks?', 23 Berkeley Journal of International Law (2005) 615.

Provost, R., 'Introduction', in Provost ed., *State Responsibility in International Law* (Aldershot: Ashgate, 2002) xii.

Pugh, M., 'Legal Aspects of the Rainbow Warrior Affair', 36 International and Comparative Law Quarterly (1987) 655.

Randelzhofer, A., 'Article 51', in Simma ed., *The Charter of the United Nations: A Commentary* (2nd edn, Oxford: Oxford University Press, 2002) 788.

——, 'Article 2(4)', in Simma ed., *The Charter of the United Nations: A Commentary* (2nd edn, Oxford: Oxford University Press, 2002a) 112.

Ratner, J., '*Jus Ad Bellum* and *Jus In Bello* After September 11', 96 American Journal of International Law (2002) 905.

Redgwell, C., 'Universality or Integrity? Some Reflections on Reservations to General Multilateral Treaties', 64 British Yearbook of International Law (1993) 245.

Reisman, W.M., 'International Legal Responses to Terrorism', 22 Houston Journal of International Law (1999) 37.

Reuter, P., *Droit international public* (Paris: Thémis, 1958).

Rice Jr., W.G., 'State Responsibility for Failure to Vindicate the Public Peace', 28 American Journal of International Law (1934) 246.

Riphagen, W., 'Second report on the content, forms and degrees of international responsibility (Part two of the draft articles), by Mr. Willem Riphagen, Special Rapporteur', UN Doc. A/CN.4/344 and Corr.1 (English only) and Corr.2, [1982] Yearbook of the International Law Commission Vol. II(1), 79.

——, 'Fourth report on the content, forms and degrees of international responsibility (Part two of the draft articles), by Mr. Willem Riphagen, Special Rapporteur', UN Doc. A/CN.4/366 and Add.1 and Add.1/Corr.1, [1983] Yearbook of the International Law Commission Vol. II(1), 3.

——, 'Sixth report on the content, forms and degrees of international responsibility (Part two of the draft articles); and "Implementation" (mise en oeuvre) of international responsibility and the settlement of disputes (Part three of the draft articles), by Mr. Willem Riphagen, Special Rapporteur', UN Doc. A/CN.4/389 and Corr.1, [1985] Yearbook of the International Law Commission Vol. II(1), 3.

Romanov, V.A., 'The United Nations and the Problem of Combating International Terrorism', 2 Terrorism and Political Violence (1990) 289.

Root, E., 'The Outlook for International Law', 9 American Society of International Law Proceedings (1915) 2.

Rosand, E., 'Security Council Resolution 1373, the Counter-Terrorism Committee, and the Fight Against Terrorism', 97 American Journal of International Law (2003) 333.

——, 'Security Council Resolution 1373 and the Counterterrorism Committee: the Cornerstone of the United Nations Contribution to the Fight against Terrorism', in Fijnaut et al. eds, *Legal Instruments in the Fight Against International Terrorism: A Transatlantic Dialogue* (Leiden: Martinus Nijhoff Publishers, 2004) 603.

——, 'The Security Council as "Global Legislator": Ultra Vires or Ultra Innovative', 28 Fordham International Law Journal (2005) 101.

Rosenne, S., 'State Responsibility and International Crimes: Further Reflections on Article 19 of the Draft Articles on State Responsibility', 10 New York University Journal of International Law and Policy (1997) 155.

Rostow, N., 'Before and After: the Changed UN Response to Terrorism since September 11th', 35 Cornell International Law Journal (2002) 475.

Roth, B.R., 'Draft Convention on the Responsibility of States for Internationally Wrongful Acts, Prepared by Professor Roth in 1932', in [1969] Yearbook of the International Law Commission Vol. II, 152.

Rousseau, C., 'Chronique des faits internationaux', 80 Revue Générale de Droit International Public (1976) 211.

Rowe, P., 'Responses to Terror: The New War', 3 Melbourne Journal of International Law (2002) 301.

Ruda, J.M., 'Reservations to Treaties', 146 Recueil des Cours de l'Académie de Droit International de la Haye (1975) 95.

Ruys, T., 'Crossing the Thin Blue Line: An Inquiry into Israel's Recourse to Self-Defense Against Hezbollah', 43 Stanford Journal of International Law (2007) 265.

—— and Verhoeven, S., 'Attacks by Private Actors and the Right of Self-Defence', 10 Journal of Conflict and Security Law (2005) 289.

Santori, V., 'The UN Security Council's (Broad) Interpretation of the Notion of the Threat to Peace in Counter-Terrorism', in Nesi ed., *International Cooperation in Counter-Terrorism: The United Nations and Regional Organizations in the Fight Against Terrorism* (Aldershot: Ashgate, 2006) 89.

Sassòli, M., 'La "guerre contre le terrorisme", le droit international humanitaire et le statut de prisonnier de guerre', 39 Canadian Yearbook of International Law (2001) 211.

——, 'L'arrêt Yerodia: quelques remarques sur une affaire au point de collision entre les deux couches du droit international', 106 Revue belge de droit (2002) 791.

——, 'Transnational Armed Groups and International Humanitarian Law', Occasional Paper Series, Program on Humanitarian Policy and Conflict Research, Harvard University 2006, <http://www.hpcr.org/pdfs/OccasionalPaper6.pdf>.

Saul, B., 'Definition of "Terrorism" in the UN Security Council: 1985–2004', 4 Chinese Journal of International Law (2005) 141.

——, *Defining Terrorism in International Law* (Oxford: Oxford University Press, 2006).

Schabas, W.A., *Genocide in International Law: the Crime of Crimes* (Cambridge: Cambridge University Press, 2000).

——, 'Is Terrorism a Crime Against Humanity?', 8 International Peacekeeping (2004) 255.

——, *The UN International Criminal Tribunals; The Former Yugoslavia, Rwanda and Sierra Leone* (Cambridge: Cambridge University Press, 2006).

Schabas, W.A. and Clémentine, O., 'Is Terrorism a Crime against Humanity?', in Doucet ed., *Terrorism, Victims and International Criminal Responsibility* (Paris: SOS Attentats, 2003) 270.

Schachter, O., 'The Enforcement of International Judicial and Arbitral Decisions', 54 American Journal of International Law (1960) 1.

——, 'International Law in Theory and Practice', 178 Recueil des Cours de l'Académie de Droit International de la Haye (1982-V) 175.

——, 'The Right of States to Use Armed Force', 82 Michigan Law Review (1984) 1620.

——, 'The Extraterritorial Use of Force against Terrorist Bases', 11 Houston Journal of International Law (1989) 309.

——, *International Law in Theory and Practice* (Dordrecht: Martinus Nijhoff, 1991).

Scharf, M.P., 'Defining Terrorism as the Peace Time Equivalent of War Crimes: A Case of Too Much Convergence between International Humanitarian Law and International Criminal Law?', 7 International Law Students Association Journal of International & Comparative Law (2001) 392.

Scheffer, D.J., 'Non-Judicial State Remedies and the Jurisdiction of the International Court of Justice', 27 Stanford Journal of International Law (1990) 83.

Schloemann, H.L. and Ohlhoff, S., '"Constitutionalization" and Dispute Settlement in the WTO: National Security as an Issue of Competence', 93 American Journal of International Law (1999) 424.

Schreiber, R.E., 'Ascertaining *Opinio Juris* of States Concerning Norms Involving the Prevention of International Terrorism: A Focus on the UN Process', 16 Boston University International Law Journal (1998) 309.

Schulte, C., *Compliance with Decisions of the International Court of Justice* (Oxford: Oxford University Press, 2004).

Schwebel, S., 'Aggression, Intervention and Self-Defence in Modern International Law', 136 Recueil des Cours de l'Académie de Droit International de la Haye (1972-II) 463.

Schwenck, W., 'The Bonn Declaration on Hijacking', 4 Annals of Air & Space Law (1979) 307.

Scobbie, I., 'Assumptions and presuppositions: state responsibility for system crimes', in Nollkaemper and van der Wilt eds, *System Criminality in International Law* (Cambridge: Cambridge University Press, 2009) 270.

Seibert-Fohr, A., 'The Crime of Aggression: Adding a Definition to the Rome Statute of the ICC', ASIL Insight, 18 November 2008, <http://www.asil.org/insights081118.cfm>.

——, 'State Responsibility for Genocide under the Genocide Convention', in Gaeta ed., *The UN Genocide Convention; A Commentary* (Oxford: Oxford University Press, 2009) 349.

Setear, J.K., 'Responses to Breach of a Treaty and Rationalist International Relations Theory: The Rules of Release and Remediation in the Law of Treaties and the Law of State Responsibility', 83 Virginia Law Review (1997) 1.

Shany, Y., *The Competing Jurisdictions of International Courts and Tribunals* (Oxford: Oxford University Press, 2004).

——, 'Know Your Rights! The Flotilla Report and International Law Governing Naval Blockades', EJIL: Talk!, 12 October 2010, <http://www.ejiltalk.org/know-your-rights -the-flotilla-report-and-international-law-governing-naval-blockades/>.

Shaw, M.N., *International Law* (6th edn, Cambridge: Cambridge University Press, 2008).

Shelton, D., 'The Boundaries of Human Rights Jurisdiction in Europe', 13 Duke Journal of Comparative & International Law (2003) 95.

Sicilianos, L.-A., 'Countermeasures in Response to Grave Violations of Obligations Owed to the International Community', in Crawford, Pellet et al. eds, *The Law of International Responsibility* (Oxford: Oxford University Press, 2010) 1137.

Simma, B., 'Self-Contained Regimes', 16 Netherlands Yearbook of International Law (1985) 112.

——, 'International Crimes: Injury and Countermeasures; Comments on Part 2 of the ILC Work on State Responsibility', in Weiler et al. eds, *International Crimes of State: A Critical Analysis of the ILC's Draft Article 19 on State Responsibility* (Berlin: de Gruyter, 1988) 283.

——, 'Counter-measures and Dispute Settlement: A Plea for a Different Balance', 5 European Journal of International Law (1994) 102.

——, 'From Bilateralism to Community Interest in International Law', 250 Recueil des Cours de l'Académie de Droit International de la Haye (1994a) 219.

—— and Pulkowski, D., 'Of Planets and the Universe: Self-Contained Regimes in International Law', 17 European Journal of International Law (2006) 483.

—— and ——, '*Leges speciales* and Self-Contained Regimes', in Crawford, Pellet et al. eds, *The Law of International Responsibility* (Oxford: Oxford University Press, 2010) 139.

Simpson, G., *Great Powers and Outlaw States* (Cambridge: Cambridge University Press, 2004).

Sinclair, I., 'The law of sovereign immunity: recent developments', 167 Recueil des Cours de l'Académie de Droit Internationale de la Haye (1980-II) 113.

Slaughter, A.-M. and Burke-White, W., 'An International Constitutional Moment', 43 Harvard International Law Journal (2002) 1.

Sofaer, A.D., 'Terrorism and the Law', 64 Foreign Affairs (1986) 901.

Sohn, L.B., 'The International Court of Justice and the Scope of the Right of Self-Defence and the Duty of Non-Intervention', in Dinstein ed., *International Law at a Time of Perplexity: Essays in Honour of Shabtai Rosenne* (Dordrecht: Martinus Nijhoff Publishers, 1989) 869.

—— and Baxter, R., 'Convention on the International Responsibility of States for Injuries to Aliens, prepared at the behest of the Director of the Codification Division of the Office of Legal Affairs of the United Nations, for the consideration of the International Law Commission', in Garcia-Amador et al. eds, *Recent Codification of the Law of State Responsibility for Injuries to Aliens* (New York: Oceana Publications, 1974) 133.

Spinedi, M., 'State Responsibility v. Individual Responsibility for International Crimes: Tertium Non Datur?', 13 European Journal of International Law (2002) 895.

Spiropoulos, J., 'Draft Code of Offences Against the Peace and Security of Mankind—Report by J. Spiropoulos, Special Rapporteur', UN Doc. A/CN.4/25 (1950), [1950] Yearbook of the International Law Commission Vol. II, 253.

Stahn, C., 'International Law at a Crossroads? The Impact of September 11', 62 Zeitschrift für ausländisches öffentliches Recht und Völkerrecht (2002) 183.

——, 'Terrorist Acts as "Armed Attack": The Right to Self-Defence, Article 51(1/2) of the UN Charter, and International Terrorism', 27 Fletcher Forum of World Affairs (2003) 35.

Starke, J.G., 'Imputability in International Delinquencies', 19 British Yearbook of International Law (1938) 104.

Stephens, T., 'International Criminal Law and the Response to International Terrorism', 27 University of New South Wales Law Journal (2004) 454.

Stone, J., 'Hopes and Loopholes in the 1974 Definition of Aggression', 71 American Journal of International Law (1977) 224.

Stowell, E.C., *Intervention in International Law* (Washington, DC: John Byrne, 1921).

Sucharitkul, S., 'Immunities of Foreign States Before National Authorities', 149 Recueil des Cours de l'Académie de Droit International de la Haye (1976) 87.

——, 'Terrorism as an International Crime: Questions of Responsibility and Complicity', 19 Israel Yearbook on Human Rights (1989) 247.

Sur, S., 'La Résolution 1540 du Conseil de sécurité (28 avril 2004): entre la prolifération des armes de destruction massive, le terrorisme et les acteurs non étatiques', 108 Revue Générale de Droit International Public (2004) 855.

Swaak-Goldman, O.Q., 'Who Defines Members' Security Interest in the WTO?', 9 Leiden Journal of International Law (1996) 361.

Szasz, P.C., 'The Security Council Starts Legislating', 96 American Journal of International Law (2002) 901.

Talmon, S., 'The Security Council as World Legislature', 99 American Journal of International Law (2005) 175.

Tams, C., 'Light Treatment of a Complex Problem: The Law of Self-Defence in the Wall Case', 16 European Journal of International Law (2005) 965.

——, *Enforcing Obligations* Erga Omnes *in International Law* (Cambridge: Cambridge University Press, 2005a).

——, 'The Use of Force against Terrorists', 20 European Journal of International Law (2009) 412.

——, 'The Use of Force against Terrorists: A Rejoinder to Sperotto and Trapp', 20 European Journal of International Law (2009a) 1957.

——, 'Waiver, Acquiescence and Extinctive Prescription', in Crawford, Pellet et al. eds, *The Law of International Responsibility* (Oxford: Oxford University Press, 2010) 1035.

Tanzi, A., 'Problems of Enforcement of Decisions of the International Court of Justice and the Law of the United Nations', 6 European Journal of International Law (1995) 1.

Thiam, D., 'First report on the draft code of offences against the peace and security of mankind, by Mr. Doudou Thiam, Special Rapporteur', UN Doc. A/CN.4/364, [1983] Yearbook of the International Law Commission Vol. II(1), 137.

——, 'Third report on the draft code of offences against the peace and security of mankind, by Mr. Doudou Thiam, Special Rapporteur', UN Doc. A/CN.4/387 and Corr.1 and Corr.2 (1985), [1985] Yearbook of the International Law Commission Vol. II(1), 63.

——, 'Twelfth report on the draft code of crimes against the peace and security of mankind, by Mr. Doudou Thiam, Special Rapporteur', UN Doc. A/CN.4/460 and Corr.1, [1994] Yearbook of the International Law Commission Vol. II(1), 97.

——, 'Thirteenth report on the draft code of crimes against the peace and security of mankind, by Mr. Doudou Thiam, Special Rapporteur', UN Doc. A/CN.4/466, [1995] Yearbook of the International Law Commission Vol. II(1), 33.

Tomonori, M., 'The Individual as Beneficiary of State Immunity: Problems of the Attribution of *Ultra Vires* Conduct', 29 Denver Journal of International Law & Policy (2001) 261.

Tomuschat, C., 'The Lockerbie Case before the International Court of Justice', 48 Review (International Commission of Jurists) (1992) 38.

——, 'What is a "Breach" of the European Convention on Human Rights?', in Lawson et al. eds, *The Dynamics of the Protection of Human Rights in Europe* (Dordrecht: Martinus Nijhoff Publishers, 1994) 315.

——, 'Are Counter-Measures Subject to Prior Recourse to Dispute Settlement Procedures?', 5 European Journal of International Law (1994a) 77.

——, 'Article 36', in Zimmermann et al. eds, *The Statute of the International Court of Justice* (Oxford: Oxford University Press, 2006) 589.

Trapp, K.N., Book Review: 'Tal Becker, "Terrorism and the State; Rethinking the Rules of State Responsibility" (2006)', 19 Revue Québécoise de Droit International (2006) 407.

——, 'Back to Basics: Necessity, Proportionality, and the Right of Self-Defence Against Non-State Terrorist Actors', 56 International and Comparative Law Quarterly (2007) 141.

Trapp, K.N., 'The Use of Force against Terrorists: A Reply to Christian J. Tams', 20 European Journal of International Law (2009) 1049.

——, 'WTO Inconsistent Countermeasures—A View from the Outside', 104 American Society of International Law Proceedings (2010) (forthcoming).

Travalio, G. and Altenburg, J., 'State Responsibility for Sponsorship of Insurgent Groups: Terrorism, State Responsibility and the Use of Military Force', 4 Chicago Journal of International Law (2003) 97.

UK Ministry of Defence, *The Manual of the Law of Armed Conflict* (Oxford: Oxford University Press, 2004).

US Department of State, Office of the Coordinator for Counterterrorism, 2008 Country Reports on Terrorism, April 2009, <http://www.state.gov/documents/organization/122599.pdf>.

Van Damme, I., *Treaty Interpretation by the WTO Appellate Body* (Oxford: Oxford University Press, 2009).

van Sliedregt, E., 'Complicity to Commit Genocide', in Gaeta ed., *The UN Genocide Convention: A Commentary* (Oxford: Oxford University Press, 2009) 162.

Verdier, P.-H., 'Cooperative States: International Relations, State Responsibility and the Problem of Custom', 42 Virginia Journal of International Law (2002) 839.

Vereshchetin, V.S., 'Some Observations on the New Proposal on Dispute Settlement', 5 European Journal of International Law (1994) 54.

Verwey, W.D., 'The International Hostages Convention and National Liberation Movements', 75 American Journal of International Law (1981) 69.

von Hebel, H. and Robinson, D., 'Crimes Within the Jurisdiction of the Court', in Lee ed., *The International Criminal Court: The Making of the Rome Statute* (The Hague: Kluwer Law International, 1999) 79.

Warbrick, C., 'Public International Law: Immunity and International Crimes in English Law', 53 International and Comparative Law Quarterly (2004) 769.

Ward, C.A., 'Building Capacity to Combat International Terrorism: The Role of the United Nations Security Council', 8 Journal of Conflict & Security Law (2003) 289.

Wardlaw, G., *Political Terrorism: Theory, Tactics, and Counter-measures* (Cambridge: Cambridge University Press, 1982).

Watts, A., 'The Legal Position in International Law of Heads of States, Heads of Governments and Foreign Ministers', 247 Recueil des Cours de l'Académie de Droit International de la Haye (1994) 10.

Wedgwood, R., 'Responding to Terrorism: The Strikes Against bin Laden', 24 Yale Journal of International Law (1999) 559.

Weil, P., 'Towards Relative Normativity in International Law?', 77 American Journal of International Law (1983) 413.

White, N. and Abass, A., 'Countermeasures and Sanctions', in Evans ed., *International Law* (Oxford: Oxford University Press, 2006) 509.

Whitt, R.S., 'The Politics of Procedure: An Examination of the GATT Dispute Settlement Panel and the Article XXI Defense in the Context of the US Embargo of Nicaragua', 19 Law & Policy in International Business (1987) 604.

Whomersley, C.A., 'Some Reflections on the Immunity of Individuals for Official Acts', 41 International and Comparative Law Quarterly (1992) 848.

Williams, S.A., 'International Law and Terrorism: Age-Old Problems, Different Targets', 26 Canadian Yearbook of International Law (1988) 87.

Wirth, S., 'Immunity for Core Crimes? The ICJ's Judgment in the *Congo* v. *Belgium* Case', 13 European Journal of International Law (2002) 877.

Wise, E.M., 'Terrorism and the Problems of an International Criminal Law', 19 Connecticut Law Review (1987) 799.

Wouters, J., 'The Judgment of the International Court of Justice in the *Arrest Warrant* Case: Some Critical Remarks', 16 Leiden Journal of International Law (2003) 256.

Young, M., 'The WTO's Use of Relevant Rules of International Law: An Analysis of the Biotech Case', 56 International and Comparative Law Quarterly (2007) 907.

Zanardi, P.L. 'Indirect Military Aggression', in Cassese ed., *The Current Legal Regulation of the Use of Force* (Dordrecht: Martinus Nijhoff Publishers, 1986) 111.

Zegfeld, L., *Accountability of Armed Opposition Groups in International Law* (Cambridge: Cambridge University Press, 2002).

Zoller, E., *Peacetime Unilateral Remedies: An Analysis of Countermeasures* (Dobbs Ferry, NY: Transnational Publishers, 1984).

Index